RI

'Fearism is a new concept; it is uti
the matrix of superiority intact in ....y ....
purpose of wielding abusive power and justifying such acts using other's fear. Identification of the practice of fearism would take us to deeper layers of psychological impact that the victims suffer from. However, the apprehension of dismay, the fright of terror, the panic and horror and all the dreadful and painful emotion will end up its threatening danger when one has realized there was this kind of dominance and one is prepared to fight against it.'

Prof. Dr Streamlet Dkhar,
Khashi Language department, Nehru University,
Shillong, Meghalaya, India.

'Fear is a founder of human emotion. It is the fear that directs human activities. If man had no fear, s/he would be dull, that is, inactive but Adolf Hitler was not inactive, for fear was existent in him and as a result of this he made an attempt to be a winner being the Second World War leader. The world would call him a coward in case of being a failure as the world winner. Hence he felt compelled to be undaunted or undeterred owing to this internal fear. By this it is clear that he was active by dint of his outstanding bravery brought out by human emotion as regards fear. It is a partial instance. Desh Subba has essentially presented the several expressions of an apt human emotion by means of convincing instances and dealt with them in parts in the instrument of fearism in which various forms of human emotion have turned into an imagery and reflection. And he has also had a thoughtful approach to the positive way for the removal of fear to render these forms explicitly. This is the fearism to be discussed and talk about. His fearism will make Nepali literary world and the world literature to have been considered and studied.'

Bikram Bir Thapa,
Indian Literary Academy Winner,
Shillong, Meghalaya, India.

'Fearism yields an alternative interpretation of class struggle.'

Prof. Dr Gobinda Raj Bhattarai,
Central Department of Education English, T. U. Kirtipur,
Kathmandu, Nepal.

'Fearism is a new perspective to look at life and the world.'

Prof. Dr Sanjeev Uppretti,
creative literary Hong Kong, Half Yearly 2008,
Central Department of English, Tribhuwan University,
Kirtipur, Nepal.

'To claim this text as the World dictionary of fearism cannot be an exaggeration in my opinion.'

Prof. Dr Durga Prasad Aryal,
Padmakanya Multiple Campus,
Kathmandu, Nepal.

'Fear is factual and ancient whereas fearism is original. It exists along with the existence of human being. Human civilization started right from fear. A ceaseless effort has been made on solution and emancipation. Desh Subba has attempted to study fear pervasively. The way that focuses on fear to interpret human life is fearism. In my opinion, a philosophical thinking didn't come into being apart from Buddhism in Nepal. Here Desh Subba has made his attempt to offer this philosophical thinking to the human civilization in the world. Its application to a literary theory is not right and just. It makes an impact on important aspect of life. All isms like spiritualism, materialism, Marxism and Freudism more than a mare aspect. Fearism is also the same. It's a new dimension to the world.'

Dr Tanka Nath Khatiwada,
Presidency College, the Head of Hindi Department,
Imphal, Manipur, India.

'Fearism makes a deep study on fear and finds out a way towards emancipation. Desh Subba has propounded an ism. It is a new experiment in Nepali literature.'

Bhawani Adhikari,
Poknafirm Daily, 6 April 2013
Manipuri language daily,
Manipur, India.

'Propounder of Fearism, Desh Subba believes on its benevolence to the human being. All people from different languages, castes/ethnicities, and religions comprehend as well as adopt this philosophy.'

Rana Kafle,
Assamese language *Dainik Pratibedan*,
3 August 2013,
Assam, India.

'To demand for an ancient Gorkhaland by Gorkhalis, attempts on preserving literature, culture and language, establishment of ethnic institutions and launching movements are guided by the fear for existence.'

Rohit Gautam,
Editor, *Sapriyar Monthly Magazine*, April 2013,
Assam, India.

'Fearism propounded by Desh Subba, a novelist and thinker is the latest philosophy.'

Pradip Manyanbo,
Kantipur daily, 18 February 2013.

'Fearism is a bright light in the literary world.'

Devendra Shakten,
Garima Literary Magazine, Chaitra, 2013.
Kathmandu, Nepal.

'Desh Subba has formulated how fear is produced – life, consciousness, knowledge, fear, cognition.'

Gyan Bahadur Chhetri,
Aamar Assam, Assamese Daily,
9 October 2013, Assam, India

'Fearism presents sincerity and elaboration through comparison and analysis between medical sciences, sciences, psychology and other empirical formulations and theories.'

Dr Chabi Gogoi.
Vol. 1, Issue 2, Sudha Assamese,
Quarterly Literary Magazine, January 2014,
Assam, India.

'I would like to appreciate from the bottom of my heart to Mr Desh Subba, who had opened "the philosophy of fearism" and to hope that one day this interesting subject will be thought as one of the most important subject in the college and university of the world.'

Dhaneswar Engti,
Dipu Darpan 26th Central General Council Assam Gorkha Sammelan,
December 2013, Souvenir Magazine,
Assam, India.

PHILOSOPHY OF FEARISM

PHILOSOPHY OF FEARISM

Desh Subba
Translated by Rajendra Subba
With Bhabindra Kumar Rai

Library of Congress Control Number:		2014909564
ISBN:	Hardcover	978-1-4990-0470-0
	Softcover	978-1-4990-0469-4
	eBook	978-1-4990-0467-0

Rev. date: 07/14/2014

To order additional copies of this book, contact:
Xlibris LLC
1-800-455-039
www.Xlibris.com.au
Orders@Xlibris.com.au
606909

CONTENTS

FOREWORD

Fear has completely surrounded all living creatures, especially man. All things, natural things, human beings, and visible and invisible things, produce fear all the time. Most of the fears arise themselves, whereas some of them exist because of external forces. It is so vast that fear appears as soon as it is added to a word. This fear has continued its existence since the prehistoric period. So, it existed with the existence of living beings in this universe. Low fear slowly and gradually grows in the cause of human civilisation as well as the existence of the animal kingdom as the fear of the baby reaches climax. High fear turns into low fear too. It is a rule of nature. War, murder, terror, etc. are produced by fear. Anger, conspiracy, suspicion, and hatred are produced by the fear of man. Then, he takes the shelter of religion, philosophy, science, etc. But the forms of religion, philosophy, and science are also supposed to produce fear. Man feels restless, tortured, suppressed, and suffocated because of known and unknown fears and searches for an outlet and emancipation. Employment, profession, invention, creation, recreation, religion, and philosophy are the ways for these outlets and emancipation. Man spends his time in these fears and makes an attempt for emancipation from such fears. He is always the victim of fear. He has been making his attempt for emancipation since the prehistoric period. Life is painful just because man is unable to utilise his life properly. Here, I have made my attempt to theorise fear, an important issue. Now, most people are familiar with fearism, a new philosophy. Many people, including teachers, critics, journalists, friends, and readers, have expressed their love, reactions, advice, and support in order to develop fearism into theory.

The fearist perspective is a new dimension to look at life and the world. The question strikes the mind: How does the fearist perspective look at life and the world? The purpose behind fearism is to conduct continuous research, investigation, and invention in order to make life more comfortable.

11

This theory is applicable to both distinct and general philosophical purposes. In fact, fear is not any external factor, but power exists within itself. If it is utilised properly, it is beneficial to man. Otherwise, it can be harmful. Therefore, its usage depends on us. This is what this theory tells us. We are users, victims, and consumers of it. Yes! Let us utilise it properly and take benefit as much as possible. This is the theory that has just begun its investigation and research. It deals with the elaboration of 'ism', linguistic interpretation, logical evidence, and their effects in life. This is a perspective to look at the world and living beings. But it has some challenges. First, it is not easier to constitute ism. Second, it is not easier to present illustrations about it for readers. Third, it is difficult to produce accessible and comfortable materials. Fourth, if the theory is not applicable to human beings, it becomes absurd. Here, I have made my attempt to combine them all in order to develop it into a theory.

February, 2014

1

Introduction of Fear

Definition

1. Fear is a beautiful consciousness.

Fear is a beautiful consciousness with different forms. We need to regard it as beautiful because our success, prosperity, and progress lie behind it. The world could be different if it wasn't beautiful. Even the world is beautiful due to its beauty.

2. Fear is a director of life.

Fear is a director of both life and civilisation. Like in the animal kingdom, human civilisation without fear could be chaotic. Fear directs even animals but more differently than human beings. It has directed the whole of civilisation to this stage of development. People have multiple options. They choose security, longevity, profit, and prosperity in their lives. Failure to choose a best option directs them to the fear of insecurity, destitution, and loss of reputation and bliss. All choices made by human beings as said by Jean-Paul Sartre, an existentialist, are not complete; yet some of them are. They suffer from various difficulties, unless their decisions and objectives are right. Their choices have been right till this time. A small range of some blows, changes, and wars in human civilisation are usual. Fear makes us alert when our decisions, objectives, and choices are wrong. For thousands of years, history elapsed along with victory over various difficulties. Even human physical structure adapted to climate change and environment. If it was not

---

adaptable, human beings and their civilisations could have disappeared by this time. These have all been directed by the fear. Thus, fear, as said in the beginning, is a director of life and civilisation.

3. Fear is a driving force of civilisation.

Fear has a dominant role in the primitive hunting age, the agricultural age, the feudal age, the industrial age, the cyber age, the age of space, the age of atomic weapons, the age of virus, the fear age, and the fearless age. In the primitive age, people had simple weapons, but later, they invented guns made of metals. They invented such powerful weapons for protection from dangerous wild animals and other enemies. It was difficult to protect themselves from storms, thunderbolts, rain, hail, snow, and winter during that period. However, they didn't have houses in the primitive age; they began to build houses to protect themselves from such calamities. Moreover, they constructed bridges and roads. They established industries. It was a way towards production growth. They did all this for liberation from fear. Pleasure, secured freedom, and other amenities, thus, are selections by human beings.

4. Fear is a universe.

Fear is as vast as the universe. It is in imagination, dreams, power of nature, consciousness, physical bodies, visibility, and invisibility. Everything in this universe has been be occupied, incorporated, and touched by it. Everything is under and around its periphery.

5. Fear is a black hole of space.

John Wheeler, an American physicist, found a vast hole and named it a black hole in 1968. It is much too vast and eternal. The earth is supposed to be plunging into this black hole in the future, and it is yet not known when it would come out. Therefore, a vast black hole of space is a fear. It is too vast; any research on it is always incomplete. It expands within consciousness for protection from every human tendency, dynamics, and the power of nature. In the absence of fear, human tendency and structure of society and the country could be different. Thus, a black hole is never completely realised.

6. Fear is an invention.

Fear is a source of all invention, construction, creation, and imagination. People have been working on inventions, creations, and constructions due to fear since the primitive age. In fact, an imagination is a predecessor to all invention, construction, and creation. Human beings did not possess good weapons, houses, scripts, languages, societies, religions, and traditions. They were unable to hunt big animals in the absence of good weapons. Similarly, they hardly kept protected themselves from storms and thunderbolts. No fire was available for cooking. Later, they learnt all of these things. These inventions, constructions, and creations were caused by fear. In this way, no invention is possible without fear—it's a source of all inventions and creations.

7. Fear is a light.

Fear is a light like the light from the sun. It gives light to the life. Perhaps people will still be living in a primitive stage in the absence of fear. The light which is essential for civilisation along with ceaseless guidance is possible due to this fear. Thus, fear is guiding every individual with necessary light.

8. Fear is a seer.

Fear is a foreseer. It predicts any accident before it happens, and it works to make us aware at present. It not only works to make human beings aware of a possible accident in the future, but it does the same to birds and animals. Birds and animals know about possible natural disasters much earlier than the human beings do. These birds and animals receive earlier indication and information about some natural disasters like earthquakes and storms, and they come back to their respective habitats as soon as possible. Because of fear, people get pre-information about chaos, war, food scarcity, money inflation, epidemics, and other severe disasters, and they seek protection.

9. Fear is a mystery.

It is as vast as the universe. It is just like a vast sea of vast planets, stars, and solar systems. These are all eternal and mysterious as well. Thus, fear is also vast, mysterious, and eternal. It constitutes an impact on human tendency, action, and activities. Human activities done knowingly and unknowingly are heading towards it. So, a claim on size, shape, sector, colour, and form is impossible. Hence, some mysterious events can happen unexpectedly.

10. God is fear.

People have faith in God. Again, the reason behind it is fear. Fear forced human beings to respect and have faith in God. God is a way of emancipation from the fear of various difficulties, hardships, and problems that they may happen to human beings. Existence of all these drives human beings to respect God. People believe that God emancipates them from suffering, difficulty, pain, and death. God exists due to fear, and similarly, fear exists due to God. So, God is a fear.

11. Fear is a superpower.

A superpower exists along with fear. It doesn't exist forever. The work which we can't do in normal time exists as a superpower in abnormal time. Such a superpower disappears within us somewhere in this universe. Its existence is more circumstantial. Lots of examples are available about the man who jumps down from the top roof or runs like a leopard to protect himself from disasters, attacks, and police lathi charges. We have seen and met those like him, who say, 'How have I done this work? I have no idea. When I remember it, I feel frightened.' He doesn't know which superpower urged him to face such challenges. In fact, it is a fear that exists as a superpower.

12. Fear is an alert indicator.

Fear works as an alert indicator too. It works to alert us to any disaster, accident, or danger before it happens to us. When people are alert earlier, they will avoid possible accidents or incidents and will minimise the possibilities. If work is done cautiously for the present, the future, family, friends, society, and country, then peaceful emancipation is possible. Whatever difficulties they are, fear always works to alert.

13. Fear is courage.

Fear is a source of courage for living creatures. Because of such courage, people do some miraculous works. Animals also do such works. When a cat is beaten in a closed room, it will start to attack whoever is nearby. The reason behind it is the cat doesn't have a way out. This courage is a product of fear. Even a man in such a trap will have such great courage.

14. Fear is an enemy of a person.

Fear is an enemy of personality development. Divergent natures and tendencies appear in a man. The fears that come out of them is human nature. It is both harmful and useful. Fear is a harmful nature as well.

There are some people who would rather die than make a speech on stage. Some of them feel uneasy to speak. Feelings of both uneasiness and fear are one out of many forms. A man with fear in his mind can't be involved in talking, writing, debating, and discussing. It is harmful to his personality development. It can cause feelings of being introverted, hesitation, and mental retardation. Therefore, fear is useful for the present, the future, property, success, and progress.

15. Fear is beauty.

Fear is beauty too. Fear occupies the mind that other people won't like one if one is not good and attractive. People always think, 'I'm good.' Beauty is essential for it. A man must be good for his personality, modesty, and gentility. 'Good' not only consists of physical beauty; it also consists of the beauty of mind. It is much more important in the modern era. Schools, industries, and businesses have been started for it. These all are the products of fear.

16. Fear is a powerful weapon.

Fear works as a powerful weapon. It is used to force others or himself to do something. Rules, regulations, acts, and the constitution should be strictly followed to maintain security, peace, and prosperity in the country. Its violation invites anarchism in the country. No one remains under any control in such a condition. Fear of legal punishment for the violation of rule, regulation, law, and constitution compels people to follow rules, regulations, and the constitution in the country. It is the same fear that is applied to different organisations, families, and offices. The seven wonderful constructions and inventions were by slaves. They worked so hard on the construction of buildings, gardens, statues, temples, musk and the Great Wall. Owners used to keep fear-inducing weapons. Those who didn't work hard used to be severely punished, and some of them used to get the death penalty too. Thus, they were successful in constructing such great and wonderful works.

Fear is very useful for personality development of every individual. Fear makes people think, 'If I don't study hard, I will fail in the exam.' This forced students to study hard. If a student works hard, s/he will succeed in his/her life. A student without fear doesn't study hard and s/he has a dark future. So fear has a dominant role behind every success. If fear drives a man into study, games, work, writing, singing, and other businesses, there lies the success. The fear weapon is being used in national and international sectors. No other power works where fear works; because fear is the most powerful weapon in this world.

17. Fear is a controlling mechanism.

Fear is an integral part of every human temperament. It exists in every human being. It works as a controlling mechanism in decreasing, increasing, balancing, and controlling such temperaments. Therefore, it is a controller of such temperaments and behaviours. Human temperament without fear is uncontrollable, neutral, and anarchic. Fear controls them all and makes them disciplined. Thus, fear controls, directs, and conducts suspicious, illusionary, envious, greedy, egotistic, and angry natures.

18. Fear is a super law.

Fear is a super law among laws. Whatever laws exist, they are either to create fear or to control fear for human beings. Legal fear prevents the involvement of human beings in theft, robbery, murder, violence, and terror. Unless law creates fear for human beings, it doesn't work at all. If people realise that the legal provision of severe punishment has been passed, they feel fear to commit any crime. Similarly, the law protects us from the fear of injustice and crime.

19. Fear is a guardian of all activities.

Fear works as a guardian of every activity. So, every human activity is guided and followed by fear. As discussed above, fear is an alert indicator for all activities. We think before we start to work—possible or impossible. We think even after we complete it—right or wrong. If the work is done right, it is all right, but if it is wrong, it will be improved later. If it remains unimproved, it merely creates fear of possible challenges.

20. Fear is a group of all psychological effects.

Different types of psychological effects exist. Here, fear is a group of all psychological effects. Fear should be understood first to make a study on psychological effects. In all diseases and problems associated with psychological diseases and effects, there lies fear. When we hide and suppress fear, fear appears. So, hysteria, depression, hesitation, suicide, and some other psychological problems are related to the study of fear as a group of all psychological effects.

21. Fear protects birds and animals.

Fear urges animals to put their ears up and produce strange sounds. Fear is not visible in all human beings. It is clearly visible in all animals and birds. The animals put their ears up and seek secured places just before they encounter other powerful animals and natural disasters. Hens makes their chicks aware when hawks approach nearer. The chicks hide as they receive a signal of fear from their mothers. These all happen due to fear.

Fear has a number of possible definitions. Powers and forms of fear exist in all disciplines, rules, languages, script, religions, cultures, directors, players, generations, the present, the future, life, and the universe. Any definition of it is yet incomplete. We can see people put notices on the wall in order to create fear—'Beware of Dog' or 'High Voltage Power' on electric pillars. When a road has a turning that is dangerous and steep, we see a notice: 'Be Careful' or 'Be Aware'. It means the place is dangerous. Signs that say 'Walk/Drive carefully' creates fear. Some notices tell us that the work is punishable. Fear the notice creates makes people be careful and aware.

Everything that is available creates fear or has a factor of fear. There are many interpretations of the universe and nihilism. The worldly form of fear has been interpreted. Fear starts with what we remember beyond the world or what comes to our mind. We worship invisible power; it was invisible in prehistoric time and still has occupied our mind. We continuously keep accepting and worshipping such powers and objects. To worship is an order of fear. Visible and physical objects are here, but their presence doesn't create fear. When consciousness, knowledge, conditional reflex, and nature interact with these objects, then they convert themselves into fear. There is a cave, but we don't know since how long it exists there. It makes no difference when we look at it. The more our nature, knowledge, and consciousness start to observe it closely, doubting and thinking about it, the more the cave looks dangerous. The more we stir our illusions and doubts, the more it increases fear in our mind. Such fear doesn't come from anywhere else but it is within us and wanders out. Several similar factors are around us—like religion, culture, language, scripture, blind belief, and superstition.

Some people made myths of some caves and some of them wove stories about them and some of them linked them to monsters and said that they would eat human beings. It slowly grows to conditional reflex and then it becomes human flesh-eating caves and habitats of monsters. Thus, the meaning of the simple cave transforms into a monster cave. Generally, the cave has a fundamental meaning, and similarly, the meaning of a man-made cave is different. Some of the meanings are perilous and others are general. General meanings never produce fear in us. A close-to-perilous meaning produces fear automatically. Most of the general meanings of the past have changed totally now.

Human beings began to be civilised since ancient periods—they were educated and enlightened, but along with these, fear increased. Invention is knowledge and education. However, the purpose of invention is to minimise fear in human beings; it is quite contradictory. Fear exists with all knowledge, education, civilisation, and invention. It appears from the forward, middle parts, and backward. Fear was in existence before the development of civilisation. A different fear replaced the previous one after the development of civilisation. The fear before the invention of weapons was different from the fear while the weapons were being invented. The fear after the invention of weapons is different from those two different types of fears. This principle can be applied everywhere. We have a fear before we earn. Our fear while earning is different, and we have another fear after we earn. Thus, fear and supply continue in our lives. These fears are suppressed under micro levels. We work on in our lives around these fears. They are not visible all the time, because they are suppressed in most cases. So, the fear is like a mountain covered by a cloud. They sometimes appear whole and sometimes partial. We can not distinctly see its shape, size, colour, and characteristics. We cannot distinctly see its shape, size, colour, and characteristics. But inside, it has melting ice and concrete stone.

Towns were expanded, roads were constructed; different religious, cultural rituals and caste/tribal groups came into being on the basis of human needs. These all, indeed, came into being for protection from fear. The competition of weapons was for protection from enemies and to be more powerful. In the name of protection from fear, fears are being invited. New inventions and technologies have invited new problems and challenges. New diseases have begun to appear. Many of them transformed into epidemics, and some of them are transferable diseases. Great wars happened to take place. Many people lost their lives from the leakage of radiation produced in nuclear reactors. These modern fears are the products of new inventions invented for the protection from fears and avoiding fears. People have been seeking ways out of fears since ages. Some fears have been minimised, but many new fears have been added. It is moving around in a full circle. We are entangled with it. Our attempts on minimising fears and liberation from such fears still and will always continue.

We hardly get solution to these fears. We never realise that we are entangled with and plunged into the quicksand of fears. A man without a certain goal is like a kite without thread. We are like a boat without a boatman which goes wherever the wind takes. We seek solution of fear. Various types of fears come to our lives one after another; they are our immediate problems. They are tangled, and in case we find solutions, it is easier to escape such complexities. We live our lives step by step. When we are on a step, many other steps follow it. In this way, we have to complete steps in our lives. When we have no idea about it, sometimes we have to step on and sometimes step down—it's an illusion. It makes our lives more difficult.

The consciousness is a major cause. It gives us both knowledge and fear. Rene Descartes, a great philosopher, said, 'Knowledge comes from wisdom.'[1] John Locke argued, 'Knowledge comes from experience.'[2] I disagree with them. Consciousness should collide with some other objects to produce knowledge; otherwise, neither knowledge nor experience exists. Imagination without such collision is sometimes possible, but it neither produces knowledge nor experience.

Knowledge generates fear. Knowledge shouldn't be for knowledge; it should be for the sake of life. Knowledge without understanding of fear is useless. Its collision with objects is necessary in constituting knowledge and experience. Otherwise, how can knowledge and experience be possible? The knowledge we get from consciousness is a message. Major sources of such messages are sense organs and muscles. Sense organs and muscles send messages to the brain and converts itself into consciousness. Consciousness does not produce fear every time—fear depends on how consciousness has been developed. The presence of an atomic weapon does not create fear. But when we acquire knowledge about its destructive potentiality, expansion of poison, and explosive potentiality, it creates fear. When consciousness and conditional reflex in all physical and non-physical objects in this universe collide with our nature and characters, then it converts into fear.

We are entangled with fear all around. New fears have been adding to existing fears since prehistoric time. People had fear of food and habitats in ancient periods—livelihood was possible with fruits, roots, and meat and caves were sufficient shelters. They had fear of storms and wild animals. When they were able to hunt, they used to eat enough to satisfy their hunger, but in case they were unable to hunt, their hunger used to hunt them. However, they had no fear of rules, regulations, cultures, blind beliefs, superstitions, and public scandal. They had very few enemies. The number of enemies increased along with the expansion of their groups. Their hostility used to particularly be related to food, territories, and lovers and their beloved.

People moved towards civilisation, and they continued invention as well as development of science. Buildings were constructed, vehicles were brought into use, societies came into being, countries were developed, national and international laws were constituted, and territorial borders were determined.

New weapons and machines were invented. Peripherally, a man makes his attempts to work for his security and increase facilities. He builds a house. Then, he manages air conditioning, heaters, stoves, ovens, gadgets, washing machines, irons, and refrigerators in his house. Sufficient facilities sometimes measure the state of civilisation. If we observe all these goods for facilities, we can see the existence of fear. Although he claims that they are for facilities and protection from hot and cold, still a major reason behind it is fear. In some cases, we wear clothes for prestige and fashion—but in most of the cases, we wear them for protection from the heat and cold. Fear makes us wear warm clothes in winter for protection from cold and sickness. We have the fear that we may die if our body suffers from imbalance of temperature, food, and weather. The 'fear of death' is produced from the combination of these trifling matters.

It does not matter whether he is healthy or unhealthy, he shows various indications. These may be because of unconsciousness or outcome of id as analysed by Freud, due to which everything is out of memory. Whatever we have in our mind comes out one after another. As they come out through varied means, they become various signals.

During the interpretation of various signals, Freud says that the signal disappears when consciousness replaces unconsciousness.[3]

That means that in the presence of consciousness, whatever signal a man has will disappear. They come to the mind when he tries to remember. Signals of fear are different. Various signals exist when a man suffers from fear: like being scared, yelling, weeping, crying, hurrying, escaping, hiding, defending, murmuring, etc. When a man knows about fear, he applies all techniques and ideas to get rid of such fear. So, to suffer from the fear is to identify problems and acquire knowledge. Knowledge produces fear and it brings solution too. This knowledge works to realise, clear, care, bring up, and liberate. A man who lives in the jungle is scared if he sees footsteps of a giant and dangerous animal. But the people in the town areas are never frightened of such footsteps. The reason behind it is their unfamiliarity to the footsteps, how dangerous it is, and how brutal the animal is.

Jhamak Ghimire remembers the death of her grandmother and writes, 'I didn't know how the life-bird of my grandmother flew away from my frontage. If I knew about it, I would have been frightened, and I would have lost my soul that night.'[4]

We find such fear in small children as well. They fear new people, new goods, and new circumstances. They vary from one another. We judge their activities as weak, introverted, and ignorant. These are not their weaknesses, but the results of their fears. Some of them feel fear even when they sleep and they ask their parents to keep chatting. They fear according to the level of their knowledge. The lower the knowledge is, the lower the fear is, and the higher the knowledge is, the higher the fear is. Sometimes we see babies climb on the window and play with sharp weapons and fire. The babysitters and parents fear these activities of the babies, but the babies don't seem to have any fear. Both their parents and babysitters have knowledge about the hazards of these objects.

People use different terms like criminal, strong, warrior, poisonous, fighter, murderer, robber, and villain in different places. These terms are often used to influence the mentality of others. These are Hitlerian words to terrorise others and rule them. Some people think if they say, 'He is superior here.' It makes others feel a fear of him. The essential meaning of such a remark is that he is a ruler there. It's a kind of psychological publicity that whoever fights against him loses his/her life or s/he never gets victory over him. Use of words like superior, villain, murderer, law, constitution, and police is to create fear (or indication of freedom from fear). People use such words to show their existence. I discuss the sliding, uncertainty, and logocentrism of meanings and words under the title 'Meaning of Fear and Meaning of Sassure, Lacan and Jacques Derrida'.

As discussed above, fear is in every living creature. It is related to the event. Events and possible events cause fear in living creatures. Human beings are the most conscious among living creatures. Therefore, interpretation of fear is based on human beings. He tries to be alert with any fear. Likewise, he tries to protect and escape from fear. If he encounters fear with any event while trying to escape, he produces signals. He seems to be attempting to escape from possible events, accidents, and problems. Attempts at prevention always take into account circumstances, conditions, and time. This consciousness belongs to disease, conditional reflex, nature, and character. The discourse on fear by the scholars continues since the consciousness was developed.

Fear is significant in life. All the time, life undergoes fear. Let us think. Are our activities possible without fear? Are the present, past, and future possible? Is it possible to reach the office after we leave home? Or is it easier to spend time from cradle to the grave? Is philosophy without fear possible? Nothing is possible in the absence of fear. If our philosophy is relative to our lives, it undergoes fear. We assume fear is an invisible power, which is sometimes good for our problems, trouble, hardship, pain, and concerns, and we escape or struggle with it, which is always impossible. In this way, fear is omnipresent. It is in our houses, offices, with families, relatives, wealth, rages, conspiracies, murders, violence, religions, blind beliefs, and superstitions. Western scholars have interpreted fear as phobia. But Eastern scholars never linked its interpretation to phobia.

Aacharya Bharat, the first thinker of *rash* (taste) theory in the East, has considered fear a fearful *rash* among many *rashes* (tastes): *shringara* (erotic), *vira* (heroic), *karuna* (pathetic), *adbhuta* (marvellous), *hasya* (laughter), *raudra* (furious), *bibhatsa* (odious), and *santa* (quietistic). All interpretations yield these tastes.[5]

Many consciousnesses exist. Fear is one of them. Fear wakes up and sleeps with consciousness; or our consciousness wakes up with us and fear always wakes up with it. We hurry up for work—we fear we will get late; we cross the road—we fear vehicles will crash into us; we wait for the bus—we fear we won't get it; when we get late to reach work—again we fear the proprietor will scold us. The same thing recurs at home. It is just like a diary. The same process continues from the cradle to the grave. Thus, fear exists with birth and ends with death. It exists and disappears. We keep swinging into events and possible events and keep escaping. Many other possible events keep following the possibility.

During the interpretation of relativism, Rahul Sangkrityan writes, 'Even a straight line doesn't appear straight if we observe it so closely.'[6]

Like impossible straight lines and possible curve lines, curve lines exist along with straight lines between lives and deaths. Unexpected events in lives are, in fact, curve lines. We think about these before investing in life insurance. It makes us feel free when we fall sick.

Knowledge is a consciousness produced by a combination of conditional reflexes and contexts. Moreover, fear with knowledge depends on conditional reflexes. For it, how much influence the conditional reflex has, is important here. The conditional reflex is related to 'conditional reflex under behaviourism' propounded by Russian philosopher Petrovic Pavlov.[7]

Two attitudes have been interpreted: spontaneous attitudes and conditional reflexes. Any attitude based on the order of the brain is a conditional reflex. A signal has a significant contribution to the conditional reflex. According to Pavlov, mental work is a combined dynamic of the conditional reflex, the brain, and cognitive organs. He conducted an experiment in a dog to study conditional reflex. The owner always provided food to the dog at a fixed time. When the owner arrived, the dog used to produce saliva. His arrival or that particular time is a signal. These signals can be used differently on the basis of convenience and needs—blowing a whistle, ringing a bell, other indicators, and the use of different colours and names. Sense organs of the dog received the message and that went to the brain through cognitive organs. Then, the brain directed it and as a result, saliva was produced. Thus, a message in the brain received from sense organs is consciousness. It is based on regular attitudes or conditional reflexes. Sense organs automatically receive it. Conditional reflex has been discussed in detail under the title 'Conditional Reflex'. If a man loves and gives us money, we expect the same when we see him. When we see him, we think he loves and gives us money. This is always the case for children, and sometimes, it happens when they grow up. The same thing happens in jobs and businesses. This is a kind of conditional reflex.

Fear is also a conditional reflex. Its meaning is based on the conditional reflex. A word does not carry meaning itself. Meaning of a word of the past keeps continuing. The meaning of any word, as we use and understand it, has been developed in this way. These meanings convert into the conditional reflex along with the individual and time. We study, write, hear, and understand the same meanings. Similarly, we teach the same meaning and debate on them. Both language and knowledge are constructed on the basis of their meanings. Fear can be considered consciousness, as knowledge and as disease. Liberation from fear needs medicine made for fear.

Seeing a snake is equal to seeing a stone in terms of events. Seeing a snake creates fears, whereas seeing a stone does not create such fear. To see both of them is to gain knowledge. However, some of the snakes are dangerous as well as poisonous. We recite that snakes are dangerous and poisonous like Pavlov manages regular signals to the dog. We have regular signals in our consciousness that the snakes are fearful and poisonous. Due to recurring signals, the fear, like the saliva of the dog, is produced in our minds. When we see and know about the snake, our sense organs send the signal of something dangerous to our brain. So, we feel fear. Nobody has taught us that stones are dangerous and poisonous. We never feel fear when we see a stone. Again, some fears come forth from mentality and heredity. Rene Descartes says that we have some innate natures.[8] They also help maximise and minimise fear.

We have passed through different civilisations from prehistoric time to the present. Fear was powerful, yet it remained invisible in knowledge. It used to exist as comprehension occasionally. Philosophers coined terms like disgust, pain, hunger, love, pity, tension, illusion, trouble, etc. instead of fear. Philosophers and religious thinkers interpreted fear merely as comprehension. Therefore, fear remained invisible in the minds of people. It did not appear even as a dream in their wisdom. A philosopher named Immanuel Kant 'has presented 12 features' to understand objects.[9]

However features do not give complete meanings to the objects. A name of an object is a sign only. A snake is a sign, but its signified meaning is different and the conditional reflex is also different. Our words do not signify accurate characteristics of objects. As an alternative to the meaning, we use a poisonous and fearful snake, which is conditional reflex, not the meaning. Our consciousness could not develop fundamental meaning.

If in case it develops, it melts with context, but still we search signals to signify a conditional reflex. First, we understand about objects, and then we automatically understand and realise the conditional reflex. When we understand all these, we perceive the meaning of objects. Like stone, the word 'snake' does not signify poison, but our understanding of the snake makes us think it's poisonous and harmful. We understand most of the words in the same way—ghost, war, murder, violence, etc.

According to Ferdinand de Saussure, 'Language is a system of interdependent terms in which the value of each term results solely from the simultaneous presence of the others as signifier and signified.'[10] In the word, signifier is juxtaposed with signified to produce meaning. Signifier and signified always have arbitrary relationships. A word does not have factual meaning—for example, we get neither ghost nor ghostliness of the ghost in the word 'ghost'. We never have fear in our minds when we read about ghosts in books, but the imaginary presence of a ghost produces fear in our minds. Fear, in fact, has existed since time immemorial. In the beginning, fear was ignored and research continued on others. Philosophers spent ages in the name of research on fear. They found various unexpected results, like Columbus, who found America: existentialism, deconstruction, nihilism, Marxism, naturalism, skepticism, theology, materialism, monism, dualism, behaviourism, etc. Is 'ism' complete without fear? For what purpose did they discuss them? These are some genuine questions for philosophers. If we exclude fear from these philosophies, they are like consciousness without the amygdala. According to amygdala health science, 'First out of four parts of the brain was developed the earliest. It causes fear. Fear ends if it is excluded from the brain.'[11]

Dr Michael Davis, a psychiatrist at Yale University School of Medicine, has written in his report that a mouse with a wound and a useless amygdala does not fear the cat. In an experiment, he kept both the mouse and the cat together. The result was dramatic—'A mouse with such a condition walked slowly towards the cat and began to lick its ear.' He further says, 'A mouse with a normal condition had never shown such behaviour.'[12]

Death is a great fear for human beings. It is not only necrophobia. We are extremely fearful of death. In fact, we die every moment. We don't know anything about it. We consider the death of the whole body as death. We have a billion trillion cells in our body. They are dying every moment and new ones are taking their place. The more those cells are alive, the more we are alive. For our longevity, our cells must be strong. If their numbers decrease, we need to work to increase their numbers. If we are able to increase their numbers, we can elongate our lives. This is the same reason behind the average long lives of citizens in rich countries and the average short lives of citizens in poor countries.

Fear is a powerful human circumstance. It has influenced most of our activities; above all, it has the biggest influence in our lives. We are walking to the future, but our journey is guided by fear. It conducts our lives. Thus, fear has widespread scope. Its measurement of length, width, and height is impossible. Its size is not smaller than the sky. We cannot go beyond it. It exists in every human. According to Rene Descartes, 'Knowledge without skepticism is impossible and it can be possible only via skepticism. So, skepticism is useful for knowledge and truth.'[13] We continuously encounter fear while searching truth via skepticism. Thus, most of research works end at fear.

As I have said above, fear exists with knowledge, but in some cases, it exists without knowledge too. Suppose we go to a new place—we have no idea about the way of life, knowledge, script, religion, culture, climate, ruling system, law, etc. in that place. Then fears start: How should one behave? How does one search for a job? How does one work? What kind of people are there? What kind of ruling system does that place have? Will we make a mistake in our work? And will friends tell us something? We fear human beings on the one hand and machines on the other. We fear making a mistake, since we don't know how to use the machine. We fear wounds and accidents.

A fear of nature in the mechanical age has also been added. Jean Boudrillard said, 'Now, if you're able to run with a machine, you can live. If not, your last day is supposed to arrive.'[14]

Here, to know about 'I don't know' is also knowledge. Many interpretations have been made on fear 'existing' and 'not existing'. To know fear 'doesn't exist' is knowledge. If in case we get an idea about work and machines, fear gets minimised. Thus, we have been surrounded by fear. When we think about all these, it suffocates us. This is a reality. We spend our lives playing hide and seek with fear.

The way we have been walking for so long is ours. So, we feel no fear to walk on it. But if murder and suicide cases happened to take place, they create fear and we would fear to walk there. We walk all around the way due to fear. Such fearful circumstances prevail everywhere in the house, the office, industries, and on the way.

We felt no fear to live in a house yesterday. We thought the house was secured and strong. It was comfortable for us. But today, a man says, 'Somebody has committed suicide here.' Then, cold blood runs through our body and our body becomes chilled. We feel as if our head is swelling. We don't like to live there any longer. We fear something unexpected will happen to us.

People with and without fear are able to do great works. It means people have lots of powers. The people who use such powers have become famous. To be crazy in work is to be free from fear. As children grow, so fear increases in them. Similarly, when a man enters into consciousness, he encounters a number of problems. These problems were various forms of fear. Fear encounters each problem. These problems revolve around fear. We spend our lives in search of solutions for these problems. We are deprived of entertainment, happiness, and comfort due to this fear. Fear originates from knowledge and we continuously work on its solution. Fear, thus, urges a man to create his own world. Even the world has been deeply influenced by this fear. He can be free from some fears, but it is impossible to be free from some of the others—although such fears can be minimised. There is a haunted house or extremely fearful place. We fear it, yet we continue to go there daily. To continue going can minimise fear. Three people have committed crimes in the place since I started my job. I know—this is the same place where three people have committed suicide. Many people like me walk daily through the same place. In the beginning, I felt fear to walk there. As soon as I reached there, the same incident used to be in my mind. Now I am habitual there. It's all right for me now. Neither do I feel fear nor do I remember the incident. But as exceptional cases, some other people still feel fear. If a man reaches the mouth of death for the first time, he feels great fear. But if it is repeated continuously, fear will be minimised. The same thing happens to people who go to the battlefield for the first time. In such a way, we can minimise all fears—they will gradually be minimised.

Prof. Dr Tanka Prasad Neupane, a linguist, tells us about the universality of fear in our lives that has been included in Eastern literature and writes, 'Fear has been considered as a continuous process in all living creatures in Sanskrit literature: food, sleep and masturbatory activities found in all living creatures including human beings.'[15]

Fear in human beings is more than in animals or they suffer from fear more than animals. Sub-fears continued to be added in fears. They are: fear of living creatures, fear of dreadful animals, fear of natural disaster, fear of heat, fear of cold, fear of storms, fear of thunder, fear of earthquakes, fear of tsunamis, fear of new diseases, fear of atomic weapons, etc. People suffer from fear of country, caste/ethnicity, language, script, religion, and culture on the one hand, and they have the fear of their own physical disease, death, events, and accidents. In this way, layers of fears exist like economic fear, social fear, relatives fear, generation fear, etc. There is a different fear from feudalist rule, rules and regulations, law, constitution, oppressor, etc.

There is another group of fears of violation made upon the weak by the strong in society. In addition to these fears, there are other fears to follow human beings. Thus, they fear even widespread, real, and imaginary fears. Besides, they fear marriage, biodiversity, and other physical fears. We make weapons for security from enemies, but at the same time, atomic weapons are feared as the whole of human civilisation could collapse. If we have a way towards social structure against oppression and domination, we still fear irresponsibility, corruption, corrupt administration, and inability. So people have no emancipation from fear. In this vast universe, even light takes a long time to reach from one corner to another. We human beings are alone and separate in this planet. This is too fearsome. We have no contact with civilised living beings from other planets. If in case we are able to contact such living beings and if they appeared more developed and civilised than us, how fearful could our hesitation be in front of them? This is an imaginary question.

The structure of the human mind is distinctive. The dynamics of fear in human beings is much wider than it is in animals. So human efforts for life security are much better than efforts by animals. The more fear is sensitive, the more self-defense is serious. Animals with developed minds suffered from fear much more than the animals with the least developed minds since prehistoric time. So, human beings suffered from fear and still they fear with other animals in this planet, because human beings are more conscious than other animals.

If the fear is divided into two parts: black and white, the black part represents negative characters like violence, murder, crime, conspiracy, ego, etc., whereas the white part includes positive characters like civilisation, progress, success, development, friendship, peace, etc.

These concepts apply from family conflicts to world wars; and from feudalists to old and unhealthy men. Similarly, it can apply from language, script, religion, culture to the development of caste/ethnicity. The same thing happens from scientific invention to the invention of medicine. It is in music, song, and art as well. It can be found from human activities to superstition and blind belief. It is in recreation, love, and happiness. Fear stirs and guides every human activity: both negative and positive. We have to minimise unnecessary fear. Necessary fear should be balanced and increased.

Fear gives birth to need, invention, construction, and creation. This fear is a universe of consciousness related to human activities. War, peace, murder, suppression, injustice, oppression, domination, etc. are black and white parts of fear. Fear occupies the human mind more than 75 per cent of the time.

End Notes:

1. Birendra Prasad Mishra, *Introduction to Philosophy*, Nepal Charity Foundation, Kathmandu, Nepal 2065 v.s. p. 39.
2. Birendra Prasad Mishra, *Introduction to Philosophy*, Nepal Charity Foundation, Kathmandu, Nepal 2065 v.s p. 25.

3. *Freud's Psychoanalysis*, trans. Madhusudhan Pande. Pairavi Publication, Kathmandu, Nepal 2061 v.s. p. 117.
4. Jhamak Ghimire, *Jivan Kanda ki Phul*, Online Nepali Literature Forum, Kathmandu, Nepal 2067 v.s. p.43.
5. Mohan Raj Sharma; Khagendra Prasad Luitel, *Eastern and Western Literary Theory*, Student Book Bhandar, Kathmandu, Nepal 2063 v.s. p. 44.
6. Rahul Sangkrityan, *Sketch of the World*, trans. Narayan Giri. Marxbad Study-Research Academy, Kathmandu, Nepal 2066 v.s. p. 47.
7. Rahul Sangkrityan, *Sketch of the World*, trans. Narayan Giri. Marxbad Study-Research Academy, Kathmandu, Nepal 2066 v.s p. 285.
8. Birendra Prasad Mishra, *Introduction to Philosophy*, Nepal Charity Foundation, Kathmandu, Nepal 2065 v.s p. 15.
9. Birendra Prasad Mishra, *Introduction to Philosophy*, Nepal Charity Foundation, Kathmandu, Nepal 2065 v.s p. 43.
10. GovindaRaj Bhattarai, *Creator and Digital Talk*, International Nepali Literary Society, Washington DC, USA 2066 v.s p. 71.
11. Rush W. Dozier, Jr. *Fear Itself*, St. Martin's Press 1998, p. 30.
12. Rush W. Dozier, Jr. *Fear Itself*, St. Martin's Press 1998, p. 30.
13. Birendra Prasad Mishra, *Introduction to Philosophy*. Nepal Charity Foundation, Kathmandu, Nepal 2065 v.s. p. 14.
14. Gobinda Raj Bhattarai, *Uttar Adhunik Bimarsha (Post Modern Discourse)*, Modern Books, Kathmandu, Nepal 2008 p. 62.
15. Tanka Prasad Neupane, *Vayabadi Aadibasi yek Anucharcha, Vayabad Baicharik Chintan*, Editor and Publisher Prakash Thamsuhang, Nepali Literature Academy, Hong Kong, 2066 v.s. p. 54.

2

Fear System and Fear

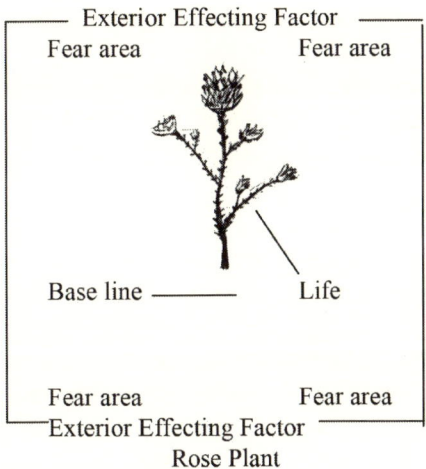

Exterior Effecting Factor

Fear area   Fear area

Base line ——————— Life

Fear area   Fear area

Exterior Effecting Factor

Rose Plant

Figure No. 1

Figure No. 1 presents a rose plant. It is just like a life. It depends on its root, bud, flower, leaf, and thorn. The exterior part that influences the plant is the fear area. When we plant a seed, it comes forth and grows. The branches grow on its body, it grows buds, and beautiful flowers blossom. The beauty of the flower attracts and entertains others. We compose songs of flowers and claim the rose is just a flower. In fact, the meaning of the word 'rose' does not limit it as a mere flower. The rose plant includes the root, bark, stem, leaf, and flower. These are all separate parts of the rose plant. So it is easier to know them separately. A combination of all these separate parts is the rose. Similarly, the earth and the universe have a similar combination. We don't care how the feelings of a rose have been incorporated into the combination. We ignore even consciousness. We ignore both the non-physical presence like feeling and consciousness and the physical presence like root, etc. and other interior parts—still, the combination of these is rose. We closely recognise its thorns and flower. The beauty of its flower is linked to feeling. We feel happy and sentimental due to its beauty. The thorn along with its flower works to keep our consciousness active. Roots hide inside the soil and its bark. Similarly, the bud hides inside the seed and the flower inside the bud. According to the consciousness of the rose, its thorns remain active. In total, the rose has sharp, pointed thorns, bark to cover its body, and roots under soil. Roots, stem, branches, buds, and flowers do not develop on its whole body, but bark covers the whole parts except the flower. The flower has a thin layer of flower bark. Its thorns develop on each and every part covered by the bark. People witness a continuous smiling in a rose. The beauty of a rose, indeed, grows in its flower. The same thing happens to the lives of human beings. Some are beautiful; some are visible; and some are invisible.

Philosophers, spiritualists, literary figures, and artists sing songs of rose flowers, but not of its thorns. Beauty does not lie in thorns; again, no beauty of the flower without thorns is possible. All others have no idea about it. Flowers can be beautiful under the security provided by thorns. Similarly, the whirlwind of fear moves around us. We prevent it by theory, philosophy, and science. A man with ego 'I' makes a way and moves around it. We come out from a whirlwind and plunge into another one. The whirlwind always follows us. We get rid of it, but immediately, another whirlwind follows us. Thus, life is a long series of whirlwinds and emancipation. We consider life as if it has been enclosed by whirlwinds, or the main theme of fear has been lightly covered inside a transparent net by the theory. Still, we are not free inside it. Everybody has seen darkness in the transparent net but yet not observed it closely. Due to the same darkness, the light is visible. Our life has light, yet it has been covered by darkness or fear. Like to the light, we are unjust to the fear, yet it has a huge role in our lives.

Like the thorns of a rose, all living creatures possess different organs, poisons, nails, trunks, horns, colours, etc. to signal the arrival of enemies and protection from them. These security organs help them keep themselves safe. In this way, the poison of snakes, the colour of the lizards, the paws and teeth of tigers, sharp pointed thorns of porcupines, the urine of wolves, trunks of elephants, etc. are security organs. When living creatures feel fear, they show these security organs.

Philosophy, theory, science, and spiritualism guide our lives, but fear is their source. 'I' exists with fear. The height of life increases along with the development of the consciousness of kids. This height shows an invisible line to encircle human beings before they encounter fear. One phase completes along with the encounter with fear or events that happen; and the next phase starts or new fears take place. A man plays this game throughout his lives. Therefore, philosophy is essential for lives to live. Fear is the foundation of all philosophies. It's just like a rope that looks like a snake crushed under walls and stones or crushed over by life and darkness. It's so much crushed, almost suffocating to come out from such a trap. We, in this way, desire liberation from theory and philosophy. 'Is' are driven away. So 'I', 'you', 'we', and 'they' are fearful.

To think about fear is to minimise fear of both universe and body. A man, at least, loves his body, loves to touch, but at the same time, he feels fear as well. Even the human body is vast. We hardly find out where and what part of the body itches, suffers, and feels pain. We feel pain, suffering, and itching somewhere in our bodies. Moreover, we feel something uneasy inside the chest, sharp pain in the heart, kidney, lungs, stomach, throat, etc. We ignore light pain and itching of our bodies, but we think we will die if any sharp pain starts. The kidney, heart, lungs, liver, and brain are likely to burst out. In such a condition, however, we are unable to diagnose illness, yet we still suffer from an unknown fear of death and lifelong damages of parts of the body. If the illness was diagnostic, the fear could be known, but it is beyond the diagnosis. So the fear is unknown in this case. If the illness is diagnosed, next, fear will start.

This universe is so vast; something beyond imagination appears, disappears, and reappears. Events and accidents beyond imagination occur. What would happen in planets, stars, solar systems, and the earth? The answer is beyond imagination. We are unable to answer such a question even about Earth, let alone about planets, stars, and solar systems. The same case applies to some parts and objects in the earth. Thoughts and feelings about the universe generate fears continuously. These are all unknown. So, people imagined their symbols: god, goddess, devil, natural force, and invisible power. Then, people began to be fearful of them and started to respect them. This universe is still mysterious.

For all people, from passengers on an airplane with fire on the tail, an old man struggling with death in his bed, and people with dangerous transferable diseases, death is inevitable. The more it is higher, the more it is troublesome. Suffocation when death is inevitable does not lower the pain, rather the pain increases—again, the more it increases, the more troublesome it is and dies soon. In such a condition, what does a man feel? What does he think? What will happen to his life and the world? Contemplation is necessary on all these things. Such moments are ahead all the time. In this situation, fear and fear-related subjects come to the mind more than anything else. Balanced thinking, consolation, and tolerance are great medicines in these moments. Activities like hurrying up, crying, and weeping do not minimise pain, rather, these all maximise pain. The knowledge of death makes man more terrified and fearful. Death does not have any relation to terror and fear. It is not beneficial to increase illness through terror and fear. We human beings should proceed through minimising terror and fear in our lives. When we are able to see fear around us, it brings comfort in life, death, and trouble.

3

Age of Fear

When human beings existed in this earth, consciousness began to increase. They began to consider the necessity of security. As was knowledge about different caste/ethnicity, life, and the world, so was fear in human minds. People started to struggle with the fear produced by appetite, wild animals, and natural forces.

While interpreting Marxism, Dr Prakash Kanta writes: 'Marxism adopts five production systems. Thus, the social development requires phases. Five production systems are: (1) primitive commune society, (2) slave-owning society, (3) feudal society, (4) capitalist society, and (5) Communist society.'[1]

Marxism has been divided into ages. I divide them from the fear perspective. These ages differ on the basis of different thoughts and faiths. This division is not based on hard and fast rules. Again, it can't be as it has been claimed. We try to justify our perspective to determine them. I present here different ages from the perspective of fear. Fears appeared in the previous age seem to be adding to the later fears. Fears are continuously added based on time and civilisation.

Ages based on fears are as follows. The following figure shows the fear of a previous age being continuously added to the later.

    a.   Primitive low fear age (primitive hunting age)
    b.   Pre-middle fear age (agricultural age)
    c.   Middle fear age (feudal age)
    d.   Post middle fear age (age of industrialisation)
    e.   Nuclear fear age

f. Cyber fear age
g. Space fear age
h. Virus fear age
i. Extreme fear age
j. Fearless age

a. Primitive Low Fear Age (Primitive Hunting Age)

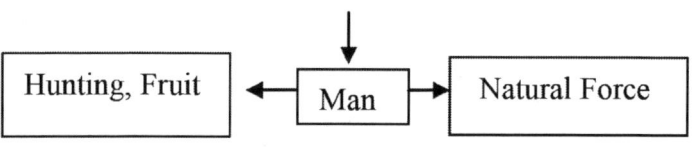

Figure No. 2

The man is in the middle of Figure No. 2. He is a man of primitive age. He is surrounded by hunting, fruits, appetite, disease, and natural forces. The figure indicates that the man in the hunting age was alone. He was with appetite, disease, and natural forces. He used to eat meat, fruits, and roots for his appetite.

The beginning phase of human civilisation development can be considered as the primitive hunting age. This is also known as the primitive low fear age. People were different physically from other animals since the primitive age and still they are different. In the primitive age, people did not have laws, rules, and regulations, religion, culture, language, script, society, country, relatives, science, and dangerous diseases. Knowledge related to an object is necessary for fear. The people in the primitive age had consciousness, but they did not have knowledge. Consciousness gives knowledge of objects and fulfills needs. Fear is maximised by knowledge. In the primitive stage, people did not have knowledge of everything. They did not have any idea of effects. As a result, they had no fear. Fear beyond possible events was hardly possible. They did not have any occupational, economic, social, political, present, future, and past fear. Nuclear weapons were not available. No fear of god, devil, paradise, hell existed nor was there the fear of generation. In the beginning, they were not in groups. Later, they began to live in small groups. During that period, one group hardly met with another. People were living individually, so suspicion, jealousy, conspiracy, superstition, and blind belief were not developed in their minds. Therefore, fear from all these was impossible. It was a classless society without division between caste/ethnic groups.

There was nothing to evaluate human temperament, so the people had temperamentally free but simple lives. Man was alone. What was there to doubt? Who was there to be jealous of? Why should one make a conspiracy? Why should one be greedy? Why should one be angry? These consciousnesses are human temperaments, yet they were not necessary for human beings. Nothing was systematic and everything was open. No police, soldier, rule, regulation, nor law prevailed. Society, like postmodern and Communist societies, was open. The only fear they had in their minds was scarcity of meat and wild animals for hunting. They used to encounter wild animals while wandering to and fro for food. They used to eat fruits, roots, and meat. The natural forces were another fear for them. A labour division did not exist during that age. Due to the absence of production and private property, oppression and domination were impossible. War among them was hardly possible. Similarly, there were a few chances of hostility. They did not have necessary instruments to fight with natural forces and for their livelihood. They did not have reservation of food. They had very simple weapons to hunt big animals. They used to hunt with weapons made of stones. They used to wander from place to place for food because they were nomads. They used to live in caves, tunnels, and underground. In fact, they had very little fear. They had limited knowledge and conditional reflexes; as a result, they had limited fear. They had only 10 per cent fear compared to the present. Therefore, it is the primitive low fear age.

b. Pre-middle Fear Age (Agricultural Age)

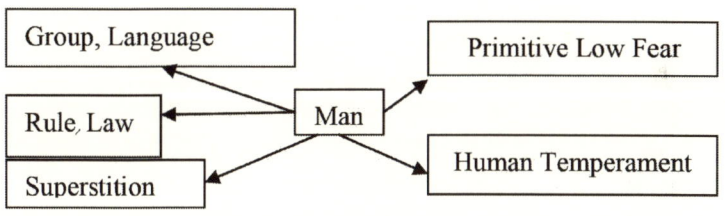

Figure No. 3

The above Figure No. 3 shows a man in the middle of group, language, script, rules and regulations, law, blind belief, superstition, human temperament, and primitive low fear age (primitive hunting age). Other fears were added to the fear of primitive low fear age.

It is a more advantageous age in terms of consciousness, knowledge, and conditional reflexes than the hunting age. But some consciousness, knowledge, and conditional reflexes of the hunting age transferred into the agricultural age. Some more were added to this age. People began to live in groups. Various groups were constituted. They left to enjoy wandering in small groups, and it was not secured in terms of security. Threats from wild animals increased even more. Similar threat was possible from enemies. Thus, they began to live in a huge group, but they were helpless in front of a natural force. They began to worship gods for security from such forces. They began to worship natural events and objects. They worshipped rains, floods, earthquakes, thunder, and storms as invisible powers. They began to fear what they worshipped. Their weapons began to be improved. In course of time, the hostility increased between different groups. They began to fight even without their groups. Slowly and gradually, human temperaments like work, anger, love, jealousy, and suspicion began to exist. Fear was continuously added due to these temperaments. Yet, social development was continuous. The more they developed and were richer in weapons, consciousness, and knowledge, the more fear increased.

They were tired, of scarcity of food, mismanagement, and difficulties of their settlements and other problems during their nomadic lives. They were in search of an alternative solution for it. Then, blind belief and superstitious thoughts began to take place. The population increased very fast. Rules and regulations and laws were enacted for prosperous and peaceful societies and proper culture and rituals. The same rules and regulations and laws to control human beings were threats for them. The population growth in a group invited conflicts among them. Jealousy, hatred, and mistrust increased. Thus, human temperament expanded. Various problems began to take place. They needed language and script for communication. Love increased among them much faster. In this way, human temperament, enemies, rules, and laws helped fear to increase. They used to be hungry most of the time when they merely depended on hunting. It forced them to consider growing and preserving food. They used to hunt in a group and divide meat among them. It was difficult to sustain lives on hunting and fruits during that period. From the group emerged some who were clever and others who were leaders. The course of developing security for them maximised fears only. Fear resulted in a new invention on the one hand, and civilisation began to develop on the other hand. In other words, fear existed along with invention and civilisation. Fear increased 20 per cent in such a condition.

c. Middle Fear Age (Feudal Age)

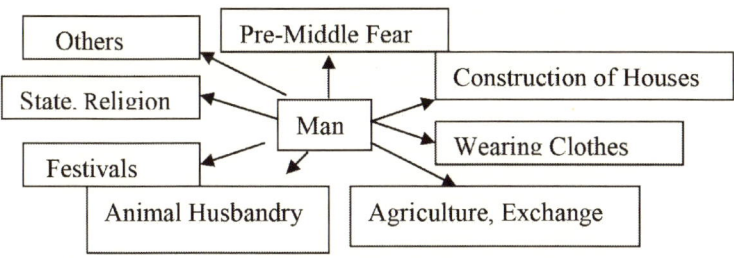

Figure No. 4

The Figure No. 4 shows the man in the middle of pre-middle fear age, construction of houses, wearing clothes, agriculture and exchange, animal husbandry, festivals, state and religion, and other things. It also depicts additional new fears to the previous fears.

Slowly and gradually, people began to adopt agriculture. They began to live in groups for agriculture. Those groups gradually changed into society. They learnt to wear clothes. Festivals, religions, and rituals began to be celebrated. As the consciousness increased, they began to understand troubles and difficulties originated from natural forces. Storms and hail ruined their crops; as a result, they feared invisible forces and began to worship them as gods. As French Marxist Luis Althusser said, some clever people in society started to weave the net of blind belief and superstitions to trap and dominate others for their security. The tradition of superstition and blind belief of the very beginning continued, and other new ones were added to them later. Population increased in society. They were divided into different caste/ethnic groups: like country, religion, and culture, etc. The feeling of mine and yours developed. In the slavery age, those who lost in wars were made slaves by those who were victorious in wars.

Many people were peasants in the feudal age and few of them were feudalists. Those feudalists were rich. They used to dominate the peasants. There used to be struggle between the peasants and the feudalists. Besides them, there were other people of different classes and occupations. There was jealousy, doubt, anger, greed, and conspiracy and treachery. All of these things caused struggle among them. Such struggle even used to happen within their groups and classes. Their competition was to be limited within their classes and groups. It exists even today. Peasants competed to win the faith of feudal people, for their benefits. They had a hierarchical social structure, both in peasant and feudal communities. Their competition was based on levels. States, security forces, jealousy, and executives were established during this age. Rules, law, and constitution were in practice. Good and powerful weapons began to develop. Thousands of years later, weapons made of stones were replaced by the weapons made of metals. Wars began to take place beyond groups between countries. Detainees used to be murdered in the beginning. Later, they were sent to a labour camp. Labour division and exchange of goods started. The system of private property developed. Likewise, private property and family developed, and oppression and domination started along with all these things. Different forms of worships of nature appeared. Changes took place in religions. Those who considered themselves great and leading figures in society appeared dominant even in religious sectors. The rich people used a religion as a weapon to dominate and control the poor. The power in society was centred in the hands of priests and popes for a long time. Suppression, jealousy, conspiracy, treachery, ego, greed, etc. appeared in society and began to appear in the country. Rules, laws, religions, cultures and disciplines in this age were more rigid than they were in the primitive age. Fear did not exist before the existence of these all. As a result, due to the fear from law, religion, culture, private property of the group, country, and family, fear reached 30 per cent.

d. Post-middle Fear Age (Industrial Age)

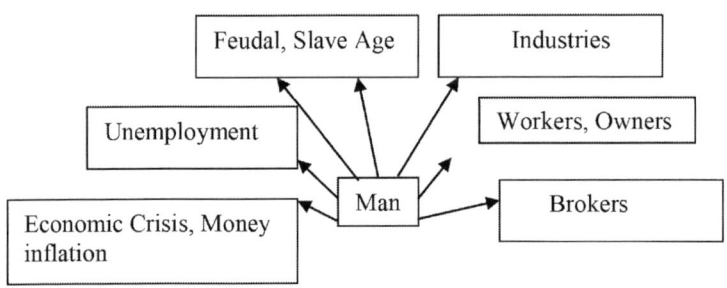

Figure No. 5

The figure shows that industries, workers, owners, brokers, economic crisis and money inflation, unemployment, etc. were added to the fears of the feudal age.

People were even more civilised. Their knowledge and wisdom became much wider. They had more knowledge and education. Agricultural products were insufficient for them. Good exchanges increased even more. People began to use money. Human needs, desires, and expectations expanded more than ever. Such ceaseless expansion of needs, desires, and expectations invited the development of industries. Owners of the industries invested a huge share of capital for their factories; they appointed workers to run their factories. The establishment of industries generated problems. With the presence of economic crisis, money inflation, and marginal productive potentiality, conflict between workers, owners, and brokers was inevitable. Economic crisis appeared in the world. The rate of unemployment increased due to such economic crisis. Workers began to unite for rights against owners. The hostility increased among the people. People were divided into classes and groups; they were fearful and aware of each other. Additional fears ceaselessly came into being. Huge walls of fears were erected all around human beings. The size of fear was 40 per cent in this age.

e. Nuclear Fear Age

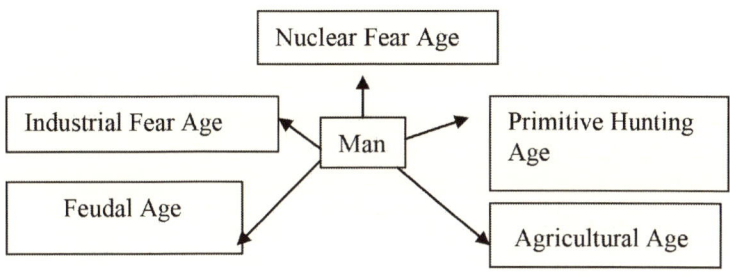

Figure No. 6

The figure shows man in the middle of primitive low fear age (primitive hunting age), pre-middle fear age (agricultural age), middle fear age (feudal age), post-middle fear age (industrial age), and nuclear fear age. The nuclear fear as an additional fear has been added to the previous ones.

Countries in the world were in competition for power. All of them understood that to be developed is to be powerful. The developed country without power cannot be considered as a developed country, because the meaning of 'developed' was mostly focused on power. Again, no other countries respected a country without power. So, most of the countries were in competition for power. A huge share of economy was invested for the production of weapons and nuclear weapons; yet they did not forget to talk about disarmament and treaty. In fact, they all engaged in conspiracy and they considered themselves superior. They say one thing and do another. The whole world was undergoing the fear of nuclear war. The fear in this age increased to 50 per cent.

f. Cyber Fear Age

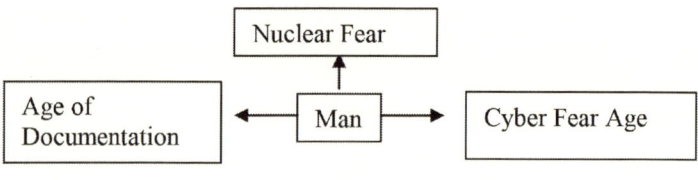

Figure No. 7

In the course of talking about the impact of cyber space, Prof. Dr Gobinda Raj Bhattarai says, 'Cyber has a big role in transplantation of psychological fear and even bigger role to wage psychological wars.'[2]

Figure No. 7 depicts the cyber fear and the fear of documents and records are added to the previous fears. Most of the works in this age are done online. This online lifestyle creates fear too.

The world is in the cyber fear age. The online world is used from general household works like reading, writing, and documentation to nuclear weapons, war ports, jet fighters, satellites, etc. Nuclear weapons of the world's powerful countries are under the control and supervision of the cyber world. Switching on a small button can collapse huge buildings and cities within a second. The cyber age, in fact, is the highest achievement of human civilisation. Its proper use enriches human civilisation, but its misuse can be a threat to the people in the world. Antagonism among the countries can possibly collapse the whole world at any time. The potential for dangerous accidents, therefore, is around us. Nobody knows when and what will happen. So the world is threatened with a big and possible accident. The fear keeps playing in the minds of everyone that such an accident will take place. Here, the size of fear extended to 60 per cent.

g. Space Fear Age

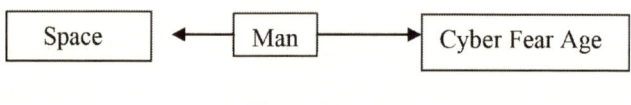

Figure No. 8

Figure No. 8 presents a man between the cyber fear age and the space fear age. In the course of development, the man started space travel. Thus, the impact and scope of the cyber world are not limited to Earth. Its scope is extending to space. The satellite is controlled and guided by the cyber. It is used in war and attacking enemies. Many works like treaties, agreements, practice of war, etc. have started in space. Most of the powerful countries are in competition to increase their impact in space. Nuclear weapon tests have begun in space. Entry of human beings into space has increased every day. It has created fear in the minds of people on this earth. In this age, fear increased to 70 per cent.

h. Virus Fear Age

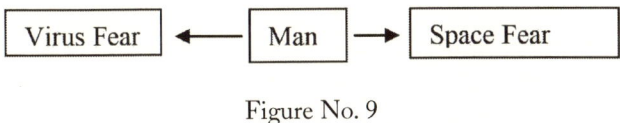

Figure No. 9

Figure No. 9 presents the space fear age, the man and the virus fear on a horizontal line together. Fears that continued from the past are always with human beings. New fears are being continuously added to them. The virus is the most dangerous disease in this world. However, there are other diseases; a virus is a serious threat to human beings. During this time, the power of human immunity has increased. Birds and animals could not remain untouched by such a virus. The bird flu (H5N1) broke out in 2003 from China and swine flu (H1N1) broke out in 2009 from Mexico and terrorised the whole world. A large number of people lost their lives and numbers larger than these were severely affected by the disease. Because of these diseases, a man was frightened to talk with a man and shake hands. Either he escaped from the man or used a mask to talk. People began to use the mask at that time and now it is compulsory. Those who walk without a mask will be attacked by such a virus at any time. So, people feel secured to walk with masks. People used the masks in dirty places, to protect themselves from smoke, dirt, and at work. They use masks at hospitals and industries. The use of masks yesterday was not compulsory. After the threats of bird flu and swine flu, its use increased and became widespread. Nowadays, some people can't walk without masks. We manage injections and medicine for our babies to keep them safe from viruses and other diseases in the future.

These indicate a big fear in the mind of a man. People did not feel difficulty eating pork and chicken before the flus existed. People don't feel sure to eat these meats after the onset of the different kinds of flu. Not only pork and chicken, they think twice before they eat any meat. If swine and bird flu cannot be controlled, such viruses will transfer to other birds and animals and finally to human beings. Then, the whole world will plunge into chaos. It makes us feel frightened, if we just think about it. Social and economic impacts of these diseases are beyond the limit. Hong Kong and Mexico are yet not completely out of such chaos. The pain left by it has not yet been recovered. What will happen if these new viruses attacking the world also had those suffering from HIV Aids?

The virus has extended fear not only in living beings, but in the cyber world too. The computers in proper use can be attacked by viruses at any time, and all documents, information, data, and recordings will collapse. These days, people store their information, data, records, and industrial and official information in computer. It is comfortable and easy. But if a virus attacks it, everything will be ruined. Thus, the threat of viruses are everywhere. People are always fearful of a computer virus. The same virus we find in computers can be found in mobile phones. New machines and instruments exist every day—their chips and software are under construction. Viruses are not limited to computers and mobiles, but they have transferred to cameras as well. It is extending its sectors every day. The fear has increased to 80 per cent in this age.

i. Extreme Fear Age

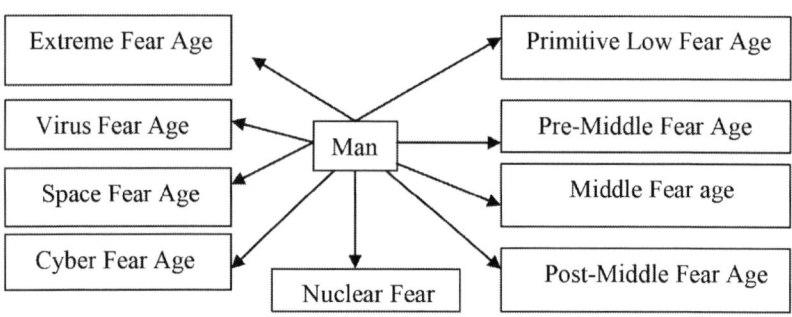

Figure No. 10

Figure No. 10 shows man in the middle of primitive low fear age (primitive hunting age), pre-middle fear age (agricultural age), middle fear age (feudal age), post-middle fear age (industrial age), nuclear fear age, cyber fear age, space fear age, virus fear age, and extreme fear age. These are the fear ages till this time in the world. There are many ages like this and new ones will continuously be added. It is a construct of ambition, desire, aspiration, and time.

It has been extreme fear age till this time. Consciousness, knowledge, fear, wisdom, and conditional reflexes have reached their climax in this age. People understand life and the world exclusively—they have experienced wars and epidemics. They have understood nuclear weapons and their impacts. They have understood religion, culture, rituals, blind beliefs, and superstition. Machines and instruments have been used to their maximum. They have undergone economic crises, money inflation, unemployment, and loss of capital. Impacts of environmental decline, depletion in the ozone layer, population growth, and new epidemics—attacks of viruses have been experienced. They have witnessed huge wars caused by ethnicity and religion, attacks, and threats. Many people in the world have experienced impacts of radiation produced from nuclear plants and nuclear weapons. Life and the world till this time have been understood completely. This is an extreme fear age. We are undergoing the extreme fear age. New fears have been continuously added. No one has an idea when and where fears get added from. Now, we are ready like a goalkeeper in a football game to fight against fears. New fears still continue to be added to the extreme fears of age. Extreme fears exist for ages. Everything proceeds with human dynamics and activeness. Our efforts on minimising extreme fears and the liberation of lives from such fears continue for ages. Fears increased to 90 per cent in this age and 10 per cent fears generate from other sectors.

In this way, consciousness increases gradually, inventions continue, and fears also increase along with them. The fear circle continues with human efforts on liberation through minimising fears.

Now, the world has been occupied by fears. Due to human activities, 'devastation' is possible. Human beings till this age like 'mice' are more frightened of human beings than natural disasters and external attacks. Therefore, fears constrict human freedom, development of civilisation, and life experience.

j. Fearless Age

The last stage of fears is fearlessness. If human nature—sex, anger, love, affection, doubt, jealousy, ego, hatred, all are in balance, minimising extreme thoughts, behaviour, and work, then limitlessness, equality, amiability, coexistence, and love, etc. prevail in terms of differences in ethnicity, religion, nation, culture, language, script, etc. These thoughts lead us to a fearless stage. Human beings then will abandon competition, hostility, anger, sex, love, affection, greed, doubt, jealousy, hatred, etc. As a result, all wars, murdering, and violence based on ethnicity, religion, culture, language, nation etc. will be minimised. Human beings will feel less fear in this stage. Heavenly imagination of religion, postmodern interpretation, deconstruction, limitlessness, Malthusian theory of population, Maslow's theory of necessity, Marxism and the ideal city of Jacques Derrida will exist in the last stage of the development and are theories related to fearlessness. We are working, running away, hiding, and fighting for the same fearlessness. This is our life. We are widely reading, writing, understanding, and teaching about it.

Thus, wars, violence, murder, ego, doubt, hatred, extremism, treachery, conspiracy, terror, etc. will continue to be minimised and will lead us to the fearless age. This is what we discuss here as the fearless age. Whatever works, we have moved towards fearlessness.

In this way, fear has been on a ceaseless journey since the beginning of human civilisation. Each step of civilisation is through fear. Some of the fears under this step cling to it and some others drop. Minimum fear existed in the primitive age and now is minimising down from the climax. Delogocentrism and borderlessness of the postmodern period, the ideal city of Jacques Derrida with citizens without citizenship and passports and a society of communism without class, police, and armies are all imaginations of the fearless age. Here lies the fear circle. Low fear reached at the climax and then went to the same low fear stage. Minimisation of fear lies behind every human activity. The process of minimising some fears is successful while others is unsuccessful. Likewise, minimisation of fear is even behind efforts on liberation from fears. Fear is a power that always attracts us.

Today, people who have undergone various fears are working on escaping, minimising, leaving, liberating, and relief from fears. Extreme thoughts on religion, culture, rituals, language, script, and caste/ethnicity are on the way to minimisation. Population is decreasing in some countries. The process of disarmament has started. Human traits like doubt, ego, hatred, greed, jealousy, etc. are being minimised every day. Everyone is working to minimise what he has understood as sources and factors of fears. Thus, some factors of fears are on the way to their ends. The low fear started in primitive age is on the way to minimisation and has been encircling human civilisation.

End Notes:

1. Prakash Kanta, Karl Marx, *Samajbadka Masiha (Prophet of Socialism)*, Hinda Packet Books 2006, p. 109.
2. Gobinda Raj Bhattarai, *Uttar Adhunik Bimarsha (Post-modern Discourse)*, Modern Books, Kathmandu, 2064 v.s. p. 77.

4

How Does Fear Occur?

On the body, sense organs, mind, and soul, Bhagawat Gita says, 'Animals with visible bodies witness and recognise through their eyes. Moreover, all organs and parts have been witnessed and recognised. Ten sense organs are over yonder the organ. The mind is over yonder the same organs. The knowledge is over yonder the mind and the soul is over yonder the knowledge.' (Bhagawat Gita 3/42) [1]

The formula is: body—organ—sense organ—mind—knowledge—soul.

But fear is a bit more different than the perspective of Bhagawat Gita. I have presented as below:

Life . . . Consciousness . . . Knowledge(Meaning) . . . Fear . . . Cognition

Figure No. 11

Figure No. 11 presents: life—consciousness—knowledge (meaning)—fear—cognition. Fear is impossible without knowledge on disease, problems, subjects, etc. Fear exists only with knowledge. Real knowledge of an object invites two different conditions: Is the object fearful or fearless? If it does not create fear, it is fearless. If doubts and illusions are added to the objects, that often creates fear. If the object is fearful, no doubt that creates fear. We have an illusion in the mind and may doubt seeing a rope as a snake from a distance. To witness nothing is also knowledge. When we approach nearer, we know it is merely a rope. It is knowledge. We don't fear the rope, because it is not an object to create fear. When we begin to wonder if the rope is poisonous (it can be a scorpion or centipede), fear exists in the mind. If people consider that a simple rope is a ghost, spirit, god, are fearful, or if it is linked with myth or story, the same rope becomes fearful. We know it's a snake; it is also knowledge. The snake is poisonous. We die if it bites us. But if in case the snake is not poisonous, then only minimum fear exists. It too is knowledge. We began to doubt—disease attacked us. We explain it to the doctor. This is knowledge. Diagnosis of disease creates fear. But real information would have avoided such fear. First, we were not sure whether it was a rope or a snake, but later, we knew it was a snake. Does what we know about the fact avoid the fear? It rather increases fear. When we know it is fearful, it adds fear. Cognition analyses and describes the fear. It tells us how to get rid of fear, escapes and measures for treatment. It happens to flower, and the same thing happens to other objects in the world. It is formulated in Figure No. 12.

Figure No. 12 shows sense organs, exterior unconsciousness, interior unconsciousness, unconsciousness, development process, consciousness, object, knowledge, and fear. The figure depicts the combination between unconsciousness of consciousness circle and unconsciousness of sub-production. I will discuss consciousness circle and sub-production later. When the same consciousness collides with an object, it creates knowledge; the same knowledge creates fear.

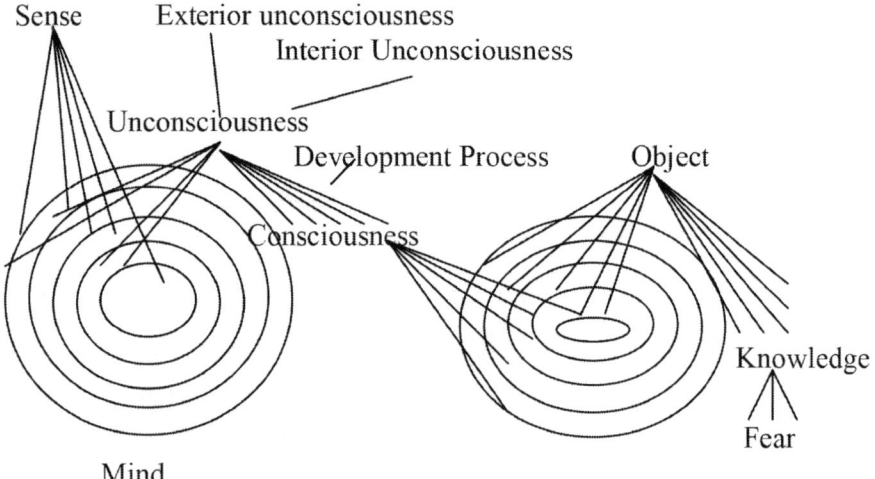

Figure No. 12

The figure depicts five sense organs. Micro level consciousness exists within layers of unconsciousness of every organ. Cells of a body have consciousness at a micro level, so they fight against an external disease. Likewise, the size of a pupil in the eye becomes small and big based on the light. The central consciousness does not control and direct every micro level consciousness. Our micro level consciousnesses of these organs remain active even if we are unconscious, sleepy, and mad. The consciousness we receive from the sense organs is geometrical, and when we gain knowledge from micro level consciousness, the micro level fear exists. Our consciousnesses becomes active when we see land sliding or a deep chasm while walking on the way. We sometimes become decisionless and speechless if our consciousnesses remain active. Any decision can happen in such a situation. It is too small that we are unable to notice it. When we know, we attempt to escape, kill a snake, or find a way out.

For example, somebody has a disease, yet he does not know about it. He is an ordinary man. He has consciousness. One day when he goes to the doctor for a check-up, the doctor tells him about his disease. Then, he gains the knowledge about the disease and he starts to fear it. Along with this knowledge, all his behaviours and activities change. His behaviour with his friends and relatives also change. Without such knowledge, he walks, eats, and drinks with friends like a healthy person; his relatives and friends don't stop him doing these things. With the knowledge of disease, restriction on what he does begins. The unhealthy man should make rules and regulations of discipline; otherwise, a critical health condition is inevitable to his life.

However, one considers himself materialistic; he seems to believe in something else. A man without conviction and faith is beyond imagination. Such a belief and faith also create fear. Some people believe in the soothsayer, witch doctor, priest, and shaman. They guide their lives. A man habituated to look at horoscopes, he can't do anything without it. The same thing happens to the man who has faith in a soothsayer, witch doctor, priest, and shaman. If something worse is written in the horoscope, he remains anxious and fearful the whole day. So the people with such conviction and faith always consult soothsayers, priests, witch doctors, and shamans before they go out to new places, build new houses, do new works, and also for weddings and the delivery of a child. Soothsayers, priests, witch doctors, and shamans observe their fortune and horoscope. Even kings used to consult soothsayers, priests, and shamans before the pregnancies of queens. These are all matters of conviction and faith. If fortune tellers, witch doctors, priests, shamans twist the matter, their good luck turns into bad luck. They stop their work. On the eve of a wedding, if somebody tells a man that the 'pairing is not good or relation *(lagan)* is not good', his wedding ceremony will be bad or ruined.

Many wedding ceremonies will stop and lives will be ruined due to fortune tellers, priests, witch doctors, etc. Many women are accused of *auseni* (born in dark night), *malabaseni* (born in leap year), being witches, and having the fate of a second wife in our societies. People fear to wed such women. People consult fortune tellers, priests, witch doctors, and shamans before they purchase a house. If they say, 'Don't buy, or it is astrologically not good', those people don't purchase the house.

Jhamak Ghimire, in her book entitled *Jivan Kanda ki Fool*, writes, 'My mind is full of fears due to talking with the priest, witch doctor, shaman, priest, ghost, soul god, etc.'[2]

Some people go out to carry out their work, but if a soothsayer, witch doctor, or shaman say to them, 'You have bad days. It is unfortunate to go to the south', they don't feel good. If at any cost he has to go, he feels fear. It's not good to walk and work with fear. Because fear and suspicion already exist, it will further increase fear, suspicion, and anxiety. Is anything we eat with suspicion sweet? In such a case, sweet becomes bitter. So, the habit of waiting for good days to start work and consult horoscopes has made a deep impact on human mentality—it is like an impact made by religion, politics, and drugs. They are so habituated; they never come out of it. They always walk with it in their minds. If fortune tellers, witch doctors, and shamans make predictions based on oracles and horoscopes, 'You live for only thirty years', that man is deeply hurt mentally by the prediction of thirty years. He suffers from mental anxiety like, 'When do I reach thirty years? Do I die at thirty? And how can I live long?' This is caused not only by the fortune teller, witch doctor. We believe anything when we are told by learned people and teachers on whom we have faith. These are all due to faith. Such beliefs can be superstition, blind belief, and spiritual thought.

This theory can also be applied in medical science. Rich people often consult a family doctor for their health check-up. The doctor diagnoses and indicates some disease after a health check-up even if the man is strong and healthy. Then the strong and healthy man also starts physical exercise and controls his food intake. These activities indicate human suspicion and fear. The same fear and suspicion make us exercise unnecessarily and have faith and belief. Above all, it makes a mental impact that makes a man be more suspicions and fearful. Such a condition sometimes leads to sickness. The man has to abandon the work he has just started and the house or land he is about to purchase. It also breaks relation. It is caused by knowledge full of fear. If the man does not consult a fortune teller, witch doctor, shaman, or doctor, he won't know the diagnosis nor the indication. So, no fear exists without knowledge.

People always want security. To have even more security, they consult fortune tellers, shamans, witch doctors, and doctors. They wash away bad days *(swastishanti)*, go on pilgrimages, and give alms. Otherwise, they fear death, trouble, bad days, and loss. It is unknown that these activities further increase fears in their minds. Every moment, we remember what a fortune teller, a witch doctor, a shaman, or a doctor said. Knowledge is behind such a fear. Bad days mentioned by the fortune teller, unfortunates as mentioned by the witch doctor, and diseases diagnosed by the doctor are all knowledge. This knowledge causes fear in human beings. If the man who the fortune teller said would die at thirty years was not told of his death, he would enjoy it. Now, he suffers from the same knowledge of death at thirty. If the fortune teller was not asked advice before purchasing a house, going abroad, marrying, all his work certainly and comfortably could be completed. Anxiety, tension, fear, and suspicion would not exist. Therefore, this knowledge merely invites fear. Rule of this fear is applied everywhere. That means every bit of knowledge a man gains generates fear, but it requires consciousness. Here, life, consciousness, knowledge, and fear are all formulated together. It does not mean that knowledge of everything is not good. Knowledge is necessary, but knowledge that invites unnecessary fear is harmful. So, what knowledge and faith a man needs depends on him.

Some of the fears exist in memory and exist out of memory. It exists much more in an unfavourable condition. It remains in the unconscious part of the brain—it exists time and again; sometimes, it exists suddenly; and sometimes, it exists in similar circumstances of incidents. Here, memory means knowledge. Some memory heads towards words to create fear. Fear does not exist without memory. When a man feels loneliness, becomes helpless, and reaches tranquility, the memory of fear is even more forceful. Our heart beats faster when we know our mistake. Fear is generated from other things that play on our mind. In the pitch dark, the situation is much more fearful. Sound produced by insects, other sounds, shadows, and tree trunks create fear. A man realises it while walking along the river, in hills, forests, seashores, deserts, farms, and graveyards. When we get a message that a member of the family is sick, we fear his death. Mental conditions become ready to face that environment before that situation occurs. It further increases fear. All fears are not equal; they depend on the level of consciousness.

Along with the knowledge of life, death, relatives, and wealth in human beings, fear starts. Information of all this is impossible at our birth. As we grow, consciousness and conditional reflexes increase. We continue to be fearful about these issues and problems. We play different roles to protect ourselves from these fears. A combination of these roles is in fact a life.

5

Fear Path

Fear is human consciousness—a natural result produced after seeing, remembering, and experiencing objects and animals. Human beings have sense organs to see objects, have consciousness, knowledge, time, and circumstance. Human beings possess tolerance, potentiality, and adaptability. Fear is an experience of reactions produced by the objects constituted from the combination of these. It depends on the individual. Every individual differs from each other in terms of perception, listening, understanding, adaptability, and tolerance. As a result, the world as thought by a man, environment, and nature are also different. So, an object has a number of interpretations. Someone experiences more problems, anxiety, and fear from the same difficulties and problems, while some others feel less. For example, two people witness a snake at the same time. Their fear is not equal. In fact, both of them do not witness the snake from the same distance and ability and consciousness. Difference in time and place makes everything different. A plausible reason behind it is a difference between two people in terms of behaviour, knowledge, consciousness, human nature, physical structure, and environment. Therefore, while interpreting the theory of relativity of Einstein, Indra Bahadur Rai writes that time is the fourth dimension of country—time probability—relativity is also understood under country—time continuity.[3]

It is impossible to understand and experience this without their division. Fear comes from the human mind—a result of memory or presence of external objects. Thus, a combination of exterior or interior factors generates fear. An external factor is insufficient to generate fear unless some internal factor remains active.

A snake is the external factor. Seeing it does not necessarily create fear. The snake we see activates our fear, consciousness, and as a result, we become fearful. There might be a number of such paths and factors to create fears. The interpretation of them all is impossible. I will discuss on the fear path:

    a.   Consciousness
    b.   Consciousness circle
    c.   Bond
    d.   Foundation
    e.   Recurrence

a.   *Consciousness*: It is a major source of both spiritual and physical thinking. Philosophical and religious people interpret it according to their convenience—the meaning is the same. It is natural too. What is consciousness? It's a flower that blossomed in the human mind since prehistoric times. The same flower blossomed in the mind of philosophers, making them look beautiful.

Various interpretations by philosophers and scholars on consciousness exist. Some of them are as below:

'The same consciousness factor had been expanded in the sky before the creation of planet. Later, the same consciousness factors determine dynamics of the smallest particle in the sky and they are called *yat*. According to Veda, invisible and smallest blowing particle is called air. So, the air is considered to have been originated in the sky. It has speed. As a result, it produces *fi* bill electronic potentiality (air and fire) has been used in the Veda. Various elements have been constructed along these three elements. Therefore, a change in these particles brings changes in matters. It's a process towards creation of "five elements (earth, water, fire, wind and sky)" and above all the creation of this universe is as mentioned in Veda.' (Satpath Brahman (10, 3, 5, 1-2))[4]

'Numerical philosophy has accepted life factor as male. Here male is consciousness. He witnesses everything. He does not accept any contact from outside. Nature is also a blind force. It is active. Male sees and knows everything but remains inactive. Thus, despite the relationship between the blind nature and the lame male, the world has been created.'[5]

'Theory of dialectical materialism by Karl Marx includes three laws. One of them is the law of transition of quantity into quality—transition of quality invites automatic transmission of quality. During the development process, whatever new qualities are produced, they are produced due to the difference of quality. There is quality difference between life or consciousness and blindness; there is quantity difference only. Due to quantity difference, the origination of life or the consciousness is possible.'[6]

While interpreting dialectical materialism, Dr Kumar Prasad Koirala writes, 'Transition of quantity does not continue forever, rather the transition of quantity into quality occurs at a point; transition of quantity into quality brings fundamental change or goods appear to be different.'[7]

'Freud has compared unconscious mind with a small room attached to a big acute room. The room has an emotive decoration. A small room attached to a big room is like a room to welcome guests. There lies consciousness. A man stands between these two rooms for patrolling. He checks up different mental emotions and censures them. Whoever he does not like, he does not allow him/her to go into the welcome room. Again, whoever is selected to go into the welcome room, s/he becomes conscious.'[8]

According to Charvaka philosophy, 'Our body is combination of earth, water, light and air. Development of consciousness is also combination of these four things.'[9]

A man dies, but his mind, knowledge, and consciousness never die. Swami Ananda Arun further writes, 'A recent research conducted on brains of the people who were declared dead at hospitals in UK has revealed that mind and consciousness remain alive even after the death. A study conducted by British Dr Piter Fenwik and Dr Sam Pariniya has proved that mind, knowledge and consciousness remain alive even after the death of human body.'[10]

Discussing reincarnation, Swami Ananda Arun remarks, 'Generally, mobility begins for reincarnation just twelve days after the death of consciousness. Reincarnation occurs any time after the death of consciousness. The worst and best consciousnesses take time to seek a proper womb.'[11]

'Scientists like Henry Modasley have proved a fact—whatever culture of the external world, the same sense organs receive in the mind, many of them remain hidden in the consciousness and silently disappear in the mind. They are not collapsed, rather it lights from the piece of fire like petrol changed into vapour and disappears in the atmosphere.'[12]

'If the substance of salt is mixed in the salty water and be left to be cold, the substance will increase and salt in the water gathers here. Whatever we see in substance, it takes close to either of consciousness and unconsciousness.'[13]

According to Rene Descartes—'Our knowledge are based on faith. We have some innate faith.'[14]

'The power of fire was hidden somewhere in nature. Something caused movement in the nature; then the fire existed', the numerical philosophy argues.[15] 'According to Bargasan, the consciousness is a widespread element that exists from inside. Like in *Upanishad*, Bargasan says—the consciousness can live in physical elements (body), however both of them are different (objects). The centre of lives is god and god is eternal life activities.'[16]

All scholars, philosophers, and science almost have the same belief. The same thoughts mentioned above are from the physical world and some others are from spiritual thoughts. It means the world is based on a combination of both physical and spiritual thoughts.

The consciousness, in fact, is a dynamic communication to give knowledge and information about objects and subjects. It includes knowledge, thoughts, sensitivity, feeling, meditation, emotion, imagination, etc. In cause of its expansion, greed, hatred, jealousy, ego, etc. exist in tendency. It is debated that there is only one consciousness. As any object or problem appears, consciousness does not limited to a single one. At once, various consciousnesses exist. Therefore, we talk about a sixth sense organ. Multi-consciousness is, thus, the combination of five sense organs, cognitive faculties, and muscle. If the combination of five colours construct, only six colours create! It can create numerous colours. So, it is written in the Gita that there are ten sense organs after the body, sense organs before the mind, mind before knowledge, and knowledge before soul.

Bacteria and amoeba are some examples of multi-consciousness. They are living creatures with one cell. Other one-cell creatures have micro-level consciousness—it is a limited effort to live and fight. Each cell of multi-celled creatures has a micro-level consciousness. The same micro-level consciousness keeps directing them. Due to the same consciousness, it fights against an external bacterium. Victory of external bacteria invites illness for human beings. A man with strong immunity power does not suffer from disease so easily. Human consciousness does not direct the cells of human immunities. They have their own micro-level consciousness for direction. In this way, as we witness an object or incident, our multi-consciousnesses remain active. The feeling of pain when any part of the body is hurt does not directly reach the consciousness; rather, cognitive faculties and muscles direct such feelings to the consciousness and then we feel pain. According to Russian philosopher Pavlov, central consciousness does not work to direct in a conditional reflex.

Natural objects give us consciousness, but human-made objects remain zero first. Size and shape begin right in zero—the consciousness worked all for construction, invention, creation, theory, philosophy, etc. in zero.

While talking about it, philosopher Jean Paul Sartre presents an example, 'Somebody has invented the knife that we use to cut paper. He had the idea or theoretical knowledge of knife before he invented it. Because we do not produce the world; it is there; but we make it reveals itself, come into "being". That means idea of knife is already there; later construction of knife is based on this idea.'[17]

Because of physical and chemical impacts on fundamental productive factors in the world, mixture, dispersal, and survival of the fittest, these two laws of nature are sufficient for the development of unconsciousness to consciousness. The law continuously creates physical factors and makes the old disappear. The next one is heir to the new form. Physical elements in the world based on these laws created an environment for the development of molecules to human beings.

Similarly, another scientist, J. B. S. Haildon, has said, 'Demarcation between chemistry and lives has been narrowed down so far. It has contributed to the research on virus.'[18]

German chemists prepared duplicate alizatin in a chemistry laboratory. All the rooms suffered bankruptcy within one generation; the plant of alizatin was not needed later.[19]

Like Sartre says, the knowledge of the knife was not limited to a single person before it was made. In fact, knowledge of many people contributed to its construction. The structure of a knife today is the continuation of an idea since the Stone Age. People did not invent a metal knife at once. Various shapes and sizes of stone knives came into the development of today's knife. In all constructions, every object has the quality of being, but the knowledge of a person cannot make it complete and perfect. For freedom and self-sustenance, a man needs heredity, conditional reflexes, and a favourable environment around him. Despite his capacity, a man is not as able as he is today.

Like the analysis made by Freud, there is no clear division. It's a process for unconsciousness to be conscious. It is as small as a frozen substance, and the cause of time brings changes in mental procedures. It is just like a straight line. It is unconsciousness on the one side and consciousness on the other. Unconsciousness increases itself and becomes conscious. It is not necessary to take permission from any gatekeeper. If the presence of a filter net or gatekeeper for filtration of consciousness from unconsciousness is possible, all living creatures could have been developed. So, the straight line exists and unconsciousness becomes consciousness.

Uncons.—Natural Process—Micro cons.Natural Process—consciousness

Figure No. 13

The figure presents unconsciousness first. It has become micro-level consciousness through natural processes. The same micro-level consciousness has been changed into consciousness through natural processes. The same process has been applied for the development of multi-celled creatures developed from one cell creature. It completes a process and becomes a 'regular casualty', a theory by a great Nepali dramatist named Balkrishna Sama.[20]

When we came out of a dark room, we can't see anything for a while. The pupil of the eye itself becomes big and small in light and darkness. It increases its size in the dark and decreases its size in the light. It can see even if it decreases size in the light, but it can't be possible in the dark. So, it adjusts its size. We can do the experiment ourselves or with the help of others. It is not directed by our main consciousness. Inability of a pupil to see in the light at once is its moment for adaptability. It's a moment taken by the pupil to transform from being of a big size to one of small size. After adaptability, we can see.

All cognitive organs, muscles, and sense organs are in the process of accommodation of all these. No consciousness is possible before the message reaches the brain through these means. Other organs remain active even if a man is sleeping, unconscious, or a lunatic.

In this way, unconsciousness may enter the consciousness. This is a natural process. I have analysed it on the basis of divisions of consciousness.

The origin of consciousness is mysterious. So nobody has entered there. Where does the consciousness power come from? This question remains unanswered for psychologists. We are in an attempt on tracing the fear path.

It's logic for all life, world, and consciousness. The matter to discuss is who is far and close to life. Everyone has their own interpretations to support their philosophies and thoughts. All interpretations are not complete and truthful. Interpretations from different perspectives are possible. It incorporates all knowledge, experience, anxiety, fear, doubt, and jealousy. Absence of consciousness does not make a huge difference. So, claim on origin of unconsciousness is natural. Both physical and spiritual views on origin of unconsciousness can be right. They can have their own logic too. Origin of fears is consciousness. I put forward two arguments on Consciousness Circle 1 and Consciousness Circle 2: sub-production unconsciousness. Others might have disagreed on it.

b. *Consciousness Circle:* Two different consciousness circles have been discussed below:

Consciousness Circle—1

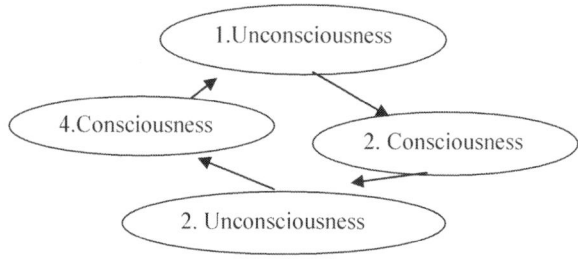

Figure No.: 14

Figure No. 14 presents 1 to 4 orders. The first presents the unconsciousness condition. The second presents its collision with an object. Consciousness, experience, knowledge, fear, and causing factors came forth in this order. Whether or not most of the philosophers have access to the point, they have made interpretations on experience and knowledge. The third presents memories in consciousness that remain disappeared or hidden—it's a stage of unconsciousness again. The fourth presents its collision with objects again, and consciousness transforms into experience, knowledge, and fear. This process continues.

Fear remains unconscious in the mind as the thing that is lost from memory, as interpreted by Jacques Derrida under eraser. Fear remains suppressed, half-suppressed, and free in some cases. Consciousness, mind, sensitivity, imagination, and thought are all like this—like desire and aspiration, that they are lost from memory, left, and suppressed but remain stored in the unconscious mind. In this way, voice, memory, and consciousness of human beings are stored in an unknown part of this world. The fear makes an impact on them all.

Consciousness Circle: 2

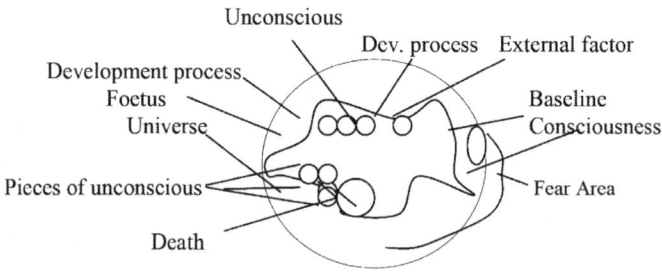

Figure No. 15

Figure No. 15 shows developed pieces of the unconscious, the development process, the external factor, the baseline, the consciousness, fear area, death, and pieces of unconsciousness, universe, foetus, and development process again. Pieces of unconsciousness in this universe are hidden, suppressed, and also, they exist as external factors. This unconsciousness enters the foetus from various forms. Here, unconsciousness is a kind of external factor. Unconsciousness produced from the body gets a fusion in this foetus. Heredity lies here. Natural objects and conditional reflexes merge together to form consciousness during the development process. This consciousness collides with other problems and objects and produces knowledge; the fear generates from knowledge. This knowledge and fear exist throughout the whole life and end with death. Again, consciousness like unconsciousness remains hidden, suppressed, and continued as external factors. This process recurs along with the development of the foetus. This is Consciousness Circle 2.

Physical Body of Human

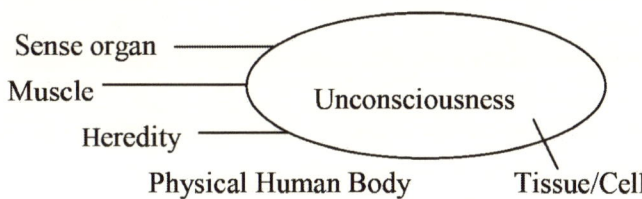

Figure No. 16

Figure No. 16 shows the physical human body constituted with muscle, sense organs, and bones, etc. Unconsciousness is a product of assimilation of these muscles, sense organs, and bones, etc.

Our body consists of salts as sub-production. The combination of salts reacts differently: It's like electricity produced from the combination of positive and negative charges. Our body is a construct of muscle, tissue, and cells. High-level production from the combination of these things is unconsciousness. Muscles and sense organs of the body play an important role for unconsciousness in human beings. From the universe of this unconsciousness, fusion is invited and generates consciousness. This is the sub-production path. It exists in every living being from one cell to multi-celled beings.

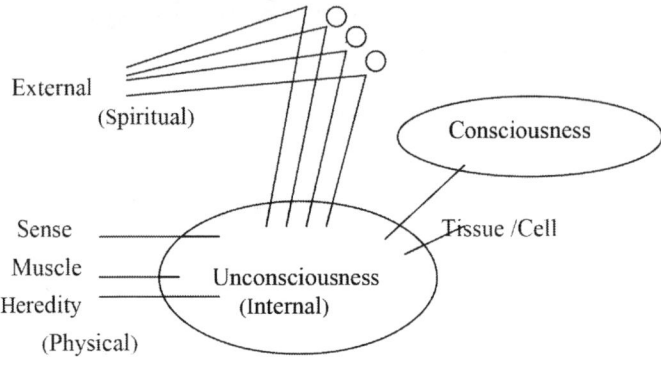

Figure No. 17

Figure No. 17 presents that consciousness has come forth from unconsciousness and the conscious circle produced from the body—i.e. one is physical and the other is spiritual. One is internal and the other is external. The consciousness is constituted from the fusion of physical unconsciousness and spiritual unconsciousness. This is the centre of fusion between physicality and spirituality. It is an initial consciousness. It develops with the foetus. Similarly, logic of fusion is in Marxism, *Charvaka*, *Sankhyadarsan*, and Freudian psychology. Only matter is not sufficient in the world to sustain it, and spiritual thought is also not sufficient. The creation of the world is supposed to be possible through the combination of both. Where both physical and spiritual unconsciousness are joined, the world lies there, and consciousness has made it dynamic. It is an Eastern philosophy.

This logic exists in every subject. The problem is in science too. The concept of Sir Isaac Newton has been replaced by the concept of Einstein. Philosophy and religious belief that the sun revolves around the earth was proved false by Galileo. Research on it is still continuous. We are like the blind. We are touching an elephant. Whatever is found, we claim it as the world and the truth. Its truth lies in perception.

Jain philosophy has presented the story of the blind and the elephant to clarify its *Syatbat*. One of the blind men touched the trunk of the elephant and understood it as a banana tree. Another touched the tusk and understood it as a thorn. Another touched the body and understood it as a wall. They understood the elephant differently.[21]

Like a person but different illusions of Shankaracharya and different people and different illusions of Indra Bahadur Rai, these illusions exist not only where eyes are closed, but also where they are open.

Thus, various arguments on consciousness exist. The consciousness I have seen is a fusion of physical and non-physical unconsciousness. The world is a combination of physics and spirituality.

Consciousness is a main path towards fear. Conditional reflexes are added to it continuously. After consciousness, knowledge is achieved related to the particular problem and we are fearful. In this way, fear increases along with consciousness.

c. Bond

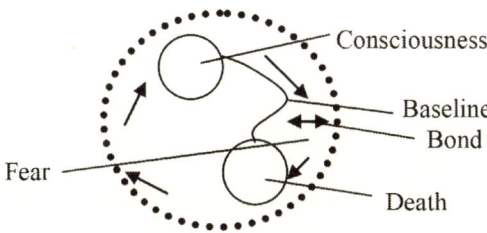

Figure No. 18

Figure No. 18 presents consciousness, baseline, bond, death, and fear. Consciousness travels on the baseline in a journey from consciousness to death. There is a struggle between consciousness and the baseline. The zigzag line is shown in the journey. Death is the end of consciousness itself. Both difficult and easy bases are possible in the journey of consciousness to death. Similarly, both hard and soft bases are also possible. Here, base is a path. Due to the elasticity of this basis, consciousness reaches at high, mid, and low levels. We struggle on our way. It is easier to work if the path is not a zigzag. Our path is like this. So, if the path is comfortable, walk comfortably, and if it is difficult, walk a little.

d. Foundation:

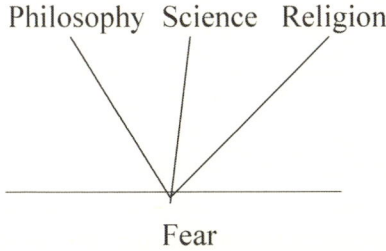

Philosophy Science Religion

Fear

Figure No. 19

Figure No. 19 shows fear as the foundation of science, philosophy, and religion.

Science: Let us consider, science has invented a powerful weapon. Foundation of such an invention is fear. Similarly, disease of serious illness is found; again, its foundation is fear. Therefore, people invent weapons, find medicines and diseases because of fear. It includes every new thing.

Philosophy: It consists of principles, disciplines, and policies. It desires life to stop going the wrong way and desires to get peace and prosperity. Again, the basis is fear.

Religion: Fear, in fact, originates from hardship, trouble, tension, and problems. People take religious shelter to get relief from fear. So, to be religious without any cause is meaningless.

Every invention of science is to make lives more comfortable. Medical science, simple tools, and vehicles are for daily use in our lives. If they could not make our lives comfortable, what is their utility? Philosophy is for policy, discipline, meditation, behaviour, character, and housework necessary for human lives. Socrates, Plato, Aristotle, Confucius, Buddha, Nanak, Nietzsche, Marx, and Sartre interpret human lives in their philosophies. Religious people perhaps easily accept theism due to fear. Reasons behind theism are happiness, peace, and prosperity. Besides these things, they must have a desire for heaven after their deaths. But religion is not in the centre of all these faiths. Fear is in the centre of faith; whether others support or oppose it.

Thus, knowingly or unknowingly, science, philosophy, and religion move around the fear. Therefore, religion, philosophy, and science are peripheral faces, whereas fear is the heart. In this way, we can understand one as a face and the other as a heart.

The above interpretation shows that the world is related to life and life is related to fear. The fear determines the future of life. Life goes ahead as the guidance of fear. No one can be free from fear on the way. So, tangible and intangible fear is a basis of our lives.

e. Recurring:

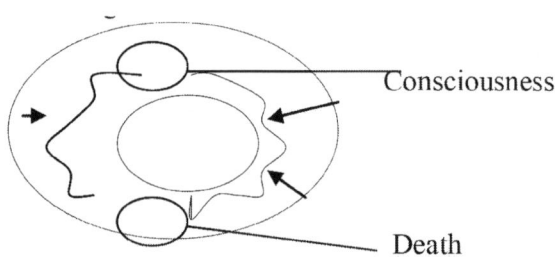

Figure No. 20

Figure No. 20 presents both consciousness and death. Here, consciousness is life. Unconsciousness forms body in consciousness, and consciousness does the same thing in the brain. Live human brains consist of museum of unconsciousness. Our desire, fear, and suppressed nature are stored in this museum. As a result, we sometimes see different glimpses. Freud has interpreted unconsciousness or id here.

Circles of consciousness originating from physics and non-physics are recurring. Fear recurs with consciousness. Reason is everything recurring in the world and remains moving in this box. It does not have any outlet. Living beings are bound by the laws of nature—birth, growth, and death. It is a process of recurrence. A man or object does not appear the same in its recurrence. It appears like another through chemical reactions during its recurrence. Whatever the chemical reaction carried out, elements of unconsciousness transfer as its external forms. It differs in its quantity.

So, when consciousness, the circle of consciousness, bonds, and foundation recur, fear completes its circular path.

End Notes:

1. Arjundev Panta, *Bedanta-Darshan Sar (Brief Vedaanta Philosophy)*, Ratna Book Store, Kathmandu: 2062 v.s. p. 166.
2. Jhamak Ghimire, *Jivan Kanda ki Phool*, Online Nepali Literary Forum, Kathmandu: 2067 v.s. p. 77.
3. Bijaya Kumar Rai, ed., *Indra Sampurna 1*, Nirman publication, Sikkim, 2004, p. 323.
4. Mohan Prasad Bhandari, Bhumi Prasad Dahal, Indira Poudel, eds., *Trend on Eastern Thinking*, Student Publication, Kathmandu: 2066 v.s. p. 17.
5. Adhikari, Bishnu, *Darshanka Kehi Anautha Pakchha (Some Strange Aspect of Philosophy)*, Ratna Book Store, Kathmandu: 2064 v.s. p. 37.
6. Birendra Prasad Misra, *Introduction to Philosophy*, Nepal Charity Foundation, 2065 v.s. p. 61.
7. Kumar Prasad Koirala, *Trend on Eastern Thinking*, Student Publication, Kathmandu: 2066 v.s. p. 119.
8. *Freud's Psychoanalysis*, trans. Madhusudan Pande, Pairabi Publication, Kathmandu: 2061 v.s. p. 123.
9. Adhikari, Bishnu, *Darshanka Kehi Anautha Pakchha (Some Strange Aspect of Philosophy)*, Ratna Book Store, Kathmandu: 2064 v.s. p. 46.
10. Swami Ananda Arun, *Santa Darshan*, Osho Tapoban, Nagarjun Hills, Kathmandu 2008, p. 176.
11. Swami Ananda Arun, *Santa Darshan*, Osho Tapoban, Nagarjun Hills, Kathmandu 2008, p. 182.

12. Rahul Sangkrityan, *Sketch of the World*, trans. Narayan Giri, Marxbad Study-Research Academy Kathmandu: 2066 v.s. p. 280.
13. Rahul Sangkrityan, *Sketch of the World*, trans. Narayan Giri, Marxbad Study-Research Academy, Kathmandu: 2066 v.s. p. 297.
14. Birendra Prasad Misra, *Introduction to Philosophy*, Nepal Charity Foundation, 2065 v.s. p. 15.
15. Adhikari, Bishnu, *Darshanka Kehi Anautha Pakchha (Some Strange Aspect of Philosophy)*. Ratna Book Store, Kathmandu 2064 v.s. p. 38.
16. Rahul Sangkrityan, *Sketch of the World*, trans. Narayan Giri. Marxbad Study-Research Academy, Kathmandu 2066 v.s. p. 287.
17. Birendra Prasad Misra, *Introduction to Philosophy*, Nepal Charity Foundation, 2065 v.s. p. 137.
18. Rahul Sangkrityan, *Sketch of the World*, trans. Narayan Giri. Marxbad Study-Research Academy, Kathmandu 2066 v.s. p. 302.
19. Rahul Sangkrityan, *Sketch of the World*, trans. Narayan Giri, Marxbad Study-Research Academy, Kathmandu 2066 v.s. p. 301.
20. Birendra Prasad Misra, *Introduction to Philosophy*, Nepal Charity Foundation, 2065 v.s. p. 174.
21. Adhikari, Bishnu, *Darshanka Kehi Anautha Pakchha (Some Strange Aspect of Philosophy)*, Ratna Book Store, Kathmandu: 2064 v.s. p. 83.

6

Source of Fear

Human beings are the most conscious animals in this world. Since we are more conscious than other animals, we are most fearful. Sources of fear are within us. Human temperament, inventions, and natural disasters, including physical and non-physical objects they strike consciousness, are the sources of fear. Our temperaments have developed with our attempts to understand life, society, and the world. Interpretation and understanding depend on individual mentality, consciousness, and structure. Some of the understandings are the sources of fear and we become fearful. The life within is harmful to person, society, and the country. Life exists with such understanding—perspective on movement, smuggling, extremism, terrorism, war, problems, objects, thinking, behaviour, and temperament has been applied for interpretation. It results in drug addiction, leaving family for the jungle, extreme thinking, and war, etc. There are branches within it. People fear the people who interpret life and the world in their own words. It has created a threat among people. It's a threat to the world. So, it demands new definitions and interpretations because the world's becoming the victim of a great fear. To rescue the world from such quicksand, its sources have to be identified and they have to be reinterpreted. Doing all this minimises fear a little. It can be a great achievement. I have interpreted some sources.

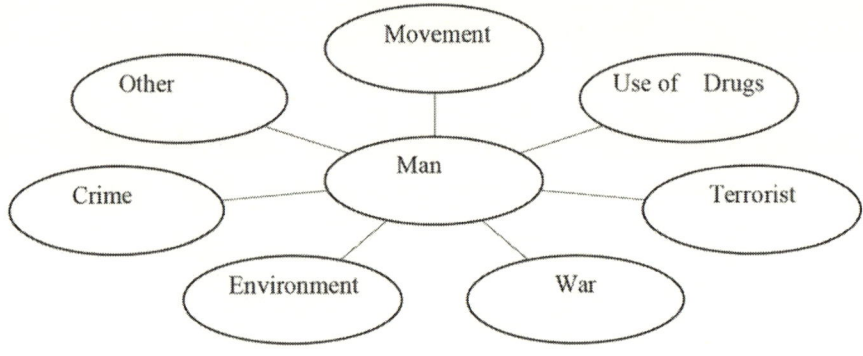

Figure No. 21

The man is in the centre of Figure No. 21 peripheral sources. They are fearful to have been presented here. These are some example of sources. These are peripheral sources.

1. Movements

Identity of movements is associated with existence. Many people express their views on identity-based movements and struggles. Elaine Showalter, Judith Butler, Gayatri Spibhak, Michel Foucault, Ranjit Guha, and Shahid Amin have been speaking from different angles. Some countries are in chaos due to movement. If dissatisfaction and inferior feeling in people are expressed collectively, that creates movements. Movements are mostly based on politics, society, race, literature, environment, labour, language, religion, and gender. The people who are dominated and oppressed go to the streets for their rights and space. Many theories and philosophies have come into being in such a condition. Even deconstruction of Jacques Derrida came into being. He said, 'Hundreds like me have been marginalised in the name of the mainstream, pushed aside and not allowed to have entry into the mainstream. Let us see. I'll show what'll happen when somebody is marginalised.'[1]

Due to these reasons, many countries have endured the Cold War and civil war. Wars in most of the countries are the result of movements. Fear generates movements. Minimisation of fear lowers the possibility of movements and wars. Again, the process of minimising movements leads to minimisation of fear.

Different types of movements have been discussed below.

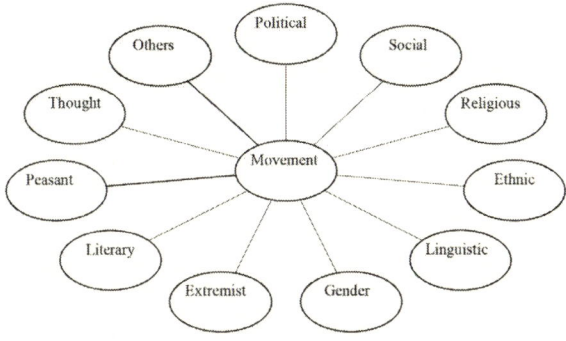

Figure No. 22

a. Political Movement

Political parties and institutions in countries have different backgrounds—ethnic, regional, proletariat, capitalist, feudal, etc. The political parties express their dissatisfaction, unrest, disagreement through movements. Initially, such movements are launched to build pressure.

If such pressure remains ignored, it turns into violence; prestige for everyone is important. Domination in such a case produces war—war of thoughts or physical war.

Thoughts, ethnicity, region, and occupation can lose their existence. So, movements are launched for the protection and respect of thoughts, ethnicity, region, and occupation. Clashes can take place in such a condition. Weapons can be used, including lathi charges and the use of water flush. Ultimately, they result in war. Knowledge that movements are launched due to fear can minimise wars and such movements. It can help maintain peace and security in society and country.

Aristotle had expressed his thoughts on revolution—general and specific causes. Specific causes according to him: 'Fear of troubles in the future can cause revolution.'[2]

b. Social Movement

People with different religions, classes, and professions live together in society. They make their own groups based on thoughts, behaviour, and professions in society. They work even with other people, groups, and nations. Agreement and disagreement continue in society. People who think they are right and have disagreements launch movements for the implementation of their issues. It creates fear of not implementing their issues and reduction of their facilities.

c.   Religious Movement

Religious movement is not dangerous, but when it reaches the hand of extremists, it can turn into civil war and the Cold War. Fear that 'my religion can be spoilt or somebody can spoil my religion' creates such religious movements. We have heard and seen the religions movements that have turned into violence. Fear that one's faith can disappear invites such a movement. If extreme thinking related to 'I' and 'my' is minimised, it can solve the problem.

d.   Caste/Ethnic Movement

This is more dangerous. When people think they are suppressed and oppressed, they launch movements for their protection. In most countries, ethnic movements have been associated with religious movements. As it continues, it transforms into civil war. It is more dangerous than political movements. They always fear that if their communities disappear, they feel insecure, deprived of their rights, and compelled to be dominated. Even dominated, people can rise up and create a threat, which is the cause of fear in the minds of rulers. Therefore, they try to suppress them more. As a result, civil war and ethnic hostilities take place. Fear exists before these wars begin, and people fear chaos after war. The feeling of being a minority has a big role in the theoretical development of Jacques Derrida. Knowledge about fear on ethnic movement can minimise the possibility of movement. Aristotle said that the state should work for minimising its possibility.

e.   Linguistic Movement

Language is the heart of the caste/ethnic community. How can caste/ethnicity be identified without language? A language dominates others. Extinction of language is the extinction of a concerned linguistic group. So, they work hard for the preservation of their languages. They fear the extinction of their languages.

f.   Gender Movement

There are two genders in the world: male and female. Now, a third gender has been added to it. Women and third genders who were suppressed in terms of fear, shame, and hatred are openly participating in movements for their rights and justice. The world is male-dominated; therefore, all religions, cultures, and laws are in favour of males. Females and other genders are suppressed. They have been dominated for centuries. Fear of continuous domination forced women and third genders into movements. This movement is a reaction against the male-dominated world. A group of males, particularly gays and queers, have experienced the same domination. They want to remain identified. They are all like third genders.

g. *Extremist*

Extreme belief on any subject is a major issue of extremism. Extreme love of ethnicity, religion, culture, language, script, and country produces extremists. These people like and love their groups and people. It has been associated with their history as well as faith and existence. They work hard for preservation. They never agree with the erosion of their ethnicity, religion, language, or script. They would rather confront others and go for it. Such a condition has brought disintegration in many countries and ethnic communities. Other communities also have the same faith and love in their ethnicity, religion, and culture. They love to preserve and nurture them. It brings clashes, war, and civil war between such extremist groups. Civil war and wars are its result. These wars are inspired by fear. They fear that their community, religion, culture, language, script, and country may become extinct. They plunge into war and civil wars for protection and preservation of these things. Thus, fear-guided war has terrorised the world. It has created discomfort in different countries and communities. Many people have become homeless. Most of the refugees in the world are due to being victims of wars. Nowadays, many countries have a refugee problem. To minimise such wars is to minimise extremist thinking. We have to develop good relationships and coexistence. All ethnic communities, religions, cultures, languages, and scripts have to be preserved. Above all, love avoids wars and minimises fear.

h. *Literary Movement*

Some literary movements support ethnic, religious, and political movements, but such movements are sombre. As a result, it is not violent and aggressive, but it has seen widespread impact. Musical movements exist with literature.

i.   *Peasant Movement*

In this industrial age, workers always struggle with owners in terms of wages, allowances, profits, and facilities. Prices are increasing every day. Incomes of workers are not increasing according to price hikes. They put forward different demands and launch movements. Owners can't fulfill their demands. So, the struggle continues between these two groups.

j.   *Thought-based Movement*

All movements in fact start with thought. Finally, they can transform into civil wars and wars. Therefore, it is a vehicle towards wars. Wars stop, but such movements continue.

k.   *Other*

Besides these, other movements come into being—time, circumstance, and necessity cause such movements. New movements exist along with problems. Such movements can cause the fear of extinction, suppression, and domination. Such movements are launched to overcome problems of justice and equality.

2.   *Use of Drugs*

The business of drugs has been increasing every day. Smugglers increased even before. Who engages in such a business becoming richer? Only rich people in aristocratic families and huge cities in the world used to take such expensive drugs some decades ago, but now it has reached every village/hut. Smugglers ruin their lives and property, give physical and mental torture, and ruin their families. It's a big problem in each and every corner of the world. Rich countries expand huge property to control it. Yet it has not been able to minimise its use and business. Its root cause has not been found. So, it is increasing instead of being controlled.

Who uses drugs? People who are tired of their lives, have family problems, are accused of corruption, have mental problems, are deceived in love, have troubles, and are indifferent to the world use drugs. Young people who understand the world negatively have become the victims of such an addiction. Being tired, enduring tension, having been deceived and becoming unhappy are factors for drug use. To become tired of family problems is to suffer from anxiety and tension. The people who suffer from what to do and how to solve problems always attempt different solutions. When they are trapped, they adopt drug use, lose mental balance, and commit suicide. Many people adopt these as an ultimate weapon in their lives. It ruins them. It's a kind of designed suicide. Fear is the cause for it. Proper counselling and advice can minimise their problems.

3. Terrorist

The world is under undeclared danger from terrorists. All countries are not secured from terrorists. Rich countries are even more unsecured. Attacks upon the Twin Towers, the Pentagon, and the White House have proved it. Chaotic situations during that period is still fresh in our minds. Since then, bombs have been exploded in many countries; many innocent people have lost their lives; and similarly, children, women, and old people have been killed. So, people do live with fear. They are not sure where these terrorists have come from. Their network has been expanded all over the world. Neither do people know when the bombs will explode nor do they have any idea how many people will lose lives in such an explosion. People suffer while travelling from one place to another. People fear possible attacks and possible accidents of vehicles. The first root cause of it is political, religious, and ethnic disagreements, and next one is fear that is in the mind. Waging war is to eradicate opponents, because people fear opponents. As a result, they see no option but terrorism. These people desire to attack all opponents and to remain secured.

It's a reflection of thought consisting of politics, ethnicity, religion, ego, jealousy, and arrogance. Fear is invisible inside them. Faith on 'I' and 'my' gives faith to extremism. Terrorism is a branch of extremism. The active role of terrorism increases the number of terrorists. They use different technologies and expand terrorism in societies, countries, and the world. To make people more threatened is their victory. There lies the fear. So, terrorism is caused by fear. Terrorist groups need to explain about fear that can minimise terrorist activities.

4. War

Fear is a major cause for wars. Both the First and Second World Wars were fought due to fear. Widespread wars fought for the liberation of fear are world wars. Causes of wars from the Vedic period to the present were ego, ethnicity, and religion, but fear was a driving force; preservation of ethnicity, religion and culture, expansion of territory, control over resources, to be egoistic, suspicious, and jealous are part of human nature. These natures become pervasive. When these natures increase, wars take place. Many countries wage wars due to politics and frontiers. People always are fearful for the loss of ethnicity, religion, culture, language, script, and country. Nobody likes suppression, harassment, and disrespect. They realise it due to human temperament and seek solutions for it. As a result, war and world wars occur. The environment before wars is much more chaotic and creates a huge fear of possible incident. People will have live pictures in their minds: running away for security, hiding, preserving food, preparing for attack, destruction through war, injury, crying for death, and shouting for water. The reason for all this is fear. The situation before a war no doubt is chaotic, but the situation after war is even more chaotic. War is always possible.

5. Environment

About chaotic situations, Prof. Dr Gobinda Raj Bhattarai says, 'People seem to be turning into unsecured and meaningless journey when they witness chaotic condition in this world.'[3]

Environment is important for animals and plants. Environmental pollution is increasing every day due to human activities. Deforestation, drought, partial rain, acid rain, soil erosion, landslides, fires, global warming, earthquakes, storms, extinction of wild birds and animals, thunder, and urbanisation are harmful to the earth and living creatures. It has caused depletion in the ozone layer and various diseases. Climate change has changed the life circle. It has brought unfavourable changes to lives. It's anxiety for the world. The environment has become adverse. If the environmental problem cannot be solved before the situation runs out, living creatures will have to face even bigger problems. Many living creatures will disappear and the ecosystem will collapse. Many countries in the world and the UNO as well are working for environmental preservation; yet no significant change has occurred.

6. Crime

Knowingly or unknowingly, people commit crime. Unknowingly, if someone is dead by the hand of another, it can't be crime, but the law regards it as crime. If a man is not proved a criminal, s/he should not be penalised. What was the condition of consciousness when the crime took place: Was it planned or accidental? No scientific invention is available to distinguish between criminals and non-criminals for justice.

Ordinary people are always fearful of criminals. They fear being a possible victim. They are always conscious and aware for their security.

7. *Other*

There are many sources of fear besides those mentioned above. Now sources keep on adding vertically.

End Notes:

1. Gobinda Raj Bhattarai, *Uttaradhunik Aina (Postmodern Mirror)*, Ratna Book Store, Kathmandu: 2062 v.s. p. 25.
2. Adhikari, Bishnu, *Darshanka Kehi Anautha Pakchha (Some Strange Aspect of Philosophy)*, Ratna Book Store, Kathmandu: 2064 v.s. p. 94.
3. Gobinda Raj Bhattarai, *Uttaradhunik Bimarsha (Postmodern Discourse)*, Modern Books, Kathmandu: 2064 v.s. p. 7.

7

Causes and Determining Factors of Fear

What produces fear? It's impossible to explain. Life is a huge form of fear. It can be produced from anything and anywhere. It has form but is not fixed. Generally, fear is produced from thoughts, incidents, living creatures, problems, diseases, relatives, enemies, property, life, death, laws, regulations, religions, cultures, disciplines, ghosts, the present, and the future. Fear produced from these factors is as vast as the sky. It is just like we are unable to tell the area of the sky. Any area, perimeter, and density cannot identify it. We are unable to tell the types of fear, its area, perimeter, colour, and form. Some causes and determining factors have been interpreted for the comfortable understanding of fear. It's a perspective. It incorporates not whole, but partial reasons and factors. The source of the major causes and factors are given below.

Consciousness

We can understand the universe due to consciousness. The universe is a combined form of all that is available here. Some of them are free from fear and some others are not. Consciousness identifies which one of them is free from fear and which is not. Knowledge is possible by seeing, hearing, and understanding due to consciousness, and no fear is possible without consciousness. So, people with mental retardation, those who are crazy, and children do not have fear as much as conscious people. Fear defers according to the straight line of consciousness. Fear depends on adaptable capacity, conditional reflexes, and heredity.

10

Figure No. 23

In Figure No. 23, let us consider 10 as a point for measurement. This is an average point. All fears in this point cannot be equal. Adaptability and consciousness stages differ from person to person. Even if the range of consciousness in every human being is 10, other and external fear factors cause differences.

Knowledge

The consciousness generates fear. Some people consider both consciousness and knowledge as the same. Consciousness and knowledge are different factors. In fact, knowledge is consciousness, but consciousness is not knowledge. Everybody has consciousness, but knowledge about everything is not possible—fear starts with knowledge. Our consciousness always sees a flower, that it does not create fear, but when we know that the flower is poisonous, then fear starts. Unless we know about death, fear doesn't exist. Fear requires knowledge first.

Sense Organs

We hear a huge roaring while walking. It is more accidental. In such a case, immediate sensitivity of sense organs is primary instead of consciousness and knowledge. This fear is produced by the sense organs. Sound is not recognised by the consciousness, and also knowledge about it is possible not because of knowledge. Rather, the sound that is heard produces fear. In this way, even the sense organs generate fear. If the sense organs do not function properly, they don't send messages to the brain for knowledge. Again, no fear is possible without knowledge. Parmenides, a thinker, says, 'Real knowledge about objects is possible from wisdom but not from the sense organs. Reason is that the knowledge received from sense organs is not real and illusory.'[1]

However, knowledge from sense organs is not real and illusory; it produces fear. That is the terrible sound of landslides, bomb explosions, crumbling of buildings, and collision of vehicles. The sound we hear can be illusory, yet that creates fear.

Sense organs acquire the following signals and produce fear.

Ear—to hear big sounds

Skin—to get pricked
Eye—to see some dreadful objects
Tongue—to taste something poisonous
Nose—to know bad smells

Messages mentioned above are received from the sense organs. Such messages can be illusory. There can be an illusion like skin getting pricked by a needle, a thorn, glass, or stone. Whatever pricks the skin creates fear, and messages from other sense organs are also the same.

Amygdala

This is first developed among four parts of the brain. Fear is under this part of the brain. Absence of this part avoids fear. A mouse has chased a cat in an experiment. For this experiment, the scientists removed the amygdala from the brain of the mouse. Then, the mouse did not fear the cat but rather began to chase the cat. Fear also depends on inactive, partially active, and active functions of this part. If this part is damaged due to an accident, fear does not occur or gets minimised. This is not whole, but part of consciousness.

Thought

Like the past, present, and future, if people began to think of heaven, hell, and incidents and relatives, it creates fear. If severe incidents make a deep impact on sense organs and consciousness, they come to mind regularly for a long time. It has a long-term effect. Such incidents include death, divorce, accidents, and they move around the sense organs and consciousness. It absorbs all at once—like sand absorbs water.

Conditional Reflex

It helps get the meaning of words and sentences. Its detailed interpretation is in a conditional reflex. Words and their meanings we use have been in practice for long. Our consciousness grasps the same meaning—for example, a ghost. We understand the term 'ghost' as fearful, horrific, and man-eating. The meaning of the word 'ghost' up until our time has been dreadful and horrific. This word may not have had the same meaning in the beginning. Now, we are scared when we hear the word. Thus, like a dog, our mind grasps the conditional reflex and we fear. Whatever meaning we know depends on conditional reflex. That makes us fearful.

Temperament

I have discussed earlier about the fear produced from temperament. A man's temperament causes fear. Many fears generate themselves within us. We know some of them. Fear can cause us to be suspicious, arrogant, stingy, nervous, angry, hesitant, introverted, shy, violent, religious, and fearful. These all create fear.

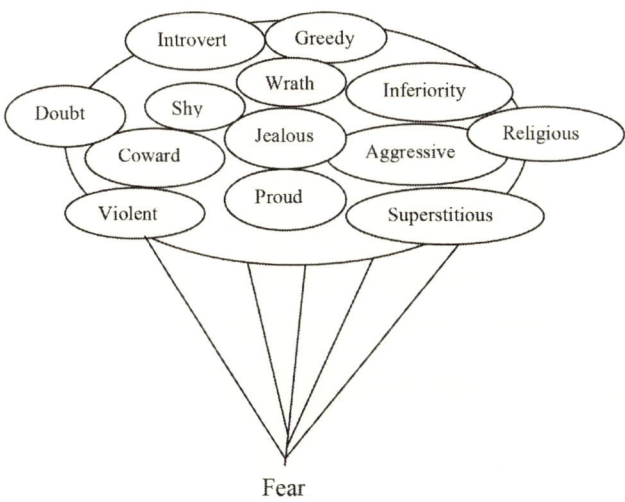

Fear

Figure No. 24

Figure No. 24 presents human temperament. It does not produce fear in the beginning, but produces it later. A little increment in our temperament brings the imbalance of peace in us. It's the beginning of problems. And they produce fear.

Like desire and aspiration, fear always remains suppressed. It is in search of an outlet. It sometimes results in war or erecting pyramids of civilisation. It can also cause the invention of atomic weapons, satellites, and new medicines. We try to suppress fear from every angle. When we try to suppress fear, it reacts everywhere. The more we suppress it, the more courageous we become. If in case we are unable to suppress it, it suppresses us. The same suppression produces mental problems, tension, extinction, hesitation, introversion, murder, violence, and terror. It encourages suicidal and violent activities. Therefore, our suppressed fear can be the cause of fear.

External Factor

In some cases, we are unable to declare the cause of fear. Factors mentioned above are major reasons. Some external factors play a vital role. Figure No. 25 illustrates some external factors.

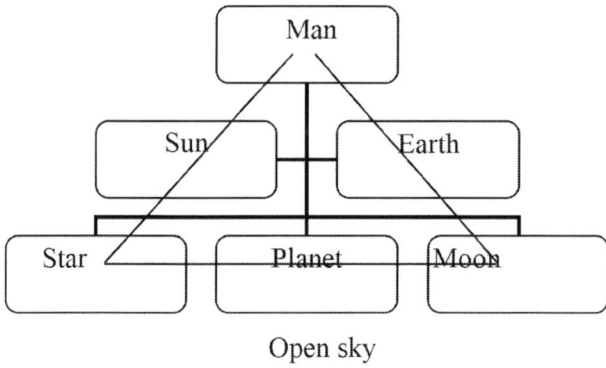

Figure No. 25

Figure No. 25 shows an open sky. There is a man in the open sky. It also shows the impact of the earth, the sun, the planets, the stars, and the moon on a man. Its impact is on his mental and physical growth. We care for the presence of planets in astronomy. Fortune tellers always observe stars and planets in horoscopes. People have a fear of the negative impact of these stars and planets. Most of us believe in blind belief and superstition. We believe in religion and consult a fortune teller. When the fortune teller says, 'You have bad days. *Rahu, ketu,* and *shani* will make you suffer', we start to fear and begin to worship to get rid of these things. We worship to avoid misfortune for peace. When we do these things, we feel protected from different problems and accidents. Many people have such faith even in the age of science. Despite the presence of these things, there are many factors to make impacts on them. They are rain, drought, storms, food scarcity, epidemics, new diseases, atomic weapons, ultraviolet rays, etc. They create fear in our minds. We adopt different measures to keep ourselves safe. In this way, planets, stars, the sun, ozone layer depletion, thunder, black holes, eclipses, etc. make an impact on us and create fear.

Whatever the consciousness, mind, and brain tell us, fear exists with those things mentioned above. Everything in this world depends on and is attached to each other. Even the solar system, the Milky Way, or all those in the whole universe are related to each other. Any change in these sectors directly influences us. There lies the fear: Earth moving towards a black hole or the ozone layer depletion, solar eclipse, lunar eclipse, typhoon, winter and summer due to Earth, sun, and moon. We determine day and month on the basis of astronomy. Similarly, fortune telling and astronomical work can be done on the basis of planets and stars. It determines bad or lucky days. Astronomy believes that gravitation, inertia, light, and revolving influences newborn babies.

So, people used to worship storms, rain, thunder, forests, hills, rivers, and wild animals as gods in the primitive age. In case of describing fears of people in the primitive age, Rahul Sangkrityayan says, 'People used to fear dark and new places and objects. They used to fear lightning and fire on the one hand, and they used to regard them as god on the other.'[2] We still worship them as god. We believe that if we worship, we get relief from scarcity, difficulties, and many other diseases.

End Notes:

1. Birendra Prasad Mishra, *Darshansastrako Parichaya (Introduction to Philosophy)*, Nepal Charity Foundation, 2065 v.s. p. 13.
2. Rahul Sangkrityayan, *Samyabatnai Kina (Why Communism)?* trans. Kashi Ram Gaire, Pragati Book Sadan, Kathmandu 1934, p. 47.

8

Scope of Fear

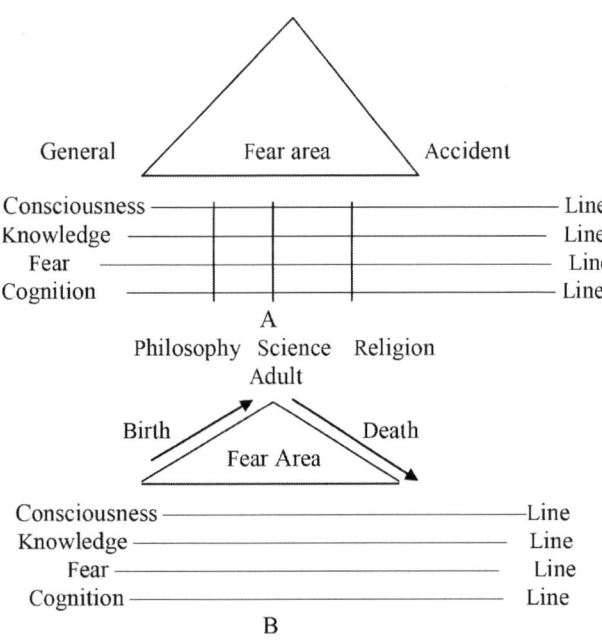

Figure No. 26

B in Figure No. 26 shows birth, adulthood, death and fear area, consciousness, knowledge, fear, and cognition. Just above those lines, there are philosophy, science, and religion. When the meaning of it exists, it continues to maturity. Unless these successes, programmes, and prosperity are achieved, we suffer from the fear of failure. That means fear starts with birth and ends with death.

In the same figure, 'A' shows general, accident, consciousness, knowledge, fear, cognition, and fear area. Both figure 'A' and 'B' are joined with philosophy, science, and religion. To get rid of our fear, we take the shelter of philosophy, science, and religion. In fact, science and religion are philosophy. We find them different when we go into detail. We have fear from general case to the accident or life to death. Figure 'A' represents a short period and Figure 'B' represents a long-term effect, but death has no time limit.

The line given above shows consciousness is followed by knowledge; knowledge is followed by fear and cognition is required to get rid of fear.

Thus, we are surrounded by the fear system from the cradle to the grave and the general case to accident. These all are under the scope of fear. Cognition helps us to get rid of fear or minimise it. It helps us. Intellect protects us from accident, incident, disease, and natural disaster. Coincidence is a different thing; we are protected by rationality, knowledge, consciousness, and intellect. Therefore, the knowledge of fear further helps us acquire knowledge. A huge sector of consciousness is the scope of fear.

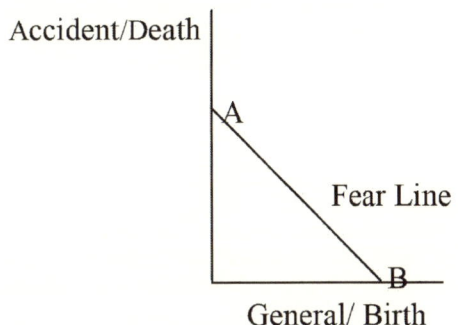

Figure No. 27

Figure No. 27 shows fear reaches a climax as soon as it collects the information about incident, accident, and disease.

Suppose a house has caught fire. As soon as we know about it, the fear reaches climax. It remains there for a long time. In such a condition, people feel frightened, shout, and cry. This is knowledge. Such a decision can save or invite accident—thinking. Such a decision can save or invite accident—death. But when time passed on, fear begins to minimise and we adopt comfortable measures. But in case tension, troublesome and uncomfortable thoughts begin to increase, fear automatically increases. If incident and accident become severe, fear increases at once. It minimises in a general case. We have been realising fear in this way in our lives. Figure No. 27 shows fear from A, the highest point, decreasing to B, the lowest point. This theory does not apply to all cases but can be applicable to more than 75 per cent cases.

A man becomes nervous as soon as he sees a snake or horrible accident. He remains horrific for a certain time. He gradually understands that wisdom instead of fear should be used. Then he sees a solution and begins to use his rationality. This is useful for the people who suffer from transferable and epidemic disease and old age. Information about death and accident on the verge of death makes the situation much more horrific. Here we search solutions and alternatives.

9

Area-based Fear Pyramid

According to Baishesik philosophy, 'Objects at micro-levels are visible. When they are invisible, they are called atoms. Therefore, everything is made of atoms.'[1]

Fear differs on the basis of place and time. When we keep on breaking down objects, they reach atomic levels and ends in zero. Baishesik philosophy considers the world as made of atoms. Science also agrees with it. Similarly, if we divide sectors, they also reach small units—villages, chowks, houses, etc.

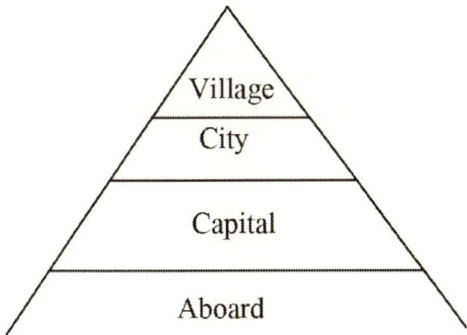

Figure No. 28

Figure No. 28 shows the pyramid of fear that takes place in villages, cities, capital cities, and foreign countries. Here, the village is in a small room, the city is in a bigger room; the capital city is in a much bigger room, and a foreign country is in the biggest room. It means that fear differs according to the size of rooms. Some examples of fear based on such sectors have been presented below:

1. *Village*

People in the village have simple lives—with much work in farms and busy in going to markets but few means of recreation. People are always busy in their fields. They celebrate together at festivals, weddings, and other gatherings at their leisure. They hardly experience the feeling of conspiracy, treachery, flattery, backbiting, etc. in their minds. They have clear and clean hearts. Robbery and theft hardly take place. Police and soldiers have a small presence. They have limited desire and hunger, but larger superstition and blind belief. They fear only the reduction of their production or crops being damaged in their fields and also with ends being meet. These are general fears. They don't have the fear of severe disease, because they have little knowledge about disease. The people in the village fear hunting gods, gods of the forest, snake gods, and natural objects and existence. Such fear is based on superstition and blind belief. Due to this fear, they worship these gods to make them happy. Even if they are severely sick, they don't spend money so much for the treatment due to the absence of sufficient knowledge about the diseases. Now, big cities, capital cities, and countries are plunging into ethnic and religious conflicts. They suffer from economic crisis. They have become the victim of terrorist attacks and also epidemics. Unemployment rates have become a big challenge. Many problems have occurred in other places, but villages are more peaceful. But these days, due to the impacts of cities, capital cities, and foreign countries upon them, villages have begun to experience fear. In the absence of these problems, people will have no fear in the villages. Limited fears in the villages consist of fears of wild animals, superstition, and blind belief. So only 10 per cent fear exists in villages.

2. *Cities*

Cities have larger facilities and population than the villages. A large number of educated people do live there. Fear exists with education and knowledge. The people in cities have the knowledge of new diseases. They acquire knowledge of atomic weapons, machines, industries, and occupations. Huge numbers of vehicles and means of communication are available there. They are busy with occupation, work, etc. They sell their time. People have different occupations and classes. They don't have agriculture-oriented lives as in villages. Some people in the cities don't have any idea about agricultural products. They learn to live with ready-made foods. Lives in the cities are more mechanical; people have lonely lives and always feel insecure.

According to Eric Fromm, a psychologist, freedom of a man increases as he grows young. He further says that on the one hand, complete power with other people, natural capacity and power increase, but at the same time, along with the increment of personality, loneliness, insecurity, meaningless role of a man in the universe, and doubts of power increase.[2]

People in the cities do not have collective feelings, closeness to each other, friendly relationships, giving and taking and a faithful environment as the people have in villages. People are suspicious of each other. They lose their self-esteem.

They are dependent. It indicates lives with jobs. People with professions are also dependent. Any incidents or events in the world influence lives immediately. Bankruptcy in America, Japan, or other countries shakes the foundation of economy in other cities. Scope of fear in cities is much wider than in villages. People are more insecure in the cities than in the villages. So, people desire to have their lives secured. They work day and night for it. Here, if we work for others, it will ruin our lives. People do not care for others. To mange time even for family is difficult. Here, life is not as easy as in the village. Life is fearful—fear of unemployment, fear of terrorism, fear of disease, fear of polluted environment, fear of theft and robbery, and other fears. Many countries have political, economic, ethnic, and religious fears. The village has 10 per cent fear, but cities have 20 per cent fears. Hence, people use their knowledge, consciousness, and temperament to get rid of these fears.

3. Capital City

The administrative centre of any country is called the capital city. Administrative, economic, political, or all other important works are conducted through this centre. The capital city is joined with other national and international cities through different transportations. Most of the important government and non-government offices are established in the capital city. Many industrial and commercial works along with seminars and workshops are conducted here. Similarly, important national and international sports are also conducted here. It has a high possibility—particularly, the possibility of job. People with jobs always fear losing their jobs. Proprietors are always fearful of bankruptcy. High living standards is a centre of fear. People fear low life standards, and they make an attempt for its uplift. People with high life standards are fearful of the degradation of their life standards. Therefore, they attempt for even higher life standards. Again, if life standards do not go up, there is fear that it will go down. Many people commit suicide when their life standards do not go up. So, people have much bigger fears than in cities or in developed villages. Fear measures here at 30 per cent.

4. Abroad

While talking about lives in foreign countries, Prof. Dr Gobinda Raj Bhattarai writes, 'Many experiences exist in foreign countries: first, geographical, historical and cultural displacements—illusion or fear of displacement, second, dualism/dual cultural consciousness, and third, fear of insecurity. We never experience such fears in our own country.'[3]

The world has become a global village. The human mind is always escaping. Most people emigrate to rich countries. More facilities and opportunities are there than there are in villages, cities, and capital cities. Fear is also greater. People run to and fro to escape fear. They work more than in one place. People emigrate from underdeveloped countries to developed countries at a great rate. People get more facilities and opportunities there. So, facilities, opportunities for economic and professional activities, and law and order also attract people. Therefore, people are hungry for such countries. When people in this way get more facilities and opportunities, they are doubtless hungry for those countries. But loneliness and ways of life have brought mental insecurity. Thinking about how to live strikes our minds. There is no one to come and help in need. Let us say there is no one to love in need. Again, they don't have time to love and care for others as in the villages. Relationships between lover and beloved, friends, and even social works are artificial. Its main reason is that neither they have their own lives nor have do they have time. They sell their labour and time. Irregular in work and inability to maintain punctuality bring the fear of termination. When one is terminated from a job, that person will hardly get a new job. If the income is reduced, one will suffer from economic crisis. As a result, life becomes more insecure. Another problem will be that savings will have been invested, or one will have sent it to relatives of one's own country. Moreover, one will have spent the money. Thus, fear always follows and haunts people.

In this way, the more facilities and opportunities are added, the more fear is increased. On the one hand, people enjoy happiness, facilities, and prosperity, and on the other, they increasingly suffer from fear. Fear increases along with the increment of facilities. People from different countries of the world come to live in rich and developed countries. We can see crowds of people there—both honest and dishonest. It creates various problems. As a result, fears like terrorist attacks, theft, robbery, ethnic and religious conflicts, including many others, exist in the country. American and British people are the most terrified people in the world. These countries have undergone many terrorist attacks. Therefore, they are like a burnt child that dreads the fire. Facilities and fears absent in villages, cities, and capital cities are present in foreign countries. Almost 40 per cent fear is with fleeing to a foreign country. The reason behind it is that the fear is continuously being added here.

Therefore, about the people living abroad, Dr Gobinda Raj Bhattrai says, 'People suffer from homelessness and also from nostalgia of the lost ways of their lives, lost culture, along with their geographical and historical displacements—fear of displacement, affection for their geography, culture, law, and religion, and fear of loneliness.'[4]

End Notes:

1. Mel Thompson, *Eastern Philosophy*, Hodder & Stoughton, UK, 1999, p. 18.
2. Eric Fromm, *The Fear of Freedom*, Routledge & Kegan Paul, London, 1942, p. 29.
3. Gobinda Raj Bhattarai, *Uttar Adhunik Bimarsha (Post Modern Discourse)*, Modern Books, Kathmandu, 2064 v.s. p. 119.
4. Gobinda Raj Bhattarai, *Uttar Adhunik Bimarsha (Post Modern Discourse)*, Modern Books, Kathmandu, 2064 v.s. p. 119.

10

Global Form of Fear

Dr Sachchidananda Misra writes about the global condition on fear in his book entitled *Iswor Mariskyo* (God is Dead):

'For human beings, the world with three different conditions has been accepted in the religion: *Pratibhasik Bishwa*, *Byavaharik Bishwa* and *Paramarthik Bishwa*.'
   a. *Pratibhasik Bishwa* (Dreaming World): When we dream, we think that everything that we dream is truth. This is a *pratibhasik* world. Neither logic nor process of thinking can abolish it. But when we wake up and our sense organs start to adopt the sensitivity of another world, this world gets self-abolished or turns into falsehood. b. *Byavaharik Bishwa* (Practical World): When we wake up from our slumber, the practical world appears in front of our sense organs. We run and spring in its specific time. This is a practical world. It is between *pratibhasik* and *paramarthik* worlds. c. *Paramarthik Bishwa* (Meditation World): If the sense organs that have experienced the practical world reawaken, the *paramarthik* world can be witnessed. We reach the second awakening through meditation, penance, and contemplation. The condition to experience this world is to some extent similar to the state of salvation. It can be achieved throughout life and even after death.[1]
   Fear exists in these three worlds—some of them are visible, while others are invisible.
   The meaning of fear is so vast, which is proved even with its changing forms. Its expansion covers the whole world. Part of it begins from the cell of

every living creature and expands throughout the whole universe. Nothing in this universe remains untouched by it. Its wave and impact are ubiquitous.

Fear transforms to apply to every human activity. A word hardly exists with such a vast meaning—fear, dreadful, gigantic, fear arouser, chaotic, full of fear, based on fear, causing fear, related to fear, mixed with fear, terror, threat, suffer from fear, terror, fright, etc.

Intermingling of fear with any other word constitutes a fear word: for example—fear of scarcity, fear of suppression, fear of failure, fear of attack, fear of fire, atomic fear, fear of weapons, fear of terror, fear of extremism, fear of storms, interior fear, fear of relatives, fear of necessity, fear of God, fear of depression, religious fear, fear of conspiracy, fear of thunderbolts, fear of death, fear of children, fear of culture, fear of drought, fear of food, fear of job, fear of life, fear of language, fear of script, fear of employment, fear of heaven, fear of violence, fear of anger, fear of nation, fear of nature, fear of enemy, fear of prestige, fear of property, fear of love, fear of extinction, fear of hesitation, fear of introversion, fear of shyness, fear of time, fear of transport, fear of identity, fear of weather, fear of journey, fear of earthquakes, fear of epidemics, fear of diseases, fear of politics, fear of the economy, fear of society, fear of floods, fear of landslides, fear of rivers, fear of devils, fear of technology, fear of electronics, fear of scientists, fear of exteriority, fear of the past, fear of age, fear of occupation, fear of caste/ethnicity, fear of civilisation, fear of education, fear of illusion, fear of doubt, fear of greed, fear of conspiracy, fear of event, fear of meaning, fear of nature, and so on. There are innumerable fears and the explanation for all of them is impossible. Any word followed by the word fear constitutes fear.

We fear different colours, places, events, and problems. Our human temperaments don't wake up except to fear when we witness colour, place, event, and problem. Similarly, our temperaments are not influenced when we see the red colour or a grave and lonely place. Red lights in airplanes and red lights on the back of cars indicate danger. Such indications create fear. There are too many things like that—they create fear.

It has many results: feeling fright, yelling, shouting, turning faces black and pale, dry lips and mouths, fast breathing, erect hair, crying, springing, running, stammering, shouting during slumber, loss of hunger and thirst, loss of sleep, etc. With such indications, we can guess how big the fear is.

We don't have any idea about where fear comes out from and disappears. Fear starts as we start to walk, speak, listen, read, work, sleep, eat, watch, touch, understand, think, believe, imagine, and so on. The same ordinary thing changes into extraordinary and creates fear. Verbally, other issues are not as vast as fear. When we study its antonyms, dread, fright, threat, and forms, fear appears too vast. If we let it expand, how vast it becomes. It is beyond imagination.

Western people classify fear as phobia. The word phobia originated from the Greek word 'phobus'. Later, the word began to be used in Latin and German languages as phobia. The fear word in English generally indicates the same sense, but it has not been explained and interpreted as philosophy. It doesn't have detailed interpretation in the East. Its vastness has been distinguished between phobia and fear in English. Phobia has been interpreted in detail in Western texts. They just add phobia to other words. It has been explained under various sub-titles. For example—fear of man, animals, insects, ghosts, friends, medicine, treatments, etc. Things to create fear in different places, countries, religions, and cultures are also different. Dracula in Western countries is a king of ghosts. We don't find ghosts like Dracula in the East. Similarly, the ghosts of the East can't be found in the West. Some of the things depend on myth and culture. I have discussed the types of fear to help diagnose what fear a man has. New fears are being added every day.

Both words, fear and phobia, are wider so that they can be added to different words. However, though it is wider, it is too strange, since it has not been interpreted as an 'ism'.

Fear is elastic, liquid, balanced, and vigorous. Its meaning is also exactly similar. It is not fixed, but variable and omnipresent. It flows on with consciousness that exists in one cell to multi-celled creatures. The gap between unconsciousness and consciousness can't be measured. Such a condition is within us. We not only suffer from the fear in the present world, rather we suffer from the fear of past, present, and future. Likewise, we fear visible and invisible things. Fear exists even in imagination, reality, and dreams. We have been afraid of birds and animals, plants, and our surroundings—from the vastness of the universe to the part of soul and from the God of our legends to the devils. It is both positive and negative.

We have been surrounded and crushed by the same vastness of fear and also we are tangled with it. We are progressing and retreating on the basis of this vast fear. As soon as we recollect doubtful things, see insects, and witness others, fear starts and also anxiety with fear starts. Fear stops us when we are on a wrong track and shows a right track. It's a special machine that alerts us when we are about to be run over, about to stumble, and informs us before scarcity of water and oil and before something is damaged. It is even vaster than it has been explained verbally—more than we have thought and realised. It is vaster than we read, write, hear, and realise. Its vastness is unidentified and eternal. We can realise and feel only those fears that appear in front of us. We may have illusions that they are the only fears. If we deeply study fear based on work, anger, love, affection, jealousy, doubt, ego, fright, conspiracy, and others, forms of fear appear different. Human life is totally tangled with human temperament, content, characters, and conditional reflexes. Therefore, the real form of fear is as vast as the universe. We are living in the vast universe of fear.

Universe and Void

We can study if it prevails or not on the basis of the universe and the void. The universe is based on the void and uncountable voids are in this universe. Invention, construction, and creation are possible only from the void. This universe was created from the same process. Most planets and stars didn't prevail before the big bang. They were the results of the big bang. The earth is one of them. The earth is itself a universe—it's so vast. Neither air and water nor creatures and plants existed in the very beginning. It was a big void. Many things began to exist gradually in the void. Human beings came into being. People didn't have language, script, religion, culture, caste/ethnicity, and groups—all they had was the void. The process of nature, necessity, fear, and desire gradually filled the void. The same things they constructed began to give them happiness, unhappiness, pleasure, and fear. Philosophers began to interpret the universe and soul and the universe and the void slowly and gradually.

Chha (Yes) .... *Chhaina* (No)

Caste/ethnicity .... No caste/ethnicity

God .... No God

Existence .... No existence

Language, religion .... No language, religion

Other .... No other

Figure No. 29.

Figure No. 29 depicts *chha* (yes) and *chhaina* (no). These are only examples. Such examples apply everywhere. Existentialist Jean Paul Sartre, in his book *Being and Nothingness,* has explained about being and nothingness. The universe, according to Shankaracharya, is in fact the universe and not beyond that. Fear in many cases starts from *chha* (yes), and in other cases, it starts from *chhaina* (no). The origin of the former is 'I' and 'mine'. 'I' is always followed by 'mine', then *chha*. I have my caste/ethnicity, language, script, religion, culture, and country. It needs to be preserved. If 'I' doesn't carry its characters, it can't be 'I'. Everything that is needed for 'I' should be preserved. It can become extinct and get attacked. Fear occurs anticipating the extinction of 'I'. It is followed by property, family, relatives, country, and society. These all have what 'I' needs. 'I' is closely attached with 'mine'. This is the identity of man. We can't distinguish a man from another in the absence of all these. Therefore, he wants to preserves his identity and he campaigns to claim that whatever he has are all good. He fears caste/ethnicity, country, language, script, religion, and culture; it has to be preserved. These are the causes of fear. We believe in life, God, and others. Fear starts from there. This fear is a product of *chha*. Many critics, writers, and philosophers like Partha Chatterjee, Shirin Rai, Julia Kristeva, Homi Bhabha, Lui Althusser, Remond William, Michel Foucault, Jacques Derrida, Edward Said, and Aijaj Ahamad have written and spoken about it. They have come either of literary criticism, Marxist thinking, gender introduction, marginalised sectors, or colonial thoughts. They are all for the man who is about to extinct, suffers from injustice, discrimination, and domination.

On the other hand, there is *chhaina* (no). It also creates fear. For example, philosopher Friedrich Nietzsche declared the 'death of God'. No God is possible after the declaration of the death of God. The place of God was vacant. There was nothing in the vacancy but fear. The world is impossible in a void. Who liberates us from our crisis?! Then, they proposed the concept of 'superman'. God didn't exist in the prehistoric period. However, though God didn't exist, fear existed. There was the fear of who would liberate us from the crisis. They didn't have knowledge about storms, typhoons, thunderbolts, rain, the sun, the moon, the stars, and the planets as well as natural disasters. They didn't have houses and clothes to protect them from natural disasters. There was no one to protect them from such disasters. Thus, natural power became the source of fear. The belief still exists.

Man is bound to suffer from different problems and calamities. People have to face various problems and crises. In the beginning, they began to worship the power of nature for protection from natural disaster, storms, typhoons, thunder, floods, landslides, starvation, drought, heat, and cold. What they worshipped became God later. Many communities in the world still worship the power of nature, plants, hills, mountains, steep lands, rivers, and streams as God. This tradition developed in the prehistoric period. Now, people can't live in the absence of God. They live and work with the faith and help of God. God is in the centre. Fear existed in the absence of God, and it also exists in the presence of God. Fear exists with and without caste/ethnicity, religion, language, script, and so on. Where does one go to live without language, script, religion, culture, country, and society? How does one recognise 'I'? There must be *chha* for self-identity and self-existence in society. So, there is fear in *chha* and *chhaina*.

There are too many gaps between *chha* and *chhaina*. It is filled with possible and real events. This fear can be experienced by living creatures, particularly by the most conscious animals, human beings. Many activities run between *chha* and *chhaina*.

Existentialist Jean Paul Sartre brought freedom to the centre of his thinking. Existentialist thinking says: 'I'm here and I'm free for choices, decision, and work.'[2] The freedom has come into being with heavy loads (bondage) since prehistoric time. Bondage and freedom have an arbitrary relationship. Bondage always strides on to freedom. The presence of bondage is the absence of freedom. Those who are living now are unable to live according to their desires. Individuals, societies, and nature are not under the control of human beings. It is impossible as well. People can have freedom of choices only if they are under the control of people.

An ordinary man can say, 'I'm the king. I'm God.' How practical it is depends on the faith of the people. In my opinion, more than 99 per cent of people are unable to have the freedom of choice. The choice of people is always to be rich, famous, and prestigious. Only a few people are able to meet their choices. That is again not sufficient to meet desire. Writers, players, social activists, politicians, and others have choices to be successful, famous, and rich. Only a few people can meet their choices. Both external and internal factors are there to influence the choice. They all have to undergo struggles. A man who has the choice of a hundred steps can walk only ten steps. Thus, he is unable to reach the destination according to his choice. In this way, the man is free for choices, yet external factors influence his choices and his choice becomes impossible. Freedom of choice for human beings, who are under the limitations of law, rules and regulations, society, country, and nature, is more imaginary and ideal. People can't live without society, country, and nature. This is a matter of theory, but it doesn't happen in practice. Many theories in fact are based on idealism—like a car running to meet the impossible mission. Fear can also be like this. Fear alone looks practical from an individual to the country. Inability of choices is due to the fear of bondage. It takes time to reach freedom from bondage. Many problems and obstacles have to be crossed. New thinking and philosophy have come up for its liberation. Nobody likes to live in bondage. Monarchy, democracy, socialism, and God are *chha* bondages. Existence is also under bondage. Our choices are in the *encircle* of bondages. Breaking out from the bondage of fear is, in fact, freedom.

End Notes:

1. Sachchidanda Mishra, *Ishwar Marisaky (God is Dead)*, trans. Balkrishna Shrestha 'Nebha', Utsarga Publication Baranasi, 2009, p. 213.
2. Mohan Raj Sharma, Khagendra Prasad Luitel, *Purbiya Darshan ra Paschatya Sahitya Sidhanta (Eastern Theory an Western Literary Criticism)*, Student Book Store, Kathmandu, 2063 v.s. p. 345.

11

Condition of Fear

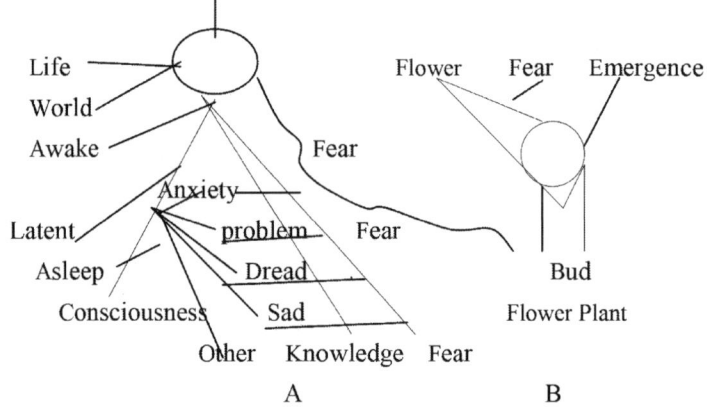

Figure No. 30

A in Figure No. 30 shows the consciousness on one side, knowledge in the centre, and fear on the other side. The line of consciousness is drawn with the combination of being latent, asleep, and awakened, and the line of knowledge is drawn with the combination of anxiety, problems, death, disease, hardship, pain, existence, ego, suspicion, and illusion and others. The line of knowledge originates from the same place where the line of fear starts. The line of consciousness has crossed the line of knowledge and has touched the line of fear. It means knowledge starts with consciousness and fear starts with knowledge. The meeting point of these three lines is the condition of complete consciousness and the condition of complete life as well. All consciousness, knowledge, fear, and so on exist in this condition of complete life. This point is the climax of fear. Life and the world are viewed from this point. Fear has a greater possibility of expansion where two lines, the line of knowledge and line of fear, are crossed. Fear appears fluctuated in the points where the line of knowledge and the line of consciousness are broken. The higher the consciousness, the higher the knowledge, and the higher the fear and lower the consciousness, the lower the knowledge and lower the fear. Thus, the condition of fear depends on consciousness and knowledge.

For easier study, A in Figure No. 30 divides the consciousness into three different conditions—asleep, latent, and awakening. As the consciousness increases, so knowledge and fear increase. Fear that starts from micro-level consciousness influences problems, anxiety, dread, suspicion, illusion, and other things. Awareness, conditional reflexes, human temperament, and environment play a vital role in the consciousness, knowledge, and fear. Moreover, fear depends on human struggle. Fear, therefore, is movable according to the structure of man.

When complete consciousness comes down, fear is also minimised. Children with low fear jump, spring, and climb on everything. The level of consciousness of the courageous people who acquire medals and jump down from the roof during mass movement has reached this point.

B in Figure No. 30 shows the bud emerging, flowering, and fear. The most beautiful form of a flower is as a bud. If we are able to lower fear to the state of a bud, our lives become heavenly, beautiful. People always want to make their lives like buds. They can't succeed due to fear.

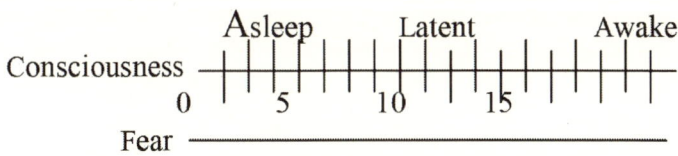

Figure No. 31

We find that some scholars have divided it into four or five parts, although consciousness has been divided into three parts in general. Four kinds of consciousness are mentioned in *Sarbasaropanishad* as 'nightmare, latent, asleep, and awakened'[1].

Figure No. 31 shows the level of consciousness 0, 5, 10, and 15. Lines are drawn between each division. These divisions can be more than they are. The line of consciousness is given just above. Consciousness along with fear has been shown dividing. Human temperaments and characters also divide like this. Divisions of all make them easier to study; otherwise, they make us plunge into puzzles.

The level of consciousness of the plant and the animal differs according to time, circumstance, and condition—particularly the condition of security and hunger. To come forth, a plant faces the abyss of land, stones, and sand and protects itself from sun, rain, and wind; these are levels of consciousness of fear. The development of civilisation has come a long way since prehistoric time—knowledge on how to make a stone weapon, how to make fire, how to cook food and eat, how to cultivate the land, how to build houses to live in and so on were all possible after a long struggle and jumped from one condition to the other.

End Notes:

1. Arjundev Panta, *Vedanta-Darshan Sar (Brief Vedanta Philosophy)*, Ratna Book Store, Kathmandu 2062 v.s. p. 150.

12

Types of Fear

A plant also tries to relieve itself from fear according to its capacity. If we cover the seed of a plant with something, it finds a way to grow. The plant starts finding a support if it is creeper. The search is for security against fear, but not for the sake of searching. Man and animal are always in search of something, if we study this from the perspective of searching. All the animals and birds seem to be walking and flying, looking for something at any time. They eat, drink, and rest if they find their food, water, and shelter on the way. Sometimes they are found to be tied to love. They don't seem to have had any particular purpose, but they always try to find their food, water, and a safe shelter, fulfil desire, and have power and position.

Karna Sakya in his book entitled *Khoj* (Search) writes: 'Seed takes sunlight from the sky and its roots go deeper down to the soil in order to search for water. When the search for sunlight and water stops, the plant dries.'[1]

Man is like this—he walks to and fro and also seems to be busy in doing something. He eats, drinks, and rests like an animal does. He always seems to be busy in search. Once he finds what he is looking for, he immediately starts another search. This process ends with his death. All people, such as social workers, politicians, scientists, philosophers, etc., are busy in search of something. The searching is of no avail without any purpose. These searches are regarding life and on what is related to life. Their search ends with fear. Most of their searches end with fear. A plant is guided by the fear of death in its search. That is why all people seem to be moving about and searching to be safe from fear. Scientists are seeking any way out to save the earth so that she may not be attacked by any other planet and end at any time. Doctors are busy in search of medicine for fatal diseases. In relation to the new search sought by the great leaders of the world, Karna Sakya writes: 'Gandhi, Nelson Mandela, and Martin Luther King eradicated not only colonialism, but also racial discrimination during their search for non-violence.'[2]

Whatever struggle they had was not just in searching. The search was for the liberation from the fear of racial suppression. All searches are attempts made on liberation from some fear. Search doesn't have self-existence. When it is associated with the fear, then it exists.

Man always keeps himself ready through his experience and knowledge to be safe from animals such as a lizard, frog, etc. and enemies as well. Chickens start crying and run to hide as soon as they see a hawk flying in the sky. Their efforts to hide show fear rather than worry, suffering, and pain. Animals try to be safe as soon as they feel the shaking of the earthquake. Similarly, man brushes his teeth and wears gloves, helmet, shoes, watch, clothes, and a mask due to fear. He eats a balanced diet and exercises for good health and longevity. He tries to make a strong house, windows, doors, walls, with bricks, cement, wood, etc. for more security. We find that there is an attempt to be safe from fear everywhere. For example, a house, clothes, food, etc. are for security and existence. Perhaps some people don't consider them as needed for security and existence. Thus, we always want to make our lives secure from all sides. Man has been taking hygienic food, wearing nice durable clothes, and making a strong house since prehistoric times. All this is because of fear. Man is looking for a good strong material, substance, building, etc. Similarly, a machine, vehicle, and any other useful things for humans are focused on considerably safety. It helps to be safe from any accident. Man always takes care of his own safety whatever he does, because he realises that he is surrounded by several unsecured situations. Indeed, he is in the middle of hazardous environments. That is why he wants to be safe from all those situations.

Thus, every animal wants to be free from fear at any cost. Man is the most rational creature of all the living beings. That is why fear affects a man very much. The types of fear also focus on man. Fear differs on the basis level of consciousness, knowledge, conditional reflexes, and level of tolerance. It is an improper thought that everyone has the same kind of fear. As mentioned above, fear requires consciousness to exist. Knowledge, tolerance, and conditional reflex must be complete for complete consciousness. Absence of knowledge on life, world, death, disease, property, relatives, etc. is absence of knowledge to some extent. For example, a man has high or low blood pressure, but he doesn't have any fear unless he knows it. He eats, drinks, walks, etc. like a healthy man. When he knows about it, he starts controlling his eating, drinking, walking, etc.

It has an enormous effect and sub-effect too. Conservational concepts, superstition, religion, culture, customs, illusion, doubt, etc. aren't real things, but they make us as fearful as if they were real things. We always fear things unless we know that they aren't real things. There is a possibility of fear in every moment in life. Some fears can't be learnt till the last. When we know that it is not really a fearful thing, we have no fear. For example, a trunk in the dark, a rope, etc. that we see in the dark, they threaten us, although they are not fearful things in practice. The fear of a trunk and rope is removed when we know the reality in the light. If that is a real snake, fear exists because it is, indeed, a fearful and harmful thing. We have such a fear even in daytime. Sometimes, a cat crosses the way, a jackal cries near the house, a crow crows, and an owl hoots. We have a bad dream etc. All these are artificial fears. Conservation, superstition, etc. in society creates such a fear. We have also found that doubt and illusion have caused big fears somewhere else. This has been categorised as a phobia in English. There are different kinds of experience of the same phobia. For example, it is not that everyone has hydrophobia. This is a phobia that exists while seeing water. Short-term fear, long-term fear, less fear, average or moderate fear, and excessive fear are artificial fears. Although there are uncountable fears, some possible fears have been classified in the following figure.

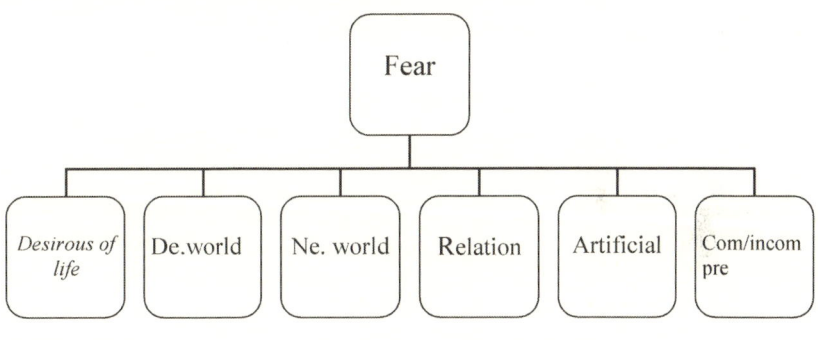

Figure No. 32

1. *A Fear of Desired Life*

Fear is always between life and death or possible events and real events. Man suffers from such fears during his whole life. Every moment we have to deal with fear in our daily lives. All these fears are the result of the desired life. Man is ready to do any kind of bad activity, such as forgery, violence, injustice, suppression, theft, robbery, etc., for a happy life. Social prestige is also a basis of life. Man is busy with his profession, job, and cultivation every day. They work very hard till the last to make the dark part of their lives bright. All the emperors, hermits, saints, great spirits, philosophers, etc. seemed to perform different activities. All the creatures are in fear until they are alive and careful. Philosophers have given us the philosophy of life. Similarly, preachers have preached a lot of sermons on a happy life. Although those religions and philosophies have existed in human life, they have caused some fearful situations. Fear lessens for the time being but not forever. Perhaps a man feels free from his hardship, suffering, troubles, problems, etc. as he worships God, yet his concentration plunges into the whirlwind of fear. Necessity, ambition, desire, freedom, existence, human temperament, religion, culture, customs are all the instruments of our lives. Fear plays a vital role in controlling, preserving, conducting, and inspiring all these instruments. All these fears are products of those desiring life, *jijivisa*.

b.   *Fear of Departure from This World*

While taking about fear, Saint Achyuta Nanda said, 'Death is the origin of fear. Man performs different functions for freedom from the fear of death. A major cause for faith in religion, incarnation, and God is fear.'[3]

Socrates said, 'I didn't give up my duty even in the battlefield with ignorance to the fear of death. Now, I have become old. How do I give up the divine order to make the citizens of Athens conscious due to the fear of death in such an old age?'[4]

During a discourse on fear, Bertrand Russell writes: 'The people realise having been enslaved by an external power due to the fear of death.'[5]

Many philosophers, intellectuals, writers, and priests have been expressing their views on death like this. This is the later part of life. In other words, it is the fear of death. Death causes man lots of fears. Man is harassed due to the fear of death. We wish old age could be delightful. It brings curiosity about life after death. Those who have a weak heart tremble even with the thought of death. It doesn't occur to us in a normal condition. If a man undergoes an accident, a disease, and is crying and yelling on his bed on the verge of death, he sees death very close to him. He is much more fearful than he was in a normal condition. It affects him severely when he suffers from AIDS, SARS, cancer, and when he witnesses a house on fire, a plane on fire, and during an earthquake. He worries much about himself first, then about his family, and lastly about his relatives in such a condition. Some people, in exceptional cases, may take the situation normally, like Socrates, but the rest can't do so. If the situation is not taken normally, life can't be easy and comfortable. Fear often lessens from the initial stage. Those who have suffered from epidemic diseases and are facing the death penalty feel extreme fear in the beginning, but slowly and gradually, they adjust to the situation. In some cases, the fear rises constantly and it can invite an accident.

c.   Fear of Differences of Worlds

No one is able to say anything yet about life after death. Certainly, no one is able to talk about it. No one has come back after death. Conservational concepts, superstition, and religious concepts are followed for both life and death. Such concepts concern heaven and hell after death. Fear exists because of the wrong promulgation about hell; therefore, people imagine going to heaven. Similarly, a wrong proliferation among people is also the cause of fear. People, indeed, are always curious to know about life after death: Where does the life go, and what suffering does one have to face? These questions haven't been answered yet. These questions stir the minds of many people. If Socrates had returned after his death, he would have told the people about life after death.

Charvaka says, 'Another world doesn't exist.'[6]

Fear after death stirs the minds of many people and this is fear after death. People contemplate on concepts of the next world in the later phases of their lives. Most people wish they could go to heaven, not to hell, particularly theists. People with faith wish they didn't have to bear hardship, torture, and pain after death. They are deeply influenced by this thought and faith, knowingly or unknowingly. Desires of happiness, peace, and prosperity along with the worldly fear often exist for them. Their wishes on peace, happiness, and prosperity and faith in another world liberate them from their fear for the time being, but increase their fear later.

d.   Fear of Relation

Everything is related to each everything else in the world. Human beings are also related to both biological and non-biological things. When a man acquires self-knowledge on 'I', it communicates fear. 'I' is followed by community, religion, culture, happiness, sorrow, relation, kith and kin, etc. Man always suffers from the temptation of his own-ness. When we utter 'I', 'you' immediately exists. These all demand identity. Mostly essentialism and constructism have been interpreted in regard to the identity. 'You' and 'I' are others for each other. Many writers, like Michel Foucault, Julia Kristeva, Homi Bhaba, Helene Siksu, Judith Butler, and Partha Chatterjee, have focused on them in their interpretations.[7] Always war and love exit between 'you' and 'I'. 'I' is the main reason for murder, war, and violence. Blacks, Whites, Nazis, Jews, Muslims, Christians, Hindus, Buddhists are all the result of this. Wars always occur due to this reason. My family and relatives exist due to this reason. America-Vietnam war, Iraq-America war, Afghanistan civil war, and Israel-Palestine conflicts are based on the fear of relation. The fear of relation is a major cause for upheavals in the world. War is born in the campaign for the preservation of 'I' and 'mine'. Reducing extremism of relation and adoption of sharing and common consensus reduce the possibility of war. It's human nature to work for 'I' and 'mine'. We can't reduce and ignore it so easily. Man is a social being. Even animals need groups. Fear exists as long as 'I' exists. We can reduce the fear produced from it to some extent. Reduction in extremism in individualism, caste/ethnicity, and religion is a way towards the reduction of fear. It is also a way towards reducing violence, murder, war, terror, etc. But what is going on in the world is due to extremism. We get at least a little relief from fear if we reduce extremism. People, caste/ethnic community, and religion go for people of other caste/ethnic communities and religions—attacking, murdering, and burning. One imaginary god is killing another imaginary god. People are nourishing groups and sub-groups within the same groups. These things occur due to the relationship between 'I' and 'mine'. Reduction in the feeling of 'I' and 'mine' reduces violence, murder, threats, attacks, etc.

e.   Artificial Fear

Fear beyond a real thing and a problem is an artificial fear. Conservatism, superstition, religion, and culture are beyond real life. They are colourless and formless. They cause fear in people. This is an artificial fear. This is a big problem to strike our mind. There is no problem when a cat crosses the road. Similarly, neither does a bad dream bring any problems nor does the crying of a jackal nor does the crying of a dog bring an omen of misfortune. They are all blind beliefs. Some of the doubts and illusions also cause fear in man. We think that we are like the donkey of Samasuddin, and we feel as if we have been chained. We feel as if we are sick; we feel as if someone is following us; we feel as if our property is ruined; and we worry about family members as we walk on the way. These are merely imaginary fears. Such fears are scattered around us. Neither do they exist nor are they real. They just give us the fear and we just feel fear. If we develop faith that they are merely illusions, some general fears are reduced. Above all, even a big scale of fear can reduce.

Thus fears of doubt and illusion exist. There are some differences between doubt fear and illusion fear. To see the stump of a tree as a ghost is an illusion, and to assume the same stump to be a ghost is doubt. Similarly, to see a husband or wife with someone at home is an illusion, but thinking about him or her, whether they are in love with another is a doubt. Thus, doubts and illusions are the causes for various fears. Various incidents occur in course of reducing fear. We find that many incidents have occurred due to these reasons; like the saying, 'To be over-suspicious is too dangerous.' We are also the victims of them. Doubts sometimes can cause war, murder, suicide, etc. Doubt looks and sounds normal, but destructive fear is hidden inside. It itself is like a tunnel. The more we doubt, the more it brings fear. Here, to reduce doubt is to reduce murder, violence, and anarchy. As the same fear doesn't exist in problems, worries, troubles, diseases, death, property, hunger, so the same fear doesn't exist even in doubts. This theory does not apply to all sources of fear, but different theories apply to the same source of fear. Low fear exists in some doubts, whereas much higher fear exists in other doubts. The same theory applies in problems, worries, troubles, diseases, death, enemies, etc. These are artificial fears.

f. Comprehensive and Incomprehensive Fear

Works are not comprehended to have been done due to fear. They are unknown in human beings. If people comprehend fear, they will stop murder, war, and violence. Events and accidents occur due to incomprehensive fear. Incomprehensive fear is larger in human beings than comprehensive fear. It remains suppressed. The world would be different if fear could be comprehended well and it would go ahead differently. The world is like this today due to incomprehensive fear. New discoveries in thoughts and theories are possible due to this incomprehensive fear. Similarly, some people go to their work, sing songs, create literary works, and get involved in politics. They don't know; there is fear behind their work and creations. Thus, some fears are comprehensive and others are incomprehensive. Fear is always moving and floating deep inside the consciousness—visible in some places and invisible in other places, like the ice floating on the sea.

These are general types of fear. Such fears exist in every step. No theory can claim the types of fear. Types of fear, we interpret, don't incorporate all. Life consists of a global form of fear. I have discussed only representative fears.

2. Escaping Fear

About eco-criticism, Prof. Dr Gobinda Raj Bhattarai writes, 'Eco-criticism includes the impact, effect, destruction, fear and worse result of immigration of creatures from the secured place where they have been living, working and spending time since long onto the new place.'[8]

People escape from boredom, sense of meaninglessness, trouble, suffering, problems, crime, punishment, poverty, mental stress, etc. Fear is a major reason. There are different types of escaping—to leave family, village, town, and country, emigration, becoming a hermit and recluse. It often happens in society. It is easy to comprehend the fragments of escaping. I want to discuss particular kinds of escaping here. When escaping is explained in detail, people who are willing to escape come to know why they are escaping. And then they may give up the idea of escaping.

We can divide escape simply into two parts: (i) physical and (ii) mental/non-physical.

(i) Physical Escape

Physical escape is to move physically from one place to another. Mental decision plays a vital role in it. When the people decide mentally, then they move from one place to another and one country to another. This escape has been explained below in detail.

a. To abandon the family

Different troubles, suffering, economic crisis, diseases, deaths, hardships, etc. occur in the family. Some people feel frightened even with the small scale of problems, hardship, pain, and suffering. Some people are ready to bear it; those who are not ready to bear it abandon the family. This is escaping from hardship, problems, and suffering. Some of those who have abandoned their families have progressed, and the rest of them are in much worse situations: they have become hermits, monks, beggars, saints, and recluses. They are dejected with worldly love and enticement.

Young people abandon their families to be free from family bondage, be liberated, and to spend a free life. They fear that they are deprived of their freedom at home. Growing divorce cases are due to the fear of losing freedom. They want to have a free life. This is also escaping.

b. To migrate

While talking about the reasons of migration, Prof. Gobinda Raj Bhattarai writes: 'To leave own place and unable to come back to the same place are due to obligation. People leave their place, escape and migrate due to war, conflicts, natural disasters, religious cause, ethnic or political cause, self desire or in search of adventure.'[9]

Migration is also an escape. People migrate to another place, village, town, or go abroad. People migrate from their places to other places, villages, towns, and foreign countries due to natural disasters such as landslides, drought, storms, earthquake, failure, insult, social stigma, economic crisis, exploitation, injustice, and suppression. People from one country emigrate into another country in search of good opportunities. Some of them leave their countries to escape from autocracy, exploitation, injustice, suppression, etc. A large number of people migrate from one place to another and one country into another these days.

c.   To wander as hermit, monk, beggar, saint and recluse

Some people are fed up with their worldly lives. Some people want to live in the world of loneliness, peace, and knowledge like the prince, Siddhartha, when they are fed up with life and want to give up on their lives, diseases, old age, family, generation, social problems, and economic problems. Sometimes they are unsuccessful in meeting their objectives for long and want to live alone. They blame their social life on an ignorant world and sacrifice everything for the name of God. Some of them are criminals. They disguise themselves as innocent people and walk secretly to be safe from rules, laws, and punishments. Therefore, saint, monk, yogi, hermit, and beggar are fearful of trouble, suffering, etc. and living a dejected life. Society can't be progressive and developed through their penance, meditation, and knowledge they perform for their dejected lives. So, those who are about to reject their lives, family, and society are their followers.

Thus, many people escape every day from their lives, families, and society. As mentioned above, people escape to be safe from failure, weakness, poverty, conservative concepts, superstition, rules, laws, revolutionary consciousness, natural disasters, scarcity, civil wars, etc. Again, fear is the heart of the causes. It is easier to understand escaping if we understand fear. Then, they can possibly give up escaping.

(ii) Mental/Non-physical Escape

It is not a physical escape. Man gives up his occupation due to various problems, hardships, pain, tortures, and threats and starts new work/ occupation. This is a process of mental escaping. Those who have escaped mentally are larger in numbers than those who have escaped physically. They change their ideas. Their behaviour and relationships change along with the change of ideas. All ideas that have been changed are not related to escaping. They are even clearer if we study them separately.

3. Fear of Depression

Like other diseases, modern medical science considers depression as a disease without clear symptoms. It has been identified as a disease for some decades. With its identification, it is much easier to conduct treatment for it. As it doesn't have clear symptoms, its treatment is based on assumption. Some symptoms are: feeling worried, being angry, feeling irritation, sadness, helplessness, convicted, humiliated, insomniac, losing weight, thinking of death, suicide, feeling dejected, considering life as meaningless, feeling irritated with friends and relatives, being too tired to talk, feeling a decrease in desire and aspiration, loving loneliness, giving up company, seeing no reason in life, feeling fear, tiredness, sweating without labour, being suspicious of others, disbelieving others, feeling as if someone is following them, doubting others loyalty, and so on. This agitation, hopelessness, and loneliness can pull people into drug addiction, drinking, and smoking. Even ordinary people have symptoms like these. We hardly distinguish whether someone is depressed or not on the basis of these symptoms.

People who suffer from depression look like healthy people. The time for his suffering from the disease can't be calculated. We don't know whether we have suffered from such depression or not. Depression sufferers don't accept illness immediately. Doctors guess the disease through symptoms. Even a healthy person suffers from this disease if he has different problems, economic loss, problems in the family relation, and deception in love. Always, these are not the symptoms of depression. The environment is certainly a cause of depression. In the beginning, particularly before identification of these as symptoms of depression, patients used to be taken somewhere else for treatment. After its identification, it is easier for the treatment of depression. Whatever symptoms are presented above are symptoms of fear as well. The number of people who commit suicide is increasing these days. It is a much severer problem, particularly in developed countries than in under-developed and developing countries. Now, life is difficult, complex, competitive, and mechanical. Life is like a machine. Those who are unable to compete here find no alternatives; therefore, they choose suicide. They are unhappy, hopeless, helpless, guilty, and depressed.

When fear and anxiety increase at a greater range, people suffer from sleeplessness and unwillingness to eat. It works to reduce memory and decision powers. People lose their honour, prestige, respect, etc. They feel greater difficulties to live in society. They work hard for their prestige and respect. Fears exist here—fear of unemployment, fear of dismissal, fear of failure to save money, fear of an unsuccessful future, fear of domination by friends, and financial fear. These are also causes of depression. If a man knows that whatever situations he has are the result of fear, then his condition improves to some extent. This illness is as a result of his thinking, wariness, heat, and mental stress. He becomes healthy as soon as these are reduced.

According to doctors, if one is successful in his or her life, the problem of depression never arises. It is said that children, youth, and old people don't have any depression, because they don't have much worry, problems, suffering, stress, burden, responsibility, etc. Fear is produced from worry, problem, anxiety, hardship, burden, responsibility, etc. A good relationship between a lover and his beloved detaches them from unnecessary thinking, since they concentrate on each other. If he thinks that nothing has happened to him and he takes everything normally, his depression lessens automatically. To lower fear in this way is treatment of depression. I have also interpreted effects of fear elsewhere in this text. Effects differ according to the nature of fear. Depression is also one of them.

Absence of depression in children, youth, and old people is because of the absence of burden and responsibility. They don't have any tensions, anxieties, problems, burdens, and responsibilities due to the household or other things. They depend on others in the family. They are still immature for household work, commercial activities, and other things. So, fear is absent in them. Depression also is absent due to the absence of fear. These all make it clear that the root cause of depression is fear. The alleviation of depression lessens suicide, violence, murder, etc. in society. Similarly, it decreases the number of drug addicts.

This is a state of mental volatility, stress, and responsibility. Many fluctuations happen to take place in the mind. There is a conflict among the thoughts. That is a fear struggle. If volatile kinds of thought overwhelm the rest in this struggle, they turn into frustration, nihilism, monotony, and depression. These decisions are destructive. He who is making such a decision thinks that he is right to do so. Actually, his decision is against his successful life. Depression is, no doubt, a difficult condition that can't easily be cured. As the man floats in thinking, the depression starts. Many people have suffered from such a condition. The number of patients is growing along with the growth of urbanisation and industrialisation.

Depression is an epidemic that has spread everywhere in this modern and competitive age. Everyone undergoes direct or indirect mental stress from early morning to late evening. Since dozens of fears between economic crises, problems of unemployment, and necessity and achievement, including competition, pollution, and ambition, are not generalised, the level of depression has increased.

Discussing depression in *Nepal*, a fortnightly paper, Rabindra Pande writes: 'Three hundred forty millions of people have become the victim of depression in the world. The scale of depression is much higher in developed countries than in developing countries, in towns than villages and in educated people than in uneducated people. Every year more than twenty millions of people become the victim of depression in the developed country like in America. The effect of depression is growing very seriously even in Europe, Australia, Africa and Asia. According to the data of National Institute of Mental Health, America, each one of the four adults suffers from depression in America. Similarly 15 per cent of the long-term depression sufferers commit suicide and suicidal rate is double in women. According to a study, 45.1 per cent of people in urban areas in Pakistan, 21 per cent in rural areas of Bangladesh, 15.5-25 per cent in India and 30 per cent in Nepal suffer from depression.'[10]

Similarly, Dr Aruna Uppreti writes, 'Depression is one among many reasons for suicides. Churchill, the prime minister of UK, famous writer Earnest Hemingway and famous writer Virginia Woolf were the victims of depression. Hemingway and Virginia Woolf committed suicide because of their depression.'[11]

It shows that people are more conscious and fearful in developed countries than in the undeveloped countries. Similarly, they have much higher competition. Therefore, lots of fears exist among them. Mostly, people in the village are less educated; they have less knowledge. As a result, they have a lower scale of fear. These data, symptoms, effects, and situations reveal problems and disease produced from depression.

4. Mental Stress

Mental stress is also one of the various effects of fear. People are under mental stress when they fear the burden of work, dismissal from work, financial crisis, family problems, social problems, etc. Similarly, they also suffer from mental stress if there is burden of work to build up their personality. We have to get success for prestigious lives in society. We can't get higher prestige in society if we can't have any progress and success. That is why we do different tasks as much as we can to get success. As a result, we are under mental stress. No doubt we fear to lose prestige in case of failure to get success. Fear exists again owing to the effects of mental stress. A man always wants to live happily and peacefully. If he can't meet his plan and get success, he suffers from mental stress. This mental stress is caused by fear. Such a stress sufferer may also become the victim of depression. It means that effects and stresses go on continually. All these problems and effects are due to fear. His stress lessens as soon as fear is reduced and depression as well.

People are very busy in the world. There are big competitions. They have problems brought about by their struggle of existence. Over-competition causes mental stress—mental stress of the burden of work, family burdens, burdens of various works, and financial burdens. These burdens are linked with economic prosperity. All people are not economically prosperous, because desires, ambitions, and needs of human beings are always incomplete. So they are always busy trying to fulfil them. In this business, fear plays a significant role. They look as if they are running to touch the horizon and to satisfy the extreme thrust. Such stress in work brings mental stress. It generates a number of diseases and problems. Some people commit suicide and some others become the victims of paralysis. Some people again escape due to these reasons. These are serious problems caused by fear. Fear, thus, should be clearly identified. In the same way, fear produced from mental stress and disease produced from fear also should clearly be identified. Only then will treatment be beneficial.

Fear is a superpower that always urges people to run. A man fears if he is incapable in such a competitive world; he is sure to fail. If he can't have any respect and maintain social prestige like others, he has the fear of being weak in others' perspectives. Even family members get a chance to express their dissatisfactions, and it brings another problem of mental stress. Like the infinite sky, these ambitions and necessities are impossible to be fulfilled. Mental stress exists when they can't be fulfilled and then several fears appear along with it. Abraham Maslow has interpreted these necessities in his theory of necessity order. Similarly, Malthus has also interpreted it in his theory of population. But people have never made any attempt to interpret it from the fear perspective. If we can reduce fear or we know that mental stress is due to fear, we can be free from mental stress. The remedy for it is its identification and reduction. A man can reduce his mental stress through reduction of his fear. The fear caused by anxiety, pain, ego, temptation, conspiracy, and doubt can be reduced as soon as they are reduced.

I have particularly focused here on escape, depression, and mental stress because of them; men feel more fear. The number of mentally ill people is gradually growing. These people don't know they are committing suicide, escaping, and suffering from mental stress because of fear. This theory, therefore, focuses on the improvement of this condition for comfortable lives. Thus, I have interpreted—the reason is, knowledge about them brings us improvement.

End Notes:

1. Karna Shakya, *Khoj (Search)*, author and publisher, Kathmandu, 2065 v.s. p. 363.
2. Karna Shakya, *Khoj (Search)*, author and publisher, Kathmandu, 2065 v.s. p. 364.

3. Gyanamitra Achyutananda, *Nagrik Daily*, Kathmandu, June 1, 2010.
4. Punya Prasad Prasai, *Sukrat Jiwani (Socrates Biography)*, Dikura Publication, Kathmandu, 2065 v.s. p. 101.
5. Bertrand Russell, *In Praise of Idleness*, Routledge, Taylor & Francis Group, London and New York, 2004, p. 150.
6. Arjundev Panta, *Vedanta-Darshan Sar (Brief Vedaanta Philosophy)*, Ratna Book Store, Kathmandu, 2062 v.s. p. 203.
7. Sanjeev Uppreti, *Sidantaka Kura (Aspect of Theory)*, Akshar Creation, Kathmandu, 2068 v.s. p 242-243
8. Gobinda Raj Bhattarai, *Uttar Aadhunik Bimarsha (Postmodern Discourse)*, Modern Books, Kathmandu, 2064 v.s. p. 120.
9. Gobinda Raj Bhattarai, *Uttar Aadhunik Bimarshat (Postmodern Discourse)*, Modern Books, Kathmandu, 2064 v.s. p. 118.
10. Rabidra Pande, *Nepal Quarterly Magazine*, Kantipur Publication, August 29, 2010.
11. Aruna Uppretti, 'Mahilama Manasik Awasad (Mentally Depression in Women)', *Kantipur Daily*, February 23, 2011.

13

Fear Circle

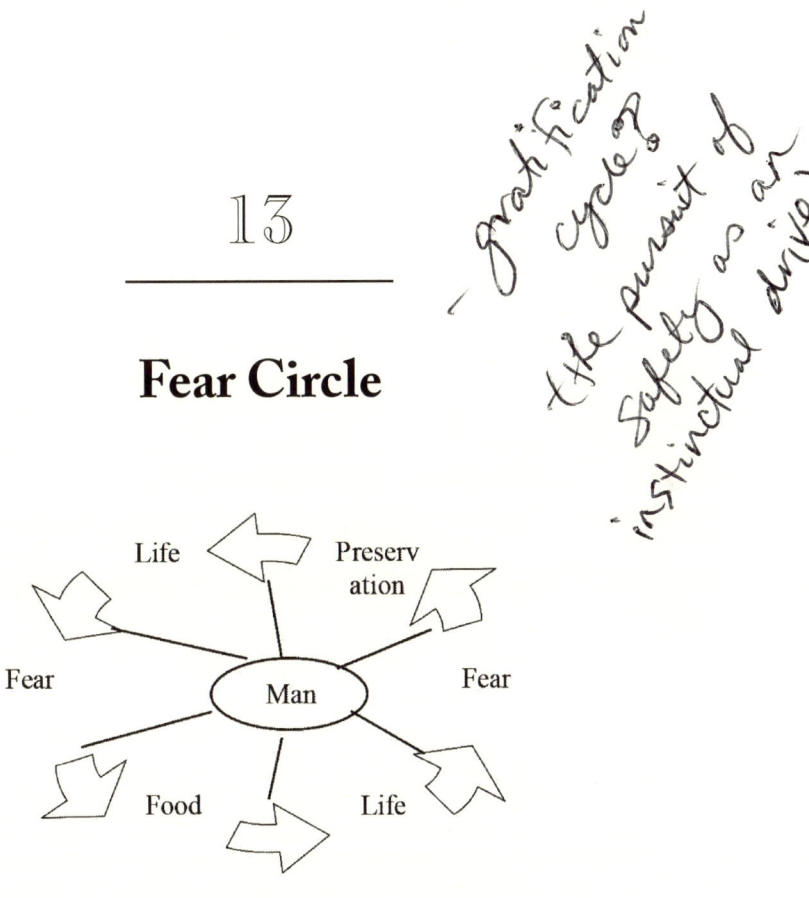

gratification cycle of (the pursuit of safety as an instinctual drive)

Figure No. 33

The Figure No. 33 shows life, fear, food, life, and preservation in the fear circle. Man fears that if he doesn't get food to eat, he will die. He then decides to take the life of an animal or plant for his livelihood. Life is possible only with food. He fears that the extinction of animals and plants surely brings extinction of human beings. We make our attempts for the preservation of these animals and plants for our food. It continuously revolves. It is a fear circle.

Man needs lots of things for a comfortable life. Firstly, he needs basic things such as food, shelter, and clothing. Secondly, he needs language, script, religion, culture, society, and country. People use forests, animals, and other natural resources for their livelihood on the one hand, and they fear a possible future impact made upon them by the extinction of animals, birds, and overuse of forests and other natural resources on the other hand. At first, man wants to live at any cost. Only then does he happen to think about ecology and environmental depletion. He fears ecological depletion. The complete and partial depletion in ecology invites a number of problems. As a result, he commences to consider preservation and then he begins to work on it. He uses them after preservation for his livelihood. Thus, he preserves on the one hand and consumes on the other. This circle revolves continuously. This is, in fact, a fear circle.

Such a circle, temptation, generation, etc. exists everywhere. We don't have property—fears exist like how we can care for our family without property and how to nourish and bring them up. We, therefore, work to earn. Fear increases as we earn property: How does one preserve the property and how does one increase the property? Fear of robbery and loot exists with our property. And it will be used up one day. It will happen sometimes before death and sometimes it happens after death. Again, fear comes forth for property and we start to earn.

Similarly, unless we have offspring, we fear that we are unable to have offspring. We suffer from the fear of sickness and bad behaviour as we beget a child. As the child grows young, the fear of his future strikes our minds. The child with bad behaviour can cause fear of misbehaviour to the parents. So, there is a saying in Nepali—'We fear that he may die when he is small and he may kill us when he is grown up.' In this way, we keep moving around the fear circle.

Many natural and biological things in this universe have such circles. My logic is that there is a fear circle in that circle. Some of the biological fear circles have been interpreted.

a. *Individual Fear Circle*

Man thinks about himself first and foremost in the world. He was alone yesterday, so he constituted a caste/ethnic group and formed a country for himself. He has a community, group, society, and country now, but again he wants his own country, society, community, and his own identity. He considers the 'other' in this world. Above all, Jewish philosopher Immanuel Levinas and his disciple Jacques Derrida have interpreted the theory of 'other' in detail.[1] Man wants to familiarise himself with everything; he tries to preserve and be secure. He can't live in the absence of his language, script, religion, culture, and country. He doesn't like others to be more knowledgeable, intelligent, and powerful than himself. He undergoes these fears. When he lives and becomes prosperous, then he thinks about his family, society, community, and country. For example, if the house catches on fire, first of all, he becomes perplexed and tries to save his life. He is not aware of his family, property, community, society, and country in such a horrific situation. When he is secure or safe from the fire, he looks for his family and property. Then he starts looking for all the things. We have heard that there are some examples where a man ate the flesh of his dead friends to stay alive, particularly in a dense forest, desert, etc. Having left all others, he alone wants to live. As he is able to live, he wants his family, relatives, kith and kin, society, country, and property, because everyone fears the death.

Man used to think of himself even in the prehistoric period. Caste/ ethnicity came into being and society was developed. These days, we can witness individuals forming groups and communities and also constituting various institutions. Despite the facts, man wants to exist himself in his group, in his society, and in his institution. Above all, people, some historical examples illustrate, have united small states in order to constitute a huge state. They even restructure the state into smaller units and sub-units. They are further divided into smaller states, sectors, cities, villages, and this work ends at the individual. Some huge countries are being divided into smaller states in the world these days. The demand on division exists in many countries. It has planted the seed of civil war in many countries. Most of the people, particularly those who suffer from the civil war, go elsewhere in search of shelter. In this way, it spreads all over the world. When the division ends at the individual, the process completes a circle. This is an individual fear circle.

b. Social Fear Circle

There is also a kind of fear circle in society. It didn't exist in the prehistoric period. The people didn't have an idea about society, organisations, community, country, and others. They used to walk alone and used to hunt for their livelihood. They used to fight for prey and food. They used to lack the idea of family and relatives. They were brutal and uncivilised and the world was the world of barbarism. They thought about how they could live. Slowly and gradually, they began to understand: What is life? What is death? What is society? They knew what the family was. They also knew what their necessities were. Consequently, they began to live in a family, and they constituted society. Then they necessitated religion, culture, customs, language, and script and they didn't delay developing them. Thus, civilisation began to develop. When it reached the climax, man didn't like it—it's an application of marginal utility. He regarded it as bondage. People

113

attempted freedom from bondage as people did in prehistoric periods. The concept of the global village, borderlessness, classlessness, and human civilisation as interpreted by different religions and philosophies signifies these things. Man searches for his existence up to a point. Whatever searches he makes are based on community, language, script, religion, culture, etc. On what the people make searches are considered bondage for them later. The people in the underdeveloped countries are more extreme in regards to their language, script, religion, culture, customs, etc. Therefore, these countries are undergoing ethnic conflicts, civil, and religious wars. The reason behind it is that they want to preserve all that they have. They all want their own language, script, religion, culture, community, and country to be more developed, powerful, and prosperous. However, world organisations and institutions also exist. They want to preserve and develop their organisations and institutions. They are all related to their identity, existence, and glory. They fear their possible extinction. Their extinction, indeed, is the loss of their identity. So, they want to preserve it by hook or by crook.

There is extreme female exploitation, community exploitation, and cultural restriction in developing countries. The women in developed countries, like in America and Canada, are advocating for freedom of their open breasts like males in their societies. At the same time, it is believed that women should be busy at home, according to their religion, and they shouldn't be provided with freedom in developing countries, particularly underdeveloped countries. Fear created by religion, culture, conservatism, and superstition lies there. Males want to take advantage of them through restriction. In fact, it's a continuation of prehistoric dogmatism. It is reduced gradually. It means we are regressing to where human civilisation began. People invented language and script, developed religion and culture, and formed a country. They established international organisations as well. Despite these facts, we are walking to and fro in search of our own country, society, etc. This is a social fear circle. Social fear circle consists of language, script, religion, culture, etc.

Man becomes separated from his society and goes to many other places from his native country to foreign countries. He is alone when he is well off and has different problems. Then he faces all the problems and eventually comes back to join his own society again. Thus, the social fear circle continues.

c.   *Natural Fear Circle*

There is always a circle in nature—the water circle, circle of the sun, etc. Rahul Sankrityayan has interpreted cycle of the sun in his book entitled

Bishwako Ruprekha (Sketch of the World).[2] The seawater becomes vapour, condenses, and rain falls and mixes with water in the sea again. Similarly, all animals, other creatures, and plants have almost the same process of circles. All these things change from one stage to another and arrive at the same beginning stage. Likewise, the creatures about to disappear are replaced by new ones or forms. If a creature dies, its particles and qualities get separated. They later assemble together and intermingle with another life. It develops, dies again, and becomes separated. Man undergoes this process. His fear lies in this process.

Man doesn't desire the extinction of all living beings. The reason behind it is that it brings imbalance in the ecological system. And sooner or later, man becomes the victim of its adverse affects. Again, the reason is fear. People desire preservation of nature in order to be safe from such a fear. Even the extinction of a one-celled creature has deep impact on human lives. We, therefore, always discuss the preservation of ecology and preservation of forests and work for afforestation. This is a natural fear circle.

d.   Chain and Circle of Fear

All living creatures are trapped within the whirlwind and circle of fear. Man is also trapped within it—he is born here and dies as well. He often spends his life with fear. Something and someone fear with him and he fears with something and someone. This is a fear produced by food. The circle of fear is also moving in numerous orbits like the moon, the earth, and other planets. When a chicken sees a hawk, jackal, or cat, they fear with them because the hawk, jackal, and cat eat them. Grasshoppers and many other insects flee when they see chickens because chickens eat them unless they flee. Similarly, a scorpion flees as it sees a frog, a snake flees as it sees a scorpion, and a frog flees as it sees a snake. All living creatures are foods for another. Strong animals hunt weak animals for their food. As an example, a tiger hunts cattle, hare, deer, and many other animals for its food. A wolf hunts other smaller animals for food. All other animals flee for their lives as they see other stronger and bigger animals are about to hunt them. This theory is applied to all the animals and creatures in the world. This is the way the world continues—some flee, some chase, some hide, while others fight. Those that can flee are able to save their lives and those that can't flee lose their lives. The winners get their lives, whereas losers lose their lives. One has the fear of life, whereas the other has the fear of hunger. One flees for life and another chases for food. In the absence of fear, it is meaningless to run away for life. To jump, to yell, to hide, and to flee are due to the presence of fear. Otherwise, they may be hunted. Thus, they have no alternatives to fleeing, yelling, weeping, and shouting. Some of them lose their lives even while fleeing. This is how nature is structured—all living creatures depend on one another. And this is a fear struggle as well. In this fear struggle, those that are able to hide, run away, fight are able to save their lives, and the rest of them that are unable to hide, flee, and fight lose their lives.

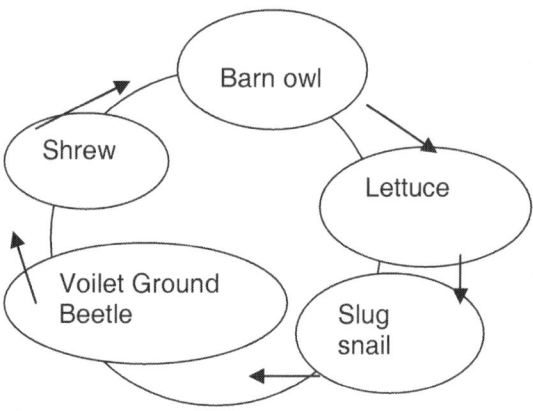

Figure No. 34

Figure No. 34 shows the circle of food. First, the figure shows lettuce and the green vegetables. It absorbs water and fertiliser from the soil. It takes the help of sunlight in order to prepare food. This is merely a plant. Consciousness and fear of this plant are not clear. More or less, every living being has consciousness. Therefore, the plant is the main source of all living beings. These plants prepare their food with the help of fertiliser, water, and sunlight as mentioned above. Other animals and birds divide food among them prepared by these plants. As Figure No. 34 shows, the snail eats vegetables. The beetle eats the snail. The shrew eats the beetle, and the owl eats the shrew. The snail flees from the beetle to save its life. The beetle tries hard to eat the snail. One fears for death, whereas the other fears for food. Similarly, shrews always look for beetles to hunt. At the same time, the beetles attempt to flee and hide from the shrews. Likewise, the shrews eat the beetles. So, the shrew fears being unable to kill the beetles for food. Owls eat the shrews. And the shrews always attempt to flee and hide from the owls. If the shrews are unable to flee and hide, the owl hunts them for food. The same owl is hunted by other strong animals, snakes, and birds. It flees and hides for life. Thus, they depend on each other for their lives. Some of them are herbivorous, whereas others are carnivorous.

A number of circles can be made on lettuce, snail, beetle, shrew, and owl. Many insects eat lettuce. Similarly, many circles of lives exist to depend on snails, beetles, shrews, and owls. Man is also included in the circle. Most of the circles of foods are according to a system. The circle revolves on another orbit as well in some cases. Man and tiger fear each other. Whichever gets opportunities to attack will kill the other. Fear strikes both of them. Man is generally an exceptional case. Animals and birds often get trapped in the whirlwind of such circles. A pyramid of power and fear appears here. This pyramid is constituted by power, and fear, no doubt, exists with other animals. It also exists within their groups as well. We see animals and birds are fighting in their own groups; the stronger ones are chasing, biting, killing, and eating the weaker ones. Some of them are found to be struggling for food, some for hunger, and some for sex. An attempt to seize food causes fights. Similarly, jackals, tigers, and so on drive vultures away if they come to seize their food. They try to take flesh from jackals, tigers, and others. Those vultures become happy when they grasp opportunities to eat food left by jackals, tigers, and others. It often happens among animals and birds. Darwin has interpreted it as a struggle for survival.

Intra-conflicts often occur in animals and birds. Stronger ones chase, bite, and kill weaker ones. Four temperaments are clearly visible in animals and birds—fear, sex, anger, and hunger. We witness males fighting for females as well as for food. Fear is clearly visible in cattle, hares, deer, chickens, etc. when they see hunters and other strong animals. Such a fear is due to another group of animals rather than the same group. When these four temperaments appear, they must have other temperaments as well. Zoologists can tell us about the other temperaments of birds and animals. It can happen to human beings too; particularly, it occurs because of professions, jobs, and the things they like very much. A businessman always suffers from the fear of the presence of another businessman as it can mean the loss of his business. It is the case everywhere. This is also true in the case of man, above all, professions, employment, and any other such things.

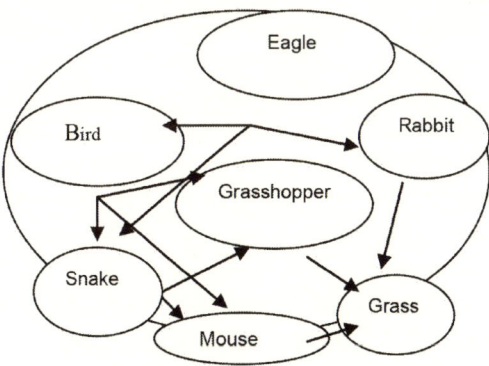

Figure No. 35

117

Figure No. 35 shows grass, a mouse, grasshopper, snake, rabbit, bird, and eagle. The mouse, the rabbit, and the grasshopper eat grass, and the snake eats mice and grasshoppers. Birds eat mice, snakes, and grasshoppers. Eagles eat birds and snakes. Mice and grasshoppers flee as soon as they see snakes. They flee and hide to safe their lives. They are safe if they can flee and hide. Otherwise, the snakes eat them. Similarly, birds and snakes flee as soon as they see eagles. If they are unable to flee, eagles eat them. Thus, creatures are food for one another. They flee like chickens flee if they see hawks. They are so terrified that they even lose their senses. They ignore their hunger and thirst as well. They are anxious only about their lives. No hunger and thirst are possible in the absence of lives. Malcolm Penny has interpreted it well in his book *The Food Chain*.[3]

Circles like this appear in all animals, birds, or creatures anywhere in water, land, hill, and mountain. Wherever it is, they have the same process of living. Man is incorporated into this circle. A difference is that the human being is guided by rationality. People use their rationality to invent powerful weapons. They are able to hunt animals for meat by the use of their rationality and weapons.

Thus, all living creatures are confined within the circle; they eat, live, rest, and die there. Although it starts from a creature, circles exist in huge numbers. All creatures are fleeing and hiding from each other. They are killing each other for their food. In such a way, creatures are trapped inside the whirlwind and circle of fear.

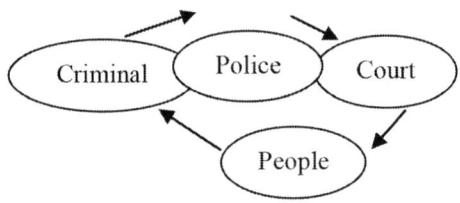

Figure No. 36

Figure No. 36 reveals different whirlwinds and circles of fears for human beings. Let us consider! It consists of criminals, police, courts, and people. The criminals fear the police. The police fear senior ranking officials. There is a unit to study the case and penalise the police if they are involved in criminal work and scandals. This is an internal unit managed for them. The police also get judicial punishment in such a case. The police, therefore, fear their internal unit and court—furthermore, they fear the people. Courts might as well make a mistake in its verdict. It can do injustice. Justices can be biased in their verdicts. So, the court manages a committee to study such a case and punish the justice if necessary. They are also bound by the law. If in case they are found biased in their verdicts, the court has a legal provision to punish such justices. They, in this way, fear the legal provision for punishment. The government conducts and regulates all administrative and judicial works in the country. They all fear the government and the government fears the people. If the government is unable to work according to the consent of the people, they can overthrow the government or can punish them in the next election. This is why the government fears the people.

In this way, the chain of command and law and order apply everywhere. They apply in the family, offices, industries, and various administrative sectors. So, criminal activities in the administration, society, and country have been reduced. Peace, security, law, and order are based on the power of fear. If this fear is powerful, people enjoy happiness, peace, and prosperity, and if in case it is weak, people suffer from chaos, violence, and crimes—a nominal circle can not minimise criminal activities.

Figure No. 37 is like Figure No. 36 that revolves around. The balance of fear can be applied to any side. It can revolve around either side. Many others are added to it. There is a single legal provision for punishment, but besides it, there are even other provisions for the same purpose for society and the individual. They are all linked to each other. So, they have a deep relationship. The police force is to persecute and arrest criminals. Yet the criminals fear each other as well, since they can be punished either legally or illegally.

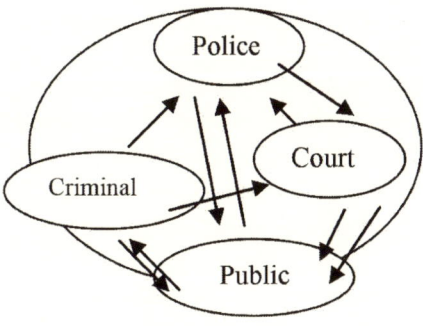

Figure No. 37

Figure No. 37 presents various circles. It presents criminals, police, court, and people. Many circles exist between them. All these are the circles of fear. Criminals often fear the police; besides them, they fear the law, society, relatives, and other criminals. Similarly, the police fear criminals, the public, law, relatives, etc. Judges fear the law, people, police and army, enemies, and criminals. Thus, man comes out of the fear circle of animals and birds but plunges into their own fear circles.

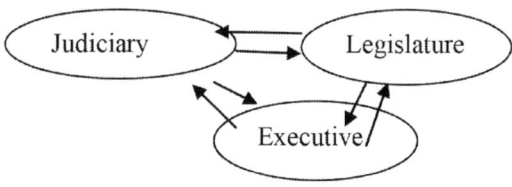

Figure No. 38

As shown in Figure No. 38, power and work have been divided among the legislature, the executive, and the judiciary. Power balance between these state organs can maintain law and order and happiness in the country. Here, power works for checks and balances. They are free to exercise power under their jurisdiction. Legislature controls executive in many cases; judiciary controls legislature, particularly in preparing laws; executive controls judiciary in many cases. In short, they all have power for checks and balances with each other. The circle of their checks and balances can revolve on either of the sides. In this circle, the constitution appears to be a greater fear than rules, laws, and acts. Any article/power doesn't work at all in the absence of fear. It means underneath power/work, there is presence of fear. Everything depends on rule and law, and the rule and law depend on fear. This is in society and the country as well.

Thus, all animals, birds, men, families, organisations, and so on are trapped inside the circle of fear. In a similar way, programmes are being conducted for controlling ecology. Such checks and balances are also applied to societies and countries too. Some of the checks and balances are natural, whereas others are human. They are all in the circle of fear. The fear circle coordinates them all.

End Notes:

1. Sanjeev Uppreti, *Sidhantaka Kura (Aspect of Theory)*, Akshar Creation, Kathmandu, 2068 v.s. p. 309, 311.
2. Rahul Sangkrityan, *Sketch of the World*, trans. Narayan Giri, Marxbad Study-Research Academy, Kathmandu, 2066 v.s. p. 18.
3. Malcolm Penny, *The Food Chain*, Wayland, Hove, 1987. p. 5.

14

Periphery and Relativity of Fear

There are many subjects in the circle of a man—his family, relatives, profession, age, and himself. More than these, other things have come to link with them. Some possible events are occasionally associated with him. Fear lies behind them. He remembers each of his family members, loves, and looks after them. He is always worried, careful about and fearful of possible problems, diseases, and events that his loving family members have to confront. He remembers everything, such as actions, life, deaths, profession, the present, future, etc. He remembers a number of such things. Some of the memories have fear, while others don't. It is impossible to interpret all of them, yet some of the periphery and relativity of fear are as shown in Figure No. 39.

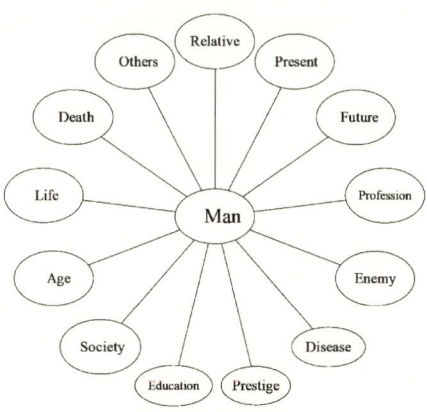

Figure No. 39

121

This is the figure of periphery and relativity. Man is in the middle of the figure. Relativity and periphery are around him.

1. Relatives

Relatives behave in a close, friendly, and loving manner. They always fear illness being endured by other relatives. They always suffer from the news of accidents, problems, and difficulties. They are always anxious about members of their families.

2. Present

Man is always fearful of crisis, problems, accidents, and other things that occur at present. We cannot definitely claim the shape, size, or the colour of present fear. It may be in any subject.

3. Future

Man always fears possible crisis, trouble, suffering, problems, incidents, etc. Security of property, insurance, care for health, the next generation, education, prestige are all for the future. Even a higher education is not for the present. Similarly, man exercises dieting in order to prevent disease, illness, and any other health problems.

4. Profession

Man doesn't live without any work. He can have a job or any profession. Many problems can occur in his job; he has to compete for jobs; and he has to work for promotions. He has to go out for national and international tours. If his family totally depends on his job, he suffers from the fear of termination of the job.

If he is a businessman, he suffers from the fear of loss in his business on the one hand and fear of possible robbery on the other. If it is an agricultural occupation, he fears drought, untimely/partial rainfall, storms, hail, and destruction of rice/products. If he has animal husbandry, he fears possible epidemics/diseases of animals and their extinction due to these diseases.

5. Enemy

Animals do have enemies, let alone the matter of human beings. We have many known and unknown enemies—they are due to jealousy, doubt, temptation, conspiracy, etc. Enemies arise due to any reason. We always fear that those enemies may attack, violate, harm, etc. On the other hand, if a person has cheated someone, committed a crime, stolen something, become bankrupt, killed a man, etc., he is always suspicious and fearful. Whoever he sees is suspected. He thinks the man has come to arrest him. So, he tries to flee and find a way out.

6. Disease

Man always fears disease. A healthy person fears that he may suffer from any disease. He takes care of his health. He wears a mask, washes his hands with soap, brushes his teeth, and keeps himself neat and clean. He controls his everyday activities like eating, walking, and sleeping. The main reason is that he wants to be healthy and have a long life.

Man does whatever he needs to be healthy, yet he suffers from any disease. If he doesn't have any symptoms, he works to prevent disease before he suffers from it because there is a saying: 'Prevention is better than cure.' Regarding the disease, man undergoes two conditions: (a) condition before the symptom of the disease appears and (b) condition after the symptom of the disease appears.

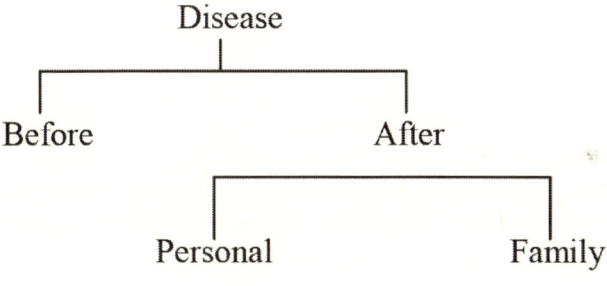

Figure No. 40

a. Condition Before the Symptom of Disease Appears

Man tries to escape even if the symptoms of disease have not appeared. The patient doesn't consult doctors until the symptoms of disease appears. He begins to consult the doctor as the symptoms of disease appear. Then, his fear depends on the level of consciousness, knowledge, and level of his tolerance. Sometimes, it also depends on the nature of the disease.

b. Condition After the Symptom of Disease Appears

As the symptoms of disease appear, his behaviour is based on type and nature of the disease. Various conditions appear in it too. Different measures are adopted in order to control, treat, and exercise it. Different interpretations, understandings, and behaviours for the same disease are because of physical strength, level of tolerance, and differences in rationality. A disease theoretically has the same definition and the same medicine has been determined. The medicine shows different impacts on patients. Knowledge of fear helps methods of treatments be more effective.

When the symptoms of a disease appear, fear increases in patients and their families. It can generate a social fear as well in some cases. Its scope can increase wider. It invites a further study. We never have consciousness and knowledge of unknown, unseen, and unheard objects, so fear about them is impossible. As I have mentioned elsewhere, fear exists only with consciousness. Hence, the sources of fear are life and death as well. Therefore, consciousness generates knowledge, and knowledge generates fear, but cognition provides us with an outlet from fear.

7. Prestige

According to Abraham Maslow, man needs social prestige after the management of food, shelter, and clothing. He always wants to be prestigious in society. He always wants to preserve his prestige. He fears losing his social prestige at all times.

8. Education

Education is essential for the intellectual development of a person. Now, the world is competitive. Therefore, people fear unemployment and loss in business. Prestige is directly linked with intellectual status, jobs, and business. Other people will dominate, cheat, and oppress in the absence of proper education on the one hand, and many people fear expenditure of education on the other. Some of them fear the possibility of failure. Again, being unsuccessful is related to their future.

9. Society

Man is a social being. He is directly related to every social activity. He is worried if society becomes the victim of ills and evils, socio-cultural damages, natural disasters, and many other problems. In this way, he suffers from the fear for society.

10. Age

Man fears growing old and the time that transfigures him. It's human nature. When he is strong and healthy, he is determined. He is ready to face any work and challenge. He loses the capacity of determination gradually as he grows old and weak. Then, he is trapped mostly with anxiety, frustration, and fear.

11. Life

Man loves his life so much. He always fears if his life is wounded; if he encounters accidents; and if he suffers from hardships. He seeks numerous ways to come out of such traps.

12. Death

Death is a great fear for human beings as well as other living creatures. Life and death are two sides of a coin. However, man contemplates an eternal life. He desires eternal life even for his relatives. Yet death is inevitable. No one can escape his/her death. So, it's a continuous natural process.

13. Other

Fears exist more than they are explained in the periphery of a man here. Economic inflation and deflation, drought, war, environmental pollution, political transition, and epidemics cause much more fears.

In addition to these, life undergoes many other incidents, accidents, hardships, pains, and anxieties. We are not sure what problems and accidents can happen to us. Thus, people always fear such unknown accidents.

Relativity of Fear

The reason behind the use of relativity of fear is—if fear is added to the human temperament, it appears even stronger. Fear is stronger than other temperaments. Various temperaments, characters, qualities, and a conditional reflex appear in human beings. If temperaments are melted with fear, only fear remains at last. Therefore, fear is invincible or relative. Fear has been taken relatively due to two reasons. First, human temperaments and characters rotate around fear. Second, a universal form of fear exists in human beings. We can study it through addition and substraction too.

First Part

Pain + fear = fear
Anxiety + fear = fear
Jealousy + fear = fear
Ego + fear = fear
Anger + fear = fear
Suspicion + fear = fear
Conspiracy + fear = fear
War + fear = fear
Extremism + fear = fear
Shame + fear = fear
Introverted character + fear = fear
Inferiority + fear = fear
Temptation + fear = fear

Pain + anxiety = fear
Jealousy + ego + suspicion + conspiracy = fear
Shame + introverted character + inferiority = fear
Anger + extremism + war = fear
Desire + ambition + fear = fear

Second Part

1. Doubt—fear: Fear exists after suspicion.
2. Fear—temptation—fear: Man earns money/property due to fear and fear exists again after he earns money/property.
3. Fear—anger—fear: Anger exists due to different reasons and fear exists due to anger.
4. Fear—conspiracy—fear: Man starts to make conspiracy due to fear, then fear exists again.
5. Anxiety—fear—fear: Fear exists due to anxiety.
6. Shame—fear—fear: Fear exists even due to shame.

Thus, whatever the human temperaments, they end at fear. Jealousy, anger, temptation, etc. are followed by fear. Jealousy, anger, temptation, and all others exist in different numbers. These are human temperaments. People generally don't like others to touch and use their things, and similarly, they also don't like others calling the people they love. They don't like their lovers and beloveds walking and talking with others. They feel jealous if they hear or see their lovers and beloveds walking and talking with others.

Suspicion happens to take place due to jealousy and the same jealousy generates fear. Man fears his beloved being lured away or leaving him. Jealousy + fear = Fear exists because jealousy is followed by fear, but fear is never followed by jealousy. This is an example. We can thus understand temperaments. All temperaments are thus followed by fear, but fear does not follow temperaments. For a further clarification, if other colours are mixed with black, they change into black. Other colours mix with black, but we cannot see. Similarly, whatever is mixed with fear changes into fear. Many temperaments are mixed with fear unknowingly. So, all merits and demerits are in fear.

Fears of different classes and ages have been explained here. This explanation doesn't incorporate all, yet it presents some glimpses. The reason for it is that fear exists anywhere and anytime.

Age	Embryo	Guardian
Embryo	Nominal	No birth/Death
5 Years	Fall down/Scold	Fall down/Lost/Sick
10 Years	Fall down/Wrong	Fall down/Break Down
16 Years	Future/Study	Drug Addiction/Sick
Adult	Future/Life Partner	Present

Figure No. 41

Figure No. 41 shows the growth of the embryo on the one side and guardians on the other side. The figure also reveals their growing fears. People, particularly those who are unwilling to have a child, fear pregnancy. Again, people, particularly those who are willing to have a child, fear with possibility of being childless. They are happy with a pregnancy. It means one fears pregnancy while the others fear the possible incapability of pregnancy. Peasants need rain during paddy planting. They fear rainfall when paddy plants blossom. Necessity on the same thing differs on the basis of time. To get it when needed is right, but the same thing terrorises when it is not needed. There are too many things like this. They are fearful according to time and its necessity.

The same Figure No. 41 shows the fear of guardians of the pregnancy of a woman. They fear stoppage in the growth of embryos, the possible attack of diseases, and the miscarriage of pregnancy. Since the level of consciousness is not grown sufficiently, the baby doesn't know about the fear. Slowly and gradually, this level of consciousness grows; as a result, the level of fear also increases. When the baby grows to be five years old, he fears falling over, getting abused, and insects biting him. As he grows to be ten years old, he likes to play and jump, but he fears falling over, getting abused, and somebody beating him. Even his guardians fear for him if he jumps a lot and goes out to play with his friends. His guardians also fear if he falls over, gets lost somewhere, and becomes ill.

Adults still suffer fears for their children until they are sixteen years old. Their guardians worry about them, since they may be addicted to drugs, ruin their lives, and moreover, their guardians worry about their future. Anxieties and fears exist largely for daughters. There are many parents who wait for their children when they arrive late at home. Fear lies behind it. Young sons and daughters also suffer from anxiety and fear, particularly for their future, their life partners, so on and so forth. Then, they gradually begin to spend their lives with fears as other ordinary people do. Fear exists throughout their whole lives. Their lives get spent fighting and playing with fears. This is a general example for ordinary people. Different people belonging to different levels and professions have their own types of fears. They are related to their levels and professions and even to their lives. It has been clearly depicted in the following figure.

Figure No. 42

1. Religious Man

A religious man fears if he doesn't follow religious rules and regulations or worship gods and goddesses; they suffer throughout their lives on the one hand and they are not allowed to go to heaven after their death. That is why man believes in God and follows a religion. Fear lies in religious practices. Man, therefore, believes religious discipline and rules and regulations and also believes in heavenly orders. He believes that God sees him whenever and wherever he is. So, he fears with God as well as harm.

2. Rich Man

A wealthy man fears robbery and the looting of his properties. He also fears being kidnapped, murdered, and attacked due to his property. Hence he adopts different methods for his security and the security of his properties. He deposits his money in a bank, and he does life insurance for his secured future. Moreover, he manages security guards and security alert bells. Above all, he manages CCTV at home, particularly in developed countries. For the security of his building from fire, he manages a fire ladder, automatic fire controlling water that works as soon as smoke comes out, and automatic bells to alert him as soon as the building catches fire. In this way, the wealthy man can save himself and his properties with the help of such technologies.

3. Poor

Many people have the problems of meeting their ends. They are always anxious for food, clothes, and good education for their children. If they are daily wage-based workers, they are worried about their work. What they think if they can't get work is that they fear how to make ends meet. They don't have as many fears as wealthy people do, but they suffer from the fear about their families.

4. Businessman

People who are involved in different businesses have the fear of their businesses—particularly their fears belonging to businesses and jobs. They fear the possible loss of their business. They similarly fear robbery, theft, and looting on the one hand, and they equally suffer from the fear of kidnapping and murder on the other. They also fear not being promoted in jobs, deprived of facilities, punished, and dismissed.

5. Criminal

The criminal flees from the police, society, and family. He can't live with peace. He is always suspicious of police and people while walking. If the police arrest him, he fears punishment and prison.

6. Superstitious

Bacon has divided superstition into four different categories.
  a. *Caste/Ethnic Superstition:* Man is superstitious by nature. He has superstitious beliefs on all natural events and incidents. He thinks there are some reasons behind these happenings. Due to such a belief, he imagines gods and goddesses.
  b. *Individual Superstition:* Man thinks and understands according to the environment, education, and culture in which he has grown up. Culture traps him inside and stops him having the ideal world outside. It's the state of being narrow-minded. Even great scholars and philosophers can sometimes be the victim of this culture.
  c. *Bajaru Superstition:* There may be two types of meanings of this word. It should be limited to particular meanings. Its general meanings merely create illusions and superstitions.
  d. *Superstition in Drama:* As Akabar and Rana Pratap appear for dialogue in drama, so the dialogue of Yagyawalkya, Vashishthya, Vishwamitra, or Aristotle, Socrates, and Plato come to the daily process of our thinking. These imitations are superstitions in a drama. All religious theories are imaginary. They are not based on facts.[1]

Thus man considers superstition as a culture. He fears what society and the god would say if he doesn't follow culture. So, he takes it as a bad omen if a black cat crosses his path; if he has a bad dream; if a jackal cries near his house; if a dog weeps; and if a crow crows. He doesn't go out during bad days and months, because he fears being wounded or harmed.

7. Citizen

Most citizens always think about the future of the country. They are anxious about how the government works and the price hike of essential commodities. In addition to these, they have internal and family fears. In this way, his anxiety incorporates economic, social, and political spheres.

8. Social

Citizens are involved in different professions. They are worried about the present and the future of society and country. They are fearful of chaos, murder, loot, kidnapping, movement, and civil war. The more a man thinks about society and country, the more he fears.

9. Community

Man loves his own community, religion, and culture. He is always anxious and fearful for the extinction of his caste/ethnicity, language, script, religion, and culture. His identity is related to language, script, religion, and culture. The community loses identity with extinction of language, script, religion, and culture. Then, nothing will be left to identify him. Therefore, he wants to preserve everything that is related to his identity. Many thinkers and philosophers like Michel Foucault and Julia Kristeva are writing and advocating such an identity.

10. Expatriate

To be expatriates is to suffer from the anxiety of the place and its future. They worry whether they get a job or not. People are fearful of shelter, food, jobs, and other things in foreign countries. That is a new place for them. They also fear what the local people say. Many things are left for them to know and understand. Since something is left to know, it automatically creates fear. While discussing it in the text of 'Postmodern Discourse', Dr Gobinda Raj Bhattarai writes: 'People are perhaps always hunted by search, thirst, desire and hope in their journey from familiar to unfamiliar places. They suffer from loneliness, fear, insecurity, indifference, and isolation there.'[2]

11. Others

Discussions of the fears presented above are some illustrations. Many other fears exist, like the fear of the hunter, the fear of the driver, the fear of the passenger, the fear of history, the fear of the present, the fear of the future, the fear of native country, the fear of a foreign country, the fear from inside the house, the fear from outside the house, and so on. These fears can exist anywhere and anytime. I have presented some major fears only. Numerous fears can exist accidentally. They have been interpreted somewhere in this text.

End Notes:

1. Sachchidananda Mishra, *Ishwar Marisaky (God is Dead),* trans. Balkrishna Shrestha 'Nebha', Utsarga Publication, Baranasi, 2009, Varanasi, p. 158.
2. Gobinda Raj Bhattarai, *Uttar Aadhunik Vimarsha (Postmodern Discourse),* Modern Books, Kathmandu, 2008, p. 120.

15

Fear Based on Human Temperament

'Human beings, indeed, are fundamental creatures. Their temperaments have made them distinct.' Human temperaments differ. These temperaments cause various problems. Man himself is a cause of fear. Due to his temperament, he plunges into problems and anxieties, and moreover, he becomes fearful. Ego, anger, suspicion, conspiracy, forgery, temptation, etc. are the temperaments of human beings. These temperaments are in the middle of fears; they grow up there, and they expand harmfully. We plunge into many problems and fears due to these reasons. For instance—we are angry very much. As a result of this temperament, the man quarrels and fights, then he is wounded; above all, he can lose his life. As a result, fear starts to appear. It is very difficult to control all these temperaments at once. Like a conditional reflex, if we keep reducing them gradually, our lives will be a bit more comfortable and fear will be reduced by a great deal. In this way, our own temperaments give us fear continuously. This can be further clarified through the following Figure No. 43.

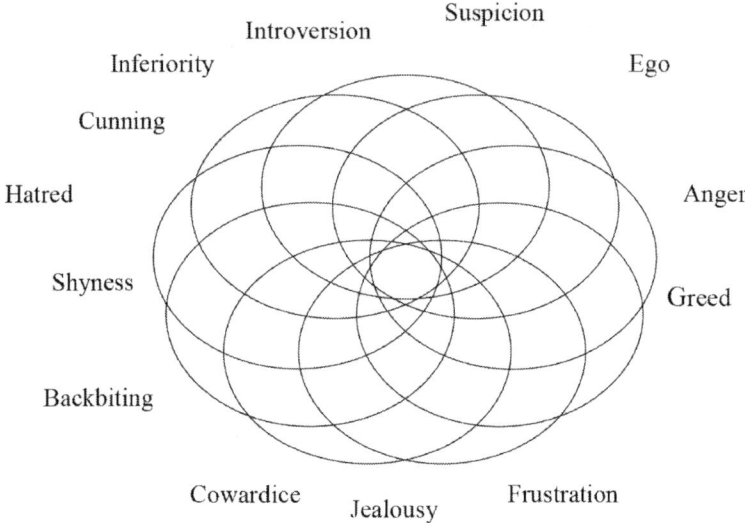

Figure No. 43

Figure No. 43 presents temperaments for a further clarification.

It shows that human temperaments overlap each other. They are created one after another. The same thing has been depicted in the figure. It is not sure which temperament exists in the same temperament. So, it has been presented as in the figure.

1. Suspicion

Some people are suspicious. They are suspicious of everyone—they are suspicious of themselves. They are suspicious of their friends, relatives, kith and kin, family members, and working friends and others. The people who are suspected are in whatever rank and businesses and have some advantages and disadvantages that influence the suspicions. Their interests, happiness, and pain are related to the suspicion. Fear begins with suspicion. Fear urges them to take initiatives to find a solution. A man, therefore, can save his life from dangerous accidents through the reduction of suspicion.

2. Ego

To show superiority among competitors is indeed a human nature. Some people are egoists, yet they don't know about their egoism. It also creates numerous problems. 'I' is so much loving for them and they don't count others. Due to this reason, man tries to show, 'I am intelligent, I understand, I'm rich, and I'm good.' He fears and hurries up so that he does not become inferior. He is, in fact, what he is, but he is jealous of his friends and relatives due to his ego. Another man also has the same mindset. He thinks, 'I'm something.' As a result, hostility, jealousy, suspicion, conspiracy, and unhealthy competition occur among the people. Here, the theory of the Jewish philosopher Immanual Levinas and theory of Jacques Derrida related to 'other' is relevant in this context. It produces fear. As a result, many problems happen to take place in countries as well as human beings. Severe conflicts take place among countries and they sometimes result in wars. Many wars occurred in the world due to ego that existed with fear.

3. Anger

Some of the people are angry. To get angry is a counter-attack to the fear. He counter-attacks his fear with anger. Some people lose their temper quickly, while others do so thoughtfully. A quick-tempered person doesn't have any fear when he is angry. Fear begins to exist as he calms down. A slow-tempered man fears all the time.

4. Greed

Greed is a main source of fear. There are many fears like the fear of the future, the fear of the present, social fear, political fear, and economic fear, including many other fears that are connected with property. He is fearful of losing his future security, social prestige, as well as honour and respect at present if he doesn't have property. He becomes greedy for the sake of his security and his family as well. So, he wants to earn and become rich.

5. Frustration

The natures of some people are always based on frustration. They always suffer from suppressed feelings. They remain unstable most of the time. They are ready to be a friar, saint, and to accept suicide as well to free them from their bondage and suppressed feelings. They always suffer from social and family responsibilities and problems internally. They leave home, family, and sacrifice themselves to get rid of all of them. This is a result of a mental depression.

6. Jealousy

People of this category are always jealous of others. They are jealous and angry with others because they fear defeat with others and loss of social prestige. The man thinks, 'I'm not weaker than him.' He doesn't want to accept defeat in any competition. He considers others merely as rivals. It brings fear. He boasts, 'I'll defeat them by hook or by crook.' This is an unfair competition due to the work and progress of others. In most of the cases, the word jealousy indicates various things, mostly negative. It indicates a few positive meanings too.

7. Cowardice

Some of the people are cowardly by nature. They don't dare to face and talk to others. They fear other people. So they can't present their talent and power at the right time. Consequently, they fall behind. They fear insects, grasshoppers, animals, etc. They also fear to walk in a lonely place and forest. All this is due to fear.

8. Backbiting

Some people always love backbiting. They play the role of an apple of discord between two persons by conveying their matters to each other. It is the nature of the people of this category. They can't enjoy their lives without backbiting others. They always fear that they may get scolded by any group and others when they are busy with backbiting. Fear is also one of the reasons for backbiting. Fear maximises if people fight and quarrel due to such backbiting.

9. Shyness

Fear is a reason for feeling shy. Man fears other people who tease and laugh at him. He makes a mistake while speaking. As a result of this fear, he feels shy as well as he hesitates to say what he has in his mind. His inability to express his knowledge and ability is harmful to him. There are many people with such temperaments in society. It is harmful to society too. Therefore, shyness is one of the various forms of fear. This temperament is an obstacle to making progress in lives.

10. Hatred

Hatred is a human nature close to ego. Some of the people hate others. He thinks, 'I'm better and tidier than others.' He hates others owing to anger, jealousy, temptation, doubt, etc. Some people are hated due to their nature, activities, etc. The reason of hating them is that they create a problem and fear.

We feel disgust when we see a dirty and undesirable thing on the way. We feel so, for the thing may touch us. If the thing touches us, we may have a problem—some wounds and sufferings from any disease. We may also feel nausea, so we hate them.

11. Cunning

Some people have a cunning nature. He thinks that if he is not clever, others may dominate and hate him. He has also the fear of being cheated and ruined. All people think they are directly or indirectly clever in society. Man is disliked if he is not clever. So, not to be clever is to be backward.

12. Inferiority

Inferiority is a great problem. Those feeling inferior fall behind in improvement, progress, and success, although they have the capacity, expertise, and talent. Most of the people have inferiority complexes. Some of them feel less inferior and the rest of them feel more inferior. Those feeling greater inferiority have a fear struggle with 'I'. If fear defeats 'I', they feel inferior. So 'I' should be very much encouraged to defeat fear and to get rid of inferiority. Enthusiasm, encouragement, and practice are required to do so. If we practice a lot, it is not difficult to overcome inferiority. Most of the people have been found to have defeated inferiority in this way.

Inferiority is a kind of problem. There is a great role of fear in it. Those having this problem live their lives with the feeling of inferiority. Psychologist Alfred Edler has also interpreted the feeling of inferiority. Financial pressure, weakness, family background, lack of knowledge, weak physical condition, and ugliness cause inferiority for man. They think that they are weak, feeble, and helpless. They hesitate to speak and express their opinion in front of people. That is to say, they fear that they may not speak, write, and sing well; others may make some comment on their performance and they may get scolded by someone else. They fall behind in expressing themselves, hide, and remain silent if they have to face other people. Those people may have a lot of knowledge, capacity, and talent, but they are not able to expose them. They are under the control of fear. Those feelings, talents, and quality should be exposed by means of their own effort. He becomes the victim of inferiority until he has the feeling that 'everyone has this problem and difficulty and I should be able to overcome all these challenging situations'. The people with feelings of inferiority are not only the characters of failure, weakness, and disgust, but also the depression and stress sufferer. As a result of this, he may commit suicide and leave his home. That is why 'I' should be made active, courageous, and strong. It is necessary to study human nature and quality as fragments to comprehend 'I' and fear separately.

13. Introversion

Introverted feeling or self-centredness is also a human nature like pride, anger, and greed. Psychologists have interpreted this nature from different perspectives. They haven't interpreted fear as a factor in the introverted attitude or self-centredness. In fact, fear makes a man an introvert. Those having this kind of nature can't express their feelings, write, and perform them. They suppress their feelings. They don't show their feelings, because they may be chaotic and unacceptable, but expose them in case of being alone. It would benefit him and others if an introvert exposes his feelings in front of others. And they would have progress, because he may have all those things such as creation, invention, construction, art, literature, and philosophy. This is the result of the struggle between 'I' and fear. He is an introvert because fear has defeated 'I'. He becomes an extrovert if 'I' defeats fear. Nature should be comprehended separately for the comprehension of 'I' and fear. There are some fundamental differences between an introvert and those feeling inferior.

An introvert can't express his feelings and show his talent. The people with feelings of inferiority think, they are weak, poor, mean, etc. All these natures are obstructions of progress, improvement, and success. Success can be achieved by both natures as soon as fear is reduced. Both of these are the sources of problems and they ruin themselves.

Man has all kinds of temperaments. The difference is that some people have more effective natures, whereas others have less effective natures. If temperaments are under our control and balance, they are like the pearls of the sea. Otherwise, they are like a snake which bites us or gives us many other troubles. There are also harmless temperaments, such as nobility, modesty, amiability, helpfulness, etc. They don't harm anyone if such a good nature grows, but if a bad nature grows slightly, fear increases and harms them and others as well. Fear is produced along with the harmful and unnecessary questions. That is why bad temperaments should be alleviated.

Similarly, human character, nature, and a conditional reflex are different from each other. It is also difficult to separate action, anger, ego, temptation, love, charm, jealousy, hatred, etc. We haven't studied different forms of these human temperaments. We should study them deeply, because different kinds of problems, especially mental disease, anxiety, and fear are produced.

Human nature is the reason for most of the fear diseases and mental diseases. What comes into the mind creates a problem. It means that it depends on our thinking process. That human temperament is a pre-signal of fear disease and mental disease. Science and technology are required to comprehend this signal. If science and technology are developed, many other diseases caused by a mental disease can be cured. It also causes fear at all times.

The symptom of fear appears in the face, nature, and activities, but the symptom of sudden fear can't be identified. Their effects are also different. Sudden serious kind of fear causes the problem of fear sickness, loss of mental condition, injury, and death. The fear caused by worry also brings about this effect. The fear and problems caused by sickness is the result of anxiety. Therefore, it is a serious kind of nature, and it has a fearful concept at the most. But the fear caused by a tiger is an unexpected one. There are also two ways: the condition in which he suddenly encounters a tiger without any information and knowledge and the condition in which he encounters a tiger about whose terrific attack he has been hearing for a long time. The patient has the symptom through thought and worry in the former condition, but the fears that exist in the later condition are like the sudden accidents. That is why fear exists: because of the previously acquired knowledge, concept, and anxiety. If quality, nature, and a conditional reflex are treated separately in such a condition, the treatment may be effective. Fear of the heart is also one of the characters.

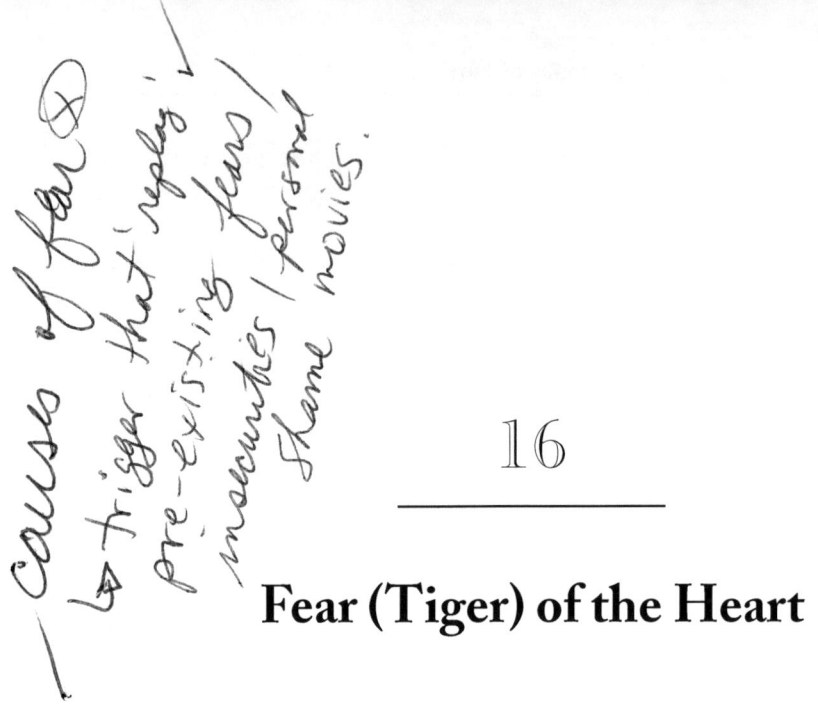
causes of fear ⊗
↳ trigger that replays
↳ pre-existing fears /
insecurities / personal
shame movies.

16

Fear (Tiger) of the Heart

I have interpreted most of the internal and external sources that cause fear, i.e. the fear caused by the thing that is far from us and the fear caused by the thing that is near us. I prefer to talk about the most powerful fear causing factor, 'fear of the heart', irrespective of all the distant and external things.

There is a powerful fear of the heart in a fearful consciousness of a man. The fear doesn't affect anyone else but himself. This fear starts growing serious when doubt, jealousy, ego, temptation go on rising. We have seen that this fear has finished off a number of people. Some people may not have an idea about this fear that always remains in the heart. This fear becomes violent in the course of existing constantly. Most of the people commit suicide because of this fear or they become the victim of depression. They are stress sufferers, remain unstable, and run and jump here and there being mentally ill. This also affects their relatives and kith and kin. Murder, violence, and crime are caused by this reason. Sometimes it turns into doubt, while during other times, it appears as jealousy. Neither our forefathers nor philosophers and preachers have said anything about the form, colour, and shape of this fear. It continued remaining like a small creature such as an ant. These fears of the heart have their respective forms, colours, and shapes in humans. They do not correspond with each other, but everyone has this fear. This fear had also finished off the lives of the great writers Virginia Woolf and Ernest Hemingway. It (tiger) also attacked the brave English prime minister, Churchill. Perhaps this fear (tiger) has attacked almost all the philosophers, writers, statesmen, social workers, journalists, and businessmen. Some of the people attacked by this fear (tiger) escaped from this problem, some committed suicide and crimes, and some waged war. There are many such events and sub-events. Many tyrants and emperors have become the victims of this. Dr Sachchidananda Mishra has written in his famous book *Ishwor Marisakyo* (God is dead), 'God Ram was also the victim of this fear. The king, Dashrath, also became faint occasionally being the victim of this problem and passed away at last. He has a logic. Ram planned an ordeal for Sita and troubled her due to his big fear.' According to Mishra, not only Ramchandra, but also his generation, were the victims of this fear. The fear of the heart is found to be everywhere in the course of studying and searching. We also have the same problem. People are found to be fleeing and hiding to be safe from this fear everywhere.

We have learnt the bad news of suicides by some unsuccessful students in examinations. Similarly, we have also heard news of suicides by some sportsmen who have not been successful. Who chased the future stars that committed suicide? This test is not a better way to finish off the whole life at once. The consciousness of a man becomes blind when the fear of the heart surrounds him. What is the treatment for this? Is there a remedy with any doctor? Why doesn't the store of philosophy say anything about this? No one can get rid of the fear of the heart as he bows his head down before God. There may be a lot of curiosity, logic, thought, discussion, but not a proper solution to the problem, because it has been a shadow and lived in the cave of the brain and the den of consciousness. It has remained in such a place that searches, investigates, invents, etc. How does one capture this fear of the heart? This is the issue for the quest. Let's study it deeply.

The origin of the fear of the heart depends on concepts, and its eradication also depends on the same concept. It appears and moves between the origin and eradication. It should be controlled through the mind slowly and gradually. It depends on the mind to follow a way. If it follows a positive way, the problem is solved. Otherwise, the problem becomes serious.

Let us consider! A person has realised that he has committed a crime. He has learnt his mistakes. In such a case, he thinks that he is a criminal, a culprit, etc. The realisation of the criminal, accused, etc. is the fear of the heart. He remains unstable due to this realisation. He feels regretful. He is in a dilemma to share it with others. 'Why did I commit the crime?' he asks himself. He says that he should not have done so. Such things come into his mind frequently. It starts troubling him. He remembers the punishment, becomes nervous, and fears internally. Doubt and anxiety also mingle with it and fear grows more serious. It finishes him off who does not have self-control. Those who can control themselves can be safe from this fear. Perhaps he may not have committed any crime in practice, but the fear of the heart can't separate truth and falsehood. There is no reason to be nervous and hopeless like this, although he has committed the crime. On the other hand, the problem can't be solved being nervous and hopeless, but man can't control his emotions when he is in difficulty. Hence, it brings big problems like a fearful event, an accident, etc. The more fear of the heart grows, the more fearful it becomes.

A famous Nepali proverb says, 'We don't know whether a tiger eats or not, but however, the tiger of the heart eats us.' Doubt, anxiety, jealousy, and temptation go on rising when he thinks about something continually in a normal, unfavourable, doubtful, and thoughtful condition. Their shapes go on spreading and get revealed in the form of fear in the mind and heart. Those having fear have another problem of inferiority, introversion, and shamefulness. Indeed, this very fear is the fear of the heart. The fear of the heart does not need any reason and event to make trouble for it. It does not come from any source. It is produced inside us and changes into a fearful situation like the change from the cub to a big tiger. The more it goes on rising, the more it carries on finishing off or troubling the person. The more it troubles, the more effect it causes. It continues troubling them. This fear (tiger) threatens a man and creates a lot of problems for him. Some people have depression and stress and some leave their home for good. Some people also commit suicide, some become mentally ill, and some suffer from fear. Doubt, anxiety, jealousy, and temptation exist individually in the beginning. Later on, they combine with each other to turn into a fearful situation. It goes on troubling them, no matter whoever has a more fearful situation than the others. The familiar thing troubles them, although no one says anything to them. If a person doubts that he has committed a mistake, done something wrong, he regrets it and starts troubling himself at first. His doubt, anger, worry, and suppression cause this kind of event. He should control himself in such a condition. Otherwise, his fear starts troubling him in different ways. A number of characters troubled by such a fear are found to be in legend, rumour, and books. So I have said above several times that man himself is the reason for fear. It does not come from any source. It exists in him. Criminal, dishonest, corrupt people, liars, doubtful people, jealous people, and bribe-givers and takers have a lot of such fears of the heart.

17

Utilisation, Effect, and Measurement of Fear

Utilisation

The poet Manumanjil says, 'Fear is a beautiful consciousness.'[1] Many problems exist, and most of the problems are also solved due to fear. Fear is the root cause of all problems such as violence, murder, war, temptation, terror, jealousy, depression, and stress. Fear is clearly visible in some of them, whereas it is invisible in others. Similarly, man acquires development, progress, success, friendship, coexistence, peace, and love due to fear. Its utilisation depends on us, because fear exists in us. Fear is revealed by the combination of perceptible capacity, tolerance, and nature based on acquired information of the brain. We are the greatest of all the sources of fear. The forms of fear, i.e. normal and serious, positive and negative, etc. depend on us. We are the guides to lead it to a positive and negative way. We beat, trap, and torture children. We trap, beat, and torture criminals. It means that we have tried to make them good. If children do not read and write well, become obedient, and gentle, etc., they will have a problem in the future. Some people might have seen their security in their future. Perhaps they have hoped that if they have built their future well, they will look after and support them when they are old. Any of us may be unstable due to fear. In such a situation, we may decide to do anything such as murder, suicide, violence, theft, and robbery. We may also have development, progress, and success in such a case. We have heard that some students have committed suicide due to this fear. We have also heard that some students have secured distinction due to the same fear. A number of people have such cases. Fear is connected and disconnected with any event, accident, success, and development.

Thus, there are a number of religions, philosophies, sciences, and inventions that have existed owing to fear. When we go back to the primary stage of different religions, we reach the same issue, i.e. fear. Fear was found to be the origin of Buddhism, Jainism, Judaism, Islam, Christianity, and all other religions in the world. Similarly, fear is the father of the class struggle of Marxism, theory of population of Malthus, necessity theory of Maslow, invention of weapons, invention of different medicines, literary and political movements, different non-governmental organisations, different institutes of insurance companies and economic development, United Nations (UN), as well as many other institutes, theories, and religions. They all utilise fear and try to reduce the fear of man. The utilisation of personal fear reaches national and international levels. The purpose of all these things is to reduce fear and make it fruitful. If fear is utilised properly, it means that fear also lessens itself, but it has been misused in many cases like in violence, murder, war, suicide, temptation, etc. There may be big changes, inventions, constructions if it is utilised properly. There were big wars, attacks, and destruction of terrorists due to the misuse of fear in the past. Even today, such activities are going on. If we were able to utilise these powers properly, we could be safe from the destruction and achieve great success.

The wonderful inventions and constructions made by slaves in the age of slavery have become part of the world's heritage now. Fear lies behind such constructions and inventions. So, fear has both positive and negative results in the world history. It is better to think about proper utilisation of fear in every moment than to present examples of huge constructions and inventions from history. Moreover, we have to think about our fears to make them useful, because they exist fragmented constantly. Every person should be able to utilise his fear at best. However, it benefits all. Low fear, mid fear, and high fear make lots of difference.

For instance, there is a student. If he is not afraid of the exam, he can't pass. His future is dark if he can't pass his exam. If he has a medium fear about his exam, he can pass. His future is bright if he obtains better marks in his exam. If he is very much scared about his exam, he can't read and write well. He is nervous, hopeless, and unable to write and speak what he knows and understands. Thus, we hear many students fail in their exams. If he fails in the exam due to his minor mistake, it affects him throughout his life. If it happens, his future becomes dark. His dreams turn into ashes. Above all, people with such a condition suffer from different kinds of fear, diseases, and mental problems. They not only suffer from depression; sometimes, they may commit suicide as well. It can badly influence their family and relatives.

This is just a case of a normal exam. Such a problem and its effect arise everywhere. Everyone has such low, mid, and high fear. Sometimes, a low fear is useful, but in some other cases, mid or high fear is useful. Above all, a medium fear is useful in our lives. It depends on the situations of fear and consciousness of the man. Thus, violence, wars, and murder occur due to their inability to keep the fear at balance.

That is why fear is of great importance in life. Every person has his life like that of the student. That is to say on the one hand, every person is a student during his whole life. We always fight for the examinations of lives, future, and societies. Those who utilise fear properly are successful in every sector. Those who ignore fear are unsuccessful. Again, those who have lots of fear suffer from fear and mental problems as well as being trapped in different problems. The people who have normal fear become murderers, robbers, dishonest, violent, terrorists, and extremists as they misuse their fear. In this way, lots of chaos and problems happen to take place due to this reason in the world. It causes fear for other people. Employees often suffer from this problem. The more a man becomes fearful, terrified, worried, and unhappy, the less he feels enjoyable. Obviously, they are not free from their fear, yet they enjoy being so. The positive fear opens the door to development, progress, invention, and construction. Consequently, it leads to happy, peaceful, and prosperous societies and lives.

We should always utilise fear according to our needs, and it should be positive. If we are able to utilise it properly, it may be property. Otherwise, it may be a poison.

Effect

Here the effect of fear means the effect produced from fear after its existence. In fact, if fear occurs once, it creates a lot of effects in human beings. They are short-term, long-term, personal, collective, mental, physical, social, economic, etc. The effect of the fear occurs throughout their whole life. New fears appear on the one hand and their effects appear at the same time on the other. Most of the effects are minor, i.e. ineffective. Only major events and accidents can create major effects. If a family member has a serious kind of effect, his relatives and kith and kin also have its sub-effects. We don't take its utility and effect importantly, as we don't value fear. Fear, its effect and utility, have their great value in our lives. The effect can be learnt through the nature of the fear. Some of the effects are sudden and unknown. Some of them are produced by our concepts and anxiety, while others are brought out by external factors. Fear is consciousness and excitement that we produce. However, the sources of some of the fears are internal and the sources of others are external. If we travel in a vehicle and an accident is about to happen, here the source of fear is accidental, which is external. The following figure further clarifies it.

Fear	Person	Effect
a	Student	
Low Fear		Fail
Mid Fear		Pass
High Fear		Fail/Mental Effect
b	Driver	
Low Fear		Accident
Mid Fear		Safe
High Fear		Extremely Unsafe
c	Ruler	
Low Fear		Careless
Mid Fear		Peace/Safety
High Fear		Suppression/Oppression
d.	Patient	
Low Fear		Careless
Mid Fear		Balanced
High Fear		Problem/Anxiety/Worry
e.	Business man	
Low Fear		Loss
Mid Fear		Progress
High Fear		Escape/Stress/Depression

Figure No. 44

a.   *Student*

Let us consider a student. He is afraid of failing in his exam and he has a lot of the effects of the fear: They are both short-term and long-term. The short-term effect includes a mental effect. As mental effects, he may escape from his study, he may give up his exam, he may become addicted to drugs, he may adopt bad behaviour, he may suffer from others, and he may suffer from depression. It has other sub-effects too.

Similarly, its long-term effect can cause his future to be dark. His future dreams may be ruined. He may be a bad citizen. His family and relatives are also badly affected if he is addicted to alcohol, drugs, and smoking, hangs out with bad company, commits suicide, escapes from his problems, and suffers from mental problems and fear. It also has its sub-effects. There are a number of parents who are worried about and fearful of their offspring's failure in the exam, involvement in alcohol, drugs, and smoking, addiction, escape from study, and depression. Some of the parents are also found addicted when their children are addicted to alcohol, drugs, and smoking. They say, 'Our children are out of control and what is left for us to do?' They do so because their hopes and assurances depend on their children and their future. They have dreams for their children. All their dreams turn to ashes. Thus, the effect of a minor fear spreads and turns into a very fearful situation.

b.   Driver

Similarly, let us consider a driver. He becomes less careful if he has low fear. He may have an accident if in case he reduces his carefulness. If he has high fear, he becomes uncontrolled and may cause an accident again. If the accident happens, it causes a lot of effects and its sub-effects for him, his family, passengers, and others.

First, it affects him physically. He may lose his life, get injured, and have mental effects.

Second, if in case he gets injured or loses his life or has any other effect, it has a severe impact on his family.

Third, it can affect passengers both physically and mentally.

Fourth, if the passengers have physical and mental effects, their relatives and kith and kin have different sub-effects.

c.   Ruler

If the administrator and the head of the government have low fear, there is carelessness and irresponsibility in administrative works, developmental works, constructions, implementations of law and order. Chaos, corruption, and bribe system can grow in such a condition in the country. As a result, people would face lots of trouble. The head of the government in many poor countries have low fear. So, the people undergo lots of problems. People, no doubt, have individual fear; the fear from the government is added to their individual fear. Such rulers are less fearful of country, society, and its people.

If a ruler has high fear, he can be a tyrant. He fears the people may revolt against the ruler, fight for their rights, and overthrow the government. Because of these fears, he tries his best to suppress and oppress the people. He tries to make his position even stronger. Consequently, there is a loss of a number of people when there is a revolution. Then the country and public always have to bear the bad effects. Due to the high fear of rulers in the past, the country is not developed.

d. Patient

If a patient has low fear, he becomes careless. He doesn't follow the food restriction; he doesn't take medicine on time; and he doesn't exercise. So, he may be more ill than before. If he becomes very careless, he may die before his time. He starts being worried, may have more anxiety, and consequently no appetite if he has a lot of fear. He may be an insomniac. Anxiety and worry are reasons for various diseases. If the patient has lots of anxieties and worry, his sickness can grow much more serious. He takes care of himself, if he has middle level fear; he takes medicine on time and exercises regularly. Gradually, he recovers.

e. Businessman

If there is low fear in business, a businessman can't run his business properly. He asks others to run his business and becomes too busy to go for a walk and a visit. Others don't run the business like him. Consequently, his business may collapse. We have seen that his business has been in loss because of being careless and being too busy in other activities to be involved. He becomes nervous and remains unstable even in the presence of minor problems if he has high fear. He may suffer loss in his business in such a case. Then, he may escape from his problems, commit suicide, and be depressed. But he may run his business well if he has middle level fear. Then it results in less probability of loss in his business. If in case he suffers loss, he chooses various alternatives.

Fear of Normal and Slow-minded People

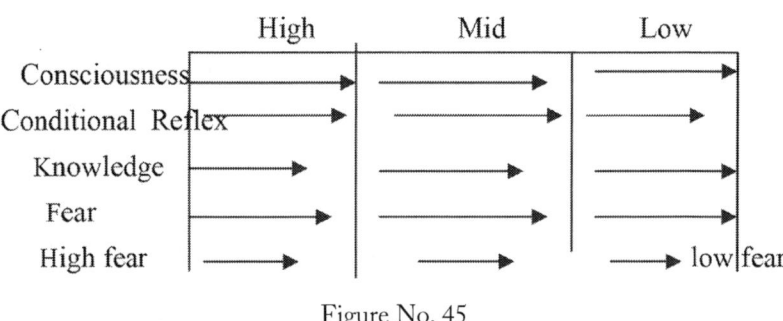

Figure No. 45

Figure No. 45 shows people with high, mid, and low consciousness. People with high consciousness are ordinary people. People with low consciousness are slow-minded people. People with high consciousness have more conditional reflexes, knowledge, and fear than other people. The less consciousness a person has, the less the conditional reflexes, knowledge, and fear. A slow-minded man has low consciousness, conditional reflexes, and fear. Even ordinary people have less consciousness when they are unconscious and intoxicated. There are variations in this fear. Fear also depends on the way a man perceives and experiences events and problems. When the mind of a normal man is distracted, he may not pay attention to an event and subject. His consciousness doesn't perceive the subject perfectly in such a case. The fear created by the situation is lower than it is. The man of high consciousness, conditional reflexes, and fear has high effects and sub-effects, and those of low ones have their low effects and sub-effects. Thus the men with 'high' minds, 'mid' minds, and 'slow' minds have different kinds of fears and their effects.

People of all classes and levels feel the impact of fear. Their effects also harm others in society at all times. Man should analyse and utilise fear properly to be safe from all these effects. The measurement of a proper fear depends on a situation, subject, and area. Various problems, such as injustice, oppression, suppression, violence, murder, war, terror, etc., arise in the country due to the misuse of fear. So, fear should be utilised carefully. It is so sensitive. Otherwise, a minor mistake may bring a major problem. In such a case, it is more harmful to us. It harms all, i.e. family, society, and country. It depends on the area, viz. country, society, etc. It means that if the head of the government and the head of society suffer from fear, it harms the country and society respectively. Yet fear is beautiful consciousness. Its misuse invites merely problems.

Measurement

The same thing creates different types of fear for the same person because of different times, places, conditions, consciousnesses, tolerance, and situations. On the other hand, the fear of a man does not correspond with that of another man at all due to various reasons. Fear that has appeared once grows very seriously in the beginning and then it begins to lessen. But some fear continues growing more serious. When we have some knowledge for the first time, fear reaches its highest point. For instance, if a doctor says, 'No treatment is possible. You are at the eleventh hour', he and his relatives fear so much that their fears reach the highest point immediately. And he starts exercising self-control and gradually he controls himself. They become tired as time passes. They know that there are no other alternatives except patience and self-control, yet they are very much fearful. No doubt, the man tries to find all the possible ways to get rid of the problem. If the man sees a violent animal, he fears a lot in the beginning. Then his fear begins to be lower or higher. Lower or higher level of fear depends on a situation. Fear begins to lessen if the animal hides somewhere, but it grows more serious if it approaches aggressively. Anxiety has its important role in such a situation. If there is the time for anxiety, the quantity of fear grows constantly. If he has no time to think about anxiety or he is busy at all times, fear gets reduced.

If the man has lots of time for anxiety, worry, and thinking, fear grows continually. It means that he keeps on being alone, hopeless, and depressed. If a man is growing old and he does not have any relatives and property, his fear grows because of the trouble that he will have to face in the days to come. On the other hand, approaching death also causes him a lot of fear. Similarly, if the problem of disease grows continually, he begins to think about his death and has death fear. When a man has fear of death, it is also related to his family. He fears, 'If I die soon, how will my family make ends meet? How will they manage clothes, and how will they spend their lives?' People give up when they undergo problems suffering, and fear. Perhaps their fear certainly reduces if they give themselves up. Everyone may not have the same situation. Some people may take it normally, whereas others may take it seriously. It depends on man and his situation. It doesn't have its clear shape, colour, and form. No machine is discovered to measure fear. Therefore, fear can't be measured in degrees, with thermometers, and millimetres. There is no development of a fear-measuring machine like the one that measures blood pressure. We don't know the quantity of consciousness and fear in a healthy man. It is easy to determine if a machine to measure fear is developed. The future problem of fear can be learnt and precautions against the diseases can be followed or had by means of this machine. Being careful is also a solution to the problems of many diseases. It eases control, preserves and balances the nature of fear, mental disease, hysteria, depression, and inferiority.

Fear has been pervasive at present. So it is the time to measure and study it profoundly. The volume and area of fear are growing seriously slow and gradual.

If doctors and medical science give up treatment of a patient who is supposed to die within three months, how does one behave with that patient? Both doctors and medical science are silent on the answer of this question. Most close to the patient is fear. The effect caused by such a sickness harms him, his family, and relatives. There is not any certain idea and medicine for its treatment. Even death can't be treated thus. The age of man is also just like the period of three months. It can't also be treated by a doctor. There are several events, such as the conditions in which houses collapse due to an earthquake, a plane crashing, and a ship being sunk, an epidemic being spread, an unpleasant event happening, war being declared, and murder, violence, suicide, and terror being committed. The concept of fear science may prove to be useful in such cases.

We have such a fear during every moment. It is so minor that it can't be expressed in terms of measurement—about life, death, and any other event. We should utilise fear properly. It can be useful for events and diseases if it is utilised properly.

Man has different types of fears. Symptoms of these fears are also different: terror, yelling, shouting, turning faces black or pale, drying lips, fast breathing, erect hair, weeping, crying, jumping, running, stammering, walking and shouting, loss of hunger and thirst, and being unable to sleep. We can also recognise the sources of some fears through a close observation of them. We can identify the attack of animals and diseases and the environment of war in general. Friends and relatives may give consolation, relief, and advice if fear is caused by an external factor. Some of the fears are minor, whereas others are major. Still, some of them are short-term and long-term. Some fears have developed themselves, and some of them have been brought about by an external thing, event, accident, murder, terror, war, etc. Automatic fear is produced by the spread of human nature and conditional reflexes. Fear begins to exist as doubt, illusion, conspiracy, and nature. Fear is also produced by the illusion of the violent animals, i.e. a tiger, bear, snake, the criminals, i.e. murderer, robber, and ghost. Similarly, fear is also produced by religion, culture, custom, acts, law, etc. In addition to these, fear also exists on seeing different things and places. Mental condition, physical condition, cultural background, and religious concepts are reasons that cause fear. The fears caused by all these situations are not the same. They do not have the same shape and symptoms. Their effects are also different. A man gets startled and fainted, loses mental condition, becomes a criminal, a murderer, rich person, and scholar owing to fear. A man whose very close relative is sick and is at the eleventh hour is worried, restless, and fearful. He can't control himself well. He also does his work carelessly, because his rationality doesn't function properly. The symptoms of fear produced by two respective situations, i.e. sickness and a tiger, are quite different. If a man is seriously sick or he is seriously injured, he becomes nervous and fearful. We know that the same thing also causes different kinds of fear, symptoms, and effect for man as we stated above. If a tiger is near, some people become nervous, some run away, some become faint, and some fall on to the ground. Those who are nervous may have injuries and fall on to the ground. Those who run away may also have the same problems. The tiger may kill and eat them. There are different short-term and long-term effects due to these situations.

The man who can have self-control and become controlled and brave has a low effect in comparison to others. The problem, no doubt, has been present in front of us. We must be ready to face it. Again, we have no other option besides our readiness to face it. It is better to choose a less problematic way to reduce physical and mental problems during that period. A man knows that the dead person can't be alive again, yet he troubles himself through the memory of a lost one, agitating, crying, lamenting, shouting, yelling, and unable to eat and sleep. If the dead person can't be alive again, why do we trouble ourselves? We need to have self-control and take it normally. If we become nervous, restless, etc. in life, it harms us. To be restless with life, yelling, and suffocation merely torture us. We are in the surround of various problems due to these reasons. If we decide to face possible accidents, approaching violent animals and other enemies, we can reduce our fears. Its sub-effects can also be reduced.

Such fear produces most diseases and mental problems. Similarly, effects and its sub-effects bring about different problems as well. Therefore, we need to attempt to utilise them properly. That is the best solution.

If we try to make people fearless and fearful, it increases chaos and anarchism in society. No doubt there is a kind of chaos produced if the man violates law, rule, religion, and culture. This is a negative aspect. They are related to concepts, philosophy, and science. If we consider religion, culture, customs, society, country, different thoughts, inventions, and civilisations negatively, they are certain to have a negative effect.

As our humanity says, we should not run or flee from the people who suffer from epidemics like HIV Aids. We need to console and help them as far as possible. If we frighten the man, he becomes restless, yells, becomes violent, and dies. Fear is an effective medicine for such problems. It helps us to be fearless and calm from birth to the cradle. There are a lot of factors that affect our actions, reactions, and processes from our births to the cradle.

If we keep searching for fears, we find them scattered everywhere. Those fears are found as infinitesimal, fragmentary, broken, partial, perfect, uncontrolled, systemless, and chaotic. They all should be utilised by means of easier ways. Then, life becomes very easygoing. Certainly thought and use can't be under our control. They fly like a bird eternally.

Life and the world are surrounded by many external and internal rings, as in above figures. These rings have networks—own networks inside and outside our bodies. Above all, these networks always affect our lives from all sides as the theory of Brown. He says, 'The second theory or Brownian motion propounded by the scientist Albert Einstein is concerned with the velocity of molecules and atoms. Many years ago prior to Einstein, another scientist, Brown, discovered that there were small molecules hanging in the moving liquid on the quick winding or zigzag path. But Brown couldn't explain why that happened. Einstein completed his incomplete explanation simply and perfectly. According to his explanation, the molecules and atoms of liquid that remain as a means constantly strike the particles that hang in it. When the magnitude of the force that comes from the opposite direction and strikes the particles is different, the particles move by the force. But this happens only in the case of very small particles. There is the possibility of such a case in the liquid, because it is impossible for the particles to be struck equally from all the directions practically."[2]

If we see a fan that moves at high speed, it looks as if it is motionless. In fact, the fan moves so fast it just looks still because of its high speed. This is the way how all others move—sea or any other object. The above theory proves it.

Thus, external and internal factors always strike fear from all sides. Similarly, lots of temperaments, merits, and demerits keep moving inside the consciousness. There should be a balance in all. It is easier to balance them if they can be measured. We have not been able to treat fear easily due to lack of its measurement. It is easy to control and conduct fear if there is knowledge of measurement. We are obliged to deal with and treat fear by means of its experience and realisation, for there has not been any method of solid measurement so far.

18

Fear in Medical Sector

A dialogue on 'mental illness' with Dr Nirakar Man Shrestha presented by Pramila was published in the national daily paper *Naya Patrika* (new newspaper). The dialogue presented as:

1. There was a goldsmith. He had a big safe in his shop to keep all the ornaments of gold. He put away all the ornaments and locked the safe every day. He was worried even though he locked the safe. He kept on checking even after he locked it. One day, the handle of the safe was broken, as he did so continually. He went to consult a psychiatrist. He said, 'You have suffered from mental sickness. Take medicine to recover from this sickness.'

2. This is a story of a lady in Kathmandu. She works in a good company. There is no problem at work. She shows her self-confidence to struggle with other aspects in the course of doing her work. But she does not sleep at night. Different kinds of thoughts come into her mind. She fears dying at once. She also fears a small wound. She feels as if the wound affects her whole body very badly and thinks about the fear of the wound frequently. So she is not satisfied with her life due to this problem. She went to a doctor some days ago and told him about her problem. She felt better in her daily life after she has started taking medicines prescribed by the doctor.

3. There is a businessman. He has his own office. More than twenty people work there. He had pain in his chest one day. Then he was suspicious and he said, 'Whole parts of my body have been damaged.

I will die soon.' He went to a nearby hospital. Everything was checked, but nothing was diagnosed. Later on, he went to the doctor and consulted him. The doctor said, 'You suffer from mental sickness.'

4. There was a man who used to wash his hands ten times when he entered into the bathroom. He used to know his hands were clean, but he did not give up washing his hands. He used to suffer from agitation and heart beating if he did not wash his hands. Lastly, he went to a psychiatrist. He was suffering from 'obsessive compulsive disorder'. He recovered from the problem after the use of medicine.'[3]

Much news like this is daily published in newspapers. Many illnesses with such symptoms are often called a mental illness. It has not been studied in detail. The goldsmith checks his locker frequently, the lady fears dying at once, and the man washes his hands ten times. They are fears, but not mental diseases. All these symptoms show that they are fears. According to Dr Nirakarman Shrestha, there is neither treatment for such a patient nor recovery from the sickness. What medicine should be given to the patient who doubts and says again and again, 'Am I dying?' What medicine should be given to a man who washes his hands ten times in his bathroom? Similarly, what medicine works for the recovery of the man who checks his locker frequently? Yes! Counselling works here, because it is the product of thoughts and it can be reduced through the process of thinking again. I have recommended primary and secondary treatments of fear during the explanation of thinking. Many patients who suffer from fear can recover from such treatment.

On the effects of fear, Carl Gustav Jung says, 'Generally, what we find on the basis of experience of mental treatment is that fear is a fundamental reason of causing a problem for a mental study and an obstruction for the knowledge acquisition of the psychology.'[4]

I have mentioned the effects and sub-effects caused by low fear, mid fear, and high fear above. In fact, fear produces lots of problems, effects, and diseases. Treatment for most diseases and problems is not possible. The ongoing treatment is also not based on the method of fear, but other methods. As a result, treatment has not been effective at this time. It is sure that fear causes a mental problem and sickness, although there is the minority of people who believe it at present. A doctor can't say anything about the reason of fear, because there is no explanation and identification of it. So it is not possible to treat the problem due to the absence of diagnosis and discover medicine for it. There is no possibility of any scientific and natural methods as well. Despite these facts, some diseases caused by fear have started by treatment in the name of mental depression as stated above in examples from 1 to 4. Above all, the patients who have suffered from depression and mental problems have been treated separately. The treatment is effective if the problem caused by fear is treated by the method of Feariatrist. There can be other reasons for depression, mental sickness, and different problems, but the quantity of fear can be excessive. If fear begins to be identified and treated, we can be safe from different problems and diseases caused by the fear.

Thus, fear produces lots of diseases and problems and it can equally produce effects as well. They are in our families, societies, and countries, yet we are silent about them. The reason behind it is that we lack a proper knowledge about them.

Now we shouldn't keep silent like this. We have to search for answers and treatment as well. It is our problem. It is the problem of society. Above all, it's a big problem for medical science, doctors, and drug specialists. We have to find out a root cause. We need to work before accidents and incidents take place.

Similarly, what treatment method can be applied to the patient whose treatment is declared impossible by the doctor? Is there any philosophy that has interpreted the patient so far? Everyone has the problem of such a fear. Moreover, a negative fear is a greater fear disease. It has different effects and sub-effects. When a man has the knowledge of a problem, he begins to fear. Some people say that knowledge of any disease ends the fear related to it. It's not fact—fear grows more serious after we know about the disease and problem. The man who has suffered from an epidemic of a disease has both direct and indirect fears. Indirect means other fears that produce fears. Even those fears produce other fears. His family, relatives, and kith and kin are all affected when he suffers from a disease. This is an indirect fear. This fear exists when he thinks about his family, life, and the world. If death occurs unknowingly, it doesn't produce fear at all. Direct fear means the fear that he has or the problems produced by his fear.

Only interpretation of philosophy is insufficient; the whole interpretation of life is also not sufficient; but all small things related to life should also be interpreted. How can the seeds of fear produced by human nature without any good knowledge of fear be learnt? Nature and external factors are the sources of mental illness. Problems arise when the quantity of human nature grows continually. Those problems bring different diseases and other problems. Therefore, we should know the main source of a disease to be treated. There is no matter of treatment without any source of the disease. We wage war and commit violence and murder because of fear. We leave for our native land or a foreign country because we suffer from the same problem. However, the treatment of the disease is meaningless until we have an idea about the search for our own identity. A man becomes startled, nervous, and fearful and runs away when someone tries to murder, rape, and rob him or her, and an animal, an accident, or any natural disaster could attack him. Fear disease and mental problem are produced by this. Similarly, we may be sick at night or in daytime when we take a stump, mountain, and hill as a ghost and then it causes a mental problem. A man also fears when a crow, jackal, dog, or fox cries near his house.

Fear disease, mental problem, tension, depression, and escape of the man originate from various sources like this. We find various techniques and methods apply to their treatments. The treatment can't be effective if a problem, disease, and sickness are treated without any knowledge and source of them. The reason why it happens is that medical science has not discovered the disease and problems caused by fear. Medical science doesn't believe it too. In fact, a number of diseases are also produced by fear. Then they expand and continue to grow. Therefore, the disease caused by fear should be studied in detail and treatment conducted accordingly. For it, there should be the diagnosis of disease, discovery of medicine, and treatment. Only then can fear and mental illness be cured. As various mental problems, fear and other problems are produced when we are afraid, so our seeds of fear grow. If it doesn't have treatment today, it will start tomorrow. How fear expands from human temperament, so its effects keep expanding. The following Figure No. 46 further clarifies it.

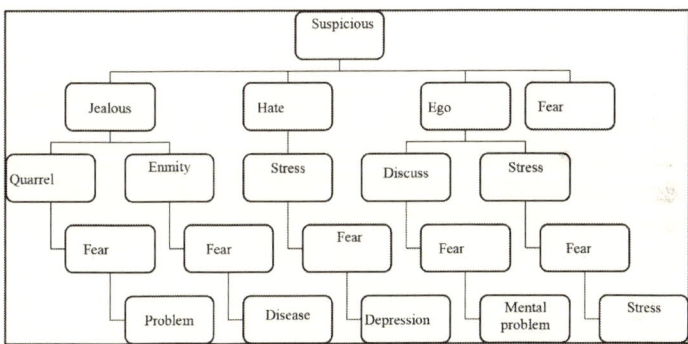

Figure No. 46

Figure No. 46 presents suspicion, temperament, effects, and sub-effects. When suspicion increases, it becomes jealousy, hatred, ego, and fear. Jealousy, hatred, and ego have turned into quarrels, enmity, and stress. Jealousy, enmity, and stress have become fear, and fear has become fear, mental illness, depression, and mental problems. Fear is mostly present in all stages. Here, fear is a medium. Fear, mental illness, and nature grow through this medium.

The effect of the problem of fear and mental illness is different from what we find. It is easier for the treatment of mental illness and depression if the problem is identified properly. This is a small example. Such seeds of fear continue to exist through temperaments. Similarly, many discussions have been carried out on the forms of fear.

Many sectors are available in medical science. Fear has a role somewhere in every sector. It's not possible to incorporate them all. I want to discuss fear and the mental illness here.

The man suffers from fear due to various reasons. Fear always affects him directly and indirectly. It is increasing. The impact of fear was low in the prehistoric period. Now, it has expanded everywhere. The reasons are growing invention, construction, and creation. Troubles, suffering, problems, etc. are also growing. The world has become more competitive due to population growth, unemployment, and financial crisis. All people want to develop their personalities and progress. Consequently, man has to work hard. His hard work and labour make his life full of tension. His failure invites fear, various problems, and depressions. New human temperaments keep on adding. Fear increases because of all this. As a result of fear, mental illness and other things affect human beings.

Doctors apply the same method of treatment to fear, suffering, depression, introversion, inferiority, nervousness, etc. Such treatment can't be effective. They should be treated separately. It means that the reason of the disease should be identified. The main source of disease has to be identified. The disease caused by fear should be diagnosed by the process of the fear treatment. Then, the treatment is more effective. Of course, it is very difficult for a doctor to identify the problem, but treatment without identification of the problem is not effective. So, treatment of some of the diseases is not effective. What we need to do first is to identify the problem. Treatment after the diagnosis as said above is effective.

We see in movies and read in books that the man who has been in an accident and lost his memory is taken to a similar kind of scene to regain his memory. Some of the patients have acquired memory when a similar kind of event is repeated. It is better to treat him by the process of fear treatment if the patient has suffered from fear because of fear. Let us consider! Someone has been sick by getting very frightened. Why was he frightened? Who was he frightened of? What was his condition when he was frightened? Who was around him? What was there? Is it better to treat him if all these details are known? The symptoms of such a disease correspond with a number of diseases. The treatment can't be effective if it is treated because he has got sickness, when he was frightened. Therefore, his treatment should start right from there where he has got frightened.

A man gets frightened after he has been attacked. He yells and becomes horrified as he gets in an accident. The man becomes unconscious when he receives news of an accident of his relatives and friends. A man who suffers from a disease fears internally. He becomes a hermit and feels loneliness because of different reasons. It produces different diseases too. If the man is deeply affected mentally, it causes different kinds of disease and problems for him. The treatment will not be effective if the disease and psychological effect caused by this situation are treated in other ways. Such a disease should be treated through its sources. There are lots of problems and diseases from fear. This obstruction has occurred, as fear has not been theorised for a long time. Fear has been interpreted a lot. It has been theorised. It will be easier to identify the disease caused by fear when its definition, condition, source, origin, effect, types, etc. are interpreted. The treatment system develops when a doctor declares that the disease is a result of fear. Medicine can be discovered for it. So, the people who suffer from this problem have relief. Therefore, it is the time for medical science to study fear from a new perspective. It is time for 'fearology' to be a study. The study on human temperaments should also be started along with these studies. Only then will it be easier to understand and identify the problem and treatment. Consequently, it develops a systematic treatment for the patient from fear. The man, then, doesn't need to suffer from various unnecessary treatments. The doctors often refer to various medicines on the basis of their guesses before the systematic study was conducted on fear. They examine the patients in various ways. They test the disease in different ways. As a result, treatment was not only expensive but also impossible in many cases.

In the past, a disease was supposed to be connected with the whole body of a man and his mental plight in the system of natural and medical treatment. There was an attempt to understand the mental condition of a man as well as the fluctuations of different elements in him to discover the disease of stomach ache. The man was categorised into different parts of the body in the course of the development of modern medicine. Diseases were categorised into different groups, i.e. stomach disease, bone diseases, heart diseases, lung disease, etc. Consequently, doctors were also categorised as a dentist, ear specialist, bone specialist, vertebra specialist, heart specialist, etc. In other words, the process of modern specialisation began through categorisation.[5]

Thus, different mental problems should be diagnosed through categorisation. Doing it is fruitful for the people with mental problems. It is fruitful for the treatment of fear as well. All hospitals are established and medicines have been discovered due to fear. Yet fear was not identified in medical science. That is why a fear patient was treated in some other places— like a man who is walking on a wrong track. As a result, time was wasted and expenditure was unnecessary. Now we have to come out from such an illusion. Fearology should be a study on fear. Similarly, a 'feariatrist' should treat the fear patient. Then, the treatment is possible. It's compensation to some extent.

As a discourse on it, Prof. Dr Tanka Prasad Neupane says, 'Fear is such a problem that certainly there is enlightenment in our whole mental lives as we find a solution to the problem.'[6]

Study, understanding, and treatment on fear have begun under different names in different countries. Fearism Study Center has been established in Dharan, Nepal to conduct study and research on it. A number of articles related to it have been published. Books on fearism are on the way to publication—some of them are psychoanalytic perspectives, some are from the perspectives of medical science, some are from the perspectives of medicines, and others are from fear analysis. Similarly, libraries have been established. Web sites have been opened. Institutes have been established. It is not clearly identified and studied yet, because during every second of time, it is emerging in different forms.

Technical Aspects Related to Fear

Fearology: Fear is as vast as the sky. People's fear comes from different sources. Man fears due to various incidents and accidents. Detailed research, study, practice, and analysis are not yet available on it. We are not informed as much as needed. Therefore, man is unable to know, understand, and utilise it sufficiently. Its effects and sub-effects remain unknown. So, fearology is necessary for it. Fearology gives us information about fear in detail.

Feariatric: We find a large number of fear patients in our societies. These patients take treatments as mental illness, depression, tension, and escapism. All the patients do not have a mental illness. Most of them are fear patients. Similarly, all people do not suffer from depression. There can be fear as well. Such diseases can also be from human temperaments like suspicion, introversion, and inferiority. They are from incidents and accidents. They are also possible from problems, mental stress, anxiety, and thoughts. Depression, escapism, and sadness can cause such illness. Feariatric should be established for such illness.

Feariatrist: Many diseases and problems originate from fear. Separate feariatrists are necessary just because various diseases, temperaments, problems, incidents, accidents, anxiety, thought, sadness, inferiority, and introversion can cause fear or problems. Here, the patient means the person who has a great quantity of fear. Generally, everyone suffers from fear. Maybe some of them suffer much and the rest suffer less. Much fear is problematic.

The human body contains things like sugar, blood, etc. If anything we need is excessive, that creates problems for us. Fear is also the same. We control sugar for diabetes patients. Maybe, fear patients need exercise or some control. Perhaps we need to take medicine. Treatment of it can be possible in some ways. To bring control in fear is to bring control in problems in order to ensure our securities. As a result, peace, prosperity, and happiness are possible in our lives.

There are lots of things in relation to hospitals, doctors, and patients. Fearology, feariatric, fear analyst, feariatrist, and different tools are required to analyse study and treat all these things. It is time for utilisation of them. It was low fear yesterday. Fear is growing and affecting man every day. We should prevent it immediately. Otherwise, there may be different negative impacts. Some of the negative effects are going on at present. On the one hand, fear is growing because of social evils, problems, drug addictions, murder, depression, caste/ethnic conflicts, terrorist attacks, etc. and on the other hand, growing natural disaster is causing fear. Fear will be reduced as feariatric is established, researched and interpretations are conducted on fearology, and feariatrists start special treatment.

End Notes:

1. Manu Manjil, *Banphool ra Usko Harayeko Thunga*, Fearism: *Baicharik Chintan* ed. Prakash Thamsuhang, Nepali Literary Academy, Honkong, 2066 v.s. p. 14.

2. *Yuwa*, Monthly Magazine for Youth, *Mulyangkan Publication*, Kathmandu, Year 10, Issue 97, 2005.

3. Pramila, *Dr Nirakarman Shrestha Inteviewed*, *Naya Patrika*, National Daily, Kathmandu, September 2, 2011.

4. Carl Gustav Jung, *The Undiscovered Self*, Routledge Classic, London and New York, 1958, p. 35.

5. Sanjeev Uppreti, *Sidhantaka Kura (Aspect of Theory)*, Akshar Creation, Kathmandu, 2068 v.s. p. 321.

6. Tanka Prasad Neupane, *Vayabadi Aadibasi Yek Anucharcha*, *Baicharik Chintan*, ed. Prakash Thamsuhang, Nepali Literary Academy, Honkong, 2066 v.s. p. 55.

19

Emergence

Eastern theory says, 'The world can be understood the best only when the atom is studied in its even smaller divisions.'[1]

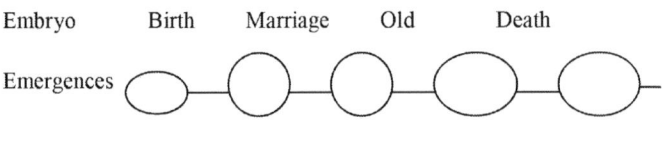

Figure No. 47

Figure No. 47 presents embryo, life, marriage, old age, and death on a straight line. Let's draw a straight line of human life from embryo to death. On the straight line, there are parts of lives more than the stars in the Milky Way. Let us divide life into embryo life, marriage, old age, and death for our comfort. Let us consider the period from embryo to birth. It takes ten months in the womb. The fetus undergoes changes every moment. The baby physically grows on the one hand and consciousness develops on the other hand. Semi-biological and biological embryos are always in fear. We don't know about consciousness, knowledge, and fear of the baby, but guardians fear for the baby all the time—they fear for the condition of the mother on the one hand and they fear for the baby on the other. The unconsciousness and consciousness of the baby move continually through sense organs, muscles, nerves, and cells. This is a risky condition. Any disease can attack the pregnant mother. There is the possibility of miscarriage. Any disease can attack the baby because he has weak immunity power. Organs of the body are soft and delicate in this period. New forms of emergence try to be safe from these risks every moment and continue growing. The emergences grow so fast that we can't see or study them in seconds, minutes, hours, and days, but we can see or study them in a long period. Birth, marriage, old age, and death are also formed of such emergences. The man gets angry, laughs, becomes happy, feels frustrated, and gets excited as a result of these emergences. New forms appear in the experience, expression, and gesture of a man after emergences. They are compared with the water that boils and appears as new forms in every second's emergence. Water starts moving to boil after a certain temperature. Later on, it changes into vapour. Afterwards, the vapour moves in the air. We can see its emergence clearly and immediately. All natural things, such as animals, the earth, the universe, etc., have emerged in this way. Our experience, knowledge, expression, behaviour, facial appearance, physical appearance, etc. also appear in very small emergences. Some of them can be seen and realised, whereas others can't be seen and realised, but changes always go on.

Every emergence means a knowledge acquisition, new experience acquisition, and new relief acquisition. Man always remains unstable and feels suffocated to have purification. He acquires knowledge by listening, seeing, touching, and smelling in a very small part of time. The yam plant emerges from the land. This is an emergence. When its first branch emerges, this is another form of emergence. Then it bears buds. This is also another form of emergence. The plant emerges in every small part of time until it exists. Such emergence also occurs in human life. Life is a long series of emergences. It has been woven just like a garland. A series of emergences are prior to the birth of a man. The acts of having care, growing, getting married, delivering a baby, etc. are all separate and different emergences. We acquire knowledge as we see, know, read, write, walk, and speak. Children always learn new things. Men acquire knowledge every moment. We are all divided into various fragments as we fragment the time. Our consciousness, knowledge, behaviour, a conditional reflex, and fear are parts of this fragmentation. One part does not transform and change into another part. It emerges into another part. There is detailed interpretation of transformation, change, and emergence in part. All these parts are related to each other. Life and the world can't be understood without dividing them into parts. Consciousness, fear, a conditional reflex, etc. can't be clearly understood. There is no knowledge of growth and reduction of consciousness. Only from parts is it possible to learn how one thing is different from another one and what the gap between them is. Therefore, an emergence is a good medium to go from one part to another. Such emergences always occur in human life. The difference is that some of them are remarkable, whereas others aren't.

Different scholars have used rhetorical words, void, difference, etc., for emergence in every series. Void (sunya) and difference are constant by meaning and word, but emergence is transformable and changeable. Living things try to remove all obstructions and bondages and go ahead in a very small bit of time. As a result, there exists an explosion of an unfavourable situation and a new emergence. The birth of a man, the emergence of a plant from the land, and the flow of water by breaking the dam are all equal processes. There occur obstructions in the course of every part of knowledge acquisition, as buds shed petals and emerge from them.

About this, Rahul Sankrityayan says, 'Whichever lives are qualified for the struggle of individual and fittest for the social forms in these changes, they exist and the rest of them disappear from this nature.'[2]

Every emergence is a knowledge acquisition as every light emerges from the dark. When that gets light, it's an emergence. Points of micro-level emergences are the study area of fearist concept. Difference can be applied to both living things and non-living things, whereas emergence is applied to life. Life values the world. Life keeps the world alive. The world is just dead (void) in the absence of life.

Every object, living being, or plant is the combined form of various parts in the universe. Unless we understand the smallest particles like atoms, cells, electrons, protons, neutrons separately, we can't understand changes in the world, the universe, living beings, botany, etc.

We should study our life with its division into parts. Life is divided into parts every moment. As a result, sometimes we are angry and other times we are happy. Similarly, we are suspicious, sometimes we are fed up, sometimes we are anxious, and other times we are dreadful. Therefore, looking, seeing, understanding, speaking, reading, and listening are also parts. Fear turns into parts because of all these parts of consciousness and knowledge. Emergence is an automatic invention that emerges from the parts. Light emerges from all these parts; that is an emergence. Life and the world are formed of such different parts.

Let us consider! The stone is still. We think how does an emergence take place in it? This is a non-living thing. External factors have remained as mediums around them striking the stone, and it gradually divides into parts every time. The stone that was seen before and the same stone that was seen later are quite different from each other. Matter, life, and the universe are the mass of emergences. Knowledge and consciousness are also the mass of emergences. Every emergence can only be acquired through a big struggle. The knowledge acquired by Gautam Buddha is emancipation, i.e. an emergence that emerged from the suffocation of life. Saint, Great Spirit, friar, and hermit perform emergence of such emancipation. Philosophers and philosophies of thinkers and thoughts are also liberation. All the liberations are in the journey of fearlessness. The journey goes on continually until it reaches fearlessness. Then, knowledge is acquired like a glimmering diamond after lots of struggles and research. That is to say the thing that was searched can be acquired in its new form. Lots of examples are available on the research conducted by the scientists for one thing but found another later. Anything covers every emergence that is there, i.e. that is blocked, suppressed, and covered. Otherwise, there is no matter of emergence. Man must struggle hard for his success like the seed breaks its husk/cover and the plant breaks soil to come forth. Like the seed covered by its husk, human life is covered by the fear. He hurries up and runs to and fro to get rid of these fears. His hurrying up brings progress, success, relief, and escape. He feels the victory of progress and success over fear to some extent. In fact, it is a sweet illusion only. Progress and success do not necessarily influence fear. Fear always moves in its own orbit. It is easy to say that we can reduce fear, but it is not so easy in practice. It is very difficult to practice in reality. Despite these facts, man tries to keep on trying. Every emergence is focused on it. Some people don't agree with it. There is newness about fear in man when it is clearly and openly expressed. If an emergence helps to make human life a bit easier, it will be a great success.

Countless emergences occur from cradle to the grave. The world of botany is also the same. Life and the world depend on this series of emergences. The emergence is not regular, but it is more causal. We possibly don't know if lives are moving towards one side and the world is moving towards another. The second emergence of the same thing is yet unknown.

The same form does not occur regularly. All of sudden, it occurs in another form, like the emergence of God. We are not sure about the form of emergence. Series of emergences are more different than their changes in forms. The difference among difference, void, and emergence is that emergence has life, whereas difference and void don't. These emergences have their important meanings, as they are related to lives. The baby whom the mother and guardians keep waiting might die in the womb as well. Although, death exists in the womb, that is an emergence. Emergence has a deep relationship with living things but not with non-living things. In fearism, we see, understand, and talk about the things that are similar to our lives. All the things are nothing if there is no life. Everything depends on life. Emergence is great knowledge. I want to present some examples of emergence here.

a. Parts of Consciousness

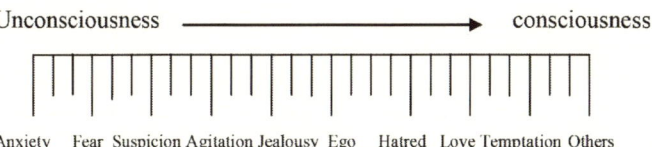

Figure No. 48

Figure No. 48 draws a line from the point of unconsciousness and it extends to the point of consciousness. It shows anxiety, fear, suspicion, agitation, trouble, jealousy, ego, hatred, love, temptation, experience, knowledge, different consciousness, and temperaments. These temperaments are a kind of consciousnesses. They move on either side and move back again from either side. An anxiety grows, it transforms into suspicion, fear, agitation, trouble, etc. Similarly, as temptation grows, it transforms into love, hatred, ego, etc. Parts may occur in the wholeness of this fluctuation exceptionally. There are small parts of anxiety. They can easily combine with each other. It doesn't have any measurement. Here, the wholeness has been divided into three parts in order to clarify the part. These parts can be either of gaps, blankness, or void. Countless parts may exist in this room. That is to say, countless parts prevail in anxiety. Some of them are small, whereas others are big. Similarly, some are fearful and some are lovely. We don't know when anxiety grows continually and turns into fear. That is to say, the border lines of anxiety and fear can't be separated. We can only identify the scene when there are changes like the change of a scene in a movie. Similarly, there is a change of scene without any idea about doubt, agitation, etc. Likewise, there are parts of jealousy as well. All of them have their parts. Those parts may attract and repel any parts and change into another experience. We can't say when parts of anxiety join fear and doubt. We can't even measure it. Neither can we divide experience nor have a new experience. When these parts join with other parts, consciousness acquires a new experience. However, any one of the experiences is an emergence. Thus, the parts of consciousness join and separate from each other, but we don't know anything about their combination and separation. This process goes on continually inside consciousness like the theory of Brown. Therefore, consciousness always transforms into different forms. All these are emergences, because we don't know which parts are connected with the other ones. We also don't know which parts separate from the other ones. They go on without any effort. It does not have any assigned way and theory. It doesn't have any scientific theory till now. After all, they transform into new scenes only after they are divided into different smaller parts. Smaller lines drawn on the line are free to move forwards, move backwards, and join with others. All plants, living beings, and other things in this universe are also free in the same way. Therefore, new emergences continue to exist. These are merely mediums. These are all moving with great speed.

b. Time

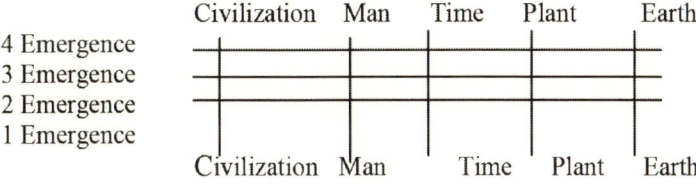

Figure No. 49

Fear and experience are different even in small parts of time. Figure No. 49 shows time in the middle of the figure. Civilisation and man are on the left side plants and earth are on the right side. The part from 1 to 2 is a small part of time. Time moves a little in this part. The consciousness of a man grows a little along with the pace of time. Civilisation has been developed a little along with the growth of the man. Plants grow a little in this period. The earth moves a little. In total, all matter and elements move in this period.

Discussing the essence of Buddhism, Rahul Sankrityayan writes: 'The whole world remains changeable every moment. This is an essence of Buddhist philosophy.' Therefore, Aristotle has said that velocities and changes exist along with the physical factors.[3] Emergences are occurring in the world. In this way, every emergence adds new dimensions.

According to the experiment by Einstein—the motion of the water flowing from the tap and the cloud flying in the sky can clearly be visible, but many things look still and seem to have zero motion, yet they keep moving deep inside. If we combine small whirlwinds, we feel as if they are still. There are many things like them that look still. Solids, liquids, gases and all other things look still, are variable. Thus, the universe and human temperaments are as they are described in the Vedas.

Marx has interpreted it in his interpretation of geometric change.[4] 'Moreover, the consciousness of a man is movable. Consciousness differs by the acts of seeing, listening etc. in the former and later parts of time, physical growth, development of sense organs and a conditional reflex. These different consciousnesses study life and the world a bit differently. Consequently, fear also differs in this fluctuation.'

This is a very small part of time. When time moves or consciousness develops in a small point of time, fear also follows the same way. Fear that moves in that way is not only limited to a man. It exists in everything, i.e. man, civilisation, plants, and the earth. The form of fear is changeable. The fear of a man and plant, the fear of a man and nature, and the fear of man and civilisation are all movable, and they move at all times. There is an internal and external conflict in a living thing. These living things are surrounded by the chains of internal and external fears. Internal chains mean personal problems, anxiety, and sorrow of a man. He always moves in the trap of such problems. His life is at an end in the effort of getting rid of the chain. His struggle continues to move with these chains, problems, sufferings, and sorrows. This is a kind of change, transformation, and knowledge.

External factors exist to affect this condition. They are climate, temperature, man, animals, and food. All these external factors affect the consciousness of a man at all times. There is also a conflict with these factors. He should be victorious over these conflicts. So, the life of a living being is risky all the time.

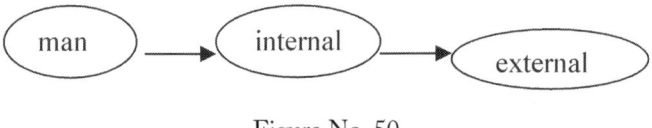

Figure No. 50

Figure No. 50 depicts internal and external fears of the man. He should come out of the internal fear at first and then the external. He should keep coming out of all these fears. The same thing has been shown in the figure.

When the man deals with all the risks, he is victorious. When the living being, plant, etc. appears in a new form in a small part of time, there is also a new emergence of knowledge, physical body, and the world. Different fears appear in the parts of every emergence. One fear emerges and gets reduced. Another fear exists over again. This process goes on continually like the sun and its shadow. Fear appears and disappears continuously. Some of the fears appear or exist for the time being, whereas others exist for a long time. Still other fears remain throughout the whole life. But it does not occur in the same way. It comes and goes like the tide when a man recalls it. Life, society, country, civilisation, and universe always depend on these series of emergences. These series of fears are also the same.

c.   Growth

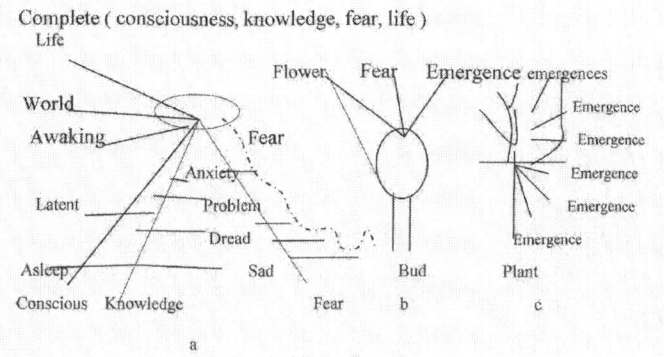

Figure No. 51

168

Figure No. 51 (a) presents consciousness, knowledge, and fear lines. Three conditions of consciousness are presented: asleep, latent, and awakened. The stage of unconsciousness is almost the condition of the first. Consciousness extends through small latent points and reaches the condition of a deep slumber. It extends from being asleep to the stage of being awakened. The consciousness has to cross many ups and downs and bends to reach stage awakened from stage latent. Quantities of knowledge and fear also grow along with the growth of consciousness. Ego, existence, problems, anxiety, doubt, illusion, and anger are the inspiring factors of fear. Several subjects that are connected with consciousness go on changing along with time and conditions and mingle with the inspiring factors of fear and then help fear increase.

In Figure No. 51 (a), consciousness is growing from one side, whereas fear is growing from another side. The line of knowledge is between them. There is a combination of consciousness line, knowledge line, and fear line at a point. Man understands life as well as fear perfectly at this meeting point. He understands, teaches, and interprets life and the world on the basis of this condition. What he understands here is the climax of his understanding. Above all, the man always thinks that he is in this condition, but there is a fluctuation. Parmenides, Protagoras, Descartes, John Locke, including many other scholars, have discussed this knowledge and experience.

When anxiety, problems, death, disease, trouble, and doubt produce knowledge, fear exists, because death, sickness or disease, trouble, and doubt are not fear themselves—knowledge gives us fear. Fear does not exist at once in the figure, but it has come into being through consciousness, knowledge, different internal and external factors. Higher consciousness and knowledge lines have caused a higher fear. This point is the height of fear. Life and the world seem to be perfect and complete from this point. A conscious being is much more affected by fear than action, anger, love, charm, doubt, and illusion. Life is not complete only by action, anger, temptation, love, charm, illusion, doubt, and sex. Fear is inevitable for a complete life. Fear emerged in Figure No. (a). Life keeps on turning into buds and babies in Figure (b). Every small part of time is in an emergence. Later on, an upcoming emergence goes on disclosing this mysterious part of time. The mysteries of time has been disclosed and shown in Figure (c).

When the condition of fear lessens continually, life turns into a bud. When the bud opens petals, it blossoms. As the petal protects the bud, so the fear protects our lives. Protection is possible only with fear. I have explained it elsewhere in this text in detail. If the petal covers the bud forever, the beauty of the flower disappears. Similarly, if the fear covers life forever, the beauty of life disappears. To take out life from fear is to take out the flower from the petal. It is like revealing the complete beauty of a flower from the bud. The same thing has been depicted in (a), (b), and (c).

Figure No. 51 (c) illustrates a plant. Emergences appear as much as plants grow. Seeds come forth from the soil. Branches, leaves, buds, and flowers emerge continually. Air, water, fertiliser, and the sun affect every emergence. The plant struggles with all of them and continues to emerge in a new form. Man also has new emergences in the same way. That is the way life is. All the consciousness, knowledge, and fear grow in that life. The consciousness gives knowledge, continues to give problems until death, and fear prevails as well.

Let us see man in place of a flower. He loves every moment from birth to death. The bud is extremely beautiful. Man is attracted to the same beauty of the bud. He struggles hard to attain it. Every change in life is emergence—birth, growth, marriage, and death. To acquire knowledge, to discover, and to develop are emergences. Life and development are the series of emergences. Different emergences occur one after another. This process goes on continually.

d.   Parts of Void or Gaps

There are a lot of parts in the emptiness or gaps of Derrida and the void of Nagarjun. It is impossible to claim the shape, size, volume, and area of gaps, voids, and absences. They may be either big or small. There is a supply of new creations, constructions, and discovery in these gaps, absences, and voids. The great form of parts is the wholeness.

Life and the world have been formed by gaps, absences, voids, continuations, changes, and transformations. New forms of these parts can't be seen at once. It takes a long time. Emergence is a coordinator to change parts into the wholeness. New changes have occurred in the former and later sections of parts. It is applied to biological and natural objects. It can be further clarified through the following figure.

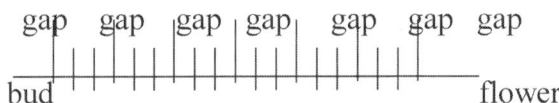

Figure No. 52

Buds have transformed into flowers in this figure. Various gaps, absences, and voids of different shapes, colours, and forms are between the bud and flower. The bud has emerged and transformed into a flower. Several gaps, absences, or voids exist here. To reach from one part to another, gaps, absences, and voids have to be crossed. Even in this condition, emergence is the coordinator of gaps, absences, voids, and parts. The continuity of emergence in gaps, absences, and voids has transformed into a flower. Life, the world, society, country, thought, and behaviour have been constituted in this way. Many other smaller gaps, absences, and voids have been constituted in large gaps, absences, and voids. Again, these gaps, absences, and voids are omnipresent. We are also emergence in the same gaps, absences, and voids. The universe is also the same. Truths are also the same.

e.   In Meaning, Experience, Norms, and Values

Jacques Derrida says, 'All meanings are under deconstruction—meanings we read write and understand, feelings, values and norms remain the same up to a condition.' We have had feelings, values, and norms so far. We have directly understood their primary meanings. They change from the old forms into new ones because of internal and external reasons when we reach another condition. Some of the meanings are outdated because of the demands of time, whereas others are affected by external forces. There is a distance between the deconstruction and reconstruction of meanings, feelings, values, and norms. For Derrida, this distance is a gap. It is not that they are reconstructed immediately after their deconstruction. A new construction may or may not be meaningful. We can't presuppose the reconstruction and come to a decision about it. Meanings, feelings, values, and norms are a kind of condition like the piece of wood lying on the ground. They lie in this way before they transform into another form. Of the pieces, we collect necessary ones, use them, and form a new meaning, feeling, value, and norm. All conditions are emergences in the course of changes. The second condition of a meaning, feeling, value, and norm is unknown. There are also gaps, absences, and voids between two or among many differences. In this stage, the second form of the meaning, feeling, value, and norm may be sameness or otherness and positive or negative. All these are emergences. All these emergences have a great value in their post-structure. Some of the parts of meaning, feeling, value, and norm may have their meanings, whereas others don't.

Let us consider a house. It has structure. The house was demolished. Materials used in the house lay scattered after the house is demolished. Every part has existence. Prevailing meaning, experience, norms, and value transform into new meaning, experience, norm, and value. They cannot cross over on to other new ones. Emergence occurs in the middle of a cross and across from the meaning, experience, norm, and value. Different human and natural processes occur while transforming meaning from one side to another. They undergo erosion and transform into new ones. It emerges in a new form. This is the emergence of meanings, experiences, norms, and values.

f.   Salvation

Terms like salvation and emancipation are often used while talking about salvation from life. Man undergoes hardship, pain, suffering, crime, sin, and debt throughout his whole life. He always suffers from all these things till the last. As all these things are relieved after death, they are bid farewell by using the words emancipation and salvation. Out of many desires, man desires emancipation for a good life. If so, what is that which we think of as salvation? What do we need to acquire salvation? What are the types of salvation? There are too many questions like this. Every human activity is oriented to salvation. Man continues to work for salvation. But he doesn't express it verbally. His works are for salvation. What is his salvation? Man works hard within this emancipation. Cognition lies there.

Generally, salvation and emancipation are found mentioned in religious texts—in the sense of emancipation for life. It's a salvation of life. Socrates has said, 'Many bad things remain in the body as long as our body exists. What we desire can never be attained. Our soul can attain what we desire after we attain salvation.'[5] Theists wish they had comfortable deaths at this stage, and they consider it as emancipation from hardship, suffering, sin, crime, etc. of their lives. In total, it's a condition of emancipation from bondage, problems, hardship, and suffering. Mostly, its interpretation is linked with death.

Nimbarka has categorised the same salvation into four different categories: *samalokya, samipya, sarupya,* and *sayujya.*[6]

We seek salvation throughout our lives. We find many small parts when we see life separately. Life is the combination of these small parts. We feel as if every moment of life and society is bondage for us. We become nervous and unstable and seek emancipation for these bondages. So, we propound different concepts, discover new things, and have constructions and creations. We feel that we have some emancipation on the basis of these thoughts, discoveries, constructions, and creations. We become social workers and make them get rid of the problems if we realise that society has several evils and follow the wrong ways. We become politicians and develop our country if the violation of rule, law, and constitution has invited instability in the country.

We are active in bringing and establishing a multi-party system in place of an autocratic system because of an unfavourable situation. We are involved in republican movement if we feel that the situation is problematic because of the monarchical system. We struggle for the emancipation of society, country, and caste/ethnic communities if in case injustice, oppression, and discrimination prevail.

Marx saw oppression and domination made upon slaves, workers, and proletariats by owners, capitalists, and feudalists. He felt suffocated by this problem. He issued the Communist manifesto and interpreted the class struggles for the emancipation of proletariats. It was, as he thought, an ultimate weapon to emancipate them from hardship, suffering, pain, atrocity, and domination. They used to think about emancipation in this way. Different thoughts, discoveries, and creations occurred then. It is only a way for them to reach emancipation. Here, man suffers from fear if the emancipation is unattainable. Marx suffered from the same fear. He feared whether people could attain emancipation. Thus, emancipation has been divided into smaller parts—second, minute, hour, day, week, month, year, etc. They have also their parts. If we study the emancipation of a day, we find that lots of problems, bondages, injustice, oppression, suffering, sorrow, exploitation, discrimination, and mistreatment appear and disappear. We go through these emancipations. These bondages are realised as the donkey of Samasuddin. We consider time, family, relatives, and actions such as financial, social, and political environment as our bondages. We get up early in the morning; we eat rice as an emancipation. We go to work as an emancipation, and we come back from our work, again as an emancipation. These are the parts of emancipation. Thus, these are emergences of the emancipation.

Jean Paul Sartre, an existentialist, didn't see any existence in society and said, 'The man, who says and feels that I exist and I have freedom of choices, decisions and works, has existence. The man, who does not have such feelings, doesn't have existence.'[7] He further interpreted existence as he realised the violation of the freedom of people, and they are restless for such freedom. He considered his interpretation as only a way to emancipation.

Albert Camus said, 'Existence of the man doesn't have purpose, theory, truth, meaning and suffers from absurdism.'[8] According to him, the man who is born here doesn't have any purpose. Caste/ethnic community, society, language, and script are all meaningless. Therefore, society should be made purposeful. It is absurd and meaningless. Family, society, and community all are absurd. He attempts to gain freedom through his interpretation.

Similarly, philosophers, writers, journalists, socialists, religious people, literary persons, and politicians use their perspectives to look at society, country, and community, and they see weakness, mistakes, absurdism, injustice, oppression, suppression, exploitation, and discrimination, etc. They want to make society, country, community, man, and discrimination free through their writing and advocacy. The difference is only technology. Although society is free from all these problems, injustice, oppression, and suppression, it is only one kind of, not an ultimate emancipation. A number of emancipations exist in society—some of them are major and the rest of them are minor.

These emancipations have been divided into two categories.

(a) Short-term Emancipation

Short-term emancipation includes all types of emancipations that occur from early morning to the late evening. We are hungry—we eat snacks. This is emancipation. We feel sleepy—we sleep. This is emancipation from sleep. We suffer from normal diseases, so we consult a doctor and take medicine. This is emancipation. Similarly, to be free from economic, social, and political problems, including the problems of religion, culture, language, script, relatives, and employment, is short-term emancipation. Scientists discover new medicines to get rid of a disease. We work to be free from financial problems. Offices also have major and minor kinds of fear, anxiety, and problems. We work continually to be emancipated from them, because such kinds of problems always occur in life. We should keep working on emancipation in this way. All these problems, troubles, sufferings, and sorrows have fear. All these create different kinds of fear for man. When we are free from these problems, we have short-term emancipation from fear.

(b) Long-term Emancipation

Long-term emancipations do not always exist like short-term emancipations. These are important parts of our lives. They affect man, society, and country for a long time. If the freedom, right, justice, and equality of a person, society, and country have not been applied for a long time, there exists religion, theory, and science. It is rare emancipation. It occurs only after a long time.

Therefore, whatever activities we do are oriented to emancipation. There lies the fear. Our attempt to come out of fear is our cognition. The same cognition helps us get different solutions. These are done for the emancipation from fear. Many people speak, write, discover, and construct in order to emancipate society, country, and the people from fear. This is, indeed, emancipation.

There are larger number of emergences than time, consciousness, growth, void, meaning, and salvation in our lives and the world. Thus, the whole universe is constructed and protected by various parts of emergences.

End Notes:

1. Dave Robinson, Judy Groves, *Introducing Philosophy*, Icon Books, London, Totem Books, New York, 1999, p. 33.
2. Rahul Sangkrityan, *Sketch of the World*, trans. Narayan Giri, Marxbad Study-Research Academy, Kathmandu, 2066 v.s p. 44.
3. Rahul Sangkrityan, *Sketch of the World*, trans. Narayan Giri, Marxbad Study-Research Academy, Kathmandu, 2066 v.s p. 44.
4. Birendra Prasad Mishra, *Darshanshashtra Parichaya (Introduction to Philosophy)*, Nepal Charity Foundation, 2065 v.s. p. 61.
5. *Plato Sukratko Aatmakatha (Autobiography of Plato, Socrates)*, trans. Ramhari Banjara, Madhuwan Publication, Kathmandu, 2065 v.s.p 110
6. Arjundev Panta, *Bedanta–Darshan Sar (Brief Vedaanta Philosophy)*, Ratna Book Store, Kathmandu, 2062 v.s. p. 43.
7. Mohan Raj Sharma, Khagendra Prasad Luitel, *Eastern and Western Literary Theory*, Kathmandu, 2063 v.s.p. 345.
8. Mohan Raj Sharma, Khagendra Luitel, *Eastern and Western Literary Theory*, Kathmandu, 2063 v.s. p. 347.

20

Flow of Possible Events

Flow of possible events always occurs in our lives. We have the day, week, month, and year. Different flows and events exist with these times. We are bound by all possible events from early morning to the late evening. These flows and events occur in months, years, and till the death of a human being as well. Our steps and the orders of these events exist side by side. Minor and major kinds of fears appear and disappear in the flow of these possible events. Some of the fears occur, whereas others don't appear. Most of them are just limited to their possibilities. Despite these facts, they occur time and again. Once when one event occurs, then another possible event appears to occur. Suspicion, anxiety, and fear take their turns in this flow. Sometimes doubt, anxiety, and fear occur, whereas at other times, anxiety, doubt, and fear exist. Still, at other times, fear, doubt, and anxiety appear. But fear continues.

We get up early in the morning. We eat; we go out; we cross the road; we use vehicles; we reach offices; and we work. Events and accidents collide with these incidents. Moreover, fear follows them. We are afraid if we get late, get abused, and our work is ruined. The same thing recurs. When our office hours are over, we go out of the office. We cross the road; we use vehicles; we get off vehicles; and we cross the road, and reach the house. During this period, we suffer from fear—we may fall over, stumble, make mistakes, lose something, and get scolded. Fear exists and re-exists at the same time. For instance, we fear the family, but at the same time, we fear the office, friends, relatives, and sickness. Countless flows of possible events occur during the whole day. Similar cases occur in weeks, months, and years. It continues until death. Possibilities, suspicions, and anxieties often occur in all these events and accidents. We often ignore small natural incidents and accidents, although they occur and hinder us frequently. They do not adjust to the mechanical science of Isaac Newton. Rather, it is like the non-mechanical science of Albert Einstein. We think before we go, but reach different circumstances and events. Nothing seems certain. When we think about doing one thing, another thing emerges abruptly. Similarly, the conditions of buying one thing, meeting a person, seeing one thing, and thinking about something emerge into other forms. After thinking, meeting, seeing, and buying, we regret what we did. We suppress most of these planned desires and ambitions. Suppressed desires, ambitions, etc. become hidden and some of them remain open. Those suppressed desires, ambitions, and thoughts appear at a glance and as glimpses in sleep and dreams. All these actions, reactions, and activities have a flow of possible events and then suspicion, anxiety, and fear emerge there. The country and time makes an impact on them. As a result, decisions, thoughts, actions, and behaviour are more dynamics. New possibilities, emergences, anxieties, fears, and problems exist and transform into other forms during this motion. This is a mass and so is the world.

Aristotle has propounded four reasons of an event and expressed them in his theory:

1. Material cause—matter
2. Effect cause—artist
3. Formal cause—artist's imagination
4. Final cause—concrete form[1]

As he says, what happens is material cause; matter lies in effect, formal and final causes; the agent is an artist; the possible event is an imagination of the artist; and the event is a concrete form. This theory can be applied to the works of constructions and creations. It doesn't apply to accidents. Material and effect causes can be in accidents, but formal and final causes cannot be there. A criminal can think of ways to commit a crime, and the final cause can be according to this plan. This theory can be applied to the process related to any construction or creation. Formal causes of events and accidents cannot be like this in a practical life. There can be more than one event—flow of its possibilities exists. If events and accidents are according to the plans of our minds, they are not events and accidents, but they are plans and projects. Therefore, events and accidents are unknown.

In fact, it is not in the minds of people. We can make guesses about possible events and accidents, but they happen to take place differently. We could control it if events and accidents occur according to our plan or we knew all things about an upcoming event earlier. Some events occur, although we control them. So that always becomes a possible flow of events. No event could harm us if we controlled them. There is no reason of being worried about and fearful of it if no event harmed us. As a possible event is unknown and deep, we always fear it. We try to be safe from it. Hence, we can't fully agree with the theory of Aristotle related to the events that occur in life. We have the flow of possible events in practice. Therefore, we fear at all times.

a. Fear in Space and Time

Certainly, we sometimes presuppose some possible events and do work carefully as well. However, all the possible events do not occur according to our supposition. We can study them along with country, time, and fear causing matter.

a. Country and time—country stable
b. Country and time—time stable
c. Country and time—both stable, fear-causing factors are unstable
d. Both stable—man unstable

a. Country and time—country stable

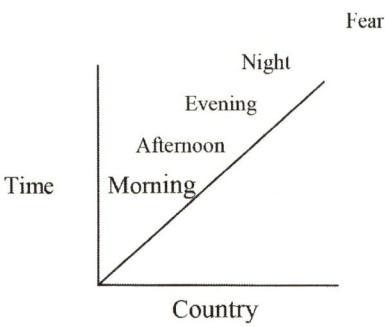

Figure No. 53

Immanuel Kant has said, 'Sensitive-power adopts all the sensitivities by means of country and time.'[2]

Figure No. 53 shows us in the grave. Here, the grave is country. It is stable. Time has only been changed into morning, afternoon, evening, and night. The fear of a man differs in the morning, afternoon, evening, and night. Low fear occurs in the morning, mid fear in the afternoon, high fear in the evening, and extremely high fear at night. The possibility of an event is always concerned with it, so fear is different from others. If possibility does not concern an event, fear does not exist.

The velocity, quantity, shape, and type of fears are different according to time and country. A type of fear may exist in the same time and country of consciousness, and another kind of fear may appear in another time and country. This is because of time and country. Prehistoric consciousness has become the same for prehistoric time. However, it seems that consciousness has also been changed due to time and country, and there have been different anxieties and fears because of these different consciousnesses.

Consciousness and fear differ due to time and country even in the consciousness in another time at present. The fear of the man living in America and that of the man living in Nepal are different from each other, although they have the same consciousness. Similarly, the fear of the man living in any village of the country Nepal and that of the man living in any town of the country are also different from each other. The quantity, shape, type, velocity, etc. of fear differs due to time, although the place is the same in Nepal. If a man has lived in a lonely place, grave, forest, or stream, his fear may start differing along with the hands of the watch. It means his fear may occur differently in the morning, in the afternoon, in the evening, and at night.

Similarly, fear also differs due to different countries at the same time.

b.   Country and time—time stable

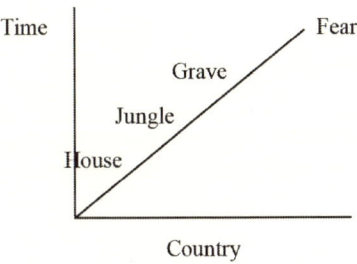

Figure No. 54

Let us make time stable and country unstable. Figure No. 54 shows midday of time. Here the figure shows country, grave, jungle, and house. Similarly, the figure shows the highest fear in the grave, lower fear in the jungle, and the least fear in the house. Let us consider! Man spends his three days in three different places: house, jungle, and grave. Then his fear differs according to time and place. It justifies that the highest fear is in the grave, lower fear is in the jungle, and the least fear is in the house.

c. Country and time—both are stable but fear-causing factors are unstable

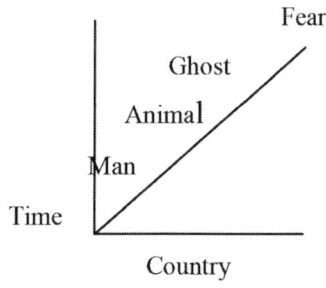

Figure No. 55

Figure No. 55 shows fear-causing factors and objects: animals, ghosts, and men. Here, both time and country are made stable. As the differences between country and time made the fears of a man different, so the fear-causing factors and objects make the fears of a man different. If the same time and country as well as fear-causing factors are different, fears of the men are also different. The above figure shows the lowest fear of man, fear of animals, and the highest fear is in ghosts. In this way, fear differs for the same man and how different it is for different people!

All people look similar outwardly. However, the consciousness, feeling, perceiving power, tolerance power, and comprehensive power of men vary due to their distinct qualities. Hence, some people fear a ghost, whereas others become fearful of animals. Above all, some people fear other people.

d. Both stable—man unstable

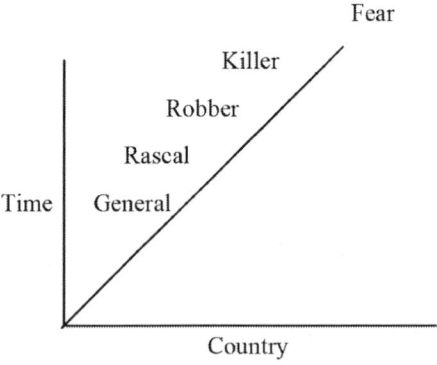

Figure No. 56

The case is the same when a man fears another one. Some people are good, whereas others are bad. A straightforward kind of man fears a murderer, a robber, and a rascal. Fear varies because of different people, although time and country are stable. Time and country are stable in Figure No. 56, except the ordinary people, rascals, robbers, and murderers. A little fear arises due to an ordinary man, a bit more fear due to a rascal, much more fear due to a robber and murderer. Thus fear differs in man because of his different characters.

Time and country have been considered stable here. It is, in fact, impossible for time to be stable.

Of course, these examples are impossible to apply to the human being. The same man also has differences on the basis of time and country. The same man does not pay attention and show his interest to the same thing constantly. In this way, the differences of attention mean the differences of his consciousness, knowledge, and a conditional reflex. The effects and sub-effects of it also vary as soon as fear differs. The fear of man also varies because of slight differences of the country, time, and fear-causing factor. Hence, fear depends on country, time, and fear-causing factor.

Marx has said, 'When a thing has a quantitative change, it has a qualitative change itself.'[3]

About the effects due to the change of one part of a thing, psychologist Gestalt has said, 'Quality and character of the whole structure can be changed through the change in a part of it.'[4]

According to Marx and Gestalt, a lot of changes occur in life and the world as soon as we change a part of a thing slightly. Fear also changes when consciousness, knowledge, matter, a conditional reflex, nature, and time moves a bit.

Anything may be a possible event. Something may catch fire. We may have an accident. Someone may die. Such possible events are countless in human life. When an event occurs, it may be bigger, smaller, and more different than the possibility. An event may also not occur. Different forms appear after one event has occurred. We are discussing the condition before the event takes place and its impact and effect after it happens.

The scope of the possible event is very vast. It can be applied to anything, i.e. from a very small thing to the whole universe and from an imagination to reality. A possible event means the condition that happens before the event, but man thinks about a possible event and fears it and starts to think about security from the event. Firstly, he becomes careful and alert to the event before it occurs. If an event takes place meanwhile, it does not make any difference, for he has already made up his mind to tackle the problem. He has both fear and worry at the same time in all these conditions. The reason why he fears and worries is that he tries to find a solution to the problem for emancipation. He does not have any trouble, suffering, sorrow, happiness, and peace, but worry and fear at the time. Different factors, viz. trouble, suffering, chaos, necessity, etc., may appear in course of trying to relieve it after fear existed.

b. Fear of Change in Circumstance

An object appears fearful in some cases and fearless in other cases. It is related to the circumstance. The same object induces fear in one man, whereas it causes no fear for another man. Similarly, the same weather may cause fear in one situation whereas it may not do so in other times. A friend in one circumstance can be an enemy in another circumstance. The same food may be tasty in one case, but tasteless in another case. A number of such things as men, animals, fire, and water exist. It is not that everything causes fear for all equally. Lots of fears exist in one case and no fear exists in other cases. All these depend on time, country, and circumstance. Change applies everywhere, but we ignore it. To change in fear requires change in place, object, and circumstance of man.

Example 1
Place—normal circumstance
There is a garden of flowers. The circumstance has not been changed in the garden. All flowers have bloomed. We go there. We feel great joy. Days pass joyfully. Nothing draws our attention. What purpose we have has been fulfilled.

Unusual circumstance:

An accident has taken place in the same garden. Some type of accident has occurred: a man is dead or a poisonous snake appears. When the man is informed about the incident, he fears going there. If he goes, the incident/ memory of the incident draws his attention and he fails to complete his purpose. The place is the same. Due to a change in circumstance and perspective, the feeling experienced while looking at the garden has changed and the man is afraid to go there.

Example 2
Food
Sugar is one among many foods. There is a high quantity of sugar in juice. People use sugar in many food items. It can be used in any food. It is

common in tea. In a general case, there is no reason to be fearful with sugar in tea. People do not care while drinking it. There can be two conditions to create fear: damages in the sugar and diabetes.

Unusual circumstance:

The first reason, sugar can be damaged due to many reasons: ants could be in the sugar and another can be the mixture of non-food items. When we know such a mixture exists, we fear using the sugar.

The second reason, a healthy man who is informed about his diabetes when he has his health check is fearful to use sugar.

A visible thing is also the same. The same thing seems beautiful in one circumstance but terrible in another circumstance. The animal, place, or thing that seemed beautiful some time ago may transform into a dangerous one later because of different events, problems, or diseases. Similar kinds of circumstances may arise in the case of man as well. The same man who behaves friendly some time ago might appear dangerous later because of his manner and behaviour. The man changes his nature occasionally in comparison to others. We not only change our perspectives to look at the man, but we also fear him if he was friendly before he starts behaving in an unfriendly manner.

Two changes occur here: external and internal. Knowledge and health change as internal changes. Due to change in former knowledge and health and change in latter knowledge and health, one thing that appeared normal before appears fearful later. When a circumstance changes in this way, the same man, thing, and place becomes fearful. It can further be clarified as:

1. Man: If an ordinary man becomes an enemy, murderer, thief, conspirator, robber, and rapist, he starts to become the source of fear.
2. Food: If the food in regular use is rotten, damaged by germs, or has fallen on to the ground, it become the cause of fear.
3. Place: A normal place becomes a dangerous one when there is a rumour of a ghost and a message of attack. Similarly, if someone commits suicide there; someone murders; cholera breaks out; an accident and landslide occur; something catches fire; earthquake takes place regularly; volcano erupts; tsunami occurs; and war or civil war starts to exist.
4. Sometimes we need rainfall and sometimes we fear the same rainfall because it can destroy crops. The same thing is useful when we need it and the same thing becomes useless when we don't need it. There are too many things and places like that.

Thus, the food in regular use, roads, good friends, relatives, and natural things transform into fearful things.

21

Probability of Fear

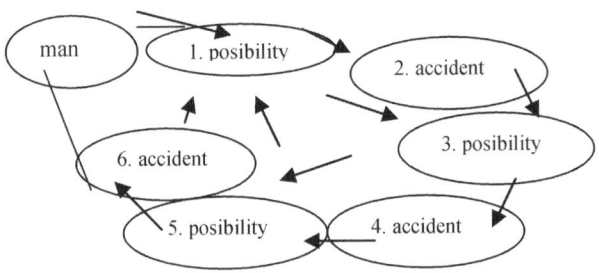

Figure No. 57

Figure No. 57 shows many accidents and probable accidents that can happen to human beings. The first presents probability. More than one probability exists in case of their occurrence. Man always suffers from probability and accident in this way. Where there is the probability of an event, there are more than one, that is, countless ones, like the arrows indicate. The event may or may not occur after its probability. Another probability exists again whether the event occurs or not. The accident may or may not occur again. Probability continues to exist like this. Some accidents occur, whereas others don't occur and some disappear. When probability exists, a number of probabilities appear.

A lot of fears appear between the probability and the accident. We continue being safe from them. Those probabilities sometimes disappear and at other times appear as accidents, like the different lines in the figure. Similarly, some events are major, while others are minor. Major kinds of events affect us badly, but minor events have a normal impact on us. Some serious impact makes us fearful every day, every month, and every year. It affects our activities and concepts. It has short-term and long-term effects. Let us consider! A man is waiting to cross the road. A motorbike and car may hit him, he may stumble somewhere, and the police may punish him in the course of crossing the road. Some of the former probabilities may disappear while others continue to exist after he crosses the road. A number of problems arise in case of an accident. If he crosses the road safely, he comes across the same kind of situation and the possibilities of a new accident begin. The series of probabilities and accidents exist continually till the last. We always walk safely. All possibilities end with death. These possibilities exist as long as lives exist in the world. As we walk, we face and are safe from incidents and accidents between probabilities and accidents.

This probability also occurs in the case of plants and animals. Plants and animals also experience fear according to their consciousness. They also struggle between probability and accidents during their lives.

End Notes:

1. Birendra Prasad Mishra, *Introduction to Philosophy*, Nepal Charity Foundation, 2065 v.s p. 119.
2. Birendra Prasad Mishra, *Introduction to Philosophy*, Nepal Charity Foundation, 2065 v.s p. 42.
3. Birendra Prasad Mishra, *Introduction to Philosophy*, Nepal Charity Foundation, 2065 v.s p. 61.
4. Pempa Tamang, *Creator*, Western Sikkim Literature, India, Sikkim, Issue 56, Year 28, 2006, p. 65.

22

Life Directed by Fear

Considerable discussion has been undertaken among people in the course of the evolution of fear. A large section of the people agree that life is conducted, directed, and controlled by fear, whereas some people disagree with it. They argue that there are some sectors and subjects out of the impact of fear: entertainment, games, luxury, love, happiness, desires, pleasure, etc. First thing! Entertainment, sports, luxury, love, happiness, desires, and pleasures cannot bypass the fear. As we listen to music, we fear ear damage, power cuts, small voices, and uninteresting songs. Likewise, fear always exists even at the time of watching a movie and playing sports. When some people live in a house, they fear that the house may crumble and an earthquake may occur meanwhile. Hence, we don't find any area or sector in life which has not been influenced by fear. However, fear affects everything in some way. The only thing is that some people accept it at once, whereas others don't. Those who don't accept it are obliged to realise the effect of fear sooner or later.

Let us consider! A man is walking on the road. Logic says that the man doesn't have fear while walking on the road. The man, in fact, walks on the road due to problems, work, or purpose. Only few people wander without any purpose. Fear is a causing factor for purpose, work, problems, anxiety, etc. When he sees a snake, ditch, steep hill, vehicle, etc. while walking, then his fear starts. They look as if they don't create fear, but the man who walks is always guided by fear. Fear directs the man to his work, business, and when he goes somewhere. However, there are reasons behind all the actions, and we find fear behind the reasons. A man proceeds with these activities to emancipate him from these problems even for the time being. Again, these subjects appear and disappear from birth to death and probability to accident. When we suffer so much from fear, we want to get involved in these forms of entertainments for the moment. People do not desire entertainment, sports, happiness, and want to be blissful without any reason. Most probably, work, troubles, suffering, anxiety, disease, fear, problems, doubt, confusion, as well as other things are behind all of them. There is a greater possibility of defeat, wounds, as well as the possibility of falling over. We have also seen, heard, and faced lots of problems occurring as we try to get involved in entertainment. If the people who play cards, drink alcohol, go for a picnic, or make a pilgrimage have an accident, a lot of problems arise and ultimately fear increases. These subjects are not only fearful, but also fear-centred.

As a matter of fact, this subject occupies a small part of life. Entertainment, sports, and tours come as a complement to fear or they take place to give relief for the time being as fear continues to trouble us. This is an attempt to hide or to have emancipation from trouble, suffering, disease, anxiety, fear, doubt, illusion, terror, problems, as we are so tired due to heavy works. They are not used separately. The rich have a lot of entertainment, luxury, etc., whereas the poor have some of them. These things give relief to life to some extent and make it a bit normal. When we play or watch a drama, movie, or game, we forget our trouble, anxiety, problems, or any other things for a moment. We just feel relief when we listen to the music. Therefore, we find a number of people who try to give relief to their mind and heart by listening to the music, as they feel that they have troubles, sufferings, tortures, etc. We try to forget them or console ourselves by means of different forms of entertainment such as cinema, music, sports, sex, etc. when we suffer from worry, anxiety, stress, problems, and fear. But it is very difficult to forget them or console ourselves with those forms of entertainment. Those problems draw our attention at all times, although we do our best. Some such games and forms of entertainment come as a physical exercise. Physical exercise is related to health, life, and death.

Many people are curious whether fear directs life or not. I claim that the fear conducts, directs, and controls life. We have human qualities, temperaments, consciousnesses with us internally. Human qualities and temperaments result in jealousy, hatred, work, anger, enchantment, ego, doubt, etc. They are the seeds of fear. Is it possible for all the things to be produced? They all have direct and indirect fears. They are all consciousnesses. Consciousness causes hatred sometimes, whereas it brings temptation and doubt at other times. Does life based on suspicion continue? Does enchantment help life continue? How does one continue? What are the conditions of roads? What are the problems? Who are the enemies? All these questions come at once. Fear exists along with all these things. We cannot reach anywhere if we cannot care, walk, and solve them. Fear controls and directs us towards the destination. These are the ways how we understand lives. Excessive quantity can cause the destruction. Anarchism takes place in society. If they remain positive, they guide society towards progress. Obviously, jealousy, hatred, sex, anger, ego, enchantment, and suspicion come and go like a game of hide and seek. Likewise, fear doesn't exist continually. Fear appears as we think about an event and thing. This is like the sun and its shadow. Where there is a shadow, there is the fulfillment of human temperaments. A shadow only appears sometimes when it is sunny, but the sun always shines. There are different thoughts to describe music, games, life, and the world. Fear seems to direct them in spite of different thoughts. Man has outwardly assumed that God and invisible powers direct, protect, and care for our lives and the world. Any power can be presented in front of the curtain, but no one can reject fear inside the curtain. The more we reject it, the more it becomes fearful. After all, we perform these activities unknowingly for protection and emancipation from the fear.

I, therefore, strongly argue that fear guides the man. Fear guides the man for what work he does, what he cares about and controls and continues and what work he conducts and looks after. What happens when we go ahead? What happens when we go back? What happens if we stop in the middle part? Fear is the astrology of these questions. Guardians, teachers, health workers, and security guards warn, control, guide, direct, and look after children until they grow conscious. The children also take care of themselves. We control and direct children after their birth until they are grown up. If he doesn't eat well and study well or become undisciplined and disobedient, we fear that his life will be troublesome, problematic, and painful in the days to come. We send him to a good school and college for his education. We also instruct him at home when he commits small mistakes and try to make him disciplined. We scold, threaten, torture, punish, and tempt him. We try our best to make him good. We do all these things so that he can't be out of track, join bad company, and get involved in drug addiction. We fear that he follows a wrong way if he joins bad company. Similarly, we provide him with different medicines, injections, and give him healthy food.

These are basic things for human beings. We continue with them in the theory of lives even if we grow up. As the man grows up, he fears, 'I may become ruined.' He fears ruin. He takes care of it and carefully works for his progress. Those who don't fear these things and become careless can't progress in their lives. We always do work like eating, drinking, walking, playing, reading, writing, speaking, and dealing, etc. carefully. We are afraid to be ruined, cheated, robbed, and to fail. We fear whether food contains nutrition or not. If food doesn't contain nutrition, we will be unhealthy and ill. Fear urges a student to choose a particular subject. His mistake in subject selection ruins his future, and a minor mistake will prove to be big later in his life. Therefore, fear is behind work, decisions, and behaviour of man.

Fear conducts, directs, and controls how a man eats, drinks, lives, walks, plays, thinks, reads, and writes from his childhood. Fear controls and warns him sometimes, whereas it guides and directs him in other times. Such kinds of carefulness, control, activeness, and balance are available in different sectors in which people are involved. We have several types of fears while thinking about carefulness, control, balance, and activeness. Housewives, officials, business people, politicians, and social workers all apply these tools of fear. Those who are out of these tools are certainly unsuccessful and undisciplined. Similarly, rascals, cheats, burglars, robbers, murderers, and terrorists have to use some more tools of fear compared to honest and straightforward persons. If they are not able to control themselves carefully, they not only get punished because of their offence, but also, they may lose their lives and be seriously injured in the encounter with the police, army, or the public. That is why we use fear weapons carefully.

Man has adopted fear normally since prehistoric times. Those who consider it normal can disagree with this theory. See! Which one is the human activity which is not guided and controlled by fear? Fear controls, directs, conducts, makes aware, and balances human activity. It is because of fear that man is controlled, aware, disciplined, obedient, and honest. Where is the destination of young people? What about the future of children, business, weather, and climate depends on fear? We work, make plans, and make rules and regulations due to this fear. It may not be an exaggeration to say that fear directs life, as everything has been guided, controlled, and warned since the prehistoric period to the present. It is applicable to society, nation, and international sectors.

23

Word as a Medium for Fear

Transformation, change, difference, void, and emergence, including some other words like these are mediums for transformations into other forms due to self or external factors. These words are often used to express activities occurring in transformation from one form into another one. Transformation and parts are possible due to this medium. To appear from one form into another is called transformation by some people and change by other people. If we study it in detail, we find some differences. Mostly people consider transformation and change as synonyms to each other. Transformation, change, difference, and emergence are often used in spoken language, whereas void and difference are mostly used in a philosophical language. We should study parts of the meanings to clarify it.

Restlessness, anxiety, suffering, sorrow, fright, terror, and fear have also been used to give similar meanings. The meanings of some words are similar, whereas others are slightly different. There are some other words that are much more different from the rest. If we take the words restlessness, anxiety, suffering, and sorrow normally, they are similar to each other. Similarly, anxiety and fear are supposed to be similar. Fear differs even because of understanding and feelings. Thus, we should study meaning as parts. Meaning and understanding becomes clear after studying their parts.

a. Transformation, Change, Difference, Void, and Emergence

Transformation *(rupantaran)*

Transformation indicates changes in forms and changes in languages. It is the expression of activities while transforming from one to another. When the word is inflected, it is *rup+antar* and becomes *rupantaran* (transformation). It is mostly applicable to visible objects. For example:— When a bud blossoms, it transforms into flower.

Change

Change is due to external but not due to internal forces. The term change is proper for weather instead of transformation. If a rock appears more different from the previous form, it's a change, but not a transformation.

Transformation and change almost have the same sense: First is a change due to external force and the second is change itself.

Difference

The term difference indicates parts. Its meaning is one object, but the meaning of the object is another. Life and the world exist due to its difference from the meaning. The same object and meaning also have lots of parts. Objects and meanings differ due to these parts. The object is formed by the combination of these differences. They are all connected to each other. The whole object made by the combination of all the differences is the world and the universe. Difference is a medium. Stone and soil are different objects. Maybe stone transforms into soil and soil transforms into stone. They will transform into another object after hundreds and thousands years. An object consists of different atoms. The water that has flown down and the water that has filled the blank space are different, although they look similar. Similarly, the meaning used a bit earlier and a bit later are different. The things that are on the both sides of the void, meaning, feeling, value, and norm are different.

A new meaning constitutes from a number of other meanings. We combine meanings to form a language to use in our lives. The real value of language is in meanings but not in letters, words, and sentences. Man is constituted with bone, muscles, senses, nerves, and blood. The word 'man' indicates a completed man, but not bone, muscles, senses, nerves, and blood. Similarly, a language is formed from meanings. It has been interpreted in this way.

Void

The word void is often used by nihilists in Buddhism. In an example of running water, nihilists say—Void exists between the water that flows and the water comes to fill the space. The new water fills that space. A gap between differences is void. The world is void. New things are supplied here. Thus, void and supply exist everywhere in the world. This void, in fact, is the world and the lives. An object that comes to fill the gap doesn't come anywhere else. It is somewhere hidden, suppressed, and blocked. A void exists as differences move. It presents itself in an appropriate period. This is the same way the meaning has been constructed.

Emergence

Emergence is the condition in which something invisible becomes visible, exists, or emerges. Emergence is the new form, meaning, feeling, value, norm, and experience that are seen, heard, and understood when they form a transition from one difference to another through a void. We see, hear, understand, and feel this emergence. It emerges from somewhere. Here, somewhere indicates the study of the parts of a straight line. If we divide consciousness into different parts and study life and the world, it becomes a part of every moment and an emergence exists continually in the part. The thing, meaning, norms, and values that have remained somewhere hidden, suppressed, and dominated emerge as new forms. In other words, existence of the same thing, meaning, norms, and values through turning over, addition, and increment due to themselves or external forces is called an emergence. Therefore, all things, meanings, norms, and values emerge differently from one part into another. Biological objects have to struggle in a transition from one part to another. It doesn't occur through a regular process, but through parts. Life and the world are made of parts. They exist from one part to another. If they haven't been studied in parts, how can we distinguish hot and cold, cold and lukewarm, and unconscious and conscious? Countless parts exist between unconscious and conscious. We should study, measure, and realise everything in these parts like the parts of a thermometer: 1, 2, 3. Object, meaning, belief, and realisation are like these numbers on the thermometer. Only then do we know emergence in every part. A new emergence exists by listening, seeing, experiencing, speaking, and reading a small part. It has knowledge and physical body, because internal and external factors always influence parts. This is a medium. These parts proceed through the medium of this emergence. It doesn't exist itself, but by means of struggle.

b. Agitation, Anxiety, Pain, Suffering, Fright, Dread, Horror, and Fear

These words sound synonymous to each other. Almost, they have similar senses. If we go deeper down, they appear dissimilar in meaning. If these words are identified in terms of their meaning, it is easy to understand fear. Thought exists in the human mind at first and then it expands and divides—restlessness, anxiety, pain, etc. They are not identified separately in the beginning. Where they go depends on conditions and circumstances. A man wears a mask, cap, and shoes because of fear at first. Then he adds his desires to it and wants their designs. Similarly, fear occurs at first and then anxiety while crossing the road. There is the fear of an accident in the beginning. Afterwards, the fear of injury arises. Then he worries and fears that his family may have trouble. Consciousness or the brain knows about it then we start to think. These are like the scenes of a movie—display of scenes one after another. Anxieties are like when sometimes the scenes of fears display on the screen of the brain and repeats itself. They are repeating thoughts. It is not homogeneous to repeat. It's so pervasive. Pervasiveness can be seen on the face or in some physical activities, but the concerned person may not know anything about it. In such a case, we often ask this question: 'What has happened to you?' We know about him only when he tells us. They can be further clarified through the activities of animals.

Agitation

Agitation is the condition of instability, embarrassment, frustration, nervousness, and boredom. This is an immediate happening caused by a bad imagination. Man is so restless in such a condition. His activities are also unstable. He walks here and there. For instance, a woman is in a delivery room and her husband is waiting outside. He is so restless. He is confused with what to do and what not to do. He is not only anxious, but he is fearful as well. He's busy thinking about what will happen.

Anxiety

Worries, anxiety, concentration, attention, thought, and concepts are sentiments. It is to think about something. A person wants to stay somewhere else to think and drinks while thinking. It is both short and long-term. This is a condition in which he struggles with his problem. He has some time to solve the problem and he carries on thinking about a way of having relief from the problem at that time. Let us think! He has a financial crisis. He deeply thinks about a solution. It's an anxiety. Figure No. 58 shows fear inside anxiety. Fear makes the man much more fearful. It is related to circumstance and condition. It's a way to be aware of fear. The brain gets information about anxiety much faster than the sense organs.

Pain

Suffering, torture, trouble, lamentation, grief or sorrow, disease, epidemic, obstruction, difficulty, mental disorder, and mental illness depend on the condition of the mind. It is related to some type of physical pain. If the body has suffered from physical pain or giving pain and being wounded, they give pain. We think less in such a condition, because it helps to produce energy to be tolerant. It breaks out abruptly in some cases and lasts for a long time. Man begins to fear because of the effect produced by the suffering or pain. He can't think a lot when he has suffering. Muscles, glands, and senses know the suffering at first and consciousness feels it later.

Suffering

Trouble, suffering, worry, illness, disease, etc. are related to grief. This is also suffering, but it is the condition in which the problem grows serious slowly and gradually. For instance, the problem of a pregnant woman in a delivery room grows serious gradually; it is assumed that she has started to be in a painful situation. Similarly, if a man who always suffers from a disease has some symptoms in the beginning, he and his relatives understand that he has started having the problem of a painful situation. At first, the sense organs receive sorrow and suffering, and then they are received by consciousness. Fear begins to exist when consciousness receives them.

According to Martin Heidegger, 'Pain/sorrow is a basic element of existence. Human life is full of suffering and pain. So, fear is a part of suffering and pain. The man always suffers from the fear of death. Thus, suffering/pain is related to death.'[1] He has considered pain as a major one and fear as minor one. I have mentioned above about pain, i.e. pain + fear = fear. Martin Heidegger, an atheist existentialist philosopher, has claimed that life is full of pain and suffering. Let us intermingle between suffering and fear and pain and fear. In fact, life is full of fear, instead of pain/suffering. Deeper meaning of full of suffering is full of fear.

Fright

Fear, dread, and suffocation are related to fright. It is a kind of realisation, thought, and reflection from listening, seeing, understanding, and thinking about a subject. It is often short-term. It is produced from unexpected calamities. If it is kept in mind, it is said, 'The mind suffers from fear.' It looks certain. For instance—it is said that we feel fright when we see a dead body, a grave, or a violent animal. We tend to be afraid in such a condition. Consciousness directs the physical organs to be careful about any situations when fright exists.

Dread

Dread is an interior feeling of fright, fear, threat, suspicion, suffocation, etc. This is realisation of fear when we hear and witness dreadful things. Facial expression also looks dreadful in such a condition. It's a feeling produced from explosion and accident that has already occurred. It is short-term. Man feels dread when he sees severe destruction due to war. When people feel dread, the consciousness alerts sense organs and muscles.

Horror

Restlessness, instability, and threat produced from dread and fright indicate the state of horror. It is like dread. This is a condition based on dreadful and unpleasant accidents. In such a situation, the man seeks a secure place and hides in the corner.

Fear

Fright + dread + horror = fear or fear is a combined form of fright, dread, and horror. Fear exists in agitation produced from dreadful imagination and mental condition for anxiety, fright, dread, horror, restlessness, suffering, pain, sorrow, etc. Fear is, indeed, a combined form of dread, fear, and horror. It is invisible. It is not immediately visible but draws the mind. Fear exists when dreadful thoughts take place in the mind of the existence of possible accidents and incidents and horrific objects. It is long-term, pervasive, and vast. Fear is in any subject. It is not clearly visible from the front, but it remains effective from the back like in the under eraser of Derrida. It exists in suspicion, jealousy, conspiracy, murder, violence, ego, hatred, temptation, anger, rule, law, religion, culture, discipline, conservation, superstition, civilisation, etc.[2]

However, fear cannot be measured; it can be understood through different activities and symptoms. We have never realized the worry of animals, but if specialists know about it, it's a different matter. We can realise that animals can be fearful, victimised, and emotional.

The weak animals erect their ears when they see hunters and strong animals. This is a condition of fear. It's a reaction against incident/accident, which has already been informed. Then, he makes his attempt for his security as far as possible, both from hunters and strong and big animals. When the hunter attacks, the animal becomes wounded that gives pain. Other animals that witness this become restless, dreadful, and horrified. Activities they perform then show fear, pain, and agitation. It shows that animals don't show anxiety. They sound the same, but they differ based on condition, action, and reaction. We can conduct a study on pain, suffering, and anxiety of man via different symptoms, and if we conduct his treatment accordingly, it could bring a huge revolution in medical sectors.

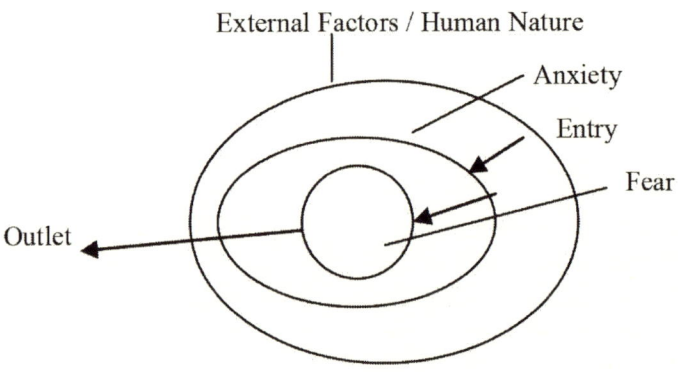

Figure No. 58

Figure No. 58 shows human nature on the outside layer. Different problems and anxieties happen to take place due to human nature and external factors—it's a way to create fear. Similarly, as the figure shows, nature enters inside and has become anxiety. Then the same anxiety enters inside and it becomes fear. We do too many activities to come out of this fear in our lives.

Human nature, exceptionally, goes to fear instead of anxiety. Thus, our temperaments generate anxiety and then anxiety generates fear. Therefore, human temperament is an exterior form, anxiety is deeper inside, and fear is the deepest inside. To look around fear is cognition. Our activities are oriented towards salvation and emancipation.

Taitariyopanishad has said that the man who knows such a bliss which is in the cave of sky. That soul or bliss of living beings and the soul of solar systems are the same. Who knows first it he remains secular to this world and remains fearless. Then he knows the soul of a grain, the soul of the mind within it, then the soul of the heart within it. Similarly the soul of science within it and finally the soul of bliss within it.(2/8/12) [3]

c. Fear in Error, False Concept, Illusion, Accusation, and Guilt

They can be seen by dividing it into four parts.

1. Fear in Error Theory of Freud
2. Fear in False Concept Theory of Francis Bacon
3. Fear in Illusion of Rope Snake of Shankaracharya
4. Fear in *Lilabhram* of Indra Bahadur Rai
5. Fear in Accusation, Guilt

1. Fear in Error Theory of Freud

Freud has interpreted small errors in his error theory that occur in our daily lives. He has divided them as:

1. Mistake in recognition
2. Forgetting names
3. Slip of pen
4. Slip of tongue
5. Misprints
6. Mislaying of objects
7. Erroneously carried out actions
8. Symptomatic acts[4]

Other errors than what Freud interpreted may occur. Fear occurs when man knows that he has made an error. Obviously, error may show other symptoms, such as doubt, anxiety, etc. However, fear is the final point for all of them and fear produces anxiety, problems, etc.

Man commits such errors knowingly and unknowingly. He knows some of his errors, but the rest of them remain unknown. It is not that all the errors cause fear. But most of the errors cause fear. There are more than eight kinds of errors that Freud has interpreted. Fear depends on their temperaments. Let us think! A man made a mistake to beat another man to death. He who beats doesn't know about it. He doesn't fear unless he knows about it. If the incident did not result in death, his fear could be based on an incident and accident. If a man is accused of murder, he feels fright and horror. The reason behind it is that it is a severe crime, unpardonable. It is related to human life. The case is appealed in the court for prosecution. Law demands proof for the conviction. It can not abide law and cannot claim that the man has not committed the crime. There is some kind of saying in Nepali that 'If you do the right thing, you don't have to worry.' It can only be implemented in general accusation, not in horrified accusation. Let us consider! Someone writes 6 instead of 5; it's an error. It doesn't have impact on every case. But if the same thing is repeated in an exam, it can be a blunder. As a result, he might fail in his exam. If somebody is paid Rs. 10 instead of Rs. 5, it's not big enough to create fear. But if in case he paid Rs. 5000 instead of Rs. 5, that creates a big fear. Severity of error depends on circumstance and condition. The sum of Rs. 5,000 is a huge amount for workers, whereas it's not a big amount for wealthy people.

'No mistake, no fear' is a common Nepali proverb. It is normal in normal cases, so people use it. If we go deeper inside the interpretation of this proverb, we find much significance in our lives. A question is, do we fear only when we commit an error?

Error can be a source of fear. Freud has interpreted error in detail. I have made an attempt to interpret fear from the same interpretation of error.

According to the Nepali proverb presented above, only those who make a mistake suffer from fear. We can analyse it on the basis of the work in the centre. The proverb seems to have two things: one commits or doesn't commit a mistake. Let us consider it again! Someone has committed a mistake, but he doesn't know anything about his mistake. He doesn't fear such a condition. He behaves as if he is innocent. He walks, eats, and drinks normally. When he knows he has committed a mistake or somebody tells him that he has committed a mistake, the fear starts in him. It continues until it is solved.

Let us consider! A man has a job. He is doubtful that he has made a mistake in his work. That suspicion creates fear. Similarly, a man feels fear when he leaves his house unlocked or leaves his children alone at home. Some of the fears last long.

It is not that only those who make an error or mistake have fear. We have said that fear exists both in *chha* and *chhaina* as mentioned above. It means fear exists in both *chha* and *chhaina* as well as in their gaps, but the possibility also exists in this gap. This gap is filled with suspicion, illusion, jealousy, anger, etc., and there exists fear. A man thinks he has made a mistake in more than 50 per cent of his work. He doesn't know whether he was right or wrong. We can claim we are right, but we may be wrong as well.

When he knows his errors, he becomes suspicious and feels sad. Different categories of errors exist. Suspicion, trouble, and fear depend on error. Suspicion and trouble originated from error that ends at fear. Think! A man has committed a mistake in his exam; his suspicion, fear, pain, and repentance appear at once. Sometimes, they can happen separately. He is suspicious of his answer. When he comes to know his error, he not only gains knowledge of his error, but also pain. He then suffers from the fear of failure in his exam. He becomes even more fearful when he knows that it blocks his success in the days to come. Then, he chooses a different track for salvation. Some of the people like him drop out of their studies. Many people leave their homes. Some of them choose business, and a few of them choose suicide. These are all results of fear produced from errors.

2. Fear in False Concept Theory of Francis Bacon

Francis Bacon has divided false concept theory into four parts:

a. First, false concepts come out from the brain automatically. People look at all objects from human perspectives and consider them for human use.

b. Second, false concepts are individual and they depend on education and temperaments.

c. Third, false concepts are the most difficult, since they are produced from cooperation or contact of names and words, as the words are used for names.

d. Fourth, false concepts originate from false theories and philosophies.[5]

I have briefly interpreted them here: a. We can study fear in parts on the basis of the interpretation of the false concept of Bacon. Socrates used a triangle for his interpretation on faith. Later, Rene Descartes agreed with it and he claimed we have inborn faith. Due to this faith, man looks at everything from his perspective and considers everything for his use. This is a human perspective. No doubt this universe is supposed to be for human use. Otherwise, who will use it? Who will interpret it? When we think it's a false concept, we start to fear. b. We have some education and some temperaments. We look at life and the world through the education we gain. It's human nature to claim what we know is right and what others know is wrong. Other people understand the same. As people understand in this way, the conflict occurs. If it continues to increase, it results in conflicts and wars. I have mentioned above that fear exists due to human causes. Extremism in education or temperament brings merely problems. These all increase fear. Fear doesn't exist unless we know our errors. Here, Bacon started his work with false concept theory. Fear appears as this theory appears. c. His third concept is based on false concept on name and word. We know that the names we have understood, heard, known, and explained are false, and if it affects someone, then no doubt fear exists. Discussing false meanings, Ferdinand de Saussure, a linguist, has also said that the word and the sign are arbitrary in relation. Similarly, a conditional reflex of Pavlov also includes this subject. Logic has also been made that no word can give the original meaning of a thing. Whatever meaning of a word we know and understand in the beginning, we understand it differently until we know it. We have understood that the meaning of the word 'ghost' is 'dangerous and man-eating' at present. Perhaps its meaning didn't exist like this in the beginning. Thus, if a word and name are wrong and anxiety and doubt grow up, it turns out to be fear. d. The knowledge we gain doesn't completely understand theory, formula, and philosophy. We perceive them on the basis of our knowledge. First and foremost, understanding of them depends on what knowledge and education we have. As we haven't studied theories of science and literature, we face a number of difficulties in understanding them. It's a human temperament not to agree with others. We fear when we know we have made false interpretation of theory and philosophy.

Our innate knowledge and faith are original. We gain knowledge on faith. Knowledge exits out automatically. Some of our knowledge is innate, and we get some of them when we are taught and we gain some of them through reading, listening, and witnessing. They combine to construct knowledge. We talk, discuss, debate, and argue about life, the world, society, and country the way how we have learnt and understood. This is how a strong foundation is constructed. We work to defend it if somebody tries to shake the foundation. When we come to know our understanding and concepts are wrong, we feel uncomfortable. Then we may get scolded and boycotted in some cases. We have to beg pardon and be ready for punishment in many cases.

The scientists of the Manhattan Project invented atom bombs, Little Boy and Fat Man, that were used in the Second World War. The scientist Albert Einstein was also involved in the project. They experimented atom bombs later. When they witnessed the horrific destruction of these two bombs, they were very afraid. As the explosion caused massacres, they thought it was a blunder to invent such weapons. There are too many theories and discoveries. They have two roads: one is to go continuously and another is to look around. If man doesn't look around and think about what he does, then the fear doesn't exist, but if he looks around and finds what he does is wrong, it brings fear. It is not only applicable to discovery, but it is equally applicable to the lives of ordinary people. Thus, wherever he finds a mistake, the fear starts right from there.

More than four false concepts presented by Bacon may occur in life. If suspicion, illusion, and anxiety are added to these concepts, they are much more severe. Then, it expands fear. Thus, knowledge after false concept and error creates fear.

3. Fear in Illusion

There are different types of illusions. Out of them, the illusion of the rope snake and *Lilabhram* are much more popular. How do these illusions produce fear? I have made my attempt to find out the answer.

a.   Fear in Rope Snake of Shankaracharya

Shankaracharya, a pioneer of monism, has presented the example of a rope snake. A man saw something like a snake in the dark and he was continuously afraid. When he saw the same thing early the next morning, he came to know it was a rope, not a snake. The same logic is often used in many countries. Such an illusion can occur in the daytime too. If he is far from the rope and can't identify it well, he may take it as a snake and fear continues to occur. A number of such snakes, tigers, jackals, etc. may be seen at night. We can't identify whether that is real or illusion. On the other hand, if we take life and the world as an illusion, according to Shankaracharya, the people who are confused can't identify an illusion and truth. The man who is free from illusion can only know illusion and truth. If we are in illusion, we only see illusion. That is to say, someone should help us to know the thing that we have seen. Shankaracharya is also an illusion if the whole world is an illusion. An illusion doesn't include the truth.

If eyes witness other things instead of truth, it's an illusion. Man sees illusion either in the dark or from a distance. He can see a stump, rock, stream, and steep land as a ghost, phantom, man, or animal. Moreover, if he is much more fearful, they appear much more horrific. This is an illusion. Such an illusion troubles man, especially in a lonely place, in the dark and in a forest, because he has already been fearful. Such a horrified man does right, wrong, and does something other. Similarly, such illusions exist in sounds or looks.

The man is afraid, as mentioned above, with a rope in the dark. This is only an illusion. He is unafraid when he sees the rope as rope, but not as a snake. Suppose he has an illusion that it remains as a snake until he knows the truth. Thus, the rope snake is an easier example to present here. It is applicable to every case. We take off our shoes when we go to a temple; we wear ritual clothes and ornaments, and we believe in unequal citizens. These are like rope snakes to some extent. Reality is beyond such an illusive world. We are trapped in the illusion. All these unreal pictures made by religious books, such as superstitions, conservatism, legends, Mahabharat, Ramayan, Upanishads, Bible, Koran, etc. are like, as claimed above, the rope snake. Ghosts, phantoms, demons, devils, and witch (*chudel*)are also like this. All of them become snakes and sting us until we know that they are just ropes and not snakes. Such superstition and conservatism are troubling us and we take them as a snake. We are, thus, living under illusion. In fact, all of them are rope snakes.

There are many types of suspicions and illusions. All suspicions and illusions don't frighten us equally. It is known that all of them threaten us more or less. It depends on rationality, tolerant power, and quantity of consciousness. For instance, all the people do not get startled seeing a rope as a snake. Some people look at the rope carefully, whereas others don't, like the clever prisoner of Plato. Some conclude that it is a rope. Some think that a snake can't be available so easily. Such suspicion and illusion prevail among husbands and wives and friends and relatives. We suffer from such suspicions and illusions. It is so pervasive in our societies.

We walk so comfortably until we witness a rope snake. Our activities get minimised as we witness it. That illusion troubles us, then—we lose our freedom. If we see a real snake, it can't be an illusion. But to see a rope as a snake is an illusion.

Consciousness and knowledge undergo illusion and deception while trying to understand life and the world. All conservation, superstition, religion, language, script, and culture are developed for bondage and illusion. We have been like the donkeys of Samasuddin in some cases because of this illusion. Several philosophies have come into being in order to interpret the illusion.

There was a man named Samasuddin. He had a donkey. He used to ride his donkey in order to go to his fields. He used to tie his donkey to a post and used to work the whole day. Then, he used to come back home in the evening.

One day, he rode his donkey to his field as usual. As he tried to tie his donkey to the post, he realised he forgot to bring the rope that day. He was in a crisis. He asked his donkey to stand in the usual place, but it immediately went to the field of another to graze. He brought back his donkey. The same thing repeated many times. He was so tired with his donkey. He could not work continuously.

Meanwhile, Sufi was going to a nearby market through the area. He was watching the game. He asked, 'Why are you doing this?'

Samasuddin explained his entire problems.

Sufi advised, 'Act as if you are tying your donkey as usual. He will stand there then.'

At first, Samasuddin didn't believe him. He acted as if he tied his donkey as usual when Sufi convinced him. The donkey thought that he was tied as before and continued to stand there. Sufi went to the market. And he started to work.

The sun set. It was time to go back home. He got on his donkey, but it didn't walk. Samasuddin had a problem again. Then he went to the nearby market to look for Sufi. Luckily, he was able to see Sufi nearby. He explained about his problems again.

Sufi asked, 'Did you untie your donkey?'

He told Sufi that he hadn't untied his donkey.

So, Sufi told him to act as if he had untied his donkey. So, he did. The donkey thought that he was untied and started to walk.

In this way, we always feel as if we have been tied to all things such as society, country, law, culture, language, script, and religion. No one has anchored us, in fact. It is just an illusion like a rope snake. This illusion brings lots of changes in our lives. We act as if we are anchored. To feel as if we are anchored is like a donkey. We regard it as a snake and become frightened.

b.   Fear in *Lilabhram* of Indra Bahadur Rai

In the declaration of *Lilabhram*, 'Bhrantiharu ra Lila Lekhan matra', Indra Bahadur Rai illustrates, 'When Krishna was entering, Mallas saw *Bajra* male, females saw statue like *Kamdeva*, ordinary people saw *Nawaratna*, *Gopas* saw *Swajan*, those who were ruled saw those whose works were to punish, old people saw murdering, *Kansa* saw *Karal Kal*, *Abidashes* saw *Birat*, *Yogis* saw *Paramtatva* and *Brishnis* saw *Istadev* in *Krishna Sabha*.'[6] Shreemat Bhagwat Gita 10/43/17

As blind people explained an elephant differently after their sensation, likewise, people saw Krishna differently in different forms. Those who examined the elephant were blind and understood it differently. They could understand the same elephant differently even if they weren't blind. Whether the eye is closed or open, it doesn't matter. It depends on sense organs. Sense organs, heredity, consciousness, knowledge, and a conditional reflex are the reasons behind it.

Thus, people perceive different forms, colours, and shapes of the same object. The reasons for it are difference of consciousness, knowledge, heredity, and a conditional reflex. Time doesn't remain still. It is not the question of different persons; the same person finds the same thing change in varying time. Either the person or the goods may move from the original place. The same thing doesn't change if the man and the object remain still. It's not possible for an object to remain stable. Any solid thing we think is still is internally moving very fast, like Brown Motion. Change is not clearly visible through the naked eye. Trillions of cells of human beings move continuously, so people witness the same thing differently at different times. Whatever messages the consciousness and knowledge receive remain unstable. The thing that was seen as red a bit earlier may be seen as light red a bit later. The food that was sweet a bit earlier may be tasteless a bit later. So, everything is unstable in the world. Again, different visual perceptions are merely illusions. No truth is final and stable. Similarly, it's not possible for people from different classes, professions, communities, and sectors to see the same thing differently.

Lilabhram interpreted by Indra Bhahadur Rai is an illusion, as mentioned above, in people. They witness the same thing differently. Heredity, conditional reflexes, consciousness, knowledge, feeling, understanding, perspective, speaking, and education change at a high speed constantly. As mentioned, people witness the same thing differently, like the rope snake of Shankaracharya. As a result, the decision of a man differs in the same movie, same book, and same game. Some people like something very much, while other people don't like it so much. It depends on the person, subject, situation, and time. The same illusion is applied when looking at Krishna. It's different from the illusion of Shankaracharya, because he says that the same man sees the same thing differently at different times and places. According to *Lilabhram* of Indra Bahadur Rai, many people see the same thing differently. Many other illusions exist beyond these two illusions.

We shouldn't feel horrified due to this illusion. We are never confined within illusion. Illusion has periphery around it. It has a way out. Many things move around this periphery. Of them, fear is very effective. Fear guided people to see things differently as illustrated above.

These illusions are not only limited to legends, but also, they are applied to our daily lives. Let us think! We have an illusion about our own wife or husband. It means that we saw him/her walking with someone else. If the man is his friend's wife, it does not draw his attention, although he has an illusion. If the friend doesn't have good manners, doubt and fear begin to exist. Similarly, a wife was seen walking with a male. It may also be an illusion. Suspicion and fear grow up along with such an illusion. If the man was already suspicious, his fear grows more serious. We have to balance and control ourselves to make sensible judgements in such a condition. We are trapped inside by suspicion, fear, hatred, jealousy, and emotion at once. It urges different events. Those events and accidents can cause fear over again.

In a paper presentation in Gejing, Sikkim, India Pempa Tamang said, 'Indra Bahadur Rai has used the term *Lilabram* instead of illusion, suspicion, doubt, and confusion or dilemma.'[7]

Fear is a medium. Illusion, suspicion, temptation, jealousy, shyness, and inferioty exist in fear at first and grow up gradually. Some of them disappear themselves, and the rest of them try to exist through fear. To live with illusion is meaningless. Similarly, suspicion, temptation, jealousy, shyness, and inferiority do not exist for long.

They enter fear and some of them grow up and try to exist out to inferiority. Fear itself mingles with inferiority. Figure No. 59 further clarifies it.

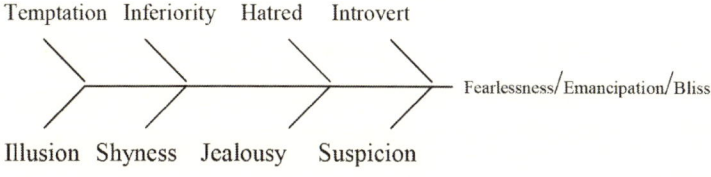

Figure No. 59

Figure No. 59 presents the man with illusion, suspicion, temptation, jealousy, shyness, and inferiority. They all intermingle with fear. They all don't intermingle at once but gradually, one after another. It helps to go from one side to another. Illusion, suspicion, and temptation can reach the other side only through this medium. Fear is a whirlwind that remains revolving in a place. Illusion exists out from the fear as it remains rotating.

4. Fear in Accusation and Guilt

Even an ordinary man who is innocent becomes fearful when he is accused of a crime. There are a lot of examples in which innocent people have been punished. He is fearful if the man who accused him is powerful. He is fearful because the police and army arrest him, send him to a prison, punish him, and torture him, society and family take him as a bad or dishonest person, and he has to collect evidence to prove himself innocent. Again, he is not sure of winning the case. Those who are accused of murder, rape, theft, and robbery are fearful. Some of them eventually and circumstantially consider themselves responsible for incidents and accidents. Thus, they are fearful despite the fact that they are innocent. Some people themselves admit their crimes and try to work for purgation. Fear starts when other people come to know about such crimes.

End Notes:

1. Mohan Raj Sharma, Khagendra Prasad Luitel, *Eastern and Western Literary Theory*, Kathmandu, 2063 v.s. p. 344.
2. Basanta Kumar Sharma Nepal, *Nepali Shabdasagar (Nepali Vocabulary)*, Kathmandu, 2061 v.s. p. 1233, 440, 843, 1232, 580, 629, 1278, 995.
3. Arjundev Panta, *Bedanta-Darshan Sar (Brief Vedaanta Philosophy)*, Ratna Book Store, Kathmandu, 2062 v.s. p. 12.
4. Mohan Raj Sharma, Khagendra Prasad Luitel, *Eastern and Western Literary Theory*, Kathmandu, 2063 v.s. p. 179.
5. Birendra Prasad Misra, *Darshan Shashtra Parichaya (Introduction to Philosophy)*, Nepal Charity Foundation, Kathmandu, 2065 v.s p. 25, 28.
6. Indra Bahadur Rai, *Creator*, Western Sikkim Literature, Sikkim, 2006, Issue 56, p. 14.
7. Pempa Tamang, *Creator*, Western Sikkim Literature, Sikkim, 2006, Issue 56, p. 60.

24

Fear Struggle

In the essence of the Communist manifesto, Marx and Engels said, 'The history of society is the history of class struggle so far.'[1]

But I don't think so. Everyone has a fear struggle in his/her life. S/he passes away one day in the course of struggling with his/her fear. Fear struggle is the life struggle of man. Man and families constitute society. They are in encircle of struggles. Therefore, the history of society is not the history of class struggle, but the history of fear struggle. Its formula is: life—internal conflict—decision—internal struggle—decision—external struggle—life.

At first, a man has life then he has to struggle with his own internal conflicts in his life. He has internal conflict with himself to do any work, make a decision, walk elsewhere, and run a business. A decision is made after a lot of internal conflicts. He follows through with the decision. That decision struggles with other decisions, for others have similar struggles as well. At first, his decision struggles with himself and then his own family, group, class, and society. Afterwards, another decision is made. The man with that decision will struggle with another class, society, and community. He struggles with another class, group, society, and external natural powers at this time. This is the thing the above formula has shown.

Why struggle if a man has no fear? That is why every creature's life is full of struggles.

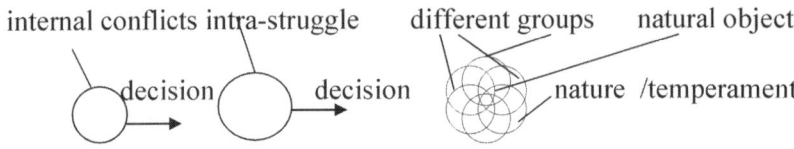

Figure No. 60

Figure No. 60 depicts internal conflicts, decisions, intra-conflicts, decisions, different groups, natural objects, and temperament. A man undergoes internal conflicts, decisions, intra-struggles, decisions, and exterior struggle. Each of them brings fear of defeat and fear of death. This is what we know as a fear struggle.

According to Freud, the life of a man develops through such series of conflicts. There can be several things causing the main tendencies—id, ego, and superego. They may also be based on id. Such conflicts or struggle can happen both at conscious and unconscious levels. Coordination through balance in conflicts can constitute personality.[2]

Decisions produced from intra-conflicts collides with exterior problems and the nature of power. The same thing has been depicted in the figure. People with similar decisions constitute their group. They conduct various activities for further development of their groups. Many groups exist in society. Discussion and disagreement among such groups result in struggle. This is an internal conflict. Exterior struggle occurs only long after the intra-conflicts. The class struggle is one of the external struggles.

All human struggles are struggles for fear—the struggle between liberation and life. Man keeps on struggling with the fear that is within him. Mobility, activity, thinking, and writing are expressions of the same fear. People are always busy playing with fear, escaping fear, and hiding from fear. Although we try our best to escape and hide from fear, it is always within us. This is a fear, and besides this one, there is another fear outside. The fear that is outside appears in different places and times. Its shape, size, and impacts constitute an interior fear. Thought, consciousness, and knowledge adopt, feel, and react to it. The fear struggle always has its own fear. Interior fear expands out and exterior fear expands inside. We are busy with this game. Politics, economics, society, and science are all in this game. Defeat with fear means punishment, failure, and death. A reward for overcoming fear is life. It is not possible to get victory over all fears, but at least we can minimise it through fragmentation and we can get a partial liberation. Fear struggle is a foundation of all struggles, like the class struggle, caste/ethnic struggle, religious struggle, economic struggle, social struggle, and political struggle. Fear is a foundation for whatever struggles exist for existence. In the present world, fear struggle includes issues about non-violence and 'others' in the coexistence of Immanual Levinash, binary oppositions under 'Structure of Language and Culture' of Derrida, 'essence' of Subaltern, Sexual Introduction of Judith Butler, and subaltern of Gayatri Spivak and Michel Foucault.

Today's struggle of fear has been expanding since ancient time. It existed even in the beginning of human civilisation, but it was not as pervasive as it is now. This struggle started out from us and expanded all over. The struggle that began at the earliest still prevails in our society. A man wants to survive himself before he talks about class, relatives, and family during the struggle. Each man struggles with himself first in his class and struggles with others later. There is a struggle with any group in these classes. It can happen to any one. He has to struggle with those who obstruct and compete with him. The reason behind it is the fear. The stronger ones used to oppress and dominate weaker ones in the prehistoric period. Only two classes did not exist in society. There were other classes, like businessmen, artists, literary men, politicians, army, social workers, students, teachers, and job seekers between feudalists and peasants. Feudalists, no doubt, used to exploit the peasants. Let us say there was quicksand and circle of fear. Above all, exploitation used to exist within the same group—exploitation within feudalism and classes/peasants exploited by peasants, politicians exploited by politicians, social workers exploited by social workers, and businessmen exploited by businessmen. They were all exploiting each other. All these people used to be present in the state mechanisms. A root cause of their exploitation was in the fear to survive. They all wanted to survive. The clever people used to use *sam, dam, danda, bhed* (attraction, money, punishment, discrimination) in the struggle. Exploited classes used to struggle with similar groups and feudalists used to struggle with similar groups. These were the struggle of fear. None of them used to desire to lose his/her prestige. They used to play a tricky game of conspiracy, suspicion, murder, and treachery within their own class to preserve their 'I and mine (ego)'. Defeat in this game used to be considered as the loss of prestige, reputation, and respect. It was a root cause of struggle within one's own group. Again, the people of a class were afraid of other classes as well.

The feudalists knew that there would be no one to work in their fields if farmers pursued their rights, justice, and liberty. They tried to suppress the farmers due to this fear, and the farmers desired emancipation from age-long suppression. It was a class in society, but there were several other classes. Some of them used to stand for peasants and the rest of them used to stand for feudalists. Non-participants in these groups used to have a bigger group in societies and they used to have powerful groups. They used to support whoever they liked. A huge struggle used to occur between owners. Their struggle was not oriented to food, clothing, and shelter. Rather, they used to struggle for their name and fame, prestige, luxury, and reputation, because there were many owners of slaves. They used to fear losing property, prestige, reputation, luxury, and name and fame. They used to engage in conspiracy, doubt, discrimination, domination, murder, violence, and treachery with the people of the same class in order to avoid the fear. As a result, murder, rape, massacres, and war among them used to occur. In history, most of the great wars were not fought against slaves; wars also were not fought against other classes.

Think! There are paddy plants in paddy fields. Those plants struggle hard if the field has limited water and fertiliser. Plants with access to fertiliser and water grow well and the rest will dry up. This is the first phase struggle of the plants. Then, they are affected by climate, hail, and storm. Similarly, man and animal also affect them. The impact made by the power of nature, birds, and animals and people is less than the impact of intra-conflicts. First struggles occur within themselves. Like paddy plants, people also struggle first within their own class, caste/ethnic group, religious group, and sector. Only then do they struggle with other classes, other religious groups, and sectors. The first inter-conflicts occur with the nearest one. This process has continued since the ancient age.

See! There are lots of orchid flowers on a tree. The orchid is a parasitic flower. They live with the limited food and water available on the tree. Struggles occur within the circle of orchids first. Orchids with access to water and fertiliser grow well and the rest will dry up. Well-blossomed orchids attract bees and people come to pluck the flowers. Bees are rarely attracted to the flowers, and people hardly go to pluck the flower. The reason is that these flowers struggle first within their own group. Pyramids of fear from the strongest to the weakest is constructed in plants and animals. Fear of birds and animals is visible, whereas fear of plants is invisible. This is a difference between them.

Slaves were like animals in the beginning—they were considered incapable of raising their voices for rights, law, justice, and life. When they were badly dominated and oppressed, they began to be organised and also they began to fight for their rights and justice. The level of the conscious increased; the state of their knowledge also increased; and ultimately, fright increased in them. Their owners were terrified with the increment of their consciousness and knowledge. They saw only domination as its solution. But that situation further organised the slaves. They began to understand life and the world. Thus, the struggle broke out everywhere.

The capitalist age came into existence after the end of the feudal age, but it was begun at the feudal age. Many big industries and factories were established during this age. Machines were constructed. Goods began to be produced in great numbers and with great variety. Those products started to be supplied to local and national markets as well as exported to the international markets. Then people began to engage in different professions, classes, and groups. It was just because consumers were larger in number than the number of workers and owners. It was a mass production that was more than enough for workers and owners. Owners and aristocrats always exploited workers, peasants, and labourers. As mentioned above, fear existed within their classes and groups.

The capitalist age is one in which the world is still standing. This is not only the age of capitalists and workers. This is the age of various classes and occupations.

Indian Marxist thinker Aijaz Ahmad says, 'Class struggle continuously exists. It doesn't matter, and either it is the first world or second world or third world.'[3]

Prof. Dr Sanjeev Upretti partially agrees with the opinion and writes: 'There are different kinds of discriminations and inequalities except the class struggle between have and have not or owners and workers in the current globalisation. Some examples are: gender discrimination, caste/ethnic discrimination, religious discrimination, and third gender discrimination, discrimination based on homo/lesbian sex, discrimination between able and disabled and other.'[4]

Out of them, the unemployment rate is very high in the world. Some of the owners are workers themselves. There are people with different professions and groups: unemployed people, government officials, army, artists, literary persons, journalists, politicians, social workers, and so on. They struggle with each other. The ruling system also varies: socialism, capitalism, democracy, republic democracy, and monarchy. All these are different classes. These classes include farmers, workers, and brokers. There is exploitation, injustice, atrocity, and struggle in their classes at first. Afterwards, they struggle with the people of other classes. Almost all countries are undergoing political stability. Politicians fear other politicians. Similarly, soldiers fear soldiers. The same problem exists in society, country, and in international levels as well. Countries are in competition with weapons, and they are testing long-range and short-range missiles. Individuals, societies, and countries are in competition to be more powerful. Otherwise, they fear that they cannot maintain their influence and others will dominate and oppress. The first condition is that the fear struggle is within them, and the second is that they have to struggle with others. The struggle of fear is the cause of all these.

The fear struggle that existed in the prehistoric period has been more pervasive today. Now, it has to intermingle with new trends and modals. Many other classes, caste/ethnicities, groups, and organisations have been added to the classes of slaves and owners, feudalists and peasants, and capitalists and workers. These fear struggles are based on straight linear, curve linear, and circle linear. We are playing in such a vast whirlwind.

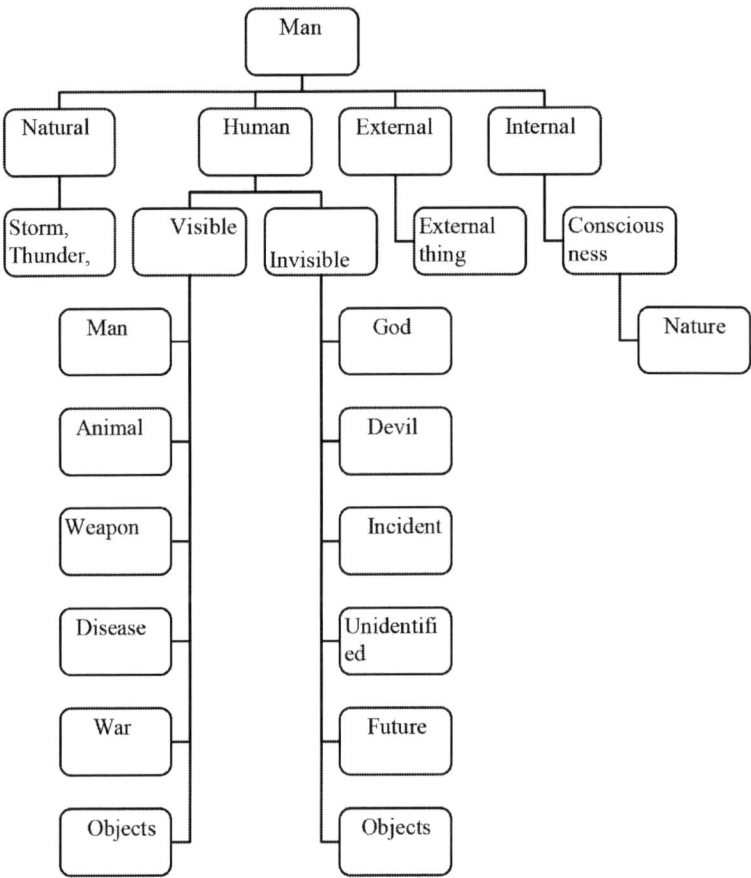

Figure No. 61

A person always experiences his fears. It has been clearly depicted in Figure No. 61 to make others understand comfortably.

The fear struggle of a man has been shown in Figure No. 61. A man always struggles with his fear. It means that he is never free from it. Gradually, he has to struggle with the power of nature, man, external factors, and internal ones.

1. Nature

Various powers of nature exist in the world—some of them are beneficial and some others are harmful. We always try to hide and escape from such harmful powers and try to be protected from them. We accept and utilise or use them if they are advantageous and useful. But these powers of nature are not under our control. We cannot control them either. We have to escape with some of the powers and we have to face some other powers. We have been discovering and following different uses and measures to get rid of them since prehistoric times. Most of the scientific discoveries are/were oriented to liberation from fear. We have learnt to build houses, learnt to wear clothes, invented medicine, and discovered energies and machines. The purpose of all these discoveries, constructions is to minimise fear. Those discoveries and constructions have become the sources of fear now. In fact, all these were demands and supply. After their discoveries, people acquired knowledge that intensified their fear. The same fear began to beget some new fears. All ages: hunting age, agricultural age, industrial age, cyber age, digital age, and others have undergone struggles of fears. Necessity, discovery, and utilisation continued since prehistoric times.

Fears of nature consist of storms, hurricanes, gales, thunderbolts, rainfall, hail, planets, stars, earthquakes, volcanos, and tsunamis. All these have their ways. They are on their own course. We are entrapped by these problems; we try to escape, hide, and face them, but people hardly get protection from them. They come and go. They produce fear when they come, and again, they leave fear when they go. Such natural happenings induce fear in us.

2. Human

A man is indeed a causing factor of fear. People had less fear in prehistoric times because all things such as demands, discovery, and utilisation were limited. Fear was limited due to the limited consciousness, knowledge, and conditional reflex. Along with the development of consciousness, demands and utilisation came into being. Consequently, it resulted in discoveries and development of civilisation. If people did not discover and develop nuclear weapons, language, script, religion, culture, caste, group, and country, fear to be produced from them could be impossible. The world has been divided into different groups at present. The world is fearful of nuclear weapons, attacks of terrorists, and several viruses. This is a collection of fear that has begun since the prehistoric period. The fear that we are undergoing today contains characteristics collected from prehistoric times—we are undergoing some of them knowingly and others unknowingly. Interpretation also is based on it. However, human philosophy, art, and literature have originated from the periphery of fear. We would suffer greatly from fear so much if people didn't start to work for construction and discoveries since the primordial age. It does not mean that there should not be any discovery and construction. All discoveries and constructions should be positive. Internal factors mean more than external factors in fear. There is no reason to be fearful as soon as we hear about the discovery of a nuclear weapon. We have to take it easy and use it positively. Its negative promulgation has made people in the world like scared deer, and it has resulted in the loss of peace, happiness, and prosperity for human beings. How to take it depends on human beings.

All thieves, murderers, terrorists, rapists, rascals, extremists, criminals, and swindlers are in society. Ordinary people always fear them. Again, those people also have the same condition of fear. They fear other rascals and criminals. The reason is that they fear becoming one of their possible victims. Nobody knows who will attack, rob, and murder whom. People always fear such people with inhuman activities. Even gentle men sometimes become aggressive and violent. So, people always fear other people.

a. Visible

Some of these human fears are visible, whereas others are invisible. Events and incidents around us create fear. This is a visible fear. These fears are natural things, man-made discoveries, human temperaments, human behaviour, human conditional reflexes, and attitudes. We feel fright with war, murder, violence, robbery, and anger. Similarly, we fear the people who always oppress, dominate, torture, and exploit others. All from seniors to juniors have experienced these visible human fears.

Similarly, there are many things to cause visible fears—stone, clay, insect, grasshoppers, grass, and others. All the visible physical things are not always the factors that cause fear. They should intermingle with suspicion and hearsay. Let us consider there is an insect. It is visible. We don't have any information about it. As we know nothing about the insect, it can't be the source of fear. We just consider it as an insect. We only fear that it can bite. But the insect specialist said, 'This insect is very poisonous and dangerous. Whoever it bites dies.' Then cold blood runs throughout the body and hair stands on end. The heart beats more rapidly. The body sweats and the person becomes happy just because their life is safe. How big is the gap between knowledge and ignorance? It can always happen. There are too many factors from one-celled creatures to multiple-celled creatures in this world. To interpret them individually is impossible. Some of the major visible things have been interpreted here.

Man

Man is the most fearful of all the visible things. The fear caused by man is more fearful than other visible factors, because man uses man as a fearful and sharp weapon. They always rule and exploit others. They impose rules and regulations on them. Fear is such a weapon that helps everyone be disciplined and progress in their lives. Small children can also be made disciplined either by means of persuasion or fear. Therefore, fear is a major instrument for human beings. That is why they use it wherever they are. We close doors and windows to be safe from other people, but not from any animals. If we do not keep them closed, we fear that there may be any kind of fearful activities such as theft, rape, or murder. To keep windows and doors open can surely cause some unwanted accidents immediately. Many such unwanted events have occurred even if we keep our windows and doors closed. Some people keep waiting for such an opportunity. If a man sees another man in a lonely place, he starts feeling fear. The man is a source of both visible and invisible fears. All inventions and wonderful and marvelous constructions were guided by fear. A man with bad thoughts in his mind is more fearful and violent than any violent and dangerous animal. People know the weaknesses of other people. They are well informed about hiding places and safe ways for them. So people fear other people comparatively more than animals. Their fear is due to their own reasons or due to the reasons of others. People always suffer with fear of the past, the present, the future, relatives, and property. The more a man tries to address his fear, the more he is trapped inside.

Animal

An animal is a visible fear for human beings. All animals are not fearful. Some animals are harmful and some others hunt human beings. They are extremely dangerous and fearful. Some insects, lizards, and birds are also fearful of human beings. They create fear for their self-defense. But these animals and birds get access to a limited place only. Therefore, we hide, flee, and fight with them. Animals are not as clever and dreadful as human beings.

Weapon

We are afraid as soon as we see a weapon and are careful about it. We try to be careful about the bare knife, axe, sword, gun, pistol, and other things before we use them. We note carefully if anyone has carried weapons. If we see children playing with weapons, we immediately seize them. When we use weapons to point at a man, he immediately becomes pale. A man takes advantage by means of weapons, but the law convicts them as criminals. Now, from general stone weapons to atomic weapons have come into use. Powerful countries always dominate other weak and small countries in the name of modern weapons. Weapons always make others feel fearful and alert. Being a bit careless with such weapons can cause wounds and severe and dangerous accidents.

Disease

We cannot see germs of disease, yet we can see the patient. When one is sick, some changes occur in the behaviour of his friends and relatives towards him. Unless we know about his illness, we behave in a friendly manner and we walk, sit, and eat together. When we know that he is ill, we feel uneasy with him. If the man is suffering from a transferable disease, we try to escape even if he is a relative or close friend. We fear that we may contact the disease. On the one hand, we have the fear of death, and on the other, we have the fear of life. We in fact never fear the ill man, but his illness. If we live with him, we fear that we may suffer from the same disease and we may die. This fear is also from man.

War

First condition: War is a directly visible event. This is previously fixed. The situation before the war and after is even more fearful. The situation before the war is not directly visible, but we can only guess. It is more chaotic. It can cause the loss of hunger, sleep, and comfort. It creates an extreme fear. People are anxious for their lives, family, and property. They are horrified, depressed, restless, and fearful in such a condition.

Armies who go to the battlefield have their own fear—enemies can attack and kill them, etc.

Second condition: This is during war. This condition presents pathetic scenes like shouting, crying, yelling of pain, bloodshed, fleeing, hiding, dying, burning, and breaking down buildings, etc. People are restless due to hunger, thirst, pain, trouble, etc. The people who gain victory engage in raping, using spears to stab, and taking enemies captive. Those who lost the war are bound to suffering and torture. It provides a fearful environment for the countries involved in war. People spend the whole day and night with fear.

Third condition: This is the post-war period. The war has both short-term and long-term impacts. The short-term impact appears and affects people immediately. But the long-term impact appears and affects them not immediately, but some time later. Everyone is frightened of war.

People, particularly those who are captives, injured, and affected, suffer from the long-term impact of war. The people who suffered from the First and Second World Wars are still afraid when they remember the past. The fear of the place where atom bombs were exploded is much more severe. Those who suffered during that period are still suffering.

It is obvious that all events endure the same impact: pre-event, event, and post-event. The difference is that they may be unforgettable like the war, but fear exists in these three conditions of events.

Objects

Objects are visible things. Any object we witness in a general case cannot be the source of fear. Let us consider a flower. No one thinks that it produces fear. The flower doesn't produce fear generally. When we begin to think about and doubt it and we are told about it, then we slowly and gradually think about the flower from various perspectives. When we doubt it, then it creates fear. Therefore, all visible things produce fear for human beings.

There are too many visible things besides those mentioned above. Many of them don't cause fear in the beginning, but ceaseless thinking, doubting, and understanding of them create fear later.

Invisible

Every human activity, temperament, behaviour, murder, terror, robbery are not visible—they are heard, doubted, and understood. We fear when we hear, understand, and believe it. Moreover, a kind of an unknown fear always surrounds us. No doubt this is human activity. We never think beyond human activities. Most of the inhuman activities such as mistakes, deceit, betrayal, dishonesty, murder, terror, threat, suppression, injustice, exploitation, etc. are invisible. We fear just on the basis of what we have heard, doubted, and guessed. Similarly, unknown powers and the power of the nature also cause fear for us at all times.

God

We have never seen God. We immediately fear when we hear his name. We try to make him happy just because we have lots of fear. As an easy way to escape, we worship him. We believe and expect that if God gives us blessings, we get rid of our difficulties, hardships, problems, and troubles. Some people believe that God saves us even from death. We have heard about *Tilasmi* (miracle) god as hope and faith.

Devil/Monster

Devil is an antonym of God. As most of the people believe, they give human beings trouble, pain, torture, etc. It causes fear for those who believe that it also troubles, tortures, and causes suffering to man in hell. We have heard and read about troubles, tortures, and sufferings given to human beings by devils in religious texts, *puranas*, and legends. That always strikes our mind. It creates fear for us continuously.

Incident

There is a possibility before the incident takes place. However, its possibility appears before; we can't be sure about all events because they are invisible. People always fear due to continuous thinking on possible events. If the incident happened before, one becomes like 'a burnt child that dreads the fire'. Many incidents happen in our lives.

Unidentified

A kind of an unidentified fear always traps man. It can't be characterised by shape, size, feature, quality, type, or colour. Such an unidentified incident can be either hardship, trouble, pain, and problems. It can't be clearly defined. The reason behind it is that we haven't heard and witnessed it, but we just believe in it.

Future

The future of man is always uncertain. No one knows where it will lead us. Fear of future trouble, suffering, hardship, and problems always alert us. He does different activities to keep himself safe and for liberation from it. All people work, run businesses, and earn money. They try to build up their secure future with their properties or money, but in fact, the same money and property suffer and torture them a lot. In this way, people dig up chasms and keep avoiding it at the same time. Such problems sometimes are avoided.

Objects

Lots of things are invisible in the world. We know nothing about their whereabouts. Neither can we see them in a picture nor can we see colours and shapes. This is the result of imagination and the thoughts of the brain. It always gives fear to human beings.

Thus, people fear many things. In a similar way, fear affects all families, societies, and countries. They all want liberation—an easy way to escape. When people have no idea about what is an easy way and what is not, in such a condition, they don't suffer from fear. Man is busy running to and fro, and moreover, he is helpless. When he knows about his liberation from fear, he feels easy and comfortable.

3. Exterior Factor

External factors refer to all physical and non-physical things of this universe. They all create fear for human beings. The universe consists of them all. With the absence of these objects, the universe is incomplete. They all run through unseen processes. Their presence is not the cause of fear all the time. Fear of their presence depends on the thoughts to create fear and thoughts that don't create fear. As we start to think about some of the exterior things that cause fear. The presence of non-physical things in our mind also becomes the source of fear for us. Then, we start to search for a way out of these fears. Ultimately, the search becomes the objective of the whole life. For example—our earth is being swallowed by a black hole. We don't know anything about what happens after the earth plunges into the black hole. Fear immediately starts when the thought of the black hole comes to our mind. The scientists are working on its solution. We are also working for the same purpose. Similarly, there are many exterior things like stars, planets, etc. The same fear of exterior things is suffered by all creatures.

Interior

Consciousness, temperament, and fear are the result of mindset. It depends on one's own thoughts. When we think about a general thing, it immediately constructs fear. Life, the world, events, ghosts, the future, generations, etc. are the external factors. They are all in their own places. They are not touching us, yet they construct fear when they come to our minds. If we take them positively and progressively, our fear lessens.

25

Pyramid of Fear

Friedrich Engels says, 'There were landowners and slaves in agriculture based medieval period; there were official artisans, trainee artisans and labourers in the post-medieval cities; there were industrialists and workers in seventeenth century; and there were bourgeoisies and proletariats in nineteenth century.'[5]

All living creatures, from human beings to the smallest creatures, live on the basis of a pyramid made of group, society, power, and rights. In the pyramid made of power, the powerful always are unjust to the weaker, and they oppress and dominate them. The weaker always fears the stronger. Other people fear rights in the pyramid of rights. People fear the people who are responsible, accountable, and honest in the pyramid of responsibility, accountability, and duty.

The history of human beings is a pyramid constituted with struggle for power, force, right, duty, responsibility, and accountability. In the world, there are pyramids constructed with force, power, and right and also pyramids of duty, responsibility, accountability, and honesty. The struggle for fear exists among them. The world depends on the construction of this fear struggle. Lots of pyramids exist in the world—most of them are constituted by fear. I have mentioned four types of fear pyramids here. They are illustrated below.

a. Pyramid of fear in civilisation
b. Pyramid of fear in power and rights
c. Pyramid of fear in responsibility, accountability, duty, and honesty
d. Pyramid of fear of renowned person

a. Pyramid of Fear in Civilisation

Discussing the beginning of civilisation, Prof. Dr Gobinda Raj Bhattarai writes, 'There was war; there was rebellion; there was fear and wish for peace since the beginning of civilization.'[6]

From the dawn of civilisation till now, our society has been developed from the pyramid of fear. There was normal fear in prehistoric times. Now the world has been flooded by fear. We invented and constructed to fulfill what we needed and desired, but our discoveries and constructions added fear and now we are in the surround of fears. This pyramid was small in the beginning, but it has become very big now.

About how our creations give us fear, Bhattarai writes, 'Mechanical world created by us is fearful to us as well.'[7]

Human civilisation has undergone the snow age, the Stone Age, and the hunting age. In this way, other ages were added one after another. We hardly find the records of snow age, Stone Age, and hunting age. The history of civilisation is explicit since the agricultural age. There were slaves and landowners in the agricultural age. Gradually, the slavery system was abolished. Conditional reflex of the slavery age still exists. The feudal age began immediately after the slavery age ended. People were not really slaves as they were in the slavery age. The slave did not own property in the slavery age. Feudalists began to provide a piece of land and little means of production to the slave to make them work. This system began when the slaves did not want to work as slaves alone. They began to acquire pieces of land from feudalists. They transformed them into *bhudas* (land slave). They began to be divided into different classes, groups, and organisations. Various groups, classes, and institutions existing already in the slavery age began to much more developed in this age. The well-off people started exploiting the poor. Consequently, the poor were victims of the injustice, atrocities, and domination of the wealthy people. Oppressors and the oppressed appeared in every class and caste/ethnic group. Likewise, oppressors and oppressed appeared in almost all classes. Then the pyramid of exploitation/oppression was constituted in caste/ethnic group, class, group, and family. Along with erection of the pyramid of oppression, the pyramid of fear was erected. The government was formed in order to liberate all poor, oppressed, and proletariats from their hardships, troubles, and sufferings and to care for them as well. There are too many examples that reveal oppression, injustice, atrocity, and domination made in one class by the people of the same class.

Many ages like the age of rights and power and the age of responsibility, accountability, duty, and honesty existed in the cause of human civilisation.

To explain them all here is impossible. I present some ages constituted by fear in the cause of civilisation.

1. Slavery Age
2. Agricultural Age
3. Industrial Age
4. Present Age

1. *Slavery Age:* Slavery Age came into existence after many other ages. Only limited fear prevailed during this age. The slaves used to fear their owners and also the power of nature and foods and animals as well. They particularly used to fear owners and slaves. Slaves used to struggle with each other. Despite these facts, they had a small scale of fears. The people in this age like the people of later ages had different temperaments, abilities, and contents of characters. They didn't have similar capacity, knowledge, consciousness, wrath, jealousy, doubt, and characters. Slaves used to exploit each other; they used to have conspiracies and disbelief against each other. They used to compete with each other in order to serve their owners and to be near them. The people of the same class used to suffer from various fears. Continuous development of human civilisation was based on the pyramid of fear—struggle for rights, power, force, responsibility, and accountability. Still it exists.

2. *Agricultural Age:* Fear increased even more in this age. People were much more conscious in this age than the people of Slavery Age. New fears continued to be added to the fears of Slavery Age. New necessities were added; compulsions and desires increased as well. As a result, discovery, construction, and creation were further accelerated. These works of discovery, construction, and creation deepened the state of fear. Fear, no doubt, existed in the Slavery Age; other new fears of the feudal age were added to them and expanded to the pyramid of fear. As the Communist manifesto was being prepared, Friedrich had written about it in a question-and-answer form. He wrote: 'We had landowners and land slaves in the agricultural based medieval age; we had artisans, apprentice artisans and workers in the post medieval cities; likewise we had industrialists and workers in the seventeenth century; and we have bourgeois and proletariats in the nineteenth century.'[8]

3. *Industrial Age:* People arrived in the industrial age from the prehistoric period in the course of developing civilisation. Many industries were established and commercial activities increased in this age—both import and export of goods increased. All commercial activities like production, sale, distribution, export, and import were performed.

Hierarchical post-structure came into being. Their work division was determined according to their rights and responsibilities. It was based on organisational structure. Rules and regulations were implemented in order to increase production, sale, and distribution of goods and to achieve goals as well. These rules and regulations were constituted on the basis of rights and duties. Other new fears were added to the fears existed in slavery and agricultural ages. As new discoveries, constructions, and creations came into being, so fears were added. They further expanded the pyramid of fear.

4. *Present Age:* Present Age is the climax age of fear. There are many associations, institutes, organisations, governments, rebellions, terrorists, etc. All are busy in their business. All are competitors and they all want to live as well. All people are involved in associations, institutions, and organisations for their works, but in fact, they all are guided and controlled by the pyramid of rights and responsibilities. The world could be different in the absence of this pyramid. The world could suffer from murder, terror, looting, theft, robbery, plotting, chaos, etc. The same pyramid of fear guided and controlled a peaceful, well-organised, and prosperous world. The fear of this age has further expanded the pyramid of previous fears. Moreover, still new diseases, problems, discoveries, constructions, and creations are being added to this pyramid. Similarly, desire and ambition are also being added. The more it is added, the more fear is added. Again, we try our best to come out of these fears. It has been the process since time immemorial. Fears will continue to be added in the days to come, and it will keep the pyramid expanding. Our necessity, desire, aspiration, obligations, and other things are still increasing. They invoke us for further constructions, discoveries, and creations. As a result, new rules and regulations are continuously evolving to regulate them all. We make our attempts to come out of these things. This process recurs eternally. This is indeed a life we have been living with.

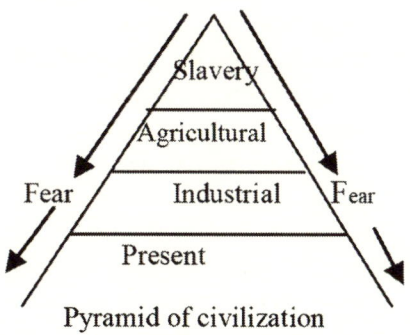

Pyramid of civilization

Figure No. 62

Figure No. 62 shows an expanding pyramid from prehistoric times to the present age. It shows a small scale of fear in the prehistoric period and also shows centrifugal expansion of fears expanding to the present age. Fears of the prehistoric and slavery ages expanded much in the feudal age; still more expanded in the industrial age, and it has become widespread in the present age—it increases along with the development of human civilisation. The present world has become the age of fear due to widespread fears and continuous addition of new fears age by age along with new discoveries, constructions, and creations. Society didn't exist in the prehistoric period. Constant growth of human population constituted society. Communist societies existed in the prehistoric period. People were not divided into different professions and productions and distributions also didn't prevail. They didn't learn how to cultivate the land. No weapon was invented. Their livelihood used to be based on yams, fruits and prey. When they found those things, they used to eat happily; otherwise, they used to live hungry. They didn't build houses—for their secure living. They didn't have any clothes to be safe from the heat and the cold. Wild animals and the power of nature used to make them suffer. They didn't know how to cook food. Fire was not invented. They didn't have the knowledge that eating uncooked food might cause sickness, disease, and indigestion. The biggest fear, above all, was about making ends meet. This fear urged them to invent new weapons, discover fire, build houses, cultivate lands, grow food and crops, discover machines, and establish industries. They began to have private property. Thus, necessities, desires, ambitions, discoveries, and constructions continued to increase faster than they did before. No doubt they continued to expand fear.

In a similar way, people began to construct language, script, religion, culture, festivals, and so on that were necessary for them and their societies. Slowly and gradually, people began to be divided according to their caste/ ethnicity, religions, and countries. Later, wars and violence took place in societies, countries, and all over the world. Similarly, struggles and chaos occurred. Then, some people became owners, some became slaves, some became feudalists, some became peasants, some became capitalists, and others became workers—they all were guided and controlled by fear. Such fears existed within them, in their classes and societies, and in other classes and societies. The power of nature existed as an exterior fear. Likewise, people were divided into owners and slaves, feudalists and farmers, and capitalists and workers. Many people and societies were beyond these classes. They were semi-owners, semi-slaves, semi-feudalists, semi-peasants, semi-capitalists, semi-labourers, politicians, religious men, artists, literary figures, unemployed people, social activists, proprietors, students, and many other classes. They all were further divided into groups. They all had their own class and group. All of them struggled for rights, power, authority, prestige, duty, responsibility, etc. in their group and class. The strongest used to dominate and oppress the weakest in society. People used to feel jealousy, derision, dubiousness, and suspicions of conspiracy against those who could not be dominated. The struggle for fear was compulsory in all classes, groups, and caste/ethnic groups. Along with this development of civilisation, fear increased.

b.   Pyramid of Fear in Power and Right

Post-structuralism, Michel Foucault says, 'Possibility of retribution exists along with the practice of power. Therefore, practice of power and its retribution are two sides of the same process like two sides of a coin.'[9]

Here, power and retribution are not on what we need to discuss. What Foucault says here indicates that fear is much more powerful than power. Fear is in every power, but every fear has no power. There is another pyramid made of power, force, and right. Above all, particularly animals have the pyramid made of force and power. The same pyramid of power and force was for human beings in the prehistoric period. Now, rule of law prevails all around the world. There is a pyramid of rights in the rule of law. Inferior people always fear superior people in terms of rights. Such pyramids exist in every institution or organisation. All the institutions run based on such pyramids. Not only institutions, the state, industries, society, administration, and others run on the basis of this pyramid. Some examples of this are:

1.   Pyramid of the state
2.   Pyramid of the organisation/institution
3.   Pyramid of the factory
4.   Pyramid of the family

1.   *Pyramid of the state*

The head of the government is at the top of the pyramid of a regime in a country in terms of power. Then, it is followed by departments, different units and levels of administration and people. According to Figure No. 63, ordinary people or the public have a much wider scale of fear. They live by fearing, escaping, and hiding. They fear that businessmen may increase the prices. They also fear a possible suffering by the administration. Those who are involved in the army, police, and administration have less fear than the ordinary people. The head of the government has the least fear, because all officials should work under his leadership on the basis of law and rights. He is everything on the basis of organisational stricture. He is the most powerful man in the country. He only fears people. This is a kind of fear circle. Only people can overthrow him if he is unable to work according to the consent of the people. Even those autocrats who claim, 'Nobody can shake the foundation of my authority' were overthrown by the people.

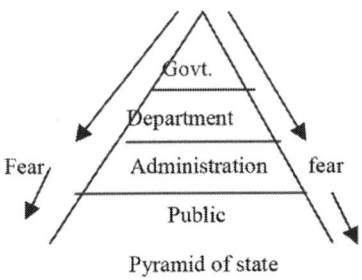

Pyramid of state

Figure No. 63

The former USSR was abolished in 1989. The people, thus, overthrew the Communist government, and the people are still overthrowing such an autocratic government in the world. Mass movements launched for democracy in 2011 in Arabian countries overthrew the ruler who ruled more than forty years. In this way, rulers always fear their people.

2. *Pyramid of the organisation/institution*

There are many countries in the world. Many social, political, economic, religious, cultural organisations and international organisations have been established in the country. There are criminal and terrorist organisations. Each social organisation has its branches. A number of sister organisations are established in political, economic, religious, criminal, terrorist organisations. Groupings are formed in the country as well. A grouping is also a kind of an undeclared organisation. Even now, countries like the people of the prehistoric period have been divided into different groups and sub-groups. The countries in the world established their own groups in the First World War, Second World War, Vietnam War, Afghanistan war, Iraq war, etc. These wars were based on visible and invisible pyramids—they were oriented to power and fear. The most powerful country remains on the top of the pyramid and other countries remain below just on the basis of their power. The country which remains on the top is due to her power. Other small countries take the shelter of the powerful country for their safety and security. Powerful countries like America, China, Russia, and India are on the top due to their powers. Other countries are under them. The whole world was divided into two poles during the Cold War period. All other small countries fear being suppressed and dominated if they don't take the shelter of powerful countries. If needed, powerful countries help them too. This is a kind of pyramid of fear. Family, society, political party, economic institute, country, and many others depend on this outline of the pyramid. All countries in the world are under the pyramid of fear.

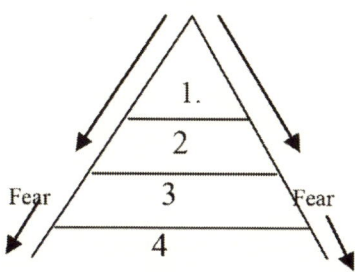

Pyramid of organization

Figure No. 64

(1) International organisation (2) National organisation
(3) Regional organisation and (4) Local organisation

There are many organisations in the world. Those organisations, whether they are governmental or non-governmental, are under the delegation of right. Figure No. 64 shows the pyramid made of powers and rights of organisations. An international organisation has a bigger scope, more region, right, and power. Then gradually, national, regional, and local organisations come in turn. Thus, all the organisations are under the pyramid of right and duty.

3. *Pyramid of the factory*

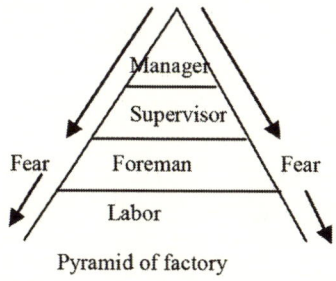

Pyramid of factory

Figure No. 65

227

Figure No. 65 shows the pyramid of the factory. Everyone fears powerful, strong, and authoritative people in a factory. There is a manager on the top in a factory. Then, there are assistant managers and other staff. The junior-most staff is very much afraid of the rest. But all of them fear the one who is in the top post. There is the matter of right rather than an individual. Whoever has lots of power is fearful to the others. For instance, the foreman fears everyone except those who are junior to him. Similarly, the supervisor doesn't fear those who are junior to him, but fears those who are senior to him. Thus, the factory is run under the pyramid of fear.

4. *Pyramid of the family*

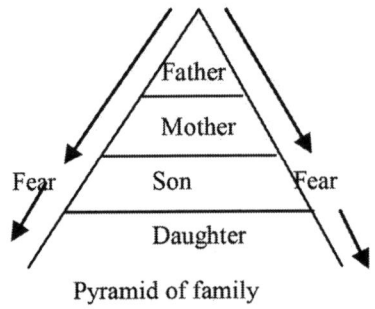

Pyramid of family

Figure No. 66

Family is an organisation. The pyramid of power and right exists in the family too. The father is powerful in the family among mother, son, and daughter. The hegemony theory propounded by Antonio Gramsci is applicable here.[10] All family members accept rules and regulations made by the father. Such acceptance is also fear. All the family members have been the carriers of the theory of Gramsci, because the father is the source of income and he is learned and experienced. Even culture has empowered him. He is physically stronger than the mother too. He is powerful, as he has had much access to physical, mental, cultural, and financial matters. Besides the father, the mother and their first issue are more powerful than the other sons and daughters. All sons and daughters have less power than the father, so they fear their father. Females are physically weaker than males. Females are very afraid due to prestige, reputation, religion, culture, superstition, law, and rights. Thus, the pyramid of fear exists in the family.

Power and fear were the reasons for the construction of patriarchal societies since ancient period. Thus, country, society, family, industry, and business are all based on power, force, and right.

c. *Pyramid of Fear in Responsibility, Accountability, Duty, and Honesty*

The philosopher Socrates had said in his conversation with Uthaifran, 'The respect doesn't always follow fear. Rather fear expands earlier than the respect'[6]

The people with many rights have lots of responsibility, accountability, and duty. He always fears that he may not carry out his responsibility. If in case he is unable to carry out his duty and responsibility, it is very shameful, insulting; above all, it influences personality development. He works very hard due to this fear. On the other hand, these people can be victims of attacks, jealousy, plots, enemies, etc. These all invite stress, depression, mental problems, as well as thoughts of escaping for the victim. People can raise a question if an honest man is unable to carry out his liability, responsibility, and duty. Honesty is indeed a great property for the man. If it gets lost once, it can't be regained. Therefore, man works for his prestige. The pyramid of liability, responsibility, duty, and honesty is everywhere. I want to present them:

1. Pyramid of the state
2. Pyramid of the organisation
3. Pyramid of the factory
4. Pyramid of the family

1. Pyramid of the state

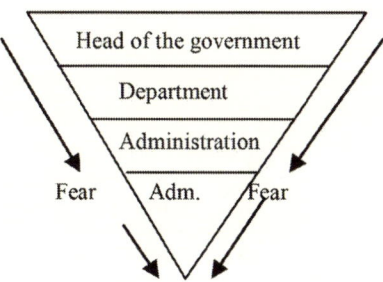

Pyramid of state

Figure No. 67

The above figure shows the pyramid made of responsibility, accountability, duty, and honesty. The people who have more accountability, responsibility, honesty, etc. have more fear than ordinary people in the pyramid of state. The head of the government has the least fear on the basis of power and right. Units, departments, and administration have more fear than the head. Ordinary people have more fear than the above. Contrary to this, the people with more accountability, responsibility, duty, and honesty have much higher fear than the people with less accountability, responsibility, and honesty. Again, the people with great responsibility, accountability, duty, and honesty fear losing his duties, responsibility, and honesty. He has to undergo many obstructions and hindrances, and his enemies might work against him. So he works very hard. But the ordinary people do not have to face such obstacles and barriers. They work when they like. They have freedom to walk anywhere they like. They don't have any fear to walk freely. The head of the government, wealthy people, popular people, kings, presidents, and others don't have such freedom and they can't walk as free as the ordinary people do. They fear attack, looting, murder, etc. An enemy may attack them at any time. The head of the government and other important persons of specific units are always worried to walk outside. If in case they walk outside, they walk with security escorting them. Yet they are in fear even with security. Many such people have been attacked even with security. Assassinations of Mahatma Gandhi, who propounded the principle of non-violence, Abraham Lincoln, who was a Democrat, including Indira Gandhi, Rajiv Gandhi, Benazir Bhutto, Jiwalahak, and the royal massacre that happened to take place in Nepal occurred within security circles. Thus, the people with more responsibility, accountability, and duty have a higher scale of fear than the people with less responsibility, accountability, and duty.

2. Pyramid of the organisation

Pyramid of organization

Figure No. 68

Organisations with higher responsibility, accountability, duty, and honesty have a higher scale of fear than the organisations with less responsibility, accountability, duty, and honesty. Like people, these organisations also suffer from the fear of failing to maintain duty, responsibility, and accountability. These organisations may suffer from various obstacles, opposition, attack, looting, etc. in the course of works. On the other hand, they have to face shame, hatred, and opposition in case of failure to carry out responsibility, accountability, and duty. That is why these organisations have to bear lots of fear. The international organisations on this basis have more accountability, responsibility, and duty. As a result, the level of fear of these organisations is much higher. Local organisations have less accountability, responsibility, and duty. Therefore, the level of their fear is lower as well. The same thing has been depicted in Figure No. 68.

3. Pyramid of the factory

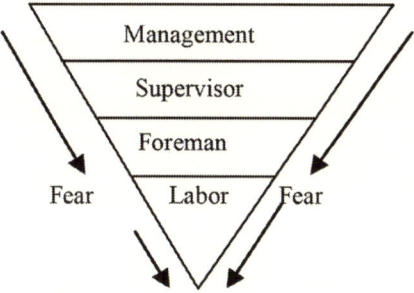

Pyramid of factory

Figure No. 69

The workers of a factory have a kind of pyramid of fear of power and right. Contrary to this, the pyramid is made of responsibility, accountability, duty, and honesty. Those who have more accountability, responsibility, and sincerity have higher levels of fear. Similarly, those who have less liability, responsibility, duty, and sincerity have lower levels of fear. Figure No. 69 shows the manager with higher levels of fear and the worker with lower levels of fear.

4. *Pyramid of the family*

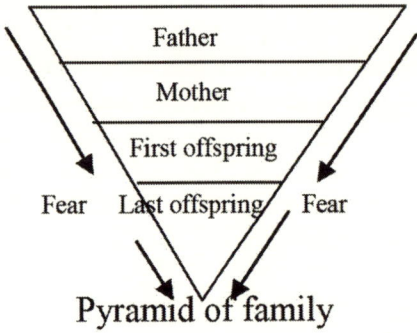

Figure No. 70

Figure No. 70 shows the pyramid made on the basis of responsibility and accountability. The father in the family has the highest responsibility and accountability, and gradually, the same responsibility and accountability are developed by the mother, the eldest child, and other members of the family. That is why they fear failing to fulfil their responsibility and accountability. The figure shows the father with the highest level of fear and the last issue with the least level of fear.

Thus, the pyramid made of right, liability, duty, and responsibility exists everywhere. The rich has a larger number of enemies. Similarly, large numbers of other people take jealousy and conspire against him. This all depends on power, prosperity, liability, sincerity, right, etc. Other people fear the people, countries, and organisations with higher powers and rights. Likewise, the same people, the same countries, and the same organisations with higher liability, responsibility, duty, and sincerity fear other people.

d. *Pyramid of Fear of a Renowned Person*

Famous people don't have freedom to walk according to their desire like ordinary people. Everyone knows them. They have prestige, money, and fame, but yet, they can't have the freedom to walk like ordinary people. They have lost human freedom because there is a higher possibility for them to be attacked and robbed. Famous people have a lot of audiences, spectators, readers, etc. They want to touch, visit, and see celebrities. It can cause crowds of people around them. Such crowded environment provides fertile ground for criminals to attack. There are too many examples of criminal attacks in such a condition. Therefore, they always walk with security personnel. It's not sure when they could be attacked, even with security. Their enemies remain all around. People always engage in jealousy, suspicion, conspiracy, and treachery against them. So, they keep hiding. Many criminals kidnap and attack them for ransom and property. The probability of attack on them, therefore, is higher than the ordinary people. Due to these reasons, famous and rich persons, though they have lots of property and fame, suffer from fear more than others. They are not only afraid of enemies, but also of journalists. So, they walk secretly. They are a kind of prey for journalists—journalists keep following them. The world knows that as Lady Diana tried to escape from journalists, she happened to die in a car accident. In this way, they lose the freedom of life like that of ordinary people under the names of property, name, and fame.

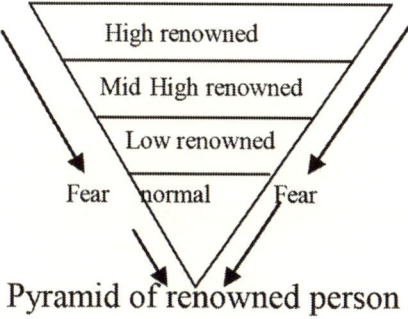

Pyramid of renowned person

Figure No. 71

Figure No. 71 shows most famous people, more famous people, famous people, and ordinary people. According to this pyramid, most famous people have the highest fear and ordinary people have the lowest fear. Since ordinary people have the least fear, they have the freedom to walk wherever they want and also they don't fear to walk wherever they like and eat whatever they like. They don't have any audiences, readers, or spectators like that of famous people. Also, they don't suffer from jealousy, suspicion, conspiracy, and treachery. Like ordinary people, famous people can't go wherever they like and can't eat whatever they like either. Rather, they suffer from jealousy, conspiracy, suspicion, and treachery. They, like other ordinary people, don't have the freedom of life. They use money and property for their facility, happiness, and entertainment.

The pyramid of animals is not like that of human beings. Their pyramid is just based on force and power. Powerful animals and birds are on the top, and the animals and birds with less power are below them in the pyramid.

The reason behind it is that the animals and birds don't have the sense of right, responsibility, duty, and sincerity that people have. They have just natural power and force. Their force and power depends on their physical structure, horns, nails, jaws, paws, poison, etc. Their lives depend on these characteristics.

Thus, everything, from human beings to animals and birds, live on the basis of their pyramids. It would be very difficult to run international and national organisations and rule a country, society, and family in the absence of such pyramids. Problems could exist as they did in prehistoric times. The world is doubtlessly well managed due to these pyramids.

End Notes:

1. Karl Marx, Friedrich Engels, *The Communist Manifesto*, Penguin Books, London, 1967, p. 79.
2. Mohanraj Sharma, Khagendra Prasad Luitel, *Eastern and Western Literary Theory*, 2063 v.s. p. 176.
3. Sanjeev Uppreti, *Sidhantaka Kura (Aspect of Theory)*, Akshar Creation Nepal, 2068 v.s. p. 224.
4. Sanjeev Uppreti, *Sidhantaka Kura (Aspect of Theory)*, Akshar Creation Nepal, 2068 v.s. p. 224.
5. Jelda K. Kots, *Jiwan and Krititwa* (Friedrich Engels Life and Contribution), trans. Sitaram Tamang, Nawdeep Publication, Kathmandu, 2005, p. 103.
6. Gobinda Raj Bhattarai, *Uttar Adhunik Bimarsha (Post Modern Discourse)*, Modern Books, Kathmandu, 2008, p. 437.
7. Gobinda Raj Bhattarai, *Uttar Adhunik Bimarsha (Post Modern Discourse)*, Modern Books, Kathmandu, 2008, p. 437.
8. Sanjeev Uppreti, *Sidhantaka Kura (Aspect of Theory)*, Akshar Creation Nepal, 2068 v.s. p. 41.
9. Plato, *Sukratko Aatmakatha (Biography of Socrates)*, trans. Ram Hari Banjara, Madhuwan Publication Kathmandu, 2065 v.s. p. 21.
10. Sanjeev Uppreti, *Sidantaka Kura (Aspect of Theory)*, Akshar Creation Nepal, 2068 v.s. p. 174.

26

Fear Weapon

To control and discipline criminals, rascals, robbers, and others, they are beaten, imprisoned, tortured physically, flushed with water, shocked with electric currents, excluded socially, and banished. Such hard punishment and torture can change the minds of people. The same formula is applied— to make the people work and disciplined, to establish peace, to implement law and order, to maintain religion and culture, and for the development of civilisation as well. This weapon is utilised for people from any class, age, group, profession, or sector.

The fear weapon is the sharpest, most effective, and powerful of all the weapons. The effective sphere of this weapon is more pervasive than the physical one. The psychological effect of the weapon invented by a nation in a corner of the world spreads quickly around the world. Iran and North Korea performed an experiment on a nuclear weapon that surprised the world. Similarly, some nations spread a rumour about such a weapon to show their power and influence. In the Second World War, some millions of people were affected by the atomic bomb dropped by America on Hiroshima and Nagasaki in Japan. More than ten million people are affected at present.

Similarly, the common people fear a lot if the country passed a bill for the death penalty. Perhaps there are fewer criminals in jail. On the other hand, it is not possible to send all the criminals into prison, but if a strict law is passed, the criminal himself abides by the law. Fear of prison is more effective than a strong and painful prison in the country. It is obvious that the purpose of the state is not that the public should be imprisoned and tortured.

However, there should be peace and prosperity by means of fear prison. Only then, the constitutional state can be established and maintained in a country.

On the other hand, even officials, whose work is to safeguard the laws, can also violate the rules. To make them disciplined, the law binds every unit, department, and branch. Even then, they might break the law. Therefore, the fear weapon is used to keep everyone in balance and discipline. It is an inevitable weapon. The judge is under the law. The judge should be punished if his verdict is not based on law. There is a unit established for petitions and to forward an action and punishment against him. Similarly, the army, police, civil service, bureaucrats, businessmen, and public are made aware of the fear of any organisation and units. Only then can they all carry out their respective duties and responsibilities.

The weapon is used on an individual, family, society, country, and international level. This very weapon is used for all ages, professions, classes, communities, religions, etc. Absence of fear in sports and other recreation, discipline, rules, and regulations cannot be maintained. No goal is possible in the absence of discipline, rule, and regulation. Fear can be minimised on the basis of circumstances in order to maintain law and order. Less fear can be applied to a very civilised and disciplined people, and much fear is essential for a very uncivilised, disobedient, and unruly people. This is the case for everyone. People should be inside the trap of necessary fears. This is a good driver of society and country. To use a fear weapon is to make man improve his habits and to maintain good discipline and to maintain peace in society. In brief, I will discuss the fear weapon used in different classes, groups, and professions.

Children: Still people have not developed the system of convincing and consoling children in order to make them disciplined, studious, and obedient in many countries. Instead of it, they are often scolded, beaten, tied, given no food, banished from home, and tortured physically and mentally. But they are given such inhuman tortures in some of the countries, completely against the children's rights. The children's rights puts bondage on such illegal and inhuman punishments. Such corporal punishments affect them psychologically and mentally. Guardians and teachers in their anger threaten, beat, entrap, and banish them and even provide them with no food. These all make them fearful. To make them fearful for work is unjust. Rather, they should counsel and convince their children in order to lure them for work. Guardians and teachers should control their anger to behave with children. It is more beneficial. Such torture and punishments make them mentally ill, introverted, and can cause psychological problems and make them feel humiliated.

Sportsmen: Sportsmen always want to win the match. They break rules and regulations during their game. They use hands if it is restricted and legs if it is restricted in the game. If they fear punishment for violation of rules and regulations, they don't violate rules and regulations knowingly. Fear always inspires them to maintain discipline while playing the game.

Justice: Court is the final interpreter of all rules, laws, and constitution. Judges can be biased in their verdict, but even laws bind them. They also fear punishment of the fear weapon. Their judgements, therefore, are always based on the law. Despite such provisions, people complain about biased verdicts and prejudices. The fear weapon is used in such a case to bring justices on to the right track. This weapon doesn't have any alternative.

People: The state writes the constitution and constitutes rules and laws to maintain rule of law in the country. People are afraid to involve themselves in criminal activities, murder, and terror due to the constitution, rules, and laws. As a result, it helps maintain law and order in the country.

Criminals threaten and warn the people for donation and to make them work. They startle and scare them even by messages through email and letters and phone calls. They fear being asked for donations or being asked to do something. They have made neither a mistake nor have they committed any crime. However, man uses this weapon to make others do his work and take advantage of others and meet his personal interests. Fear causes different problems and effects. Sometimes, he is obliged to give the amount and give what he is asked for. The criminal also suffers from the same fear.

Criminal: Police, army, and men beat, tie, hang, and give physical, mental and electrical torture to a convicted man to make him confess his criminal acts. Most of the criminals explain their crimes. But some of the criminals are so rude and rigid that neither do they confess their crimes nor do they explain their criminal acts even if they are physically tortured. Professional criminals are so rigid that they never confess their crimes, but ordinary people confess their crimes due to fear. Some people, though they are innocent, are obliged to accept the crime due to fear. They confess to crimes, although they are innocent, to be free from torture. Criminals and rascals are given punishment to improve their habits. Punishment improves habits, but in some cases, it worsens habits due to its bad impact.

Prison: There are prisons in all countries in the world. Prisons house criminals. For the people who violate rules and laws, prison is an ultimate punishment. Most of the people are scared as soon as they hear the word 'prison'. Criminals are imprisoned there on the basis of their crime levels from some years to life imprisonment. They are deprived of the right to freedom, like right to speech, right to walk, right to visit, right to write, right to read, right to play, etc. Above all, they lose unalienable rights—right to life, liberty, and pursuit of happiness. Moreover, they lose their prestige and reputation. They live in the prison like animals. There is no other alternative for their crimes. Some countries have the provision of death penalty too. The provision of prison is to make people feel fear for an inhuman life. So, people fear to violate rules and laws due to the fear of prison.

Thus, the fear weapon has been used in all groups, classes, institutes, and sectors. Fear is, no doubt, the most useful and helpful weapon to maintain law and order in societies, nations, and at international levels, and even to make the individual more disciplined.

27

Organisations for Fear

'The man inspects and calculates on how the soul remains apart from happiness, emotion, fear and other but when he becomes the victim of happiness, emotion, fear and other then he begins to acquire what bad things he had doubted on them before.'[1]

Socrates on the verge of his death had frequently used the word fright while talking with Simmiyas and Sibis, who had come to the jail to visit him. But words like fright, happiness, and sorrow were used in a normal sense. It means they had not emphasised fear.

Unlike Socrates, fear has not been taken as theory; so much information about it is not available. But many works on fear are being done directly or indirectly.

As a matter of fact, it may not be an exaggeration that organisation, wildlife conservation, natural conservation, river, and channel conservation, rule, law, language, script, religion, culture, etc. are related to fear. Again, these organisations are related to war, disease, peace, happiness, wild animals, environment, caste/ethnicity, language, script, religion, and culture. All those organisations work to minimise fear, to work for relief, and work to rescue. I want to explain some of the institutes here.

a. Organisation for Peace and Security

The United Nations (UN) is the umbrella organisation of all the nations. There are many other sister oganisations under the UN: General Assembly, Security Council, Economic and Social Council, Trusteeship

Council, International Court of Justice, and Secretariat. Other organisations, like International Labour Organization, World Bank, World Health Organization, and International Monetary Fund, etc. are under the UN.

The First World War and the Second World War were the climax of wars. It is not possible to calculate the loss of lives and properties. The condition before the war was dreadful, and similarly, the condition after war was also dreadful. People only saw death, injury, hunger, disease, murder, destruction, etc. in the environment of war. The heart leaps up in the recollection of this fearful condition. It is not possible to explain how fearful the people were. The people used different means during such a period to save their lives. Thousands and millions of people lost their lives in the war. This all happened due to ego, temptation, fear, wrath, etc. of people. The war left destruction, dread, disease, etc. They are all dreadful to recall. People were not so dreadful in the past.

All the nations of the world assembled together to establish the UNO for peace and prosperity in the world. Now, the UNO takes initiatives for peace, war, and mediation. It works to intervene in some of the countries for peace and sends peacekeeping armies in order to maintain peace. It helps minimise fear. Therefore, the UNO is established to liberate people in the world from fear, minimise the fear, and to provide relief. There are organisations related to security. Objectives of these organisations are to maintain peace, law, and order in the world. There are other institutions in the world besides UNO to work for peace and security. Government, police, army, court, etc. are institutes for the same peace, security, and prosperity.

b. Organisation for Preservation

All the wild animals, plants, and the community, language, script, religion, culture, etc. are disappearing from this world. The ecological system is badly affected due to the extinction of animals, birds, and plants. According to the theory of Malthus, population growth has deeply impacted on every sector. Similarly, the consumption of water is doubled every fifty years. Fast growth of population and overuse of water are about to cause critical crisis of water every day. We have 54 per cent water to drink, 70 per cent of water for irrigation, and 20 per cent water in industries and household works. The lack of water is causing chaos and war, and swamp land is getting dry. As a result, the animals living in the swamp land are disappearing. This is also inviting chaotic conditions in the world.

In this way, the extinction of community, religion, culture, language, script, etc. have deep impacts on human beings. Many species of wild creatures have already disappeared from this world. Many others are on the way to extinction. Preservation works for them are going on at national and international levels. Attempts are made on the preservation of beautiful mountains, lakes, forests, large virgin lands, and heritage. Those organisations and institutions are established for the preservation of wild animals, plants, natural beauty, man, and language, script, religion, culture, and community. These institutions have preserved animals and birds that are about to be extinct. So, these institutions are guided by fear.

c. Organisation for Health

Many health-related national and international organisations, along with hospitals, health centres and health posts are established. These all are established with the fear of human injury, illness, wounds, and death. Different kinds of diseases break out at once in society. Such epidemics can cause the death of thousands and thousands of people. Swine flu and bird flu terrified the whole world some years ago. These diseases create worse situations if they are not prevented before the situation turns dire. Cholera and other diseases are breaking out time and again. Similarly, different diseases, wounds, problems, etc. also cause fear for man. Millions of people get injured, become the victims of different diseases, and die during war. There have been governmental and non-governmental associations established to give them relief and alleviate fear. World Health Organization, Health Ministry, etc. are the examples of such associations. If there is an epidemic of any disease and it is prevented at once, man is free from the fear of the epidemic. Some of the diseases can be cured immediately, and some others need regular treatment. If the disease is incurable, the fear of the patient can be alleviated through consolation and counselling. These health-related institutions are to minimise the fear of man.

d. Organisation for Implementing Rules and Regulations

There are many institutions to implement rules and regulations. Some of them have been presented below:

Government: People began to practice different institutions for rules and regulations in the country. There is the government in the names of different political parties in the world at present. The government may be either Republican, Democratic, monarchic, Communist, or socialist. The duty and responsibility of any government is to establish peace and security, to conduct development, and to care for its people. People face lots of problems in the absence of the government. So, people try to form a capable government. In the absence of the government, criminal activities, murder, terrorist activities, robbery, and theft increases. The government is proposed due to these things. The government compels the people to accept rules, regulations, and constitution and punishes the violation.

Army: Every country has an army. The army also works to implement rules and regulations and also works to maintain law and order. These armies work to maintain peace and law and order internally and work for the security of the country from the attacks of enemies from other countries externally. They also work for peacekeeping armies under UNO. They are mobilised particularly for defence of the nation along with its borders during civil wars and chaos in the country. The country also always undergoes fear: external and internal. The military force is formed in order to lower and control the fear. It is an ultimate national force for the implementation of laws, rules, and regulations. Violation of these rules and regulations and law creates chaos, uproar, and disorder. So, the government spends huge amounts of money.

Police: The police force is formed to maintain discipline along with law and order and establish peace. What happens if no police force is in the country? Which unit takes the responsibility if some one is murdered, raped, robbed, and threatened? The police force is formed to prevent these events, and if in case events happen, to bring them under control. This force has the responsibility to maintain law and order and implement rules, law, and constitution. In this way, this force is to minimise and liberate fear.

Court: The government establishes a court to punish the criminals in society. The court is the final institute that gives final punishment to the criminal. The government divides works among different units. They have their own assigned works. If the criminals are not punished, it will increase robbery, looting, incidence of rogues, criminals, and murder. The criminals always try to give trouble, pain, threats, torture, anxiety, and fear to the people. That is why the court is established for happiness, peace, and security. People fear violating rules, laws, and regulations due to the fear from the punishment by the court. The court makes people follow rules, regulations, and laws of the state.

The purpose of executive, legislature, and judiciary is to lower the fear of people, liberate them from the fear, and give relief. Laws, rules, and constitutions are effective due to these levels of the state. Implementation of rules, laws, and constitution lower the fear of the human beings. Thus, all institutions around us knowingly or unknowingly are related to our fears.

e. Institute for Insurance

Many huge insurance companies have been established around the world. The purpose of these companies is to reduce risks for human beings and to help those who are at risk. The reason is that people can be injured, they happen to suffer from accidents and even deaths. If major organs of our body that support lives are broken, the life will be ruined. When the family members who earn for the family die, the lives of dependents will be ruined. Therefore, life is insured to help during harm, accidents, suffering, and hardship. Those insurances bear our risks and reduce problems, crisis, anxiety, and fear. We pay premium for insurance.

Not only people, but also their property, business, etc. may be destroyed due to any accident. They invest their property anywhere else. If their properties are destroyed and damaged, they will be ruined and bankrupt. They insure most of their properties to reduce the risks in the days to come. The insurance company compensates damages of insured goods. In this way, insurance companies have worked to reduce fear.

f. Fire control

A man's house may catch fire due to carelessness, storm, electrical problem, etc. Fire is so dangerous or harmful that it can destroy even a hard substance, i.e. iron, within a while. There is a saying, 'Fire never says unripe.' If fire cannot be controlled timely, everything, i.e. house or building, village, etc. turn into ashes. So there is the fear of fire in the house, settlement, and village at all times. The government provides accessible fire control services to the people in order to control fire like fire extinguishers, fire engines, and other human resources related to it. These are for rescue if accidents take place.

g. Organisation for security of property

People always fear that their properties can be destroyed and stolen as well. So for the security of their properties, banks are established and manage the locker system. Again, the bank is for the security of all properties. People want to be sure of the security of their properties through depositing them in the bank and keeping them in a locker system.

h.   Other organisations

Many other institutions related to fears besides those mentioned above have been established. There is no certainty of fear. Nobody knows when and where it comes forth. Other institutions have been established on the basis of situation and necessity. People don't want to exchange information about their whereabouts with others. The law is enacted and made for personal security and information in developed countries. It helps people to be fearless to some extent. People want to conceal their personal details. People fear that if others come to know about their personal details, they will torture, backbite, and tease them. Let us consider that monkeys are about to disappear from this earth; an institute for the preservation of monkeys is necessary. Similarly, if the organs of the human body like a heart, liver, nerves, tissues, lungs, and others are out of work or damaged, then health institutions for them are necessary. Institutes for blood and bone marrow have already been established. Thus, institutes keep on establishing them on the basis of necessity. And it continues forever.

End Notes:

1.   Plato, *Sukratko Aatmakatha (Biography of Socrates)*, trans. Ram Hari Banjara, Madhuwan Publication, Kathmandu, 2065 v.s. p. 100.

28

Fearism Dephilosophy

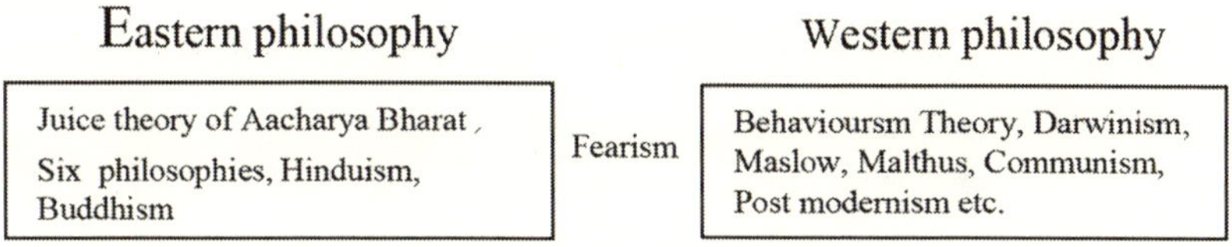

Eastern philosophy		Western philosophy
Juice theory of Aacharya Bharat , Six philosophies, Hinduism, Buddhism	Fearism	Behavioursm Theory, Darwinism, Maslow, Malthus, Communism, Post modernism etc.

Figure No. 72

Figure No. 72 shows fear between Eastern and Western philosophies. Eastern philosophy is close to spiritualism, whereas Western philosophy is close to materialism. These philosophies have presented various ways of lives and the world. These philosophies have realised fear yet not felt—what it is. How is it? It has been interpreted in detail. Wherever life exists, no matter how far away it is, still the main road is fear. It is the greatest road. All other paths of life come to join the greatest road.

Philosophies might have their respective powerful logic on lives. But the fearism gives new dimension to the logic and interpretations. Life is like the Milky Way in the sky, constituted with a series of images. The world depends on it. All consciousnesses revolve around its orbit. Fear is a guide to life and also the greatest orbit of a series of consciousnesses.

'Many years ago Plato had declared the state terror to protect from the true terror. But contrary to this, Aristotle developed understanding on fear, pity and purgation is for good health and promoted them as the theory of catharsis.'[1] No other philosophy in the name of fearism existed before it.

Those with comprehension of fear brought forth many philosophies and developed them parallel to life. Much discourse exists on policies like how to be free from fear, how to maintain free existence, and how to light a candle for life through spiritualism on the matters of disciplines and particularly on philosophy and spiritual thinking. Philosophies talked about peace, but invited wars and made the world plunge into the quicksand of wars.

Many thoughts and literary writings are available. Let's say! Fears are scattered everywhere—they are comprehensive and incomprehensive. It is risky to be anarchic if it remains only as comprehensive. Fear exists comprehensively and incomprehensively behind war, violence, murder, doubt, illusion, conservation, superstition, etc. Fearism is a means to lower the possibility of war, violence, murder, suspicion, and illusion.

Fear is expanded up to where we are working, where we are earning, and where we are reading and writing, and thus to our every step. We stride on fear in order to come out of it. The difference is we argue for fear with its comprehension. This argument is sure to bring some positive changes in our lives.

The one important thing is that all new and old philosophies—whether comprehensive or incomprehensive—are followed by the shadow. In the absence of fearist perspectives, the foundation of all philosophies—no matter Eastern or Western—will collapse. Their foundation is fearism. The fearist perspective, however core in lives and literature, is left behind. Literature and philosophy, both are impossible unless this perspective emerges in consciousness. Fear criticism did not exist, since it lacked philosophical interpretation. It is an easy and comfortable perspective. It works just to simplify life.

Separate interpretation on fearism as a philosophy doesn't exist. The world is with world philosophies, science, spiritualism, and lives. Since life is guided by fear, music and arts are also guided by fear. All theories, philosophies, and science are in fact competing to reach close to life. They all claim closeness to life. Life is quite beyond all these things, so there is continuous curiosity, eagerness, and research on it. Jacques Lacan says, 'The symbolic world of language is the world of absence.'[2] Life is absent, as it is also the construct of language. Therefore, we reach far beyond it in search of the presence of life.

In fact, eternal truth, existence, and certainty are all temporary camps for permanent camps. We think life is a permanent camp and the rest are temporary ones. There are lots of such temporary camps—for example, words like illusion, *lila*, *britha*, game, etc. have been constructed. But all these are the world forms of fear. Analysis on the power of Michel Foucault and domination of powerful man and domination over the powerless of Jacques

Derrida are all based on fear. I present interpretations on some philosophies close to fear as:

a. Conditional Reflex

In fearism, I want to interpret the conditional reflex first, for it is an apt experiment for the interpretation of fearism. The conditional reflex experimented by Russian scientist Petrovic Pavlov is under his theory behaviourism.[3]

What I prove is that word (meaning) exists with conditional reflex itself. Most meanings are under conditional reflex. We have known that death is fearful, painful, and cruel, and we have been facing the problem of fear since the primary stage of human civilisation. Thus, we have been living our lives with the fear of life, universe, future, present, etc. Above all, all meanings are considered to be conditional reflexes. We have been carrying such meaning. We spend whole lives in seeking the way out.

Pavlov managed a special experiment for conditional reflex in the laboratory. He made a room in which there was the absence of outer light and the word from which attention could not be distracted. There was a dog kept in the room. So as not to let the dog sleep, its front two legs were fastened, and it was made to stand with the help of one rope dropped from the third floor. Then two small pipes were put into both sides of the mouth of the dog; the saliva dropped from the tongue and was collected in a pot by means of the pipes. Then, the first experimenter sat in front of the dog, but no effect of signal could be seen at the time. Therefore, living arrangements for the spectators was made in the outer room. Food was also sent to the dog by dint of machines. A signal was sent to the dog for producing excitement in it. Based on the signal, the muscle, tissue, and sense of the dog were noted.

We can also apply such an experiment ourselves. Any event can be made as a pre-signal to make the dog drop his saliva for the conditional reflex. For this, a whistle can be blown by mouth, a bell can be rung, one hand can be raised, red or any other colour can be shown, electric shock can be used, or his body can be scratched. Quick electric light can be made a signal. Similarly, there was a dog kept in a room in Pavlov's experiment. If the switch was pressed, the room lit up and a thirty-second pause was managed. The machine sent a plate with delicious food to the dog again. The dog ate food within thirty seconds. The room was lit like that after a while again. Similarly, the machine sent the small plate with food to the dog and let him have it for thirty seconds. As this process was repeated for several days, the electric light became the signal that made the dog aware of food, and he started salivating as soon as he saw the light in the room. Pavlov had measured its impact on the basis of drops of saliva. As the impact increased, the dog dropped up to ten drops of saliva in the experiment.

The dog was provided food with the signal of electric light continually for some days. So, the dog caught the signal. The conditional reflex can also be abolished or alleviated. If the dog was not provided food with the presence of electric light several times, automatically the dog would give up salivating in the light. This experiment can be applied to avoid bad habits and improve good habits of a man. Regular practice changes it into a conditional reflex. Pavlov had also done the same.

We can reduce or finish conditional reflex through regular practice. This example proves that fear is merely conditional reflex. Suppose it is not conditional reflex, but our sense organs always carry it. We can easily get to have a sound sleep in our usual bed, but it is very difficult for us to get to sleep in a new one. Maybe some people can easily sleep, while others feel uneasy to sleep. The reason is that the man who has become accustomed to the bed can sleep easily and those who are not habituated can hardly sleep. If sense organs, glands, muscles, and consciousness are regularly practiced, they will grow accustomed to any kind of situation, like sleeping in a new bed. This habitual action is referred to as the conditional reflex.

Owing to the vital roles of words, fear, sense organs, and glands, they are always in connection with fear. Let's consider the word 'ghost'. It could mean stone, clay, or flower in the beginning, but we didn't try to understand it as stone, clay, or flower. Rather, we understood it as a very fearful spirit of a dead person, with dangerous teeth, blood-sucking, something that haunts at night, that troubles, and gives us pain or death. This is the meaning we have been using. Its originality may be far beyond what we have understood. We have been familiar with such meanings for long. We have been afraid since we have heard about it. So the message of the word, whether it appears or not, is instantly sent to the brain and it turns into knowledge. The conditional reflex is not only applicable to a ghost, but also to phantom, demon, snake, murderer, conservatism, and superstition. Therefore, fear is a word which is a conditional reflex. The conditional reflex is also a kind of imitation.

If the word ghost, like the dog, is not provided food with the presence of light continually and the dog stops salivating even with light in the room, it is thought not to be as harmful or dreadful; the fear it brings decreases gradually. This conditional reflex has been applied to everything, including religion, culture, conservatism, and superstition. We have been living with this knowledge, meaning, and conditional reflex since time immemorial.

End Notes:

1. Rishiraj Baral, *Pratinidhi Nepali Samalochana (Representative Nepali Criticism)*, Bibek Shrijanshil Publication Private Ltd. Kathmandu, 2068 v.s. p. 163.
2. Sanjeev Upretti, *Sidhantaka Kura (Aspect of Theory)*, Akshar Creation, Nepal, 2068 v.s. p. 55.
3. Rahul Sanskrityayan, *Biswako Ruprekha (Sketch of the World)*, trans. Narayan Giri, Marxbad Study-Research Academy, Kathmandu, 2066 v.s. p. 285.

b. Meaning of Fear and Meaning of Fear of De Saussure, Lacan, and Derrida

The conditional reflex propounded by Russian scientist Petrovic Pavlov did not regard the meaning of language, but had connection with the meaning of psychology. Most of the meanings are doubtless the conditional reflex, developed from prehistoric times or inventions. All the meanings, based on previous inventions that we have been reading, hearing, and getting, and being clear about, are not our inventions. We continue learning the same meaning at all times. The meaning of the word 'ghost', not produced by us, has already existed, fearful, man-eating, hunting at night, walking in a silent path, frightening, troubling, and causing illness and death. This is the thing we have ever figured out and passed down. The meaning of the word 'ghost', by whom it was used for the first time, could be used for flower, but now it is not possible for us to define it as flower. They used it in the sense of ghost, but not flower. We have been following it since then. It just became an indicator taught us in our childhood by our parents, relatives, and teachers. We grasp that very meaning by means of our sense organs and teach it to others. We bank on others' uses and follow some of the meanings, even without knowing them properly. The conditional reflex goes on spreading, sliding, becoming uncertain, as Lacan said, and transforming into binary opposition, as said by Derrida. There is no binary opposition in the initial stage of a river, but when it flows down, the bank of the river, stone, clay, and sand transform into binary opposition. The meaning is also the same. There is no matter of sound and letter when a new meaning is coined. The user of a new word disregards both the sound and letter.

Brown Motion was formulated by the name of the scientist, Brown, and Marxism is by name. Thus, words have their own meanings, and the words and meanings are not combined individually. The meaning of a word becomes the conditional reflex. Many others do not need to think on words very much, but they know ready-made meaning and meaning gradually slides on—becoming uncertain. There exists a centre and a periphery. A word is coined due to reason, necessity, and desire, and the meaning the word carries becomes the conditional reflex for others. Let's consider—there is a cave. A man is dead in the cave due to some reason. His friend outside said, 'The cave ate the man.' Other people believe what he said. They start expanding and spreading the same news. Afterwards, the cave is known as 'Man-eating cave'. That means the cave eats whoever goes inside. People easily understand the meaning when they hear about it. The meaning of the word is clear. Then man starts to fear the cave. As for this, linguistic science may study a wide vocabulary, investigate in the library, discover molecules and atoms, and take out DNA. Similarly, Lacanians may search for uncertainty, whereas

Derridas's followers search for binary opposition. Others may study the word and meaning, but the meaning is the conditional reflex.

Thus, the meanings of words have been in use by means of conservatism, superstition, legend, and oral myth. The meanings of the words such as birth, death, heaven, hell, giant, life, etc. that cause fear also have existed like this. If not, these meanings could have come into being through other ways or sources. They have come into being through what we have learnt and heard. We have been using them, and the later generations will continue the same. The meaning is the conditional reflex, like the flowing river. Many new different meanings, like the process of the flowing river, go on existing, expanding, and their fundamentality gets lost while sliding meanings in course of time. Thus, meaning has its existence—from its discovery to extinction.

We can consider the dogmas of the world-famous philosophers. Of them, the three philosophers and their roles or theories in relation to meaning that I have selected are as follows:

1. Combination of signifier and signified for meaning, as said by Ferdinand de Saussure.
2. Sliding and uncertainty of meaning, as said by Jacques Lacan.
3. Binary opposition, as said by Jacques Derrida.

Saussure, Lacan, and Derrida have cleverly played with meanings—foregrounding, backgrounding, paradigmatic, and systematic. They have separated word and its meaning and studied their fragments carefully and thoughtfully. For instance, what is signifier? What is signified? What is the difference between signifier and signified? What are langue and parole? They have interpreted each of them. Many linguists have considered it the Olympic torch, and they are busy in their race. Now, they have been wrapping the world all around it. Meanings are now far beyond the meanings of cat, rat, and hole, and thus, the meanings are sliding. When a meaning is constructed once, all these are possible through the meanings. The creation or origin of a meaning is the most important thing. They, with some outer knowledge and more self-knowledge, have interpreted the meaning according to their own theories and concepts. This is the thing everyone performs. I'm also doing the same. They have interpreted the same meaning in different ways. D. Saussure, Michel Foucault, Kant, and Derrida have done the same. I think that a meaning is basically formed in two ways.

a. Origin of meaning of natural objects
b. Origin of meaning of man-made objects

Meanings of man-made objects exist much later than the meanings of natural objects. A word is suitably and meaningfully given to an artificial word on the basis of quality, merit, experience, and thought of man-made objects. Afterwards, that word carries the same meaning. A natural thing is given a word that can be used meaningfully according to the quality, merit, colour, and shape or size of the object. Thus, meanings are based on:

1. Sense organs
2. Environment
3. Incident
4. Necessity
5. Conditional reflex

1. Sense organs

I often argue that sense organs and consciousness should be studied differently. If that was the same, there would not be a different name and a different meaning. Name and meanings are two different things due to their differences. We get different knowledge from our sense organs: some for taste, some for sound, some for hotness and coldness, some for sight, and some for smell. Many names and meanings have been formed on the basis of these experiences and knowledge. We have been learning these meanings and words.

2. Environment

All what we find in our surrounding is environment. Everybody has his respective environment, and it does not correspond with others. Almost all natural objects are older than humans. These non-living beings don't carry their own meaning instinctively. Man gives names to them for their suitable meanings. In the beginning, a man or a group gives a name to an object meaningfully, so that object clearly can be identified by the name. Similarly, all objects were named according to their meanings. Wherever the people live, they named objects in their local language in order to carry out a suitable meaning. Names and meanings given by them transferred to us. We were able to understand them ourselves, and we didn't have any mental trouble for the meaning. Everything, such as state, clay, water, rainfall, also came into being in this way. We understood that water as an odourless, colourless, and tasteless liquid substance that flows down. Nobody tried to make us understand. We, like Pavlov's dog, have understood them via conditional reflex.

3. Incident

An incident happens to take place while walking and working. We can also use a word and its meaning based on such incidents. Some of the incidents make our sense organs puzzle. The sense organs may have been active in any incident. But sometimes, there may be confusion by means of knowledge acquired through sense organs. For instance, when an object explodes, both sound and light are emitted by the explosion at the same time. We can see some sight or glimpse and hear some sound too of the incident, but can't be clear about it. The situation also calls for a word and suggests a meaning. There are too many words and meanings like this.

4. Necessity

We try to discover, construct, and search for objects when we need them. When we get it, it demands words and we aspire a complete meaning for the word to carry. Sometimes, we discuss a lot while naming a person, a book, or an institute, for that word ought to carry the full sense. For this, we may have disagreement and conduct discussions as well as assembly and seminars. The reason behind it is the word should carry out complete meaning. There are too many words based on necessity, desire, and attraction.

5. Conditional reflex

We can't construct and use meaning immediately. Most of the meanings we are using have been developed gradually. The previous meanings are being used as conditional reflex. Most of the meanings constituted today are being pushed back. We continue them through writing, speaking, and listening as a conditional reflex or imitation. We never invent meaning. Rather, it has already existed, and we continue it from generation to generation. We share the same meaning with whoever we meet through writing, speaking, imitating, and using signifier. We happen to see different signals when we are on the road or on the way to the office. Having seen those signals, we automatically understand their meanings. When we see the red light, we know that we should not cross the road, as it may cause a risk and accident. The people who kept light for indication taught others about its meaning, and the same thing was transferred to the later generation. Thus, meanings continue as a conditional reflex—caricature and imitation. A deaf person understands these meaning through signals and he/she shares with others. Even in this context, the meaning continues as a conditional reflex. A deaf man can understand the meaning after transforming it into a signal. Animals and birds, particularly monkeys, chimpanzees, and dogs understand the similar meaning according to the level of their consciousness. Some of them imitate sounds and others imitate actions. Only a few of them can imitate meanings. Even people can't understand an initial meaning equally. People, animals, and birds understand the meaning on the basis of consciousness via signal, sound, and symbol. Those who understand on the basis of signal, sound, and symbol are imitators, and their meanings are imitations of meanings. All these indicate meanings and information are many imitations—cultural imitation, political imitation, imitation of personality, imitation of activity, imitation of idea, etc. Julia Kristeva, Homi Bhabha, Richard Dyer, and Rey Chow have interpreted such imitations. We have left these all imitations and talking about the imitations of meanings.

The original meaning continues according to our situation, need, sense, and time. It slides on and transforms into a binary opposition. Then, it becomes uncertain. We also teach our children to understand, read, and write a meaning like this—through imitation or conditional reflex. They learn, read, and understand the meaning and teach the same thing to others. This meaning is not regularly and equally used or practiced at all times and places. It goes on sliding as mentioned above. Despite its changes, the red light on the road gives the same meaning of danger. If someone adds a new meaning to the meaning of danger, it goes on changing. All the meanings are like the red light on the road, and they prolong via writing, speaking, signalling, and imitation. The meaning of conservatism, superstition, religion, and culture are also not different from this.

The conditional reflex itself is not an origination of meaning, but it is a carrier of the same meaning that has already started. Unless and until it carried the meaning, the meaning could have disappeared at its origination. Neither could it transfer, nor could it continue to the later generation. The meaning continues due to this carrier. The vehicle for it is imitation, writing, sound, signal, caricature, and signifier. Thus, meanings are learnt by heart, listened to, taught, and written. It transforms to us. The carrier does nothing to the meaning, but just carries it. In course of carrying and conveying, some people pick them up, some play with them, some ask about them, and others give different meanings. On the basis of this perspective, some people find illusion, while others witness binary opposition. What they witness and find are based on their own structure and cognition. Originality of meaning remains with the meaning. People understand meaning like how they understand objects based on their structure, interest, and objective. But the meaning is sometimes used very often (for different purposes) and highly valued, and sometimes, it is not practiced repeatedly and becomes outdated before long. Sometimes, it is greatly exaggerated and its real sense gets lost. The meaning carried by him extends to us. We have already been familiar with some of them. We are told about the unfamiliar one. What we understood is taught to others. It expands everywhere—the tides of the sea and tremors of the earthquake. How long it extends depends on the power of word, necessity, and its context. Impacts of all of them are not the same. They vary. All the meanings we have understood have continued in this way.

To understand in this way is, in fact, a conditional reflex. Again, the conditional reflex of meaning is a caricature of meaning. As a deaf person is unable to hear, so he is unable to speak. Thus, a deaf person understands with the help of signal and caricature and makes others understand with the same help of signal and caricature. In the absence of both signal and caricature, to understand meaning is impossible for them. Even Braille used by them is a signifier and imitation. All meanings we speak, write, study, or read are meanings under conditional reflex. We have been continually taught the meaning of the conditional reflex, like the dog of Pavlov.

Julia Kristeva, Homi Bhabha, Richard Dyer, and Rey Chow have expressed their opinions on caricature or imitation.

Feminist Julia Kristeva writes, 'The women, who work in male dominated fields particularly in journalism, business, politics and law always fear—if their male rivals take them as characterless 'have male natures'?'[1]

Post-colonial thinker Homi Bhabha says, 'Like browns/blacks imitate symbolic whiteness of the western civilization with white mask, the whites themselves attempt to imitate "ideal whiteness".'[2]

According to Richard Dyer, 'Ideal whiteness itself was a cultural concept. Perhaps western people were/are not as white as Jesus Christ. They were not ideally white. A complete whiteness was impossible on the one hand and unattainable on the other. Therefore, the white people themselves used to and had to imitate "ideal whiteness" and work accordingly to show themselves symbolically ideal.'[3]

Prof. Dr Sanjeev Upreti reaches a conclusion based on the view of Homi Bhabha and Kristeva and writes, 'All kinds of cultural, sexual, political and communal identities are the result of the processes of different kinds of imitation or caricature. Every day we adopt the imitation of the social functions and customs that denote ideal woman, ideal man, ideal whiteness, ideal brownness, ideal Nepali, ideal Indian and ideal opposite sexual mindset or mentality.'[4]

According to the post-colonist and the feminist Rey Chow, the Easterners and the Africans, who have been living in the community with the majority of the Western people, have two main alternatives of the cultural caricature. The first is an imitation of activities and ways of lives of Westerners. They have to present themselves as the people with 'white mask of civilisation' through cultural imitation. Second, they should imitate Easterners or Africans admiringly.[5]

Jacques Lacan presents similar caricature and imitation in his mirror stage in post-structural psychoanalysis. The baby sees himself/herself in the mirror and thinks, 'That is me.' Later, the baby keeps on searching uniformity with new people, objects, and groups and adds a new dimension of introduction. For example, he may like a hero of a film or television. Then, he thinks, 'I'm the hero or I want to be like him.'[6]

Lacan's mirror stage is also a kind of imitation. Lacan indeed made his attempt to project his image in the mirror and the hero of the TV as the same. But his image and attempt to be like others are quite different things.

From all these opinions, we know that all the social activities continue through imitation. Thus, meanings prolong with an imitation or caricature.

Meanings are not only developed from the resources mentioned above. They rather prolong with many other resources and transfer to the later generation.

Research on meaning of fear in fearism

Huge, robust definitions of meanings, its basis, analysis, and interpretation exist here. Like the formation of other meanings, the meaning of fear is also formed. Is fear or the word first? We have this question. The experience of fear was transformed into a word and a signal, which carried the meaning of fear. The meaning slides on or transforms into conditional reflex. When we utter a word 'ghost', the meaning of fear is understood itself. There are some words that are always attached to fear—ghost, phantom, Dracula, snake, tiger, bear, murder, and criminal. These words themselves are clear to be understood for the meaning of fear. Similarly, some colours and signals also carry the same sense of fear. If a 'Beware of dog' sign along with the portrait of a dog is written on the wall of a house, it indicates a violent and dreadful dog. Some houses have only the picture of a dog on the door. If the red light is on in an airplane, submarine, or ship and any machine, it is a signal of danger. This is not our product. This is what we have been hearing and learning. Such words that produce danger or fear have come down from different sources, especially from the above five bases. Fear is such a subject that can clearly be understood by a word, signal, and indication. Some actions are necessary for jealousy, wrath, temptation, and doubt, but they work even in the absence of fear. As a matter of fact, most of the jealousy, wrath, worry, inferiority, doubt, and temptation are the binary opposition of fear.

Somebody sees a black fearful thing or imagines it. He thinks—what name should be given in order to carry its meaning? Name is given to meaning as well. Sometimes, name demands meaning, while other times, word demands the meaning. Changes occur in signifier and signified according to context. It is not that a signifier and signified should always exist. When Derrida reversed D. Saussure's signifier and signified, fluctuations occurred in meanings.

All the meanings are subjective but not objective. These meanings differ according to person, race, caste, time, and space. They are uncertain, slide on, narrow down, and are added. Then they disappear in a void, like an electron and a proton. In an interpretation of the 'abstract thinking and onion' of Shankar Lamichhane, Prof. Dr Sanjeev Upreti writes: 'If we keep on peeling the layers of an onion, new layers appear and there remains void at last.'[7] Meanings are also like solid things—they have existence till a certain period. Gradually, original meanings become extinct and new ones start. This is how a meaning is used.

The meaning of fear is also the same. We fear due to the meaning that we have heard, understood, and known. The meaning that we have known for a long time causes us fear. We fear death, but actually, knowledge about the death is a meaning. It causes fear for us. If it was known as flower, there would not be any reason for fear. There would be an easy acceptance. We have been hearing many painful legends and folklore about death. We have seen a painful death of a man. We fear hearing the news and seeing the incident. We would not fear if we did not learn the meaning of a fearful disease, an explosive weapon. Fear begins to exist after knowing about the thing. Knowing something is the way of learning the meaning of the thing. Knowledge cannot be acquired in the absence of meaning of a thing. Therefore, I have formulated life—consciousness—knowledge (meaning)—fear—cognition. Thus, when the meaning of a thing is clear, the meaning, if it is fearful, itself turns into a fearful situation, causing fear for us. If the meaning does not have a fearful situation, doubt, anxiety, and charm are added to it, and the meaning starts causing fear. The meaning that slides on from D. Saussure, Derrida, including many other philosophers, to the later generation, can also be studied in the sense of fear.

This rule does not apply to events and accidents. If all of a sudden a bus somersaults or a building catches fire, there is no meaning here at first, but an accident. This accident produces fear. Then, this incident gradually transforms into fearful meaning. This is how the meaning is formed and it slides on. It gradually transforms into binary opposition, and the old is continuously replaced by a new one. Derrida says in *Under Eraser*, 'The letter written on a paper once can never be rubbed at all. When we write new letters, the former letters become invisible and neither get erased nor lost.

Rather they internally affect the meaning of the word and the layers of the ideas continually.'[8]

They make a deep impact internally on new letters written on the same paper. Meanings are also the same. And so is the meaning of fear. We fear the meaning of fear.

Derrida has used binary opposition to clarify the meaning of things. The same thing has been applied in nature, culture, oracles, writing, male, and female. Binary opposition is insufficient to indicate the meaning of fear in fearism. Tripartite opposition instead of binary opposition is necessary for the interpretation of fear. Our study on binary opposition of peace concludes in chaos. Fear is the tripartite opposition of chaos. A lot of effort is made to establish peace. If not, there exists chaos that causes fear. So many institutes have been established in the name of peace to relieve fear. Many works have been done. The United Nations (UN), religious institutions, social institutions, and religious priests always wish and work for happiness, peace, and prosperity. They want to establish peace and prosperity in society. The constitution, law and order, government, police, and court all have been established for peace, happiness, and prosperity. In the absence of these, people fear murder, violence, theft, and robbery. Therefore, fear has tripartite opposition.

c. Bhaya Rasa (Fear Taste) Theory of Acharya Bharat

Fear Taste is the first eastern literary theory deals with an interpretation of fear. The theory has been developed by Acharya Bharat. Later, great scholars like Bhatta Lollata, Shankuka, Bhatta Nayaka and Abhinavagupta have further interpreted this literary theory. Fear taste is one of the nine tastes. Factors that produce tastes are called taste materials. Taste is produced from the combination of determinants *(vibhava)*, consequents *(anubhava)* and transitory mental states *(vyabhichari bhava).*'Taste materials are:

1. *Taste* (permanent taste): The inner intention that exists from beginning to end is known as taste. It includes nine permanent tastes and nine interpretations of tastes.
2. *Determinants (vibhava)*: The reason and cause that disclose permanent tastes are known as determinants. It consists of two categories: supportive and provocative.
3. *Consequents (anubhava)*: Trials that express already produced tastes are called consequents *(anubhava)*. They are, for instance: trembling, sweat, romance, stammerring, addiction, heat, curiosity, laughing, amazement, etc. Consequents has categorised this *kayik, bachik, satwik,* and *aaharya.*
4. *Transitory mental states (vyabhichari bhava)*: Temporary tastes that support permanent tastes are known as transitory mental states. It is temporary in nature; so, it appears somewhere in the mind and develops permanent tastes and disappears itself. Thirty-three different types of transitory mental states have been interpreted in taste theory.

Fear taste: Introduction and Example

Fear taste is permanent in nature. In it, dreadful animals, like the tiger, snake, ghost, phantom, soul, and atrocity, are supportive tastes. Similarly, fear, terror, suspicion, ghost, and activities are provocative tastes. In the same way, being pale, trembling, stammering, terrified, sweating, crying, and yelling are consequents and threat, pathos, emotion, temptation, anxiety, and suspicion are transitory mental states.[9]

Interpretation of taste categories by Bharat is a great discovery in the Eastern literary theory. Aananda Bardhana propounded phonetics based on this theory. Similarly, Abhinavagupta propounded rhetoric; Kuntak brought *bakronti* on the basis of this theory. Thus, taste has been established as prominent and powerful theory in the Eastern literary genres. This theory includes interpretation of fear as fear taste. Like in other theory and philosophy, this theory consists of comprehension of fear and fear taste. It has some important aspects worth considering.

Four conditions of fear

1. Condition of an appearing fearful object.
2. Condition of fear after fearful object appears.
3. Condition of impact after fear.
4. Condition of attempt on its solution.

Acharya Bharat has interpreted these conditions on the basis of various tastes. I said fear requires knowledge before it exists. Bear, snake, ghost, phantom, and so on produce fear. Knowledge about them is a source of fear. He called it determinants *(vibhava)*. This is a first condition of fear. He has divided taste into two parts—supportive taste related to fear produced after knowledge and provocative taste related to fear produced after dread from animals, threat, doubt, and others. The experience of seeing a fearful animal or thing is under this provocative fear taste. Different kinds of symptoms appear after the fear exists. He has described all these activities like being pale, trembling, stammering, threatening, sweating, crying, shouting, and running as consequents. These feelings are based on our experiences. As a man witnesses dreadful things, he starts to fear. It produces various symptoms. We think and do different activities for its solution. It is a state of transitory mental states.

In this way, Acharya Bharat has incorporated four conditions into his interpretation. In it, fear is a permanent taste. It is constant and its form never changes. Its taste is fearful.

In this theory, he has assumed tiger, bear, etc. as being present physically, whereas the fearful ghost and phantom are sources of fear. But fear, in fact, is nothing other than the product of thinking. It comes to mind as a tiger at first. Normal things also become fearful ones if they are thought to be serious and doubtful. He has not interpreted about thought. About how taste is created, Bharat says—as the combination of different kinds of letters, medicines, and matters work to produce taste; *gudadi* materials, letters, medicines, *shadbadi* tastes are produced; so different tastes: determinants *(vibhava)*, consequents *(anubhava),* and transitory mental states *(vyabhichari bhava)* combine themselves in order to produce permanent taste which ultimately transforms into dramatic taste.

I have interpreted fear as the outcome of consciousness, knowledge, conditional reflex, human temperament, and other external things.

In the first condition, fear does not occur unless a conditional reflex in tiger, bear, ghost, and phantom is produced. Tiger and bear may not be so violent and fearful. All tigers and bears are not violent and fearful as well. Some people who are fond of tiger, bear, and snake keep them at their homes. They are made domestic. But we consider them as dreadful, large, and flesh-eating. They are heard and understood to be dreadful and violent, and they are thought to attack wherever they encounter us. Although we see tigers, bears, etc. kept at home, we apply the same concept to them. If someone calls a bear a dog with long fur, we don't think it so dreadful. Fear depends on the message sent to the brain by the tissues of knowledge, sense organs, muscles, and perception of our sense organs, muscle and tissues of our brains. As a result, our consciousness alerts organs of our body according to the message.

Fear is not only products of animals, ghosts, phantoms, and so on. All people may or may not have seen wild animals such as tigers, bears, snakes, etc. People who live in the hills and near the forest may have seen such wild animals, but the people who live in cities may not have seen them. Despite the fact that they are unable to see them, they create fear in the minds of the people. If they really encounter them, they get scared, faint, and become sick. We can run away for protection or fight and kill for security. Besides these animals, we also fear relatives and society.

Thus, we have many other fears, like economic fear, social fear, present fear, and future fear. We are continuously trapped by fear one after another. According to Acharya Bharat, *alamban bibhava* is the source of all these fears. As he says, even the normal things transform into fear when suspicion, illusion, anxiety, and pain are added to them. Perhaps he has not interpreted a normal thing which goes on causing fear in his theory. He has included sources of fear which he has seen as a whole, but he has not incorporated fear caused by suspicion, illusion, human temperament, and conditional reflex. These are also fears related to tastes.

He has interpreted the process of transitory mental states in tastes. A transitory mental state is a way towards emancipation. When a man sees a tiger, he is fearful above all. He trembles, worries, and tries to get rid of it. More than transitory mental states, its effects and sub-effects exist. Fear is not a solution. Their effects can cause problems and diseases. It has not been interpreted in the taste theory. Maybe, the reason is that the theory is only related to literature. It has been limited only to tastes. He interprets it in a dramatic writing. For example:

> Stripped, a giant tiger came,
> Attacked a cow, I trembled and lost my sense.

Trembled my legs, heart beating about to leave the place.
Let's flee to home, the third fled at once.

(Medinath Sharma)

These lines of poetry further clarify fear taste and fear.

Stripped, a giant tiger came.—*Alamban bibhava*—knowledge

Attacked a cow, I trembled and lost my sense.—*Uddipan bibhava*, consequents—fear,

Trembled my legs, heart beating about to leave the place—*Udipan bibhava*, consequents—symptom.

Let's flee to home, the third fled at once.—Transitory mental states *(vyabhichari bhava)*—cognition.

According to Acharya Bharat, animal, ghost, phantom, atrocity, and so on are *Alamban bibhava*; fear, anxiety or worry, terror, suspicion, and terror produced by these things are *Udipan bibhava*; reactions shown by him, i.e. trembling, becoming pale, stammering, hair standing on end, sweating, crying, shouting, running, jumping, and nervousness after fear are consequents; and fleeing, attacking, falling, asking for help, and confronting are transitory mental states. Regarding it, in recollection of the night when Grandmother died, Jhamak Ghimire writes: "I had fully been overcome with fear, the door was open, through which nothing could be seen except a complete dark'.[10]

There is no other interpretation of fear in detail in the Eastern literary theory prior to Acharya Bharat. Therefore, it is the most prominent interpretation in Eastern literary theory. Of course, fear has been interpreted even in trouble, pain, anxiety, violence, murder, and terror.

Fear tastes and fearism

Sources of fear	Reason of causing fear	Contribution of Acharya Bharat	Effect of fear
Movement, drug addiction, terrorism, world war, environment, crime, visible and invisible thing.	Consciousness, knowledge, sense organs, amygdala, thought, conditional reflex, attitude, temperament.	Fear taste—*bhava*, permanent taste, determinants *(vibhava)*, consequents *(anubhava)*, transitory mental states *(vyabhicharibhava)*	Mental disease, meanness, introversion, depression, different disease, etc.

Figure No. 73

End Notes:

1. Sanjeev Uppreti, *Sidhantaka Kura (Aspect of Theory)*, Akshar Creation, Nepal 2068, v.s. p. 237.
2. Snjeev Uppreti, *Sidhantaka Kura (Aspect of Theory)*, Akahar Creation, Nepal, 2068, v.s. p. 239.
3. Sanjeev Uppreti, *Sidhantaka Kura (Aspect of Theory)*, Akshar Creation, Nepal, 2068, v.s. p. 239.
4. Sanjeev Uppreti, *Sidhantaka Kura (Aspect of Theory)*, Akshar Creation, Nepal, 2068, v.s. p. 240.
5. Sanjeev Uppretti, *Sidhantaka Kura (Aspect of Theory)*, Akshar Creation, Nepal, 2068, v.s. p. 241.
6. Sanjeev Uppreti, *Sidhantaka Kura (Aspect of Theory)*, Akshar Creation, Nepal, 2068, v.s. p. 53.
7. Sanjeev Uppreti, *Sidhantaka Kura (Aspect of Theory)*, Akshar Creation, Nepal, 2068, v.s. p. 101.
8. Sanjeev Uppreti, *Sidhantaka Kura (Aspect of Theory)*, Akshar Creation, Nepal, 2068, v.s. p. 161.
9. Mohan Raj Sharma, Khagendra Prasad Luitel, *Purbiya ra Pashchatya Sahitya Sidanta*, Eastern and Western Literary Theory, Bidharthi Book Store, Kathmandu, 2063 v.s. p. 40
10. Jhamak Ghimire, *Jiwan Kanda ki Phul*, Online Nepali Sahitya Forum, Kathmandu, 2067 v.s. p. 43.

d. God, Religion, Peace, and Fear

'*Rishi-maharshi* (Saints) used to consider great power of nature as God in Vedaic period.'[1]

There has been written in chapter Sukta 27 of Rig Veda, 'We human beings are the worshipers of power, we are the servant to all powers, we perform *yagya* (worship) for power. All kinds of meditation, chanting and penance have been performed for power. May almighty God bless us for food, shelter and cloths! It was People wish.'[2]

Chapter fifteen of YajurVeda says, 'Oh, fire (God)! Free us from both known and unknown enemies.'[3]

Chapter thirty six of YajurVeda says, 'Oh God, as you desire for good for us, so you give us relief of fear as well.'[4]

Sukta 7 of fourth part of Atharva Veda says, 'There was the serious problem of a snake and other poisonous animals too like threats of violent animals.'[5]

The eighth section of Atharva Veda has begun from praying to the god of death. This chapter includes a very long prayer. The first two *suktas* deal with longevity.[6]

These extracts are taken from the Vedas. The Vedas include fears caused by hunger, violent animals, untimely death, and praying for relief from those fears. It also includes *Karmakanda, Gyankanda,* and *Bhaktikanda*. In the Vedic period, people did not have fears of nuclear weapons, ultraviolet rays, viruses, different diseases, and pollution like the people of today. They only used to fear the power of nature, violent animals, enemies, and scarcity of food. Therefore, they used to worship different gods, the power of nature for food, and used to perform *Karmakanda, Bhaktikanda*.

While talking on the origin of God, Prof. Dr Birendra Prasad Misra says, 'In prehistoric period, people used to worship gods and goddesses for their betterments and gods and goddesses used to be happy with it and they used work for the betterment of the people. As there were the lords in different places, they used to be considered as the causes of natural calamities and accidents like earthquake, draught, flood and so on. For instance people used to worship Zeus and Apollo during that period.'[7]

In the prehistoric period, people did not have God, religion with them, except fear. Again, fear did not exist as much as it does now. Fear used to exist only due to the power of nature, hunger, and wild animals. When those powers began to give trouble, pain, and many other problems, people began to fear. Then they started worshipping God for their protection from those powers. The God the people worshipped in the ancient period was different, but gradually, they changed its forms and shapes in favour of their desires. The difference between ancient statues and present ones clarifies this. Close study reveals a vast difference between them. People began to worship God and express their trouble, suffering, and pain in front of God. People who worshipped God made a huge group. It was changed into a religion as time passed on. Religion is a group with faith to establish and preserve God. Rules and regulations were constituted for the religion.

In the prehistoric period, God was worshipped as an invisible power. Human civilisation continued to develop. Development continued on the one hand, and people plunged into the quicksand of conservatism, superstition, and blind belief. Therefore, conflict, quarrel, war, murder, and violence used to occur in society at all times. Pioneers of society began to instruct, teach, and give education, knowledge, discipline, truth, character in order to rescue society from such superstition and blind belief. According to their sayings, the number of people with such faiths increased. Later on, what they said was the sayings of God and they were God's messengers. The ideas, message which they established in their lifetime were interpreted by the followers in their own ways after their death. Their concepts and thoughts were contested. Those who opposed their messages and thoughts made groups, and different interpretations and misinterpretations continued. They began to dispute on their heirs. They divided gods on the basis of their interest, desire, faith, and aspiration. Consequently, a tree produced different branches and fruits. Everyone had his own fruits. It means they all had their own gods.

On religion, Bertrand Russell says, 'Religion is based on fear and the fear is the father of cruelty. So it is not necessary to get surprised when religion and cruelty go hand in hand, for both the religion and cruelty begin with fear.'[8]

Thus, God and religion came into being. In this way, Hindus, Jews, Christians, Muslims, Jains, and Kirat have been divided. Beforehand, society and country had been engulfed by war, violence, murder, and other things. Society was undergoing chaos, robbery, and violence. The pioneers of society attempted to find relief to these problems. Similarly, country, society were involved in war even in the times of Confucius and Buddha and Vedic period. They ceaselessly worked to rescue society from such quicksand. People began to respect their contribution and expressed gratitude. Gradually, they began to see them as gods as well. However, war, violence, murder, and atrocity could not be minimised; rather, they increased and war occurred perpetually. The reason behind it was that God was not the solution. Peace is impossible unless there is a proper solution to the real problem. Absence of trouble, pain, anxiety, worry, and fear is the presence of peace.

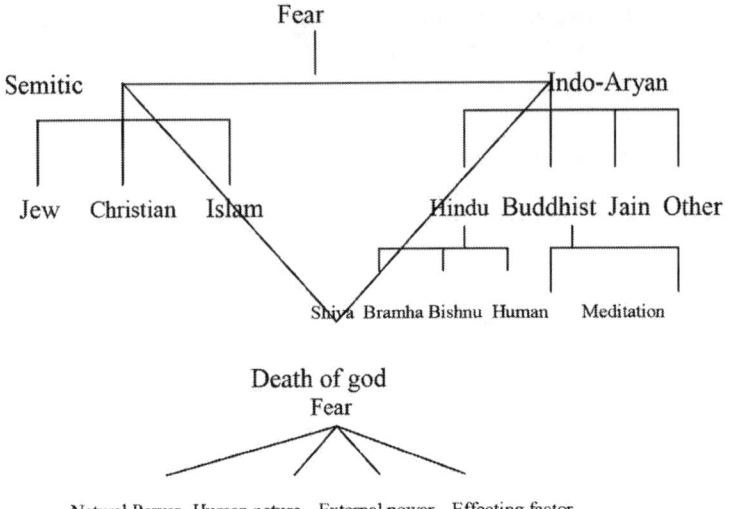

Figure No. 74

Fear is on the top of the figure. Different religions existed due to fear. Of them, Semitic and Indo-Aryan became major religions. Other small religions also came into being. Jews, Christians, and Muslims were under Semitic religion, whereas Hindus, Buddhists, Jains, Confucius, and Tao were under non-Semitic religion. Out of them, many other small and big branches and sub-branches existed. All of them had their own gods in the centre. Nietzsche, a philosopher, declared the death of God and shook the foundation of the world. As a result, fear existed. The reason was that trouble, pain, anxiety, fear, and problem did not minimise; rather, they increased. After God was declared dead, it created even bigger problems. All the people with faith in God had to face a critical condition. They could not exist without God. On the other hand, they all could not believe in God, who was declared dead. According to them, God was a faith which could never die. So, the faith of people in God still exists.

Here, I want to discuss religions related to fear.

Buddhism, among religions, is related to peace. Therefore, I exclude other religions and gods and incorporate perspectives of Buddhism and Hinduism. The gods in Hinduism are connected to nature, but in Buddhism, they are connected to peace.

Some of the gods of Hinduism are Vishnu, Shiva, and Brahma. They were supposed to be the symbols of water, fire, and air in ancient period. So, the colour of Vishnu is like water. According to myth, Brahma is a symbol of air and is considered to be originating from the navel of Vishnu. Shiva is the symbol of ferociousness. Therefore, he is furious as thunderbolt. When he is furious, everything is ruined. Again, Brahma is known as a creator, Vishnu as a protector, and Shiva as a destroyer. Whatever names they had, they were connected to nature in ancient times. People used to fear with the power of nature like fire, water, storm, hurricane, thunderbolt, earthquake, flood, and landslide because they were troubled by these powers. They used to be troubled with these powers, time, and occasions. They used to believe that to worship them was to get rid of trouble, pain, and suffering. As a symbol of all this, people used to worship fire, water, and air. All mantras, praying, chants, and devotion mentioned in Vedas prove it. As time passed on, these were linked with myths, legends, *purana,* and they have adopted different colours and forms till this time. In the beginning, people accepted God to get rid of fear. Still, we worship God to get rid of fear, but the difference is that its forms and colours have been changed. Faith on it is still constant.

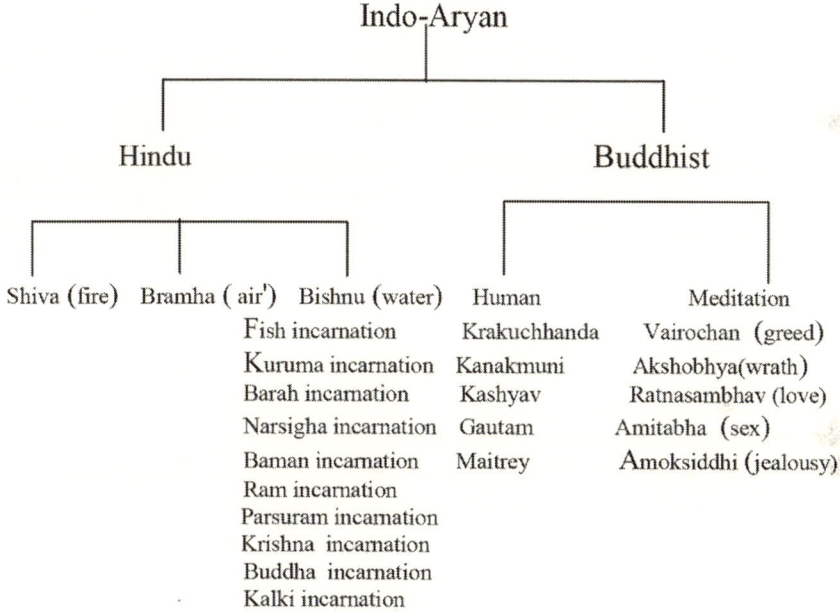

Figure No. 75

This figure depicts the Indo-Aryan religion. It also presents Shiva, Brahma, and Vishnu as symbols of fire, air, and water. Vishnu has been compared to the theory of evolution. Hinduism is a major one among Indo-Aryan religions. Shiva, Brahma, and Vishnu are major gods among thirty-three *kotis,* gods and goddesses. Hindus believe their gods and goddesses are thirty-three kotis. Out of them, Vishnu took many incarnations. He took ten incarnations. Many stories, myths, and legends are based on his different incarnations.

Those incarnations again are based on the theory of evolution. Many people disagree with these ten incarnations of Vishnu. I have interpreted them in brief.

1. *Matsya avatar:* This is the first incarnation of the Hindu god Vishnu in the form of a fish. First of all, water animals were developed in the course of evolution of living beings. Fish live in water only. So, this incarnation indicates water animals.

2. *Kuruma avatar:* This is the second incarnation of Hindu god Vishnu in the form of a tortoise. In the course of evolution of water animals, amphibian animals developed. Such amphibian animals live in both water and on land. This incarnation represents amphibian animals.

3. *Barah avatar:* This is the incarnation of Hindu god Vishnu in the form of a boar. *Barah* mostly live on land. Sometimes, it lives in water. It represents land animals.

4. *Narasingha avatar:* This is the incarnation of Hindu god Vishnu as half-lion and half-man. Animals began to live on land. Living creatures continuously evolved. Evolution of human beings started out of these living beings. Narasingha is a combination of half man and half lion. Thus living creatures developed into human beings.

5. *Baman avatar:* This is the incarnation of Hindu god Vishnu in the form of a dwarf. An animal developed from half-man into a human being. Still, a complete human being was not evolved. *Baman* means a small human being. Human form has been developed in this incarnation. So this incarnation indicates human being.

6. *Ram avatar:* This is supposed to be the incarnation of Hindu god Vishnu with bow and arrow. Ram used to keep hunting with his bow and arrow in the jungle in search of prey. In the hunting age, people used to hunt prey and wander in search of yams and fruits. They used to have simple stone weapons and bows for hunting. Ram also had the same weapons. In this way, Ram represents the hunting age. It is the seventh incarnation, but in my opinion, Ram must be the sixth incarnation.

7. *Parshuram avatar:* This is supposed to be another incarnation of Hindu god Vishnu as a man with a plough. Plough is the weapon of Parshuram. It is used in the farm by peasants. Still, the plough is used to plough and cultivate barren lands in agricultural countries even today. So, it is a symbol of the agricultural age. People started agricultural works in this age. So, it represents agriculture.

8. *Krishna avatar:* This is supposed to be the next incarnation of Hindu god Vishnu. Human civilisation was developed to the maximum in Dwapar age. All the people were well off and powerful. No one was weaker than the other. Everyone was proud of power and property. No one used to respect each other. Due to this temperament, the age had to undergo the state of war. All the states were involved in the Mahabharata war, a famous war during this age. Some of them supported the *Pandava* (five brothers), while others supported the *Kaurava* (hundred brothers) during this war. Huge amounts of property and lives were lost in the war. The whole civilisation was in crisis. Thus, Krishna avatar indicates the climax of human civilisation.

9. *Buddha avatar:* This is supposed to be the ninth incarnation of Hindu god Vishnu. Buddha is also supposed to be the incarnation of Vishnu. Buddha has been considered the incarnation for peace. People aspire for peace after the destruction due to war. The same thing happened even after two world wars. People were so afraid due to the great destruction caused by the first and second world wars that it was possible to establish the United Nations (UN). Since then, Buddha has been propagated as a messenger of peace around the world. Therefore, Buddha has been considered the ninth incarnation of the god Vishnu for peace and reconstruction after the war.

10. *Kalki avatar:* This is supposed to be the last and tenth incarnation of Hindu god Vishnu, like the fifth incarnation of Maitrey Buddha. It's just like Maitreya Buddha—an incarnation of the future. Nothing can be said about the future and evolution of living beings. It cannot be said even about the tenth incarnation of Vishnu. But it is believed that if people face problems, trouble, and suffering, Vishnu will be reincarnated to help the people in the future. So, this is reincarnation of Vishnu that will take place in the future.

In the beginning, these gods were worshipped to be safe from the power of nature. Later, they transformed into different forms and incarnations. These are still unable to work to protect human beings from the power of nature. The problems are still the same. People have discovered clothes, houses, and other things for their protection from such powers.

On the other hand, Buddha exists with meditation. A pictorial understanding on it is to make an attempt to understand the meaning of peace. As Buddha is linked with peace, so I want to discuss it. The reason behind it is that fear is linked with peace in various forms.

Today, the whole world is busy with the slogan for peace, worship, politics, religion, an social service. The world has made a common voice for peace, but the question is which one is peace? Or why do they speak for peace? About which peace did Buddha speak and why did he speak about it? Why do people require peace and what is the reason behind searching for it? The reason for it is chaos. What is the source of disorder? There may be questions like these that invite debates and produce disagreement. Again, there is a possibility of chaos, because the crux of the matter is fear. All the sources of fear, like human temperament, external factors, and natural disasters are the sources of disorders. Likewise, other examples are murder, terror, violence, war, theft, robbery, and kidnap. These are the products of human temperament. Circumstances play a role for such temperaments. When such a temperament exists in the human mind, then he becomes the cause of trouble, pain, suffering, torture, anxiety, and fear for others. Is a solution possible in the temple or worship of God? Why don't people seek a real solution and surrender themselves to God? The reasons behind it is that finding out real solutions and seeking and dealing with it are difficult tasks. People always seek easier outlets; they choose God and worship him for it. Everyone worships God, whether he is the oppressor or the oppressed/criminal or non-criminal. No discrimination is possible there, and he expects to wash away his hardship, troubles, and crimes. Still, our hardship, trouble, and pain are not minimised. God, whom we have believed in for so long, is merely void.

There is a huge discourse is on peace. People have their own definition, understanding, and interest about it. After all, murder, violence, war, bloodshed, quarrels, theft, robbery, dishonesty, treachery, backbiting, drugs, human temperaments, and other hardship, pain, and trouble are the sources of disorder. What peace do A and B want? Similarly, what peace do C and D want? What a man desires, he should determine it himself. It helps find solutions. Desire for peace depends on the individual. So, peace cannot be limited to a formula. Peace that depends on Buddha is naturally different but not always the same. As are the forms of fear, so are the forms of chaos.

While talking about Buddhism, Dr Tulasi Bhattarai writes: 'The crux of Buddhism is to find out emancipation from great troubles like old age and death.'[9]

Similarly about nature, Dr Bhattarai writes: 'Buddha was thoughtful from his childhood. He did not pay much attention to his regime. He did not want to be confined within worldly pleasure. So once he saw an old man and began to imagine—perhaps he was lovely child and young and handsome like him in the past. He has become old as his time passed on. Once when he saw a sick man, he thought—perhaps he was healthy and strong like him. He was shocked when he saw a dead man and he thought—what a surprising! He was speaking and walking just before. How has he been dead? He was even more upset and restless.'[10]

Lines mentioned above show that Buddha was very much fearful of the scenes. He, in fact, had left his palace due to family and social fear. He did not acquire knowledge when he left his palace. Rather, he left due to fright and fear.

The world knows that Buddha was fearful of being sick, old, and dead. Death, sickness, and old age are factors to cause fear. These three things cause fear and fears cause hardship, and the grief invites research. It can be formulated as fear-grief—search. The grief invites research and research gives us fear, but cognition is necessary for liberation from fear.

On fear from grief, Dr Tulasi Bhattarai writes: 'All living creatures fear with word and meaning grief. Even simple creatures fear with grief, let alone the matter of human beings.'[11]

The same thing happened to Buddha in his life. Hence, he left his palace in search of it. He walked all around the jungle in search of a remedy for disease, grief, and death. He could not find it, but found grief through his intuition. There is no relationship between old age and death. Many reasons lie behind grief, and a man becomes unhealthy and old but not dead. Old age and death are more related to fear than grief. How does old age give grief? This is a condition of age. To be old does not mean to have grief. Nobody says, 'I'm so sad due to my old age.' Similarly, nobody says, 'I'm sad because I'm unhealthy.' They don't mention their fear, yet they feel fear but not grief. There are some basic differences between grief and fear. Study on its parts makes it easier to understand. People say that they feel grief on the death of somebody else and 'I'm so fed up with his/her death.' They say this to relatives and friends. He never feels grief for his death; rather, he feels fear about it. Most of the people say, 'I fear to die.' Everything is buried with him after his death, but they produce fear.

Then we try to find out our emancipation from fear. We start to use artificial medicine and massage to prevent old age. We pray to God for security from all things, including disease. Buddha didn't write books in his life; instead, he gave religious speeches. He didn't mention peace in speeches. 'The word peace is not mentioned in *Char Aryas Satya* (four aryas truth), *Dashshil* (Good behave), *Char Darshan* (four philosophies), *Aatha Samyak* (eight samyak), Tripitak, *Om mani padme hun*, *Buddham saranam gachhami* (I surrender to the god, Buddha), *Dhyani* Buddha (Buddha on meditation), Hinyan, Mahayan, Bajrayan and *Terha Bhuvan(Thirteen world)* and *Battis lakchhan (thirty two good character)*.' Therefore, how can we understand that Buddhism gives the message of peace? Instead, great saint Laotse, during the time of Confucius, had mentioned the word peace repeatedly. While talking about ego, he said, 'Give up your ego and follow the true path of peace. This is a way of life.' Similarly, he said, 'Peace is the music of life.'[12]

In this way, Buddhism gives one message and people understand another one. Signifier indicates one thing, but signified indicates another. Whatever activities take place with religion and God, they are oriented to liberating one from fear. This is how the meanings are on construction: Real meanings are on the one hand and constructed meanings are on the other. Other religions and their philosophies are also the same.

Five *Manusik* (human) and five Dhayani (meditation) Buddhas including God, Buddha are in practice. Dhayani Buddhas, with its various forms have come up with consideration of work, anger, affection, greed, and jealousy as enemies of human beings. Are these five human temperaments are the cause for disorder? This is a genuine question. Again, does it lead to peace? I don't think so. Human temperaments and the power of nature as I have mentioned above are the chief factors to cause fear. These all possibly cause fear. When fear is minimised, the possibility of peace increases in individuals, society, and everywhere. It is because minimising fear is a balance in human temperaments. Again, balance in temperaments is to bring balance in the world.

Ten Buddhas as depicted in the above figure are in practice—five *Manusiks(man)* are Crakuchanda, Kanakmuni, Kashyap, Gautam, and Maitreya and five Dhayani Buddhas are Bairochan (enchantment), Akshyobhya (anger), Ratna Sambhav (love), Amitabh (action), and Amok siddhi (jealousy). *Manusik* Buddhists have gone through mediation and penance and they taught and gave education to others. But it has not given any religious speech for peace in the world. Again, *astanga* (eighths organ) of Buddha does not include peace. What astanga speaks is spoken by *rishimunis* (saints). Many religious priests and philosophers have spoken about grief and hardship. We have studied major religions under Indo-Aryan religions and gods, but peace is mentioned nowhere. Buddha also has not uttered a word of peace. He has mentioned non-violence and asks his disciples to speak truth, but they don't mean peace. They don't completely help maintain peace. Peace is a candle of the heart, and it should burn out from the inner heart.

'Rules and regulation is mentioned in salvation as a general one for households and strict one for monks constituted by Mahabir Jain. The same rules and regulations of Mahabir were presented by Parswanath in *Chataryam-samber sambad* as suggestion in religion.'[13]

Of course, Buddha has given knowledge and moral lessons, but he hasn't prescribed a way to peace. My study on Buddhism shows that the religion does not talk about peace. If in case it has, peace is assumed against turmoil and turmoil merely creates fear. That means we always propagate peace as we desire nationally and internationally. So, we speak one thing and do another thing here. What and where is the peace we desire? People worship whatever shape and size, as God is shapeless inwardly. We always express our hardship, troubles, problems, and tension with the same shapeless God. Despite the fact that we express them with God, they have never been minimised. A chief reason behind it is that we never try to solve our problems; rather, we seek shelter.

As stated above, there are a lot of sources, such as violence, murder, ego, wrath, doubt, jealousy, and so on for causing turmoil. How is it possible to acquire peace unless we control them first? If the head of a powerful state adopts an extreme way or becomes egoistic, he starts to wage wars against other countries, and above all, even his citizens will be the victim of atrocity, suppression, and injustice. Unless unnecessary sources of fear are minimised, no peace is possible. At first, these unnecessary sources of fear should be alleviated and eliminated for the establishment of peace in the world, country, society, family, or every individual. Only then is peace possible. To surrender with Dhayani Buddha is a way to extinction. To be a saint, hermit, and yogi is also a way to extinction. It does not help solve any problem. Perhaps everyone says, 'Our god has given us peace and prosperity.' It is just a sweet love, but not reality.

Gods including Vishnu were linked to nature in the past, but now they have been modified to the faith on the basis of necessity. We teach and understand one thing, but the reality is quite different.

Monism presents the same thing as: 'At first, Brahma is marvelous, grandeur, ultimate truth, pervasive and joyous. Even scholars are fearless with the knowledge of Brahma.'[14]

We always seek a fearless path, and our civilisation has developed continuously along this path. We imagine God due to fear. We, the victims of fear, search such a shelter where we expect to be fearless. If the shelter is superior to our inferiorty, limitations, powers, it can certainly provide us the relief. We assumed a symbol with such a superpower as God. We assume that God is ours. We try to minimise our fear through such thoughts. Our extinction in this interpretation has come forth as God.

To be devoted to God is a kind of extinction, laziness, and cowardliness. For many people, it looks right, and for many others, it looks unbelievable. This is indeed a truth. We have the fear of death if any of our kith and kin fall ill. No doubt a man with high mentality measures his temperature, manages medicines, and does whatever he can to save his life. Moreover, he does each and everything for the life of his friend. Thus, he starts to fight against fear, but a lazybones leaves such circumstances in the name of God and fate and starts penance and worship. Isn't it a move towards extinction? When we surrender, even gods are sure to be extinct, let alone the matter of ordinary people. God intervenes in our attempts of a planned scheme to avoid the fear. So we believe in God. It is all due to our attitude of extinction, and we are unable to seek permanent solution and we always ask for help from God. Since the very beginning of civilisation, some people made their attempts to seek permanent solution rather than extinction. Their research became philosophy, science, literature, music, and many others later. No new inventions are possible if all the people had surrendered during that period, and it could deprive them of many facilities and opportunities. The people who thought an attempt to find out solutions is meaningless surrender to God. The monks and nuns were also found to be devoted to God to relieve their fears even in the times of the Vedic period, Latin stories, folklores, and myths. The great men in religious texts and great narratives had fought with the consideration that God is powerful. Victory or loss of victory is supposed to be based on God, but to surrender to God is to lose self-confidence and to become a coward.

People and other creatures were victims of fear, so they imagined a God that could provide a little solace to them even if they didn't do anything. However, it was not an effort for a permanent solution. It was not an attempt for avoiding anxiety, worry, grief, and pain. Devotion to God was merely imaginary *laddu* for them. That was a kind of superstition for their solace. Conditional reflex of God that began since the prehistoric period is still in continuation with additional faiths. Even today, God is secured shelter for protection from fear. In this way, people walk through the divine tunnel to flee from their fears. But their fears, however, exist even in the divine tunnel. Consequently, people started to invent new things for their security. Thus, they exist out from one fear and enter a new fear. This process continues from the past to the present. The god for those who have faith has become merely a shelter of faith from fear.

Neha Bhikramanashosti pratyavayo na biddhate.
Swalpamapyasya dharmsya trayate mahato bhayat (Bhagawat Gita 2/40).

Similarly, Bhagwat Gita says, 'Whatever work is performed that can never be destroyed in this world. There is no any obstruction on the path of karma (work). Even a little adoption of karma (work) in religion protects us from dangerous fear.'[15]

End Notes:

1. Bishnu Adhikari, *Darshanko Kehi Anautha Paksha (Some Wonderful Aspects of Philosophy)*, Ratna Book Store, Kathmandu, 2064 v.s. p. 1.

2. Bishnu Adhikari, *Darshanko Kehi Anautha Paksha (Some Wonderful Aspects of Philosophy)*, Ratna Book Store, Kathmandu, 2064 v.s. p. 5.
3. Bishnu Adhikari, *Darshanko Kehi Anautha Kura (Some Wonderful Aspects of Philosophy)*, Ratna Book Store, Kathmandu, 2064 v.s. p. 17.
4. Bishnu Adhikari, *Darshanlo Kehi Anautha Kura (Some Wonderful Aspects of Philosophy)*, Ratna Book Store, Kathmandu 2064 v.s. p. 21.
5. Bishnu Adhikari, *Darshanko Kehi Anautha Kura (Some Wonderful Aspects of Philosophy)*, Ratna Book Store, Kathmandu 2064 v.s. p. 29.
6. Bishnu Adhikari, *Darshanko Kehi Anautha Kura (Some Wonderful Aspects of Philosophy)*, Ratna Book Store, Kathmandu 2064 v.s. p. 31.
7. Birendra Prasad Mishra, *Introduction to Philosophy*. Nepal Charity Foundation, Kathmandu, 2065 v.s. p. 101.
8. Sachchidanda Mishra, *Ishwar Marisaky (God is Dead)*, trans. Balkrishna Shrestha 'Nebha', Utsarga Publication Baranasi, 2009, p. 116.
9. Tulasi Bhattarai, *Purbiya Chintan Parampara (Eastern Study Tradition)*, Student Publication P. Ltd., Kathmandu, 2009, p. 287.
10. Tulasi Bhattarai, *Purbiya Chintan Parampara (Eastern Study Tradition)*, Student Publication P. Ltd., Kathmandu, 2009, p. 275.
11. Tulasi Bhattarai, *Purbiya Chintan Parampara (Eastern Study Tradition)*, Student Publication P. Ltd., Kathmandu, 2009, p. 274.
12. Bishnu Adhikari, *Darshanko Kehi Anautha Kura (Some Wonderful Aspects of Philosophy)*, Ratna Book Store, Kathmandu, 2064 v.s. p. 73.
13. Kavitaram Shrestha, Mahabhiniskramanka, *Aswikrit Paila (Budhha's Biography Novel)*, Bibek Srijanshil Publication, Kathmandu, 2010, p. 205.
14. Arjundev Panta, *Bedanta-Darshan Sar (Brief Vedaanta Philosophy)*, Ratna Book Store, Kathmandu, 2062 v.s. p. 48.
15. Arjundev Panta, *Bedanta-Darshan Sar (Brief Vedaanta Philosophy)*, Ratna Book Store, Kathmandu, 2062 v.s. p. 95.

e.   Fear Struggle in Existence of Darwin

Charles Darwin has included interpretations on 'struggle for existence' and 'survival of the fittest' in his book *Origin of Species*. The 'struggle for existence' has been interpreted as the struggle of plants and creatures for existence. This theory is applicable to human beings. All the creatures and plants struggle for their existence in the world. They engage in a struggle with the power of nature, hunger, and their own rivals. They all have to win in this struggle. Those who lose in the struggle get their lives finished. Plants do not have any class and group like that of human beings. When we plant seeds in the field, they grow, then starts the struggle for fertilisers and for their lives. Whichever is able to absorb sufficient fertiliser and water grows well and others no longer live. Thus, they have to engage in the struggle for survival. Cows and others hardly go there to destroy the crops.

If living creatures don't die, their numbers increase fast. A pair of species can cover the whole world. People used to struggle for food in ancient times. Similarly, every living creature will hurry up one day for food. It consists of human beings. They will hurry up from rural areas to urban areas and from one country to another. The population growth in the world affects their foods and habitats. The climate change affects agricultural products. Similarly, human activities affect ecology. 'When we go from south to north or damp land to dry land, we see numbers of some living creatures are minimizing to extinction,' Darwin writes. Even the plant that is about to dry can be alive in a suitable climate. Green and healthy plants dry if the climate is unsuitable. If plants and living creatures are provided with food and shelter and they are allowed to grow freely, species of the plants and living creatures will increase sufficiently to cover the whole world within some centuries.

When we plant the seeds of maize, some of the seeds do not produce shoots. Some plants dry due to the lack of fertiliser, some dry due to the unfavourable climate, and we take out some of them while we prune. Only few maize plants give fruit. Those plants have to struggle for survival if the fertiliser is insufficient. Maize plants in a favourable place look green and others no longer look green.

As mentioned above, plants with sufficient fertiliser and suitable climate grow well, but other plants beyond such environments dry soon. People swinging into two poles, death and life, are restless to get food, and if they are provided a little, they start to struggle for survival. The TV also shows such pictures of people fighting for a little food in distribution centres.

How terrible the fear of hunger is! While clarifying it, Rahul Sankrityayan writes: 'In station and cities, you can see some people who eat food stuff thrown on the ground and they even snatch food from the mouth of dogs to eat.'[1] The TV, radio, and newspapers show such pathetic pictures. Such struggle for hunger always exists.

When there is a struggle, there is the possibility of fear. Everyone wants to live longer and feels fright with fear. Perhaps the creatures having a little consciousness have a little fear. But human beings are rational as well as conscious animals. So, people struggle more than any other animal. We can witness such symptoms in every human activity. Yet, we ignore them in our daily lives. For example, limited vacancies in good posts have been announced when unemployment rates are very high; then we can see tough competition for jobs. They try to grab opportunities via different means: nepotism, favouritism, bribes, and servility. We can see the similar diehard struggle of people in underdeveloped countries to go to developed countries.

We can present some examples here—parasitic plants, dogs fighting for bones, and unemployed youths fighting for good jobs.

1. Fear struggle in parasitic plants

There are a lot of parasitic flowers on a big tree. They have limited food there. They have their food from the tree, and they have competition for food. These plants have no idea of life with and without food. What they want is life. Creepers move towards food. These plants also have competition and struggle within their circles. The plant which gets a good opportunity eats and drinks and becomes healthy. To be healthy means to live longer. The rest of them become unhealthy and dry soon. Even they have knowledge that scarcity of food causes death for them. They don't move to and fro for food without knowledge. I think they have fear rather than worry. People fear with the same process. The same process applies to plants in forests, dry land, paddy fields, hills, and in other places. They survive with the same process— struggle for survive.

2. Fear struggle of dogs

While talking about food stuffs, Darwin says, 'Animals struggle with each other for food and their lives when they lack foods.'[2]

If a piece of bone is thrown into the midst of hungry dogs, they attack each other and try to grab the piece. All dogs try to eat the bone. They bark at and try to bite other dogs that come closer. The stronger ones bite and chase the rest and take control of the bone. It invites a terrible brawl. Some of them die in such a brawl, and many others will leave seriously injured. Perhaps all dogs know much better than any plant that they die if they suffer from a food crisis. This is a struggle for food to survive. The winner among them gets the opportunity for food and drinks; its health becomes good and it lives longer. The rest of them suffer from food scarcity, hunger, and worse health and die earlier. This theory applies to domestic and wild animals like tigers, bears, and others. Their lives undergo this theory struggle for survival.

3. Fear struggle of job seekers

The rate of unemployment is rising in the world. It is more intensive in underdeveloped countries. We can witness long queues of job seekers with application forms for jobs if in case a vacancy is announced. The scene is worse than the dogs fighting for bones. They use nepotism, favouritism, bribes, conspiracy, and servility for the job. Moreover, the job is linked with their present and future. So, a man with a good job has high prestige and living standards. They seek jobs to avoid the fear of hardship, trouble, and suffering. Many other people lack alternative resources of their incomes in their lives. Again, life without income undergoes hardship and suffering. They fight against each other about jobs due to these reasons. Unemployed young people do not fight for jobs visibly like dogs; they fight invisibly.

Fear struggles mentioned above are similar in nature but different in form. They all fear to die. So, they struggle for survival.

1. Fear in animals and plants

About how creatures struggle for survival during food scarcity, Darwin writes: 'If the production is reduced due to climate change, creatures struggle inside and outside their groups for foods to survive.'[3]

Darwinian Theory makes various interpretations on fears of creatures and plants: struggle for existence and survival of the fittest. His book *Origin of Species* consists of many other interpretations. Animals struggle, become jealous, and they doubt. They fight to capture food. They never feel right to distribute foods among others. Nature—'it is for me to eat' belongs not only to animals; that belongs to human beings as well. Such a human temperament was clearly visible in the past, and it is not so much visible at present. Self-centred thoughts—'I'm to eat' and 'I'm to live' still exist as in the past. The reason behind its invisibility today is that people produce or earn sufficient incomes for themselves. Still, many countries suffer from starvation and food crisis in the world. We have heard and seen people fighting for a piece of bread through different medias. Sufficiency of food for animals prevents them from struggling for food. When they are busy eating, they have no time for fighting. Thus, this is a struggle against scarcity.

They all want to eat and live longer. Above all, this is a struggle for food and survival. This is the momentum, yet they are to overcome death.

Living creatures don't have any necessity for living nor have human beings. Existentialists say, 'People do not have rights over their births. Rather, they have been thrown into the unwanted world.'[4]

Living creatures, including human beings, have no certain purpose for living and eating, but they want to live after their birth. There is no meaning of what life is for. No creatures or animals live due to any meaning. Living ones fear death. Food and shelters is necessary for living. Insufficient food and shelter causes ill health and brings untimely death.

Darwin says, 'Some creatures remain alive while others disappear on the basis of survival of the fittest in the nature.' I disagree with it. All creatures should choose their existence themselves. They must have the capacity of adaptability according to nature. Those without the capacity of adaptability disappear gradually from this world. All the creatures and plants should develop their physical structure, immunity, sense organs, and adaptable capacities of other organs, and other changes that occurred in nature. Those without such adaptable capacities will disappear due to their weaknesses. Nature does not help them to be alive any longer in storms, earthquakes, floods, and landslides. They should be responsible for their security. Nature makes them unable to take their own responsibilities. So, selection is based not on nature, but on the desires of creatures and plants.

Many animals have disappeared from this world within ten thousand years. The reason behind such extinction is their inability to adopt the adaptable capacity. In such a condition, the desire of being alive does not work. Their extinction is indeed depletion in nature. Such depletion exists in some parts of nature, while construction exists in some other parts. There is the selection of nature in non-living things and the selection of creatures and plants in living things. This is proved by events and incidents. Creatures run away whenever incidents and accidents occur. A man who is on the verge of death, he still desires life. This is not the selection of nature, but the condition in which he is unable to live. He is very fearful of death at that time. He wished he could be alive. All unhealthy creatures, as well as plants, despite their desire to live, live no longer either due to the scarcity of medicines or due to other reasons. Therefore, they should adopt adaptable capacities to accommodate the changes in nature. Invention, construction, and creation to some extent are for security and adaptability. It helps us to protect ourselves from natural and human-caused disasters. If they are able to protect themselves from such disasters, they continue to live, whereas others disappear from this world in the days to come.

2. *Survival of the fittest*

If creatures and plants adopt adaptable capacities based on the changes occurring in nature, they remain alive. They have to increase their capacity of adaptability on the basis of necessity. The medicine used for eradicating fleas and bugs in the past is ineffective to work now due to its adaptable capacities. Many changes have occurred in nature and continue to occur—climate changes and chemical changes. Due to these changes in nature, adaptability is a must. In such a condition, fear compels them to make attempts to live. To live is not necessity, but living ones fear death; change is urgent. People adopt different measures to live—they steal something, lie to others, and murder others. The reason is he has to live by hook or by crook. Flexibility supports them to live. If non-vegetarians suffer scarcity of meats, they start to eat the available food. When a man suffers from famine, he eats alternative food that he has never eaten.

Only those who can struggle with crisis and problems can live and the rest of them die. Jobs, work, and occupations are for living. Those who succeed in getting jobs live with jobs, and those who fail get no jobs—this is the case everywhere. Frogs spray their poisons and lizards change their colours for living. All creatures are full of specific characters as gifts of nature, and to leave them unused can cause extinction. Animals receive pre-signals of earthquakes due to their specific characters. When they receive signals of possible disasters, they prepare for their protection. Thus, selection of lives should be based on our desires.

The surroundings of Earth are the nature of Earth, whereas surroundings of human beings are the nature of human beings. The nature of a man in one place is different from the nature of man in another place. The natures of two people in the same place are also different—unless the time, the sun, the air, and the nature are the same. Again, the nature that influences a man does not influence others. Two different people standing in the same place can differ in feeling hot and cold. In such a condition, who does nature select? A man who feels hotter and colder than the other feels fright, fear, and dies sooner. If creatures die in a certain time, it will be possible for us to argue for the selection of nature. Death is uncertain and the age of nature around the earth is also uncertain. If living creatures increase their adaptable capacities, they can live longer. The average age of people was fifty yesterday, but it has increased to eighty today, particularly in Japan, America, and Hong Kong.

Widening this thought, Prof. Dr Sanjeev Upretti further writes: 'With further development of technology, in addition to heart and kidney, is transplantation of brain possible? Perhaps, memory and thought will also be transplanted. People may live centuries due to the transplantation of new heart, hands and legs, nose, eye, brain and thought after two centuries.'[5]

How can it be selection of nature? This is a selection of man. Hence, the selection isn't based on the selection of nature, but based on the desires of man, other living creatures, and plants. If they are unable to live, they die and disappear one day.

'When we review on struggle, we faithfully console ourselves. Both the struggle of nature and feeling of fear don't continue forever. Generally they die, healthy, strong and happy creature can survive longer.'[6]

Fear is hidden in this statement of Darwin. His statement can be justified as:

a. Fear of hunger
b. Fear of defeat in struggle
c. Fear of death and existence

a. Fear of hunger

First of all, living creatures fear hunger. They work day and night to get food. When they are in search of food, they encounter different animals in some places, they entertain, and they take rest in other places. They entertain when they get food and they doze when they get no food. Generally, they spend their days in this way. Scarcity of food brings fear of hunger. Then, it constitutes grounds for struggle for food. Similarly, struggle is necessary for searching for food if other creatures are also in search of food. Availability of food saves one from worry, but its scarcity invites anxiety, worry, and fear of death.

How living creatures struggle for fear of hunger, so do the people. Due to consciousness, people have much fear. This struggle is the product of fear of death. If people didn't have fear of death, they would not struggle so hard and they would not fight till blood is shed. No one struggles if the fear of death is absent. They have to struggle for food with animals and nature. They are thus ready to face risks to live.

b. Fear of defeat

Struggle is in connection with victory and defeat. There is a possibility of defeat in any struggle. Defeat means injury, lack of food, and death. Each of these three things has a constant fear. Fear of death is the final one. The rival may kill and eat up if he is more powerful in struggle. If they have equal power, both of them fear injury and death again. Similarly, they can die if there is no food in the struggle for food. There is a struggle with nature also. There is also the possibility of fear caused by nature. It is possible that nature also defeats them. We have to win in all these struggles from any angles. We should take another thing in place of one. Only then, can we live. If not, there is the possibility of the fear of death.

c. *Fear of death and existence*

There is the fear of possible death in any struggle. Several struggles and problems are brought due to desire for survival. This desire bears innumerable problems. To fulfill this desire is the purpose of the man. Attempt to achieve this desire is linked with prestige and existence.

People must struggle more than birds and animals due to their levels of consciousness, necessity and problems. For it people have too many things like their societies, ethnicities, religions, cultures, languages, scripts, countries, prestige, property, relatives and friends. Several things are necessary to maintain them all and establish good relationships. Fear is associated to them all and struggle is necessary for them all. Animals have only struggle for food but human beings have beyond mere food. Darwin is said to have interpreted struggle for existence widely. He says, 'I use struggle for existence widely as well symbolically. It deals with not only one generation but also the whole generations of living creatures. It also deals with the dependency of one upon another.'[7]

But man is a distinguished and civilised creature. He has to undergo many struggles. All things, such as nature, desire, aspiration, science and technology, invention, and astrological research, cause fear, and he has to struggle with them to live. These are the result of knowledge. Animals don't know: 'Why do I eat? What happens if I don't eat? What is lineage?' They eat for the sake of eating. Animals hardly know about life and death, but human beings are different from animals. People fear losing respect, reputation, prestige, caste, language, religion, culture, and country. They always struggle for protection and preservation of these all. Their existence is based on them. Food and shelter maintains the existence of animals. Only these two things can't maintain the existence of human beings. When people were like animals in the ancient period, only food and shelter could help their existence. Now, their existence is not merely limited to food and shelter. Their existence can only be preserved with their language, script, religion, culture, country, caste, society, and family.

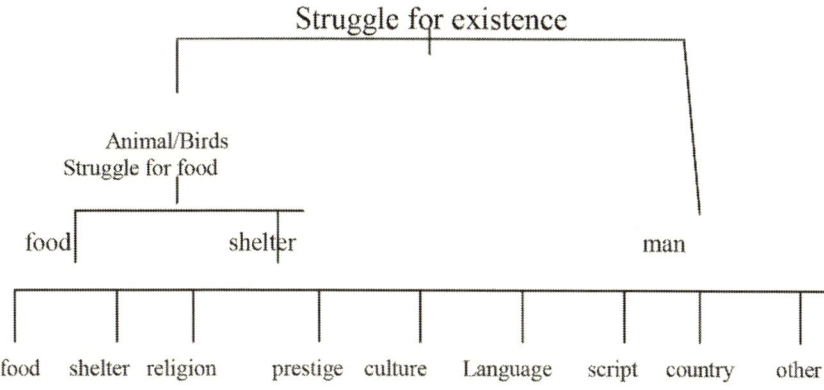

Figure No. 76

The struggle for existence by animals along with struggle for existence by people have been depicted in this figure. The struggle of existence by animals consists of food and shelter. They don't have more existence and struggle than these. Darwin incorporates people with animals and birds in his interpretations of struggle for existence that includes merely struggle for food and shelter. People need all that is related to their identity and existence. They need food, shelter, and clothing as well as community, religion, prestige, culture, language, script, and country for their existence. They fear that all these things may end as time passes on. Extinction of these things invite crisis in their existence. Struggle for food doesn't count when the existence of human beings is in crisis. In the past, people used to struggle for food sufficient for one meal. Now, such struggle has been minimised. The search for identity is the reason for struggle, war, murder, and terror in the world. The identity distinguishes them from the rest.

This is not the struggle for food like that of animals. When he is separated from one line, he spends his life for the preservation. He interprets, loves, preserves, and respects his community, language, script, religion, culture, and country. He considers it a great ideal. Above all, these things have great existence for him. He is not ready to tolerate anyone who does something to dominate it. People engage in discussion, argument, and moreover are in war for it. All wars fought in the world are due to these reasons, because they fear that their country, language, script, religion, culture, and prestige may become extinct. Fear urges them to work for their preservation. The involvement of all in preservation for the same purpose results in war. Wars due to these reasons in fact are struggles for existence. Thus, important aspects of human beings have been missed in Darwin's theory, 'struggle for existence'. People hardly struggle for food. Therefore, they always struggle due to the reasons mentioned above.

End Notes:

1. Rahul Sankrityayan, *Samyabad Nai Kina? (Why is Communism?)*, trans. Kashiram Gaire, Pragati Book Sadan, Kathmandu, 1934, p. 34.
2. Charles Darwin, *The Origin of Species*, Penguin Books, London, 1968, p. 117.
3. Charles Darwin, *The Origin of Species*, Penguin Books, London, 1968, p. 117.
4. Sanjeev Uppreti, *Sidhantaka Kura (Aspect of Theory)*, Akshar Creation, Nepal, 2068, v.s. p.145.
5. Sanjeev Uppreti, *Sidhantaka Kura (Aspect of Theory)*, Akshar Creation, Nepal, 2068, v.s. p. 320.
6. Charles Darwin, *The Origin of Species*, Penguin Books, London, 1968, p. 121.
7. Charles Darwin, *The Origin of Species*, Penguin Books, London, 1968, p. 116.

f.   Fear in Necessity Order by Abraham H. Maslow

In relation to the power of hunger, Abraham H. Maslow has said, 'When a man is very hungry and thirsty, he does not see and think about anything. He only contemplates on eating and drinking. He dreams about food and water.'[1]

Similarly, in regard to desire he has said, 'When man's desire is fulfilled, another one comes along. Even after the desire is met, the next one comes up again. Thus, this process goes on. This is a life-long process of human nature. Man always necessitates something.'

According to Maslow's theory of necessity, man has the fear of lack of food at first and of security, prestige, and respect later on. This fear leads to necessity. Man always lives in constant fear of lacking food, shelter, and clothing and losing society, kith and kin, and prestige. Relief from these fears turns out to be his necessity. This is the way prosperity comes along after the crisis. Maslow has interpreted it as a necessity order. When a man is well off, a lot of fears start arising, but he hasn't included it in his theory.

Thus, he has interpreted five necessities, viz. health, security, relation, prestige, and self-esteem. This theory of necessity can also be studied in the sense of fear.

1.   Health necessity

As I have mentioned above, every cell of the body has their respective senses. Those cells pass messages to the brain about food scarcity. The information passed by one or two cells does not result in any effect in the brain. So when the brain senses the information passed by all the necessary cells, the function begins and we feel hungry, thirsty, and sleepy. If hunger, thirst, etc. depended on our sense of perception, we would feel hungry, thirsty, and sleepy willingly, but it can't be so. We can't eat, drink, and rest according to our own will. The reason cells function together is that they perceive that they die out in the absence of eating, drinking, and sleeping. This is the primary need for health, which is brought out by fear. We are afraid of death and necessity produced by the fear of death. We eat and drink to live. These are basic needs of living beings. Everyone, including relatives, is ignored to fulfil the basic needs, for he has to live his life at first. There is no value of the whole universe if he is not alive. He has his logic about health necessity for humans at first. This necessity includes air, water, and nutritious food. In case he does not have any food and water, he passes away. Man always fears death. He wants to live because of fear. He has health necessity due to this fear. If earthquakes, big natural disasters, etc. occur, he has no sense of hunger, thirst, and rest. He only feels hungry, thirsty, and sleepy in a normal condition. That is why fear is greater than hunger.

2. Security necessity

Man believes security to be important after food management. He feels insecure due to various reasons such as murder, violence, theft, robbery, crime, natural disaster, storm, hurricane, thunderbolt, rainfall, flood, famine, disease, explosive weapon, and war. Health necessity is just an internal one. He has to be safe from external forces as well. Man makes arrangement for safe shelter, healthy life, life insurance, job guarantee, and financial fund for his life. In addition to this, he has to be also safe from other factors such as disease and enemies that affect his life. If he has no security, there is the possibility of problems of trouble and death. He needs the security of everything, i.e. desire, ambition, freedom, etc. He suffers from all these fears. If a man has no fear of death, it is not necessary for him to take care of all these things.

When a man feels secure, he requires many other facilities to live a prosperous life.

He does not remember anyone if a big natural disaster arises somewhere else. He runs around, losing his senses. A man tries to save himself first if a house catches fire or there is the occurrence of the earthquake, flood, etc. Only then does he remember his family members and his property. There are many examples of people who at the time of the sudden occurrence of earthquakes may have been sleeping and rush out of their homes without their clothes and later become aware of being nude. A number of such incidents have occurred at other places too. So a man seeks his family and property only after saving his life and having security. When a man is free from the fear of hunger, he has the fear of security. He needs several materials and things for his security. That is why things are required so that he can be safe from this fear.

3. Social necessity

Man has the fear of his family and property after he gets relief from the fear of health and security; it is very difficult for him to live his life alone in this immense world. He always has the fear of lacking property and of being alone. Loneliness and poverty bring out fear. Man needs everything, i.e. friends, relatives, family, and property. He also expects love and care from them. How can he live alone in this vast world? It's really difficult to live alone. On the other hand, the age and health of a man don't always remain the same. He grows old and becomes sick. If he falls ill, there will be no one to take care of him. Therefore, he needs a person who can take care of him. Everyone has their own nature. He wants to share his feelings about his work, wrath, love, temptation, jealousy, and doubt with others. So he wants someone in his life. He has no worry about his life after he has all these things.

4. Social prestige

No one can be fully satisfied with respect to family and property. He needs his family and property till he has them. When these necessities are fulfilled, he requires right, prestige, reputation, identity, importance, commendation, respect, etc. Such prestige is categorised into two groups: internal and external. Internal prestige refers to self-esteem and self-encouragement that help to get success. There are different kinds of people in society. They carry on competing with each other as regard to senior versus junior and rich versus poor. Everyone always wants to be a senior and prestigious person in society. He is always busy as he has to maintain this social status because he has the fear of being dominated and treated badly if he is unsuccessful and powerless. Then he appears to take on different roles to relieve this fear. The main purpose of all these roles is that he wants to be a prestigious, rich, and successful person in society.

5. Self-esteem

No one is satisfied with the fulfilment of the above things alone. After that, he wants to be distinguished in society. This distinctness inspires him to create, construct, and find out the truth. All people cannot meet this quality, and no man is satisfied with his own creation, construction, justice, and truth. That is why he gets involved in his activity continually. In such a case, he feels like doing or taking part in social services, donating, etc. He cannot do anything for his social prestige unless he is free from the above fears. It is also known that some people have done distinctive work by breaking rules and regulations. So he sacrifices everything for social work. But all people cannot do so for the sake of society. It depends on the success of his contribution or service towards their society.

This theory of necessity is based on fear. A man keeps on increasing his needs as a result of successive or consecutive fears. He himself carries on bringing out this fear. A higher position produces more fear; consequently, he becomes the victim of fear to a larger extent. It had been just so even in ancient times. Food was the primary need for a man in the past because he knew that he would die if he did not have anything to eat. He required shelter after having arranged for food. Similarly, he kept on feeling the necessity of having friends, group, society, country, and law after getting shelter. In the course of meeting all these objectives, some people became slaves while some owners. Different people hold different kinds of job, such as feudalist, capitalists, workers, brokers, journalists, literati, and politicians. It is still prevailing in society. All this is a result of the chain of fear. The theory of necessity is just like this. If there is not this chain of fear, a well-off man will not have any reason to have fear. This theory doesn't fit in all other cases. The lives of most of the people are like that of Sisyphus. Sisyphus climbed up and down the mountain. The act of going up and down continued. That is to say, the act of climbing up and down the hill continued. Thus, he went down after one or two achievements. Some people, after carrying out the second task, are able to get their success directly or reach their destination. His ideology depends on his self-pride, desire, ambition, commitment, sacrifice, and penance.

A man moves to a town, a foreign country, etc. owing to fear. Those who arrive in a foreign country have high prestige, but he becomes dissatisfied with what he has got because his desires have been met according to the theory of necessity. Still he seems to seek some better opportunities. He seems to try and gain more and more benefits in his life by ignoring his kith and kin and relatives. All the fulfilled desires have to be initiated from the beginning again as soon as the country and time change. Their fears do not subside at all. Instead they go on to grow more fearful. The village people may not have high prestige and all the requirements, but they don't have to wander without any gain as in the town. As a rule, they work from morning to evening and comfortably rest at night.

All the stages of necessities that Maslow has interpreted concerning a well-off person are accomplished. After the fulfilment of all these stages, they live their lives happily. But they are more aware of some things than the common people and run here and there in search of more facilities. Money attracts and blocks money. They take necessary or unnecessary medicine, get addicted to drugs, and are sent to prison for different crimes. Some of them commit suicide and some suffer from mental illness because they have a lot of stress as regard to the security of property, necessity, and increment of investment. They always have the fear of downfall from the present position. If they have a little loss in their business, they feel as if they are completely hopeless. That is why they are hard-working; they work day and night at the cost of their health.

Maslow's theory can be seen in the context of time and country. This theory can be only applicable to a constant condition of time and country. But the theory of hunger is repeated again when the situation of a country remains unstable. It means that this order can be applicable if a person has lived in a certain place. If he moves to another place, his position is not different from the previous one. He has to start his life from the hunger struggle again.

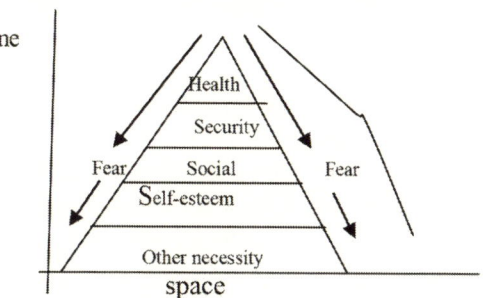

Figure No. 77

The figure shows time, fear, necessity, and country along with pyramid.
(1) Health necessity, (2) security necessity, (3) social necessity,
(4) self-esteem, and (5) other necessity that can't be fulfilled.

Here the necessity has been shown between time and country. The five necessities are based on Maslow's theory of necessity. Maslow, in the course of fulfilling the consecutive fears, stopped putting his interpretation on necessity after completing those five. In fact, man's necessity, ambition, desire, and temptation can never be fulfilled. They are expanded like an open and infinite sky. Room 5 in the above figure is big and spacious. This room is concerned with this matter. It has been clarified that there is fear in these necessities that cannot be fulfilled.

Let time be in a constant condition and the country in an inconstant one. If a man who has been living in Nepal with high prestige starts living in England, his life begins with health necessity again, because he has to make food arrangements there at first. After the arrangements of food and shelter, he has to think about security, prestige, and self-esteem. Those who migrate to another place pass their days like this. Man's life begins with hunger struggle wherever he goes. There is the fear of death in case of food scarcity. Therefore, leaving all other work and concern he struggles for food all the time. Those whose necessities have been fulfilled in one place should start their lives from the beginning again.

Let the country be in a constant and time in an inconstant condition. Change of time also affects this theory in the same country. This theory can be applied to a normal condition, but different kinds of incidents have occurred in the world. There has been money deflation several times in several countries in the world, mostly since 2000. Similarly, the outbreak of SARS epidemic in 2003 and fowl epidemic in 2009, economic crisis, tsunami, natural disasters have had an immense impact on this theory because the world economy and capital investment have turned on each other. All these things are interconnected with each other like around a ball. If one of the parts is badly affected, the whole parts will collapse soon after. As soon as the investment of a country collapses, it affects another country as well. Nobody knows anything about where and when it happens. Nothing is known about war, fearful attack, and natural disaster. Man always has the fear of all these things. In such a case, he has fear of death at first. When there is a strong fear of security, other necessities become minor. However, he wants to strive to live. Having left everything else, he wants to live.

Fear has been shown in the five necessities in Figure no. 77. Firstly, necessities are the result of fear. Secondly, fear goes on exiting, although all necessities are fulfilled. There is no certainty that human life will live at present. We may deviate from our original plan. Political change, civil war, natural disaster, epidemic, etc. are the reasons for causing this situation. World investment is at in a great loss at present. This theory can be applicable when all the social, political, and economic aspects come a long way as a rule. But if economic, social, political, etc. problems arise; natural disaster, epidemic, etc. break out; fluctuation occurs due to any reason; and war, civil war, etc. take place, a man ignores everything and wants to live at first. An invisible fear seems appear at any time. That is why time and country should remain unchanged for this theory to be applied. Even a slight change has an effect on this theory. If time and country are in a constant condition, man also remains unchanged, but it's impossible.

According to Maslow's theory of necessity, a man can live a pleasurable, happy, luxurious, and comfortable life after meeting all the five stages. This is what the theory deals with. But their reality is quite different from that of the theoretical concept. Afterwards, they seem to become more restless. His necessity of money can never be fulfilled. If money is just required to accomplish this theory, there will be no reason for wandering. Similarly, ambition, temptation, and necessity are also never fulfilled. That is why a man seems to be very busy at the cost of his health. There are a majority of wealthy people rather than poor who always run after money without caring about their health. If we look at the richest people of the world, they are found to be busier than ordinary people.

Another reason man is so much busy is that he has the fear of losing his prestige and property that he has earned. On the other hand, his earnings may finish at any time. What happens then? The more he earns, the more he suffers from fear. That is to say, the more income he has, the more fear he suffers from. Therefore, although he earns a lot of money, fulfils his necessities, and has a high prestige, he cannot live, eat, and walk peacefully and happily because he is surrounded by fear at all times.

End Notes:

1. Abraham H. Maslow, *Motivation and Personality*. Longman, c1987, Third ed. p. 7.

g. Fear in Population Growth by Malthus

I'm trying to interpret the theory of population promulgated by Malthus, supposing it's important from the perspective of fearism. Population is increasing day by day according to this theory. The growing population is occupying and overusing fertile land, dry land, forest, country, sea, and desert. Land and forest are being destroyed by the overuse of human activities. Streams and channels are drying up and rainfall is eroding the soil in the country. The population has doubled in some countries in fifteen years while in others in twenty-five years. If the rate of population growth remains the same, the whole earth will gradually be occupied by the population. People will be moving to every part of the world like insects. There may be a situation of 'human bomb explosion' in the world and it will affect everything. And there will be a serious problem of victuals, ecology, animals, and plantation in no time. The theory of Malthus has presupposed that this fearful situation will come about. As this theory has illustrated the fearful situation of the presence of people and the lack of food, it has been quite contextual. I put forward my own interpretation on fear in this theory.

In his book entitled *An Essay of Principle of Population*, he has mentioned, 'If there is no consideration of population growth in time, it will bring about a major problem in the future, for the rate of population growth is going on geometrically whereas the rate of production is going on arithmetically.'[1]

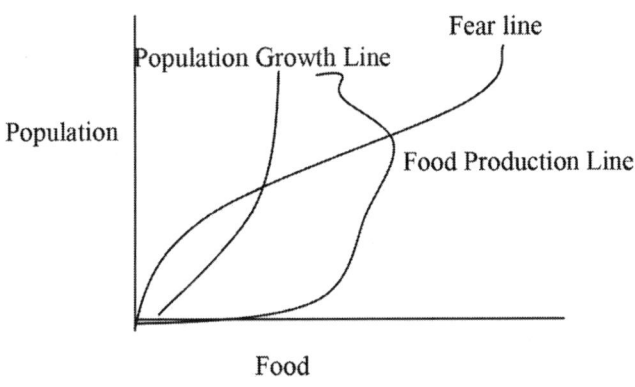

Figure No. 78

Figure no. 78: Population, fear line, population growth line, food production line, food. In the figure, population has been shown on the one side and food production on the other. The growth of population is in geometrical proportion whereas the production of food is in arithmetic proportion. The fear line touches both the lines and rises up. It has been proved that fear is also caused by the growth of population and the lack of food production.

This is the heart of his book. Many interpretations are based on this. The most rational and powerful creature protect themselves from any danger at first. They make food, shelter, and security arrangements. Man is the most rational creature, so he is powerful. He can keep away from the attack of natural power, animals, and different diseases. He tries to save himself from different crises, natural disaster, etc. On the other hand, he keeps on increasing the rate of population. As a result of this, the death rate is decreasing and the growth rate is increasing. Concerning this, in the course of giving an interpretation of Darwin's theory of evolution, I've said, 'Nature does not choose any creatures but creatures choose themselves.' Man is continually increasing the population even also because of religious belief, conservatism, and superstition. Their necessities are also growing along with the rate of population growth. All things such as food, clothing, and shelter are growing as well. The more the population increases, the more they overuse, dig, plough, and destroy forests, hills, mountains, peaks, seas, deserts, streams, channels, etc. Therefore, all of them are becoming extinct. People are overusing them in those areas and problems are getting more serious. This activity is having an adverse effect on the ecological system and the environment is being polluted. The ozone layer is depleting and ultraviolet rays of the sun are directly passing through, so different problems have started breaking out. Various new problems have arisen so far.

Many houses are being built in all the areas, viz. forests, hills, seas, deserts, plains, which we have seen in our lives. The fertile land has been occupied by houses. The area in which there would be a house has been occupied by a village. Similarly, villages are continually turning into towns and towns into big metropolitan cities. We know that the price of land and everything in the market has risen. A land that was worth about one hundred thousand Nepalese rupees ten years earlier costs ten million rupees at present. All this is because of the population density and growth. The overuse of air, water, land, and forest affects everything badly in all the areas. Accordingly, food production is diminishing due to the rapid growth of urbanisation. Still there is some barren land in some parts of the world and people are heading for the remaining virgin field and overusing them to meet their respective interests. Victuals are lacking owing to uncontrolled growth of population. It is obvious that there is lack of food for sure, for houses are being built in rice paddies. Likewise, there is lack of grass and meadows are not available anywhere. One day there will be only people after the remaining part of land, sea, and desert has been used up and look like the skeleton of a dinosaur. This is the fearful situation Malthus had already presupposed.

Thus, lack of food and growth of population have brought about many problems. The ecological system has been affected by deforestation. There is no rainfall at the right time. Snow has started melting and the earth is suffering from global warming. As a result of this, new problems seem to be arising. If this growth rate goes on like this, the condition of people will be like that of the dogs that fight for a piece of bone. The issue about food is the basic need. Maslow's theory is applicable only with regard to the solution of food. Otherwise, man will always suffer because of the problems of food. All things such as society, country, caste, religion, culture, relatives, and kith and kin made by men are for normal condition. He wants all things, i.e. entertainment, games, relatives, kith and kin, in normal condition. They do not suffer from hunger and disease if they have a good relationship with each other. When they are hungry and suffer from disease, the fear struggle begins among all family members and kith and kin. Yesterday's good friends turn out to be unfriendly. What was good yesterday turns out to be bad. Everyone fears death very much. They want to be alive. Of course, they compete with each other as they are jealous in a negative manner. He always wishes, 'May I eat and wear!' Therefore, tussle begins and they fight against their enemies. But this can't be seen in a normal condition. It is clearly learnt when man suffers from hunger.

We have come a long way at present because there is a permanent solution to the problem of food. If the same problem arises again, we will turn up the previous situation, i.e. the problem of food. Some of the countries have declared themselves bankrupt and gone through their downfall. They have had the same problem of food again. We have recently seen people struggling very hard for bread and butter in a very powerful country, Russia. So man only thinks about himself when he lacks food. He does not care about his family and kith and kin. He plays his role like a dog when food is lacking. Growing expensiveness, unemployment, murder, terror, etc. are all connected with hunger in the world. All these problems are because of lack of food, clothing, and shelter. People may also eat up each other if this problem grows continually. There is great competition everywhere due to overpopulation. This problem is growing and getting more serious day by day. On the other hand, there is the overuse of fertile land, desert, sea, peaks, etc. All this is caused by the fear of lack of food, clothing, and shelter. Those who manage their basic needs have the fear of social prestige and self-esteem. Fear is surely due to the occurrence of this problem. People are cutting down trees for their security because of fear. They are destroying jungles in trying to be safe from any danger. But for how long can this activity make them safe? The world becomes ugly when there is only the presence of people in the world. People have a lot of fear even in the present times. There will be an outbreak of plague, murder, terror, theft, robbery everywhere if the world is occupied because of the rapid growth of population. Killing will become a normal occurrence due to lack of food, shelter, and clothing. The earth will turn out to be the hell as mentioned in legends. Even now, man-dogs can be seen in the country where there is lack of food. He does maximum struggle to find his food. This situation has become very fearful. That is why Malthus says, 'Population should be controlled to be safe from this fearful situation.'

Some people are involved in the control of population owing to this fear. As a matter of fact, the crisis has been controlled for their sake but not for the world's sake. If everyone controls the crisis that will come about in his life, it will control the problems of the world. The growth of population starting from grandfather to grandchild is by at least twenty-five in a family. If there is only one child in a family, one of the family members is required to look after the baby instead of going to work. It is a loss of income in the family. Then it becomes difficult to run the family. There are a large number of people in the world who have low incomes. So they have babies according to their income. If they are unable to have a baby, they keep some domestic animals and fulfil their desires. Babies are born because of superstition and conservatism in some of the countries. According to Malthus's theory, the family that has more than one child is compelled to live painful lives even now. Those babies, like piglets and puppies, seem to suck at their mothers' breast, quarrelling with each other and crying. Both the baby and mother suffer from malnutrition due to lack of food and because of the compulsion on the mother to give birth to a child. Their health is not good. If this situation goes on, it will become a hell for living. Some people have a baby due to illiteracy and religious belief. An educated and superstitious family has a fear of conservatism and superstition rather than of trouble and malnutrition. The village people do not have the fear of trouble, although they have many children. Marxists have their respective opinions about this.

Classical Marxists say, 'Rulers have spread this kind of illusive sense. They suppose the sense true and accept it.'[2]

French Marxists Louis (Pierre) Althusser expanded on it and said, 'Ideology cannot be taken as illusion and pack of lies made by the ruling class. It has indeed its real effects. These effects influence every day thinking and activities of a man in life.'[3]

Marxist Antonio Gramsci Hegemony propounded or proposed a theory and said, 'I'm ready to be exploited; to be ruled will be welfare for one' This statement made by the people can be heard everywhere.[4] People are having many children and facing a lot of troubles owing to these reasons.

But people living in a developed country and having a certain income have to think about the reproduction of generation. Firstly, the mother has to take care of her health and beauty. As the world is competitive, she has to be aware of how to maintain her personality. According to Darwin, we have to struggle for existence. We know that they have a problem of having babies. After having a child, the mother has to take care of her child and educate him or her. Also, she has a lot of problems that needs to be tackled at the time. Therefore, the family having low income does not decide to have a baby soon. If they make a decision of having one, it will be a fearful situation for them. That is the reason the rate of population growth is negative in a developed country. The number of old men and women is positive. Above all, the number of young generation is negative. These countries have a fewer workers. Hence, people of a developing country move to a developed country for a better job. They migrate there. There won't be a high density of population in the world if the rate of population growth is low everywhere. If the population growth is not controlled in time, it will not take a long time for people to occupy this world. The world will be full of various problems such as disease, conflict, murder, terror, robbery, burglary, and wickedness. There will be just fear in human life everywhere. Human life is not free from the chain of fear anywhere. Man has no peace and comfort due to this fear. This is the issue that Malthus's theory suggests. Growth of population should be controlled to keep the world safe, fearless, and peaceful. Otherwise, there will be a big human tidal wave in the near future.

Here according to Malthus, population may grow till one point, then stop and start diminishing. If the population growth is high, it is for sure that people will have problems such as trouble, pain, and scarcity. Babies that are born cannot be killed. That's why population is controlled using the means of family planning prior to birth. Population will be doubled if there is no attempt to control it. But many people have started slowing the rate of population growth. They have started using many kinds of preventive medicines that keep them safe from the fear of the rate of population growth because life is full of problems, i.e. expenditure, intervention, etc.

'The life of a man is like that of spider due to generation,' some people say. Because of this, many people seem to live alone without any generations to follow. This problem is very serious in a developed country rather than in a developing one. In 1960, population increased continually when there was load-shedding in New York. It also means that the population grows at a high rate when there is no alternative for entertainment. It has been clearly interpreted in regional fear. There is no competition regarding performance in a developing country. There is also no need for being showy, fashionable etc. The first condition of Malthus's theory of necessity is applicable there.

Thus, fear minimises. But everyone takes care of their personal development in a developed country. So there is control of population. That's why population has started decreasing in those countries. There is a vast difference in the living standards of those who come under the three conditions, viz. no child, a single child, and more than one child. Perhaps it does not affect the rich like 'Kuber', but it is very difficult for the poor like 'Sudama' of *Puran* to struggle for their survival. Parents should manage their time to bring up their children. Again, managing time for their children minimises the sources of their incomes. Therefore, the people of developed countries remain free from raising a generation due to these chains of problems. Lovers and couples live together, but they don't have any child. Although people are superstitious about no off-spring and generation, but this is not in practice now. Still they expect a son but not a daughter. But such concepts have been broken these days.

Impact of population growth

All living creatures share this world. All these creatures have equal participation in ecology and balance. A fluctuation in balance and ecology, no matter whether small or big, has a deep impact in our lives. Man is one of the most sensible and powerful creatures. He is able to keep himself safe from any danger and continues his generation. Some of the major impacts are given below.

Ecology

Forest, plantation, and animals are the sources that provide all the necessary things to man. A land that was consumed by ten people twenty-five years ago is consumed by twenty people after twenty years. In these twenty-five years, the growth of victuals, plantation, and animals is not according to the proportion of population growth. The growth of all these things yields bad impacts due to overpopulation. Thus, increase in population has a direct impact on ecology. Many animals, birds, and plants are becoming extinct due to lack of enough shelter, meadows, and preservation. That's why there is fear of depletion of the whole ecology.

Living creatures

Living creatures particularly animals and birds have crises of habitats and foods due to overgrowth in population. Deserts and barren lands now have to be used for settlements. People, no doubt, want to live in a place full of facilities. They manage their food, shelter, and clothes, but all these can cause deforestation. As a result, many wild animals and birds have already disappeared from this planet, and many others are said to have been disappearing within a century. It is indeed a dangerous indication for the future generation.

Forest

People are overusing forests and plantation for their livelihood. They have cleared the forests for agricultural products and settlements. If we do not control or minimise overpopulation, we will have no other solution except clear the forests, which will certainly bring about an imbalance in ecology and environment. If human activities for deforestation continue, one day the world is sure to be treeless.

Climate change

Increase in population, as mentioned above, is a challenge for animals, birds, ecology, and environment. It's a major reason for climate change and untimely rainfall—no rainfall in rainy season, long drought periods, and partial rain. Because the world is overpopulated, it has caused environmental degradation. So people are victims of acid rain, heavy rain, partial rain, drought, and ozone layer depletion.

Various diseases

There is increase in lack of victuals with the increase in the number of people. Malthus says, 'Appetite is the most dangerous thing in nature.'[5]
Various diseases break out as soon as appetites increase. Similarly, new diseases arise with the growing problems of heat, imbalanced environment, untimely rainfall, starvation, cholera, diarrhoea, etc. Environment pollution has also affected the ozone layer. As a result, ultraviolet rays of the sun directly reach the earth. It leads to new skin problems. The environment becomes polluted due to the destruction of forests and ecology and extinction of wild creatures. Environmental pollution is a source of various diseases.

Global warming

There is increase in temperature due to the overuse of fuel, electricity, growth of population, and destruction of forests. The use of fuel produces carbon dioxide. Snow melts and the sea level rises due to this global warming.

The land near the sea sinks into the water. Swampy land dries up. Some land gets burnt due to drought. It brings about climate change—it's a burning issue in the world. This global warming has severely affected all living things, particularly, plantation, animals, and birds. The world will not be a good and favourable place for all living creatures if wilderness, famine, desertification, and warmth continue.

Thus, the increase in population affects everything badly. Malthus had figured it out many years ago. No effective preventive measures have been made yet. This problem has also not been taken seriously. The world is not yet fully overpopulated right now. But the present imbalance between population and resources shows symptoms of overpopulation. There must be immediate discussion on control, prevention, and family planning for the future people. If there is no serious discussion about the geometrical growth of population and arithmetical growth of food production, man will destroy habitats, animals, birds, and plantation and the earth will be like other planets without any creatures and plantations. Therefore, the future of the world is very fearful.

Malthus's theory includes interpretation of causes and effects of increase in population. This theory is very close to fearism. In this way, I have interpreted about all these here.

End Notes:

1. Thomas Malthus, *An Essay of the Principle of Population*. Oxford University Press, 1999. p. 13.
2. Sanjiv Upreti, *Sidhantaka Kura (Aspect of Theory)*. Akshar Creation Nepal, 2068 v.s. p. 165.
3. Sanjiv Upreti, *Sidhantaka Kura (Aspect of Theory)*. Akshar Creation Nepal, 2068 v.s. p. 165.
4. Sanjiv Upreti, *Sidhantaka Kura (Aspect of Theory)*. Akshar Creation Nepal, 2068 v.s. p. 174.
5. Thomas Malthus, *An Essay of the Principle of Population*. Oxford University Press, 1999. p. 61.

h. Fear in Marxism

About the class struggle, Dr Rishiraj Baral writes, 'Marxism believes fear is compulsory result of the class struggle.'¹ Communism is the ultimate goal of Marxism. Marxism has been interpreted above in the fear age, a pyramid of fear and fear struggle. I want to talk about communism in brief here. I have made an attempt to clarify it in the following Figure no. 79. This is like a life pot and vase of the world.

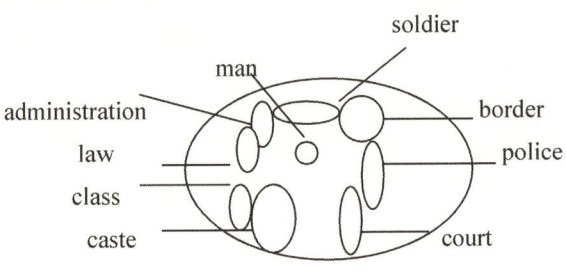

Figure No. 79

There is a man in the centre or middle of the above figure. He is surrounded by country, administration, border, police, army, class, caste, court, etc. All factors that surround him are also men. The man has been surrounded by a line of other men who are also surrounded by the next line of men. Thus, all men have been surrounded by lines of each other. All these men have been made for men by men. In the distant past, man was the problem and the chain of man, and they caused trouble, pain, suffering, torture, etc. It started producing fear. Men became active again for emancipation from this fear.

When people separate from each other due to frontier, caste, class, army, police, etc., it causes the problem of fear of injustice, atrocity, crime, etc.; then the struggle begins and it turns out to be war. In ancient times, there were few sources of fear such as caste, class, border, police, army, administration, rule, law, language, and script, so there was no fear owing to this. All these things came into existence along with the development of human sense and knowledge; consequently the problems of worries, struggle, war, injustice, atrocity, exploitation, and suppression arose. That is why, there was the presupposition of a theory, i.e. communism.

This theory does not yield border, caste, class, army, police, court, and government. All the problems, struggles, and worries get abolished in the transition from socialism to communism. It is believed that everyone is happy and has no enemy in this stage. Society loves peace and has no jealousy and war. Everyone does not believe in enemy, crime, injustice, atrocity, murder, and violence. And society is peaceful, harmonious, and helpful. Everything has already been finished in the class struggle in socialism. This is a classless society—it's a fearless society.

In reality, police, army, act, law, religion, and God cause fear in society. All these lines of demarcations that cause fear should be abolished in order to establish a borderless society for a comfortable life. Borderless means the state of communism. On the other hand, it is a fearless stage. This is impossible in real life. The more the border line is reduced, the less the fear will appear.

End Notes:

1. Rishiraj Baral, *Pratinidhi Nepali Samalochana*, (*Representative Nepali Criticism*). Bibik Creative Publication Private Ltd., Kathmandu, 2068 v.s. p. 163.

i. Periphery of Fear in Postmodernism

On the presentation of his paper *Lila Lekhan* at Gejing, Sikkim, in India, Prof. Dr Sanjeev Upreti writes, 'Ghost dreadful fears are existing in the present world. The existence of fears sometimes transforms the playful post-modern laughing into the fearful cry of death.'[1]

Having included the possibility of murder and terror, Upreti writes, 'There may also be murdering or massacre in the Royal palace and the common people may be killed in the road, school and private houses. The pre-modern activities of massacre, murdering and terror may also be seen in the modern society. In such a case, some people of the world, having celebrated the festival of the breakdown of economic centre, can only enjoy post-modern games. The ways of the lives of the rest can be broken down by the fears that cause unexpected incidents and transform the post-modern linguistic play into the fearful cry of death.'[2]

On the verge of death, while talking to Sibis, Socrates says, 'Which power is doing good they anchoring us indeed.'[3]

We feel that there are circles around us, such as family, society, country, international communities, religion, culture, custom, language, and script. When we are trapped in the lift, room, toilet, etc., we feel suffocated, sick, nervous, and restless. Then we feel as if we are sick and become nervous and perplexed. We feel as if we are dying in the trap now. We cry and ask for help. We feel that one minute is more than a year. In ancient times there was no trap. Everyone was free and open. We have let ourselves be trapped in the name of civilisation, discovery, and creation. Our lives have been tied, blocked, making us feel suffocated and restless. We have been simply theorising to relieve these ties or chains. Thus, postmodernism and communism have been propounded or developed for openness, freedom, no border, and no centre because we have been in the trap of all these lifts.

One of the interpreters of postmodern theory, Jacques Derrida has this logic, 'The assumptions of literature, philosophy and culture are based on the authority of some concepts and the suppression or replacement of others.'[4]

From this statement of Derrida, it is understood that 'authority' and 'suppression' are the strong bases or foundations of postmodernity. Those who suppress or are powerful have the fear of losing their authority and those who are suppressed have the fear of being more suppressed. In the course of reversing this, he applied the reverse to Ferdinand de Saussure's signified at first and began to test or seek a meaning. Then it brought about binary opposition. Those who were ignored, marginalised, left, and dominated seemed to be in this binary opposition. The signifier and signified were reversed and the role of the signified began to be emphasised. All these ignored, marginalised, and suppressed voices are in the centre of discussion in postmodernity at present. The fear of injustice causes the voice of suppression. The suffering experienced by Mahatma Gandhi in South Africa, the injustice faced by Martin Luther King in America, discrimination put up with by Ambedakar in India, atrocity confronted by Einstein, Freud, Derrida while being Jews are all the feeling, voice, jealousy, etc. evoked by suppression. It has been known or learnt that there is suppression, injustice, atrocity, discrimination, etc. in the centre of war, movement, civil war, etc.

On the other hand, the supporter of this theory, Michel Foucault, has forwarded the logic of power. 'Finance is the prime source of power for the Marxists and it is in connection with the existent economical and financial class struggle.'[5] This is the primary issue of Marxism.

Michel Foucault criticised this construction and started studying the practice of power not only in an economic sector but also in various sectors such as office, school, family, and organisation and interpreting them. Most of the chains such as authority, suppression, power, injustice, atrocity, discrimination, plot, doubt, temptation, jealousy, centre, and margin are all the binary oppositions of fear. Here fear is a signifier and the rest are signified. Man reserves power because of fear of suppression, injustice, atrocity, etc. Institute, association, country, organisation, etc. have been run for this purpose or reason. I've interpreted this in the pyramid of fear.

All the minor concepts, human activities, cultures, customs are tied to the power and concept after their declaration as the attraction of a magnet. Everything is chained, and a man cannot be out of the chain at all. He is like a parrot in a cage which cannot move outside the circle. He is compelled to adjust to the situation like Antonio Gramsci's hegemony, i.e. the compulsion for living, eating, etc., and Louis Althusser's concept on awareness.

Thus, a powerful man with his personality, creation, discovery, and contribution influences everybody. These are the ways he gets all these things. We believe them and claim what can be done and what cannot be done on the bases of religion, culture, history, theory, etc. All the things spoken and written by him turn out to be a limitation.

Some intellectuals and philosophers are found to be in the trap of the circle of these limitations. There was a construction in everything such as theory, religion, literature, art, culture, language, script, and customs. Everybody was trapped in this construction. They attempt to be free, be borderless and be decentralised from this trap. Fear is all-pervasive in all these things. All animals, birds, and insects want relief. When we keep them in a trap, they are restless to fly, flee, run; they make haste, strike, fall down, and face death. Man, like them, is also in the chain of the visible and invisible walls made by him. So they want relief. The concept of postmodernity and communism is the perspective of the very relief.

Plato has given an interesting example: 'Ordinary people are like permanent prisoners in the dark cave. They are taught to understand the dance of puppet as ultimate truth and they continue such beliefs. One day a prisoner runs away from the den or cave. That man sees the real nicer world outside.'[6]

Similarly, Plato compares an ordinary man with such a man in the same place. 'They have been chained and imprisoned from their birth in a cave in such a way that they haven't seen anything else except the front walls. Some shadows are displayed on this front wall. The prisoners take the shadows as truth and they spend their lives in the passion but some of them are intelligent and turn back to see the truth that what they've taken or supposed truth is just a shadow of an object but the truth is behind them. The shadow was seen due to the burning fire behind the walls. When such men come out of the cave, they learn a lot of the truth and understand the reality of the objects. Then they are not enchanted by a shadow again.'[7] It means that they know about the new world. If the prisoners don't come out of the cave they will live there, taking the puppet or shadow as ultimate truth. That is to say, that shadow would always be true for them. But when he comes out of the cave, he will come to know that the world is quite a different one.

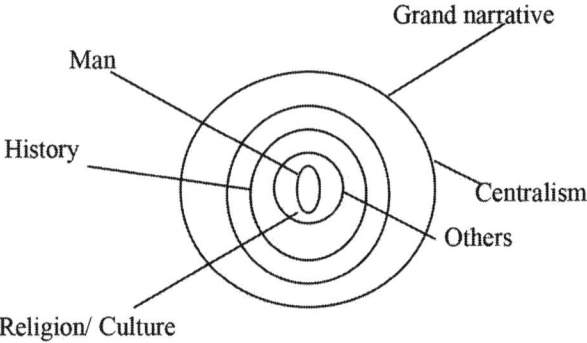

Figure No. 80

Figure no. 80 has a man in its centre. The man has been circled by lifts such as history, grand narrative, centre, religion/culture, others, etc. He is restless and feels suffocated in this lift. The sufferer can only feel the torture house at this moment. He feels as if he is sick, suffocated, and dead at the same time. The man wants relief from such a torture house. The end of history, the end of grand narrative, death of God, death of writers, decentralism, and deconstruction are for emancipation.

We feel as if we may die when we are trapped in the lift because the reaction and effect are instantly known due to it being a small place. If the lift is vast like the world, we will not be much affected. History, grand narrative, and decentralism are the lifts like this. We are suffocated by all these, so we want to get relief from it. About freedom and natural condition, the philosopher Jean Jack Rousseau (1712-78) had said, 'Man is born free but he is in chain.'[8] In Figure no. 80, there are circles such as religion, culture, history, centrality, and grand narrative. Man realised that they were trapped there, so they developed a theory for emancipation. In fact, as a man internally feels restless and suffocated, he wants relief. We enter another circle as soon as we are free from this one. We have to try for a long time to be rid of the circle again. When the layers of lives go on disclosing or unfolding, we find several things such as hope, fear, and many wanted and unwanted things. To live in an uncertain situation is fear. We are living in these uncertain situations and possible incidents. This process has been going on since time immemorial. We are just complementary to it.

In this time, closed room, suffocating environment, global warming, SARS, AIDS, tsunami, explosive weapons, anthrax, erosion, computer virus, space satellite, cloning, hybrid, test tube baby, cyber virus, etc. are causing the world to be fearful. All these are chains. We have many such chains. We are trying to be free from all these chains by means of different concepts, philosophies, arts, and literature because it has been tying us for years, but still we have the fear of being in the chain. It might not be an exaggeration to say that postmodernity and communism have been brought or developed to relieve and free us from this fear.

Postmodernity has dealt with local truth, unstable local, central, decentralised, and marginalised people. No truth is only local, but it is also self-centred. Peace, murder, crime, violence, terror, law, language, script, religion, culture, superstition, conservatism, philosophy, and science are all self-centred. The peace and philosophy of a person do not correspond to that of another one. Ferdinand de Saussure has said that grammar is langue as a whole, but it is not like that in a language. This is the way a person speaks, writes, and uses a word individually. The environment and nature of a person does not correspond to that of another one. Philosophy and region are also just so. Conservatism and superstition are not different from them. When all these are centred around a person, fear is also the same.

Suppression, injustice, and atrocity are the reasons for local, decentralism and margin brought out by postmodernity. Most of the parts of it have been done for relief from fear. Fear is the foundation of all: Michel Foucault's concept of power, Jacques Derrida's domination or suppression, Showalter's essential study, Gayatri Spivak's interpretation of subaltern, and Edward W.

Said's interpretation of colonialism. On the whole, it is an attempt to relieve us from postmodern fear.

End Notes:

1. Sanjiv Upreti, *Srasta (Creator, Publisher Western Sikkim Literature)* Sikkim, India, 2006, Issue 56., Year 28, p. 53.
2. Sanjiv Upreti, *Sidhantaka Kura, (Aspect of Theory)*. Akshar Creation, Nepal, 2068 v.s. p. 126.
3. Plato, trans. Ram Hari, *Sukaratko Atmakatha (Autobiography of Socrates)*. Banjara Madhuwan Publication, Kathmandu, 2065 v.s. p. 117.
4. Sanjiv Upreti, *Sidhantaka Kura, (Aspect of Theory)*. Akshar Creation, Nepal, 2068 v.s. p. 40.
5. Sanjiv Upreti, *Sidhantaka Kura, (Aspect of Theory)*. Akshar Creation, Nepal, 2068 v.s. p. 48.
6. Dave Robinson, Judy Groves, *Introducing Philosophy*. Icon Books, London; Totem Books, New York 1998, p. 24.
7. *Punya Prasai, Sukaratko Jibani (Autobiography of Socrates)*. Dikura Publication, Kathmandu, 2065 v.s. p. 84.
8. Ninu Chapagain, *Pratinidhi Nepali Samalochana (Representative Nepali Criticism)*. Bibek Creative Publication, Kathmandu, 2068 v.s. p. 65.

29

Fearless Path

While talking about fear, Rahul Sankrityayan writes, 'In the ancient period, people used to have the fear of darkness. There used to be fear not only of imaginary ghosts but also of living enemies as well as violent animals at night. The full moon night used to help them to have a relief from this fear to a greater extent.'[1]

Fear has different fragments in human life. We have to be out of each of these fragments. We are free from some of the fears automatically whereas we get relief from others by means of a lot of effort. We have a lot of fears and it is not possible to be rid of all of them. There is no necessity of being out of all the fears. We should not avoid some necessary fears. The fear we try to remove is the fear that is unnecessary. What we try to be rid of is an unnecessary fear. We can be free from normal fears. When it is very difficult for us to get rid of any fear, we can alleviate it by changing its form, facing it, and considering it a minor one. If fear exists as we think and follow superstition and conservatism, it can be removed through deviation and negligence, respectively. Fear can be alleviated according to its nature. It cannot be alleviated without any idea about it. Fear is a kind of problem, a mental disease. It is also a kind of treatment. The disease should be diagnosed for its treatment. The problem of fear, after knowing it, should be identified according to its nature. Then it will be easy for the treatment. If a doctor also finds the source of a problem or fear, it will be easy for him or her to treat a patient or the fear of the sufferer and cure the disease.

Small children feel afraid while sleeping at night. They are afraid because of the dark. Their fear subsides after switching the light on. But this normal fear can cause a serious mental problem if it goes on growing. That is why the problem should be completely done away in that time. We should not let it beget other problems of fear. We should get them into the habit of sleeping alone for this. Even young people have this kind of problem. Some people feel fear while walking through the jungle. If he is compelled to go through the jungle, he goes with his friends; he walks, singing a song, making noise. These are also ways to get rid of and eradicate fear from its roots.

I have already interpreted above—every human activity is oriented for relief. No activity has been oriented for killing time in human life. It is not just for a walk for the time being. We feel as if we are suffocated, imprisoned, tied to conservatism and superstitions and feel uneasy due to religion, culture, customs, constitution, rule, law, act, economic, social, family burden, trouble, rain, etc. Of course, we try to be liberated from the very uneasiness, chain, trouble, and grief. We, no doubt, feel that we are surrounded by several fears, i.e. fear of life, death, family, disease, present, future, language, script, religion, culture, economy, poverty, unemployment, etc., and for relief from all the fears, we hold a job, earn money, get married, and have many activities as if we are sincere citizens. Such fears always occur in life or surround our lives. Some of them are eradicated, some alleviated, and some extended. In this way, life and world continue their existence.

Most of the problems, worries, stress, jealousy, and doubt become serious if they go on spreading. The more it grows, the more serious it becomes. So it is better to eradicate it for its prevention. If it is not eradicated, it grows continually and becomes serious like cancer and it spoils everything one day.

As regard to the relief of fear from death, the philosopher Bertrand Russell says, 'There are many ways to fight with the fear of death. We can ignore it and mention nowhere. We can divide our thought from this context.'[2]

a. Primary Treatment of Fear

There are many treatments for short-term and long-term fears 1, 2, 3, and 4. Short-term fear 1, 2, 3 can be relieved. There is a long-term fear at 4. It cannot be relieved.

1. Fear that lessens itself

This fear is concerned with thought and reminiscence. If the person who has the fear of scolding is not scolded, the fear itself subsides. Similarly, if somebody has doubt but there is no proof about it, the fear is removed itself.

Fear does not last long when there is no mistake in reality, although he feels that he has made some mistake. Such fear is normal and worldly.

2. Fear that can be minimised

Some children whose parents are not at home have fear of something. Even adults have such fear. A man is afraid when he stays in the room alone and while walking along the way. If you are afraid in the dark, stay in the light. Similarly, if you have fear while staying and walking alone, stay and walk with your friends because your fear can then minimise. Some fears are caused by superstition, some by extremism. They can be removed like this although they are because of superstition, religion, extremism. Fear caused by smoking, alcohol, drugs, bad company, and food can be removed by controlling them.

3. Fear that is removable

We can get emancipation from some of the fears. We should give up the habit of eating and drinking for relief if it produces fear. Similarly, we should improve our habit or mind if fear is caused by our nature, habit, or behaviour. If a man is faced with the problem of an epidemic of any disease, then he has a fear of it. If a scientist invents a cure for the disease or problem, his fear comes to an end. If the bomb that is going to be exploded is deactivated and if fire is put out when a house is burning, the fear produced by the bomb and fire no longer exists. If there is fear because of animals, it gets reduced after killing them or driving them away.

4. Fear that is not removable

This is a long-term fear. This long-term fear also exists when somebody or something is recollected or they are very much troubled by pain, trouble, etc. Fear of death is a long-term and permanent fear. It is felt at the time of recollection and forgotten in other times. It is felt again at the time of remembrance. Fear exists when disease, trouble, and pain attack us again. If a man commits a serious crime and he has not been punished, he has the problem of fear in his lifetime. As he has seen the police, society, he always has this fear. Similarly, fears about heaven, hell, future always appear as fragments. If somebody reminds us of any incident, accident, etc. we have the fear of them. These fears are not removable. They always come out. They can be removed only for the time being. This process goes on repeating.

b. Secondary Treatment of Fear

Method A.
Changing form

Suppose we have a serious problem like a dangerous animal, tiger, or anything that produces a dreadful situation. We can't face it in the same manner. If we think the tiger to be a cat, by means of our mental effort fear itself dies away. It means that a major problem should be taken as a minor one. It is possible as it is the result of the mindset. Suppose somebody owes five hundred thousand Nepalese rupees and is threatened day and night by the person to whom he owes. Although unable to pay off the entire amount at once, if he gets the creditor to agree to him making payment in instalment, it is a way of dividing fear into small fragments. If there is fear of death, we can relieve it thinking, 'Death is nothing. It happens to all.' Someone has the fear of being injected. If he is convinced that everybody gets injected and it does not harm anybody and if he is physically and mentally ready, his fear lessens. Similarly, if a person has never spoken on stage, he feels nervous and has a fear of speaking. His fear fades away when he is mentally ready and says that if everyone can speak he can also easily speak. Thus, if the problem, fear, thing can be directly faced, they can be removed by changing their forms through strong thought and courage.

To be faced

Suppose a serious problem, i.e. earthquake, has occurred. The idea of escaping from this problem is not a proper solution, and even the concept of transformation in the form is also no way out. We should have self-control in such a situation. Self-control doubtless helps us to be safe during the incident. That is why self-control that is of a great power plays a vital role in solving any problem. There are many examples of self-control that has saved us from different problems, i.e. anxiety, fear, etc. Self-control suggests that we need to have courage and rationality. Our rationality doesn't function properly in the absence of self-control. Similarly, courage without rationality is also of no avail. We can have relief from problems if we perform our task in combination of self-control, rationality, and courage. If we come across a tiger and do not see a way out by fleeing and hiding, we'd better encounter him courageously and rationally. All the problems that we come across are just like this.

Escaping and ignoring

According to Bertrand Russell, we should escape from some of the fears so they are removed, especially those produced by conservatism, superstition, religion, culture, etc. The fear gets removed if we take it normally. Inter-caste marriage, which is banned or prohibited in some societies, is a cultural fear. But having disregarded this ban or prohibition, if a marriage ceremony is performed, everything will be acceptable by and by. Some of the people have done so whereas others are unable to ignore the cultural ban. Some of the societies try to harm the couple, and this kind of activity may take place anywhere. There is a legal process to be followed in defence of it. This problem should be solved by means of law.

Method B
(a) Fear that is removable

We can relieve most of the fears. The fears that can be relieved are minor and less effective. Some of them are done away with by our activities while others get eliminated itself. It is not that there is the presence of another fear after the relief of one. Furthermore, different kinds of fear arise because fear begets fear. The occurrence of fear and relief goes on side by side.

1. Suppose a man is suffering from a disease. He has a lot of fears about the problem. He does not receive any treatment due to scarcity of medicine. His fear is minimised only after the discovery of medicine and he gets treatment of his problem.
2. A man is thought of making a mistake. He has been suffering from this fear. His fear ends when he learns that he has not committed any mistake.
3. A man has taken his exam. He suffers from the fear of failure. When he gets success, his fear ends.
4. A vehicle on a journey is about to meet an accident. All passengers fear about this possible accident. Their fears end when the accident does not happen.
5. A bomb is said to have been kept somewhere. Such a rumour produces fear among locals. When the bomb is reported to have been disposed by a disposal team, the fear of the people ends.
6. Somebody is doubtful about someone else. The same doubt can cause fear. His or her fear lessens if that doubt is false.

7. Similarly, we always fear that we may have an injury if we stumble and fall over while walking somewhere. With the absence of its possibility, the fear gets abolished.

There are many fears that are removable, but our emancipation is followed by another fear.

(b) Fear to be minimised

We are not free from some fears. Such fears always surround us. That is a result of thought. The more we think, the more it increases. It continues to minimise with its absence. Therefore, thinking about fear should be minimised as far as possible. The absence of thinking about fear continues to minimise it. We have many such unnecessary fears that should be alleviated continually.

1. A man has committed a crime. If he has not been punished for his crime, he always fears about the police and thinks they may come to arrest him. He always feels that somebody is following him. He doesn't feel easy and comfortable on his way, at home, and even in his dining room. He always has fear about the crime. He becomes a victim of his crime. As soon as he stops thinking about it, he gets relief from such fear.
2. A dreadful incident has occurred in life. The incident causes the death of people and he himself has a narrow escape too. If this incident makes a profound impact on him, anything like this kind of incident causes fear for him. He doesn't have any fear if that doesn't occur to him.
3. Man always fears a supernatural power. This power neither exists anywhere nor harms anyone. Man just contemplates about such power and fears it. Fear passes away as soon as the supernatural power is ignored.
4. Someone is in need of a lot of money. He will have a big problem if he is not able to manage the amount. His fear lessens if he is able to manage some amount in lieu of the required amount. So the fear does not turn into a serious one if a big problem is taken normally. Otherwise, the fear becomes more serious. Fear itself passes away automatically if any problem is taken lightly and normally. As a matter of fact, most of the fears are so flexible that they can be expanded and constricted.

There are many such fears which are caused by thinking, but they can be alleviated.

(c) Incessant fear

The fear that plays a vital role in the improvement, progress, success, development, discovery, creation and construction of a person, society, and country can be balanced or continued to increase. The fear that a man suffers from should be removed at best. As stated above, construction, discovery, development, and progress also cause fear. Continuous work also produces fear. It is necessary to think about keeping a balance between them.

1. A student has an exam. He can be successful if he has a balanced fear for his exam. He fails in the exam if in case he lacks fear. He becomes perplexed and can't give right answers to the questions if he has more fear. However, a student requires a balance of fear. If he fails in the exam due to much fear, it may lead to different incidents, accidents, etc.

2. Positive fear is essential to acquire success in life. Again, nothing is possible to do without fear.

3. If the government works with fear of development, peace, and security, it can provide peace and prosperity to the people. The government should maintain such a positive fear continually. If the government works without the fear of anyone else, the people are unable to have peace and prosperity. And people in such a country face only trouble, pain, torture, injustice, suppression, etc.

4. Fear should be taken for environmental preservation. All living creatures will have a great crisis in the near future, if the destruction of the ecology goes on at this rate. That's why there should be the fear of the preservation of the ecology.

Method C
General instances for management:

If you fear to live in the dark, switch on the light.
If you fear to walk alone, walk with a friend.
If you are sick, live with others.
If you fear about superstition and blind belief, ignore them.
If you fear about conditional reflex, understand the meaning differently.
If you have diabetes, eat less and do exercise.
If you fear about blood pressure, control food and do exercise.

If you want to avoid normal diseases, take care of cleanliness.
If you fear about extremist thought, try to minimise it.
If you fear about greed, control it.
If you fear about nuclear weapons, ignore it.
If you fear relatives, face them normally.
If you have fear of thought, give it up.
If you have fear of religion, minimise religious activities.
If you have fear of depression, try to control it.
If you fear of death, try to generalise the fear of death.
If the doctor has diagnosed an incurable disease, control yourself and generalise death.
If you are old and you fear death, think that it happens to all living creatures and accept it.
If you fear about a possible event, work wisely. Man becomes nervous, fears, jumps, escapes, decides unwisely, etc. when he has an incident, accident, and any other disasters. There is no rational decision in such a case. Try to have self-control and relieve fear in an unexpected situation.
If you fear about natural disasters like earthquake, flood, landslide, tsunami, etc., protect yourself and your family.
A proper solution to all these problems is that we have to be self-controlled, wise, and brave. He who is able to have these things always becomes successful.

Method D
Formula to minimise fear

Human nature is added to the periphery and relativity of fear. Addition (+) causes and produces fears and problems. We have to travel from addition (+) to subtraction (-) to reach fearless stage. This subtraction leads to solution of many problems on the one hand and reduces fear on the other. If we are able to accomplish it according to our plan, fear can be zero (0). If it is not reduced to zero (0), fear becomes fewer than before.

Source	Aim	Achievement
Trouble-fear	= 0 zero	less
Anxiety-fear	= 0 zero	less
Jealousy-fear	= 0 zero	less
Ego-fear	= 0 zero	less
Wrath-fear	= 0 zero	less

Doubt-fear	= 0 zero	less
Conspiracy-fear	= 0 zero	less
War-fear	= 0 zero	less
Extremism-fear	= 0 zero	less
Shy-fear	= 0 zero	less
Introvert-fear	= 0 zero	less
Inferiority-fear	= 0 zero	less
Greed-fear	= 0 zero	less
Coward-fear	= 0 zero	less

Our aim is zero. It is not cent per cent possible. However, this formula can be useful enough to alleviate fear.

Thus, problem of fear can be solved in different ways without any medicine, expenditure, etc. We can doubtless relieve unnecessary fears by means of different ways. Consequently, we can have happiness, piece, relief, and ease in life. Man is concerned about these things. We always strive to achieve these things. We do different activities for this. We commit different kinds of crime, i.e. murder, terror, war, plot, doubt, etc. We can achieve our goal if we are able to improve our concept, courage, self-control, tolerance, etc.

30

Examples of Fearless Path

Fear and fearism are always in use in our lives. Fear exists, and there is always an attempt to remove it. However, there is relief at length. Life is trapped in it, and man tries to be rid of it at all times. This is life's compilation of the paths for relieving fear. Some examples of this are as follows:

1. **Accusation**: When a man is accused of committing the pettiest crime, he is fearful of it. He can't even bear to be in this situation. The man who can't tolerate the situation may suffer from various kinds of diseases, problems, etc. Some may commit suicide. Everybody is generally the victim of fear, but some people can tolerate it. Immediately after being accused of the crime, it affects his family, relatives, society, and others. People start making different kinds of assumptions. The family members become the victims of doubt, fear, anxiety, etc. They require evidence to prove his innocence. The accuser may have already had fake evidences. In case he loses the case, he is sentenced to life imprisonment. That is why accusation of crime, corruption, racism, etc. naturally makes one's hair stand on end. In society, there are several examples of poor people who, though they are innocent, become the victims of different kinds of crime and are compelled to lose their cases because of an eloquent speaker. Some of them are cruelly punished. As a result of this, man becomes restless, nervous, and fearful as soon as he hears this kind of news. Our case is also the same when any of us is accused of this crime. Agitation, nervousness, etc. bring about some more terrible problems.

Enemies are pleased in this situation. Therefore, it shows that we should be self-restrained, calm, and rational to get relief from fear.

(a) Example—accusation—murder

A man is blamed for murder when a short description of him is given. The police start searching for the man and doubt anyone who looks similar to the alleged criminal. The man, who is the innocent one before the arrest, becomes like a criminal.

Then he begins to think:
I've been punished. My life will be ruined.
Who'll look after the family and children?
How can I prove myself innocent?
What does the family think of me?
What does society think of me?
How to see the family and society?
How to manage financial case?

There are many such kinds of trends, doubts, accusations, etc. in society. He cannot be free from the law although he says, 'I'm innocent. I haven't committed any crime.' As he is blamed for the crime, he grows more and more worried and terrified. A man always has to face this kind of problem. So the problem of fear should be interpreted because life is a compilation of such fragments. Then his fear will be reduced and he will be free from this problem. When he is proved innocent, his fear will finally come to an end.

(b) Example—accusation—rape

Incident—A man is blamed for rape. If the police arrest him, he'll fear:

What'll my prestige be like?
What do the family and relatives think of me?
What'll my future be like?
What does society think of me?
What'll happen if the case is lost?
How to pay the lawyer's fees?
What'll be my family's case if I'm sent to prison?

Such kinds of major and minor incidents occur in our daily lives. As mentioned above, a man should carry out his plan while being brave and self-controlled at such a moment.

A majority of mischievous persons who provoke anyone to carry out such incidents are found in society nowadays. If an accused man is further blamed for crime, his fear increases terribly. As a result, he can make several risky decisions. As he himself is the cause of the problem, he should be more and more controlled, self-controlled, balanced, and tolerant. It helps his fear to reduce. It helps his fear to abate. The reduction of fear leads to the removal of all possible risks.

2. Types of doubt: positive and negative

Doubt leads to negativity in general. When the family, neighbours, and relatives are doubted, it causes various kinds of problems—the husband doubts his wife, the friend doubts his friend, etc. As a result, they quarrel and beat each other. They can also divorce at times. Suppose the husband sees his wife walking and talking with the man about whom he has already been doubtful, then he thinks that his doubt is right. Then it produces several problems—divorce, murder, violence, etc.; as the proverb says—'to be over suspicious is too much dangerous.' So such harmful doubt should be reduced to make us safe from possible incidents of murders and accidents.

(c) Example—doubt

'K' and 'G' are husband and wife. He is suspicious of 'G'. One day he sees 'G' with a new person. 'K' is in a state of shock. Such a situation may cause incident, accident, etc.

'K' feels the following:
Who might that boy be?
Wasn't he G's relative?
She wouldn't sit together if he was her relative.
She was so much excited.
She might leave me.
The property deposited in her name would be lost.
Who'd take care of the children?
How could I let her do so!
I should control her.

Then he will grow more and more suspicious, worried, and terrified without being thoughtful. From the point that he thinks, 'I should control her', 'G' may be beaten and banished from the house. Violence, conflict, and murder may break out. Previously, there was just fear that she would elope with the man. If their conflict causes murder, fear will turn into something more serious.

If murder occurs, the result will be:

Oh, I've murdered her in anger.
My life will be ruined in prison. I'm worried.
Who'll look after the children?
What if somebody saw it?!
What if police come up?!
I'd better escape or surrender.
What does society think of me?
G's relatives would take revenge.
Oh, what did I do?!

Such fears come to him. This is also a part of life. However, the incident has occurred, so what will be a proper solution to the problem? What about a doctor's treatment? Many such incidents exist in society. These kinds of incidents are also complementary to life. As for the incident, doubt arises in the beginning; worry, anxiety, and fear appear later, and then the situation produces wrath and at last fear exists at any rate. Thus, several scenarios of the same incident appear in every moment. In such a case, he regrets it, yet he gets punished. No doubt, he would not have this accident and fear if he had subdued his doubt. Man has such different kinds of nature. If they are more than is necessary, several kinds of problems such as worry and wrath arise and they turn into fear at great length. If his nature is mild or equable, he is close and friendly to the family, friends, and society. Everybody treats him well and his fears lessen. Therefore, human nature should be controlled before letting it turn into any emotional activity.

3. **Epidemic patient**: Man can suffer from any kind of disease after all. Some of the diseases are incurable. A doctor fixes the date, for example, three months, six months, etc., for the patient to live when the disease is incurable. In such a case, the patient has different problems such as worries, fear, pain, and stress at the same time. Then he may become nervous, discouraged, and hopeless. He needs consolation, relief, love, and care at this time. He should try to be self-controlled, console himself, and spend the rest of the time taking part in entertainment and being involved in sports. His friends and relatives should also relieve his anxiety

and console him. If he has much pressure of worries, fear, and other problems, he may have an untimely death.

(d) Example—epidemic disease

A man named 'K' suffers from cancer. The doctor says, 'You can live just for three months.' How does he feel now? How does the family feel? What do his friends realise? Which theory and psychology can be used to treat him for the disease in such a case? Is there any theory to understand it? This is a very serious thing about life. There are two stages here—the stage before the diagnosis of the disease and the stage after the diagnosis of it. The symptom of the disease has also been interpreted or mentioned above in the boundary and dependence of fear.

1. Stage before diagnosis

He is an ordinary man. He does everything such as eating, drinking, and walking like others. He does not know death, which has already attacked him and there is no fear of cancer in him as well. All his friends and relatives behave as usual and he enjoys his time.

2. Stage after diagnosis

After the diagnosis of his disease, he becomes nervous and afraid and his nose and mouth become dry. It is usual for him to show this reaction in this situation, for all his plans and aims are going to be over very shortly. Some people lose their senses and faint, while others are brave enough to hear this kind of news. Some people's plans and dreams turn into ashes. All the golden opportunities are of no avail. The situation changes within a while. Consequently, brightness turns into darkness. Afterwards, he has no idea at all.

3. Friends' reactions after diagnosis

The behaviour of his friends change and they show different reactions after the diagnosis of his disease. In the past, he was healthy, but at present he is unhealthy. All his friends and relatives look after and control him while eating drinking, walking, and playing. Furthermore, if he is the victim of a communicable disease, they leave him alone completely. There is a vast difference between the past and present.

Our life is very short. It seems as if life is just for three months. It is a guest, like Albert Camus's man, for a certain period. What about the treatment at this stage? Which theory is fruitful? How is he treated in such a condition? The treatment should make his life easy-going.

(e) Example—incident

Suppose passengers get aboard an airplane. The plane takes off for its destination. A bit later, they are informed that the plane has caught fire. Some passengers faint as soon as they hear the news, some start crying, some start praying to God, some become restless, and some are nervous. Some passengers embrace each other and pray to God very seriously. All this is because of fear. The passengers don't think about or care whether the plane is really burning. They panic as soon as they hear the news about the fire. They don't care for themselves. They are so much discouraged or disheartened that their senses or minds do not function and it is empty. Some of them may die untimely while crying, uttering cries of ache or woe. If the plane does not land safely in time it can explode and the explosion will shatter their lives. It is quite natural to show these kinds of activities. It may further bring about a major problem. If they are self-restrained, controlled, and brave, that incident will not occur. There are many incidents in which people die when they are crushed and trodden over while running away from the football ground or the cinema hall due to fear.

If the plane cannot land, death is sure to happen. Then:

1. Becoming nervous, yelling, and crying may cause death.
2. Even being restrained, rational, calm, and patient bring about death.

This is the choice of death. Even in such a dreadful situation, a man can use his mind for two options:

1. Death can be normal. It is also one of the beautiful choices of a man. He has seen that a man can face death after having tolerated a lot of pain, torture, etc. No doubt this kind of horror brings fear to them. So they wish for themselves a usual death.
2. If thinking power is under our control, we can be safe from any danger by means of different ways.

Not only a plane crash but also a bus accident, an occurrence of earthquake, and any other incident also cause this kind of horrific situation.

Although death is inevitable, we'd rather die a usual death than face an unusual death for the peace of the soul if it admits it.

4. Crime

Crime also varies according to its nature—theft, robbery, violence, rape, insolvency, lie, etc. Although no one blames him for his crime, he himself feels guilty of it. He knows the crime that he has committed. Nobody knows anything about it, but he also supposes that everybody knows it. So he walks secretly, silently, and cunningly. He thinks that the person who knows about the crime will capture, punish, and scold him very badly. As a result, he can't eat, sleep, and walk comfortably. Even in his dream, he feels that someone is running after him, following, calling, and scolding him. He also feels afraid of the worker or security guard whose dress is like that of the police. He hides somewhere else when he sees a van, car, or motorcycle similar to that of the police. He walks silently when he sees the man whom he has lied to and harmed him by committing a crime, while walking and talking with a known man. Thus, he happens to lose his wonderful time. He spends his time being scared at all times. Furthermore, if he commits a serious crime, he is so terrified that he can be the victim of many physical and mental problems. These criminals indulge in all kinds of major and minor crimes; namely, they are pickpockets, gangsters, drug smugglers, arms black-marketers, corrupt people, thieves, robbers, murderers, etc. They gain some profit, but they are not free from the fear which always troubles them very much. Most of these fears can be minimised by confrontation. Those who gain profit carry on with this benefit although they are terrified at all times.

(f). Example: corrupt people

Ram is a corrupt man. He takes some bribe from Hari on the condition that he will find a job for him. But unfortunately he neither does the work nor returns his money. Hari and his relatives try to see him several times to take his money back, but Ram does not willingly or compellingly give him his money back. He always fears while going somewhere. If somebody visits his house and knocks at the door or his phone rings, his heart starts beating and he thinks that the man has been sent by Hari for the amount. Similarly, he feels afraid when he supposes that they are some officials or police. Sometimes he lies to them whereas at other times he says that he is out. He is also afraid of the man whom Hari knows because he thinks that the man can tell Hari about it. He is very much worried that somebody may come and capture him while sleeping, as well as when he is up, walking and eating.

When he sees the police and their van or the man whose dress is like that of the police's uniform, he starts fleeing and hiding somewhere else because he thinks that they have been sent by Hari. He can't enjoy walking anywhere and eating anything else. He feels as if somebody is coming and calling him. It is all because of his wrongdoing. If he had been one of the sincere staff, he would not be a victim of fear and his life would go smoothly.

Many criminals, viz. rapist, robber, thief, liar, cheat, persecutor of corruption, etc., feel guilty and are afraid of others as Ram does. Despite the fact that they are pleased outwardly, they suffer from fear inwardly. However, a man often lies to others and commits offences whether they are minor or big ones. This is the source of problem that exists in mind and heart and it goes on turning into a serious problem by and by. Consequently, they are always terrified of fear. Fear is done away with after speaking the truth and paying off the debt. If the accused has committed a crime of corruption, he can only be free from his fear only after getting punished in the name of corruption. Till he does not get punished, the problem goes on troubling him very much.

(g). Example—loneliness

A man named 'A' is going somewhere else. The path is deserted and in the wilderness. There are streams, deserts, stones, forests, and bamboo groves on his path, which are completely silent. He already knows something about it, but it is essential that he should go there. He himself is obliged to go there. He is very much fearful. In such a case, his senses and other parts of the body related to the brain and mind are all alert and careful and his/her heartbeat increases. He walks while looking around, singing a song, and making a noise. He reaches out his hands to touch the weapon or stick frequently, if he is carrying one. Even a small sound of something can be heard clearly, owing to him being much alert. He also sees the leaves of trees and plants shaking far away in the distance. He gets startled when he hears the onomatopoeic sounds of something. He feels as if it takes him a long time to cross the path. Everything, i.e. rock, stamp, cave, etc., appears to be a ghost. If he meets a man in ragged clothes, holding a bag, on the way he is quite afraid of the man. Moreover, if he is on the one side and takes out his weapon and starts cutting bamboo, plants, etc., he is so fearful that he may also lose his senses. On seeing A's condition, we believe that he is fearful about a ghost and troubled by the Hunting God and Forest God. He is in such a condition that he may lose his senses for any reason at any time because he is already extremely terrified. This incident may cause mental problem sickness, fear, and paralysis to A.

When he is treated for this problem, the main focus of attention should be on fear as it is the source of A's sickness. It is sure that his songs and weapons, though they are helpful to him to some extent, can't help to get rid of his fear at all. This kind of lonely environment can be at any place such as palace, industry, and building. His fear is further pervaded by rumour, conservatism, incident, etc.

This story is of a man who was proud and showed off by talking about himself and his bravery to his friends. His friends were also fed up with his talk about his heroism. Then they made a plan jointly. One of his friends said, 'You're so brave that you aren't afraid of anybody. You aren't fearful of ghost, a wild animal, etc., are you?'

Being brave, he said, 'There is no doubt about it. I'm not afraid of anybody. I've slain many terrible animals and fought ghosts and demons.'

Another friend said, 'We're proud of your bravery. We're glad and lucky to have a brave friend like you.'

He proudly nodded his approval and slightly puffed up his chest. Another friend said, 'We've planned a small test for your bravery.'

He said, 'Yes. Why only a small test? You can run me through a big one.'

The first friend said, 'Today there a dead body has been buried far away in the cemetery. Strike this nail with a hammer on the coffin. We will see it tomorrow.' Then they told him the whereabouts of the cemetery and coffin. They decided to give him the materials in the evening. According to their agreement, they gave him the nail and hammer and parted from each other.

They pretended to give him the necessary materials and returned home at that very instant. Each of them knew that he was a coward. He loved to brag, so his friends had planned a test for him. Actually he was not brave, although he pretended to be so. He was obliged to go to the cemetery at any cost. He left for the place, carrying the materials. While he was walking there, he was quite fearful, but he controlled himself with great difficulty. He had gone there because of his arrogance, prestige, etc. Most of the people are just like him. They want to be proud of their knowledge, property, etc. by bragging about themselves. Their bravery is artificial, showing their prestige, reputation, arrogance, etc.

The clock struck twelve midnight. Dogs could be heard barking in the distance. The sound of insects around the cemetery could also be heard in the pervasive darkness of the night. He headed for the cemetery with heart beating rapidly. Everywhere it was pitch-dark and quiet. He was afraid of losing his prestige, belief, etc. in case he didn't finish the assigned task. He felt so much suffocated by fear as he had to perform the task. No doubt, man has the fear of losing his prestige, esteem, etc., so they get involved in all kinds of legal and illegal actions. Then he decided to strike the nail on the coffin. He laid the torch down on the ground. Because of his fear, he started striking the nail with a hammer without looking at the coffin. He was surprised to find that the nail penetrated the coffin box easily. He was confident about striking the nail successfully, and yet he was terrified and his body trembled with fear. He was in a rush to leave for his home and get rid of his fear. As he was about get up from there in a hurry, the coffin pulled him down. He thought it was the dead body that pulled him so, and he got nervous and started shouting as he was frightened; he then fainted. When a man is very much afraid, even a small thing makes him lose his senses, and his case was also the same. His friends were hiding nearby in a secret place, looking at his activities silently. When he did not come for a long time, they came to look for him. He was found lying there senseless. He had not struck the nail properly. They also found that all his plans for striking the nail had gone awry. Furthermore, one side or corner of his shirt had got stuck to the coffin along with the nail and the corner of the shirt pulled him down when he tried to get up. But he thought that the dead body awoke and pulled him so. It was all owing to his fear.

Many such incidents are found to exist in society. We also come across this kind of situation. If he had not been fearful, he would not have lost his senses like that. If it had been daytime or he had been with his friends, he would not have come across this situation at all. All of this happened because of fear, which makes a lot of difference between him and environment. If he had been in a normal condition, he would have seen what pulled him down. He would have found what was pulling his shirt. He didn't dare see anything, for he had already been terrified of the dead body. He lost his control and patience. Man often has a mental problem due to such an incident. If somebody tries to violate, murder, rape, and commit any sort of crime, he may lose his senses and speech and get paralysed with fear. That is why the sources of these problems are required to receive proper cure.

5. Illusion

Illusion means a false idea or belief, especially about somebody or about a situation. In other words, illusion denotes something that seems to exist, but in fact it does not or it seems to be something that is not. To take a cat as a cub and to take a cub as a cat both are illusions like Shankaracharya's rope snake and Indra Bahadur Rai's *lilabhram*. If we see a beloved walking with the man whom we have doubted, it is an illusion. It produces a lot of doubts and the doubts cause anxiety and fear. Consequently, various incidents may occur. We should not doubt anyone and make any decision banking on the only doubt unless it turns out to be true. The scene behind the curtain is quite different from that what the audience imagines. It means that everything is different from a doubt when reality is disclosed.

(h). Example—illusion

A man named Ram was walking in the semi-darkness in the evening, lost in his thoughts. He was thinking about his concerns, plans, and family. Many things were happening to him. All of a sudden, he happened to see a black snake slithering, making a hissing sound, but he lost sight of it immediately. He was so much afraid of the snake that he almost fell down and lost his senses. He was in a soulless condition. He was speechless for some time. His mind was empty, and in fact, he could not think about what he had seen there. He started trembling. He got fully drenched in his sweat until he was able to control himself. Then he ran towards his home without looking at anything. All the family members were surprised to see him in such a condition. Some of them started pressing his forehead and some made him drink water. They all started to give first aid to him. After a long time, he felt a little relieved and uttered the word 'snake' with difficulty. The people around him made different assumptions. Some of them doubted whether a snake had bitten him, but there was no sign of snake bite on any part of his body. It took him a long time to become normal. He told everything after he became normal. Afterwards, the incident drew the attention of the whole family. The incident about the snake always came to his mind. He told whoever he met about the big snake that he had seen on the road. They believed what he said about the snake. Then they slowly left, walking through the way.

Time passed on. Shyam also heard the news as it spread throughout the places. He was surprised to hear it. He understood how the news was spread all around the places. He went to see Ram; there he came to know that the rumour was spread by him (Ram), and he asked, 'Where did you see that big snake?' He told him everything as he had told others. After listening to his story, Shyam smiled. Everyone knew that Shyam was funny man. Ram was also familiar with his habit too. Shyam laughed and said, 'What a thoughtless man you have been! What you saw on that day wasn't a snake but a rope. I stayed there to startle the people walking through the way.'

In the beginning, Ram did not believe what Shyam said to him. He widened his eyes and looked at him. After Shyam added evidence to his remark, Ram, however, believed it, but actually he had no full faith in it. In fact, that was not a snake but Shyam's rope. This was an illusion. Man believes in what he sees. It appears that something seems to exist but in fact does not, or it seems to be something that is not. This is an illusion. Ram was also in an illusion and he was afraid due to this illusion. Everybody believed Ram and had the fear of the snake. He was very much affected by fear, so he could not relieve the fear as soon as he was told the fact by Shyam. We have many such kinds of illusion at all times. This illusion turns into belief which produces many doubts and assumptions, but the reality or fact is beyond us. We always take a rope as a snake in life and consider and discuss it like the man in a den. It might be due to this that Shankaracharya has said that the world is an illusion.

Thus, an illusion also causes fear in man. If Shyam would not have told him the fact, the normal rope would have remained a snake in his life. Some of the illusions can never be removed because we don't know whether that is reality or illusion. We see our family member walking with someone else and believe it is an illusion. But those who see and believe it without any evidence have many problems. That is why we should try our level best to understand an illusion. If we understand it well, we can remain safe from a number of problems, anxiety, fear, etc.

There are many examples of fear caused by doubt, illusion, mistakes, error, accusation, etc. We fear because of these factors.

End Notes:

1. Rahul Sankrityayan, *Biswako Ruprekha (Sketch of the World)*, trans.-Narayangiri. Kathmandu, 2066 v.s. p. 20.
2. Bertrand Russell, *In Praise of Idleness*, Routledge, Routledge Taylor & Francis Group, London and New York. 2008. p. 148.

31

Concluding Remarks

In the world, several theories and philosophies have been formulated under different titles and subtitles, which have been found to have played a vital role for the removal of human fear. Jacques Derrida also wrote a book entitled *On Cosmopolitanism and Forgiveness* as regard to the topic nearly four years before his death. His study and writing shows that there may not be any social harmony among human beings again owing to inner conflict and jealousy. Do we really prefer to live like this till human civilisation exists in the world? Of course not; it is obvious that we want to be tied to love, patience, tolerance, human chain, and law. And we want to get rid of chaos and brutality.[1]

The reason he wrote in the last stages of his life is an unknown issue, i.e. fear. He was curious as to why people were always worried and terrified due to various reasons. He indicated that this was not how life should be.

Considering he's learnt the growing world-wide problem of refugees, he, while proposing an open town to the world, wished, 'May an International Community sign the writ of Refugees' Town. May the refugees have the guarantee of relief from torture, pain and fear in the town. May they not only relieve their fear and be provided with the arrangements just for spending their days and nights but also be with no worry about basic needs, i.e. food, clothes and shelter and have the guarantee of health, education, prestige and other civil rights as well.'[2]

Both in the beginning and at the end, Derrida's theory stresses on fear. Although a lot of people do not bank on it, this is the reality the theory generates.

There are a large number of theories brought out by fear. All these fears cannot be done away with at all for good, although we try to alleviate it or get relief from it, or it subsides by itself. While one disappears, the other exists. That is to say, when we solve a problem the other one appears again. However, fear arises in different situations, for everything is unstable and changeable. When it comes as a terrible incident or a normal one to us, we realise that volatility causes it (fear) but constancy doesn't. It means that the same fear does not continue to exist because it itself is the result of consciousness, recollection, and thought. Hence, life is beyond its absence. All these fears should be dealt with by means of having a positive attitude, great courage, much patience, and meaningful thought, which is a proper solution to the problem. Above all, it occurs in a normal situation rather than in unusual situations, i.e. an incident, disease, natural disaster, etc. A normal fear that always occurs abounds in life. Terrible events occur unexpectedly either to ruin our lives or leave a very unpleasant memory in our lives. That is why fears should be turned into positivity and courage. Those who are able to do so can live their lives easily while the rest have to admit defeat in life. This is indeed how life is.

Fear is the result of our mindset, so balance of mind is a prime source of power to control it. Those having a balance of mind can control themselves in a difficult situation caused by fear. If one can be under his/her balance, control, and restriction, nothing more needs to be done. He can be safe from any danger or unpleasant happenings, viz. serious incident, natural disaster, war, murder, violence. When a bad or unpleasant happening occurs, he becomes nervous and loses his senses. As a result of this, a further problem may arise and cause serious injuries as well as death to him. This very fear may spread and turn out to be various physical or mental problems (diseases). Furthermore, worry, fear, and thinking can be the factors that would add to the problem (illness). Therefore, to gain self-control is a solution to various problems. To control ourselves is to control the sense. Here, the terms sense and I are two different things. Similarly, the term sense differs from mind. It is quite tough to be interpreted in words. Many intellectuals have claimed that mind and brain are the same and brain and sense are also not different from them. As a matter of fact, mind and sense are different from each other. It is the mind that controls the sense. Suppose if a bad thing is being done, it is the mind that orders, 'You should not do this.' Then the sense finds a means of identification or recognition. It is possible to figure out mind and sense only from the study of different parts. If not, then everything is a puzzle in lieu of clarity of any ideas. Nothing is clearly grasped. By means of balance of mind, fear itself subsides. There is no need to take medicine or apply ointment to remove it. And also there is no need to practice yoga, meditation, and any physical exercise. No one knows where and when it occurs and what it is like. It is just known as fear at present. It may become specialised after its study and concept have come a long way. Then fear will be studied in parts. Then it will be easy for us to find a solution (treatment) to the problem of fear. It is very difficult to diagnose any disease and problem at first, but it is easy to learn and solve this problem after its diagnosis or identification.

Michel Foucault says, 'A lunatic, a culprit, a leper and a job seeker would be kept in the same group in Europe seventeenth century ago. They would be categorized into special groups according to their involvement in different activities. The main cities in Europe would be surrounded by big walls at that time. And those victimized people would be left in the same place outside the wall which surrounded an urban life or civilization.'[3]

With regard to how a mad man, who was afraid, worried, puzzled, etc., was treated before Freud's psycho-analysis was developed, Dr Gobinda Raj Bhattarai writes, 'They would be locked and chained, stoned, banished and imprisoned.'[4]

Even in Aristotle's time, the concept about the mighty citizens and the power of a powerful state spread during the periods of Roman and Greece imperialism. Based on the same concept, Aristotle, in his book entitled *Politics*, declared, 'May there is such a law which should not be in behalf of a disabled or handicapped child!'[5]

Unless a mental illness was diagnosed, the mentally ill, as Freud said, would be treated inhumanly. The methods of treatment were developed after diagnosis and then the patients began to be treated well. At present, they don't have to face the problem as in the past. They can easily receive treatment for their illness. A fear victim can also be treated well to lead a normal life.

Tolerance, a great power of balance, plays a vital role in fearism. It can control and balance emotional problems of fear caused by several incidents, problems, human nature, etc. It is very difficult to control emotion produced by different kinds of human nature such as action, wrath, love, and charm. Tolerance, a deep meditation, the upper level of knowledge, the path of relief from fear, the peace of mind, balances and controls them. It is possible not only through mind but also through every part of the body, which should be involved for its acquisition. It does not mean that we should put up with unnecessary things, i.e. stones, soil, etc. We should only tolerate necessary things to make our lives easier and more comfortable.

As all these things are the results of mindset, fear can be removed through the balance of mind. A man has great courage and an enormous capacity to make use of them properly, but he is unable to do so. Instead, he seems to be incapable of living a normal life and says, 'I can't do anything.' There is no absence of fear; he/she is in its chain at all times. That is why we should struggle hard, have power of control, and be brave and self-controlled to alleviate fear. Indeed, a real man always tries to overcome it and strives for a normal life. Those who cannot confront their fears cannot live their lives easily in practice. There is no need for an outer source of power for the alleviation of fear. As man has great power and sense and knowledge are the major sources of it, inner power should be evoked and made active, thought should be strengthened, and mind should be rationalised for its abatement. Thus, the problem of fear can be solved by dint of the changes in sense and knowledge.

The problem, whether it is major or minor, depends on the person. Indeed, it turns on the person who overcomes it or fails to deal with it. If a man dies, some people take his death very seriously, cry their eyes out, lament a lot, and cause various problems while others take it normally and pass their time as usual. In fact, death is the same as faced by all, but it depends on the acceptance, experience, and realisation of a man. That is why, death, however terrible and painful it may be, turns on us and our response. If death is taken normally, it lessens by and by. Similarly, we can alleviate the fear of family, relatives, language, script, religion, culture, politics, economics, society, etc. If we are able to do so, our life becomes easy-going. All these fears can be minimised and transformed.

Thus, if fear is alleviated, life goes on smoothly and death becomes a normal part of life. Then a man is considered to be able to value and experience different stages of life. Sorrow, pain, etc. are not based on the concept of its removal. There should be an increase in tolerance for this.

There are many fears to be faced in human life. Some of them are essential while others are dispensable. Unnecessary fears should be reduced for an easy and happy life. Fear, the result of concept, can be subdued even by a little zeal and effort of thought. There is no need for having anything else, i.e. power, money, etc., to control it. Positive attitudes and meaningful thought in life and increased tolerance can be helpful and useful for the solution to the problem. It will be beneficial for human beings and make their lives easy-going. Afterwards, there will be peace and prosperity. It means that we don't have to escape all the fears. Unnecessary fears, which we have more than necessary ones, should be identified for their reduction and removal for betterment.

The term 'fearism' refers to the interpretation, analysis, application, investigation, research on the issue of fear or thesis, antithesis, and synthesis of fear. In fearism, fear, its condition, types, disclosure, etc. are investigated and analysed. It is applied in order to find out an easy access and a solution in all kinds of situations—above all, disease, murder, terror, life, death, anxiety, problem, worry, trouble, doubt, illusion, etc. that occur in our lives. It has continued since the prehistoric period. Comprehension of fearism alone is insufficient in life. It is difficult to comprehend due to its wider impacts. Life is surrounded by fear. It is trapped inside. In fact, fearism denotes excavation, investigation, interpretation, understanding, word, meaning, substance, thought, behaviour, application, and so on. Still more investigation and research on it and its application are necessary. This is the first step of the new investigation and research. The more we study fear in depth, the more mysterious it is found to be. Vast knowledge is still being acquired. It can have a huge contribution to making life brighter.

The following points have been presented to sum up the discussion:

1. Fear was taken to be a negative factor yesterday. It has been negatively interpreted in many religious texts, philosophies, and literary texts. Fearism has a positive perspective towards it.
2. Like Marxism and existentialism, fearism interprets both life and the world.
3. Fear existed yesterday, it exists today, and it will exist tomorrow. Religious people, philosophers, and literary figures have spoken about it yesterday. But it was in a small range. They did exist separately. Now, fearism exists as a theory in order to interpret those understandings and statements.
4. Fearism as a theory has been interpreted everywhere: In particular, it can apply in literature, philosophy, criticism, and medical science.
5. When fear is applied as a theory in medical science, the disease can be understood as a result of fear. The disease also expands due to fear. There are separate doctors for fear and its hospitals have been established and medicines developed. A fear patient is categorised under groups of those suffering from depression and mental illness as no theory related to fear has been developed. Consequently, the treatment has not been fruitful. Therefore, it is essential in medical science.
6. Fear is the cause of civil war, caste/ethnic conflicts, and world war. They must be interpreted through fearist perspective, yet it has not occurred.
7. Fear is the reason for murders, suicides, and migration. Nobody has attempted to interpret them from fearist perspective.
8. Fear has played a dominant role in civilisation, development, and progress since the prehistoric period. All works, invention and

constructions are oriented to reduce fear. In fact, they help reduce our fear as well. What we need is the fearist perspective.

9. Fear is a foundation for almost all philosophies and theories. We have never tried to understand the dominant role of fear till this time.

10. Philosophies can be studied or de-philosophised through fearism. Then it is easier to understand the reasons and circumstances of invention of philosophies.

11. Constitution, rule, regulation, act, and law are constituted and court, government, police, and army are also formed due to fear. Fearism helps us to further understand them.

12. We try to construct strong windows, doors, and walls to reduce our fears.

13. Fearism is a philosophy that tells us about where fear begins, what fear does, and how we can reduce it.

14. Many philosophies and religions in the world ignore the daily activities of human beings in their interpretations. Interpretation of fear is incorporated from morning to late night and from the cradle to the grave.

Thus, fearism interprets, investigates, and analyses many things in this way. It unfolds the folded aspects/sides. It also opens closed doors.

End Notes:

1. Gobinda Raj Bhattarai, *Uttar Adhunik Aina (Postmodern Mirror)*. Ratna Book Store, Kathmandu: 2062. v.s. p. 70.

2. Gobinda Raj Bhattarai, *Uttar Adhunik Aina (Post Modern Mirror)*. Ratna Book Store, Kathmandu: 2062. v.s. p. 71.

3. Sanjiv Upreti, *Sidhantaka Kura (Aspect of Theory)*. Akshar Creation Nepal, 2068 v.s. p. 320.

4. Gobinda Raj Bhattarai, *Kantipur Daily*, Kathmandu, June 3, 2005.

5. Sanjiv Upreti, *Sidhantaka Kura (Aspect of Theory)*. Akshar Creation Nepal, 2068 v.s. p. 259.

APPENDIX

Phobia List

A

Ablutophobia—Fear of washing or bathing.
Acarophobia—Fear of itching or of insects that cause itching.
Acerophobia—Fear of sourness.
Achluophobia—Fear of darkness.
Acousticophobia—Fear of noise.
Acrophobia—Fear of heights.
Aerophobia—Fear of drafts, air swallowing, or airborne noxious substances.
Aeroacrophobia—Fear of open high places.
Aeronausiphobia—Fear of vomiting secondary to airsickness.
Agateophobia—Fear of insanity.
Agliophobia—Fear of pain.
Agoraphobia—Fear of open spaces or of being in crowded, public places like markets. Fear of leaving a safe place.
Agraphobia—Fear of sexual abuse.
Agrizoophobia—Fear of wild animals.
Agyrophobia—Fear of streets or crossing the street.
Aichmophobia—Fear of needles or pointed objects.
Ailurophobia—Fear of cats.
Albuminurophobia—Fear of kidney disease.
Alektorophobia—Fear of chickens.
Algophobia—Fear of pain.
Alliumphobia—Fear of garlic.

Allodoxaphobia—Fear of opinions.

Altophobia—Fear of heights.

Amathophobia—Fear of dust.

Amaxophobia— Fear of riding in a car.

Ambulophobia—Fear of walking.

Amnesiphobia—Fear of amnesia.

Amychophobia—Fear of scratches or being scratched.

Anablephobia—Fear of looking up.

Ancraophobia—Fear of wind (Anemophobia).

Androphobia—Fear of men.

Anemophobia—Fear of air drafts or wind (Ancraophobia).

Anginophobia—Fear of angina, choking, or narrowness.

Anglophobia—Fear of England or English culture, etc.

Angrophobia—Fear of anger or of becoming angry.

Ankylophobia—Fear of immobility of a joint.

Anthrophobia or Anthophobia—Fear of flowers.

Anthropophobia—Fear of people or society.

Antlophobia—Fear of floods.

Anuptaphobia—Fear of staying single.

Apeirophobia—Fear of infinity.

Aphenphosmphobia—Fear of being touched (Haphephobia).

Apiphobia—Fear of bees.

Apotemnophobia—Fear of persons with amputation.

Arachibutyrophobia—Fear of peanut butter sticking to the roof of the mouth.

Arachnephobia or Arachnophobia—Fear of spiders.

Arithmophobia—Fear of numbers.

Arrhenphobia—Fear of men.

Arsonphobia—Fear of fire.

Asthenophobia—Fear of fainting or weakness.

Astraphobia or Astrapophobia—Fear of thunder and lightning (Ceraunophobia, Keraunophobia).

Astrophobia—Fear of stars or celestial space.

Asymmetriphobia—Fear of asymmetrical things.

Ataxiophobia—Fear of ataxia (muscular incoordination).

Ataxophobia—Fear of disorder or untidiness.

Atelophobia—Fear of imperfection.

Atephobia—Fear of ruin or ruins.

Athazagoraphobia—Fear of being forgotton or ignored or forgetting.

Atomosophobia—Fear of atomic explosions.

Atychiphobia—Fear of failure.

Aulophobia—Fear of flutes.

Aurophobia—Fear of gold.
Auroraphobia—Fear of Northern Lights.
Autodysomophobia—Fear of one that has a vile odour.
Automatonophobia—Fear of ventriloquist's dummies, animatronic creatures, wax statues—anything that falsely represents a sentient being.
Automysophobia—Fear of being dirty.
Autophobia—Fear of being alone or by oneself.
Aviophobia or Aviatophobia—Fear of flying.

B

Bacillophobia—Fear of microbes.
Bacteriophobia—Fear of bacteria.
Ballistophobia—Fear of missiles or bullets.
Bolshephobia—Fear of Bolsheviks.
Barophobia—Fear of gravity.
Basophobia or Basiphobia—Inability to stand. Fear of walking or falling.
Bathmophobia—Fear of stairs or steep slopes.
Bathophobia—Fear of depth.
Batophobia—Fear of heights or being close to high buildings.
Batrachophobia—Fear of amphibians, such as frogs, newts, and salamanders.
Belonephobia—Fear of pins and needles (Aichmophobia).
Bibliophobia—Fear of books.
Blennophobia—Fear of slime.
Bogyphobia—Fear of bogeys or the bogeyman.
Botanophobia—Fear of plants.
Bromidrosiphobia or Bromidrophobia—Fear of body smells.
Brontophobia—Fear of thunder and lightning.
Bufonophobia—Fear of toads.

C

Cacophobia—Fear of ugliness.
Cainophobia or Cainotophobia—Fear of newness, novelty.
Caligynephobia—Fear of beautiful women.
Cancerophobia or Carcinophobia—Fear of cancer.
Cardiophobia—Fear of the heart.
Carnophobia—Fear of meat.
Catagelophobia—Fear of being ridiculed.
Catapedaphobia—Fear of jumping from high and low places.
Cathisophobia—Fear of sitting.

Catoptrophobia—Fear of mirrors.
Cenophobia or Centophobia—Fear of new things or ideas.
Ceraunophobia or Keraunophobia—Fear of thunder and lightning (Astraphobia, Astrapophobia).
Chaetophobia—Fear of hair.
Cheimaphobia or Cheimatophobia—Fear of cold (Frigophobia, Psychophobia).
Chemophobia—Fear of chemicals or working with chemicals.
Cherophobia—Fear of gaiety.
Chionophobia—Fear of snow.
Chiraptophobia—Fear of being touched.
Chirophobia—Fear of hands.
Chiroptophobia—Fear of bats.
Cholerophobia—Fear of anger or the fear of cholera.
Chorophobia—Fear of dancing.
Chrometophobia or Chrematophobia—Fear of money.
Chromophobia or Chromatophobia—Fear of colors.
Chronophobia—Fear of time.
Chronomentrophobia—Fear of clocks.
Cibophobia—Fear of food (Sitophobia, Sitiophobia).
Claustrophobia—Fear of confined spaces.
Cleithrophobia or Cleisiophobia—Fear of being locked in an enclosed place.
Cleptophobia—Fear of stealing.
Climacophobia—Fear of stairs, climbing, or of falling downstairs.
Clinophobia—Fear of going to bed.
Clithrophobia or Cleithrophobia—Fear of being enclosed.
Cnidophobia—Fear of stings.
Cometophobia—Fear of comets.
Coimetrophobia—Fear of cemeteries.
Coitophobia—Fear of coitus.
Contreltophobia—Fear of sexual abuse.
Coprastasophobia—Fear of constipation.
Coprophobia—Fear of faeces.
Consecotaleophobia—Fear of chopsticks.
Coulrophobia—Fear of clowns.
Counterphobia—The preference of a phobic for fearful situations.
Cremnophobia—Fear of precipices.
Cryophobia—Fear of extreme cold, ice, or frost.
Crystallophobia—Fear of crystals or glass.
Cyberphobia—Fear of computers or working on a computer.
Cyclophobia—Fear of bicycles.
Cymophobia or Kymophobia—Fear of waves or wave-like motions.

Cynophobia—Fear of dogs or rabies.
Cypridophobia or Cypriphobia or Cyprianophobia or Cyprinophobia—Fear of prostitutes or venereal disease.

D

Decidophobia—Fear of making decisions.
Defecaloesiophobia—Fear of painful bowels movements.
Deipnophobia—Fear of dining or dinner conversations.
Dementophobia—Fear of insanity.
Demonophobia or Daemonophobia—Fear of demons.
Demophobia—Fear of crowds (Agoraphobia).
Dendrophobia—Fear of trees.
Dentophobia—Fear of dentists.
Dermatophobia—Fear of skin lesions.
Dermatosiophobia or Dermatophobia or Dermatopathophobia—Fear of skin disease.
Dextrophobia—Fear of objects at the right side of the body.
Diabetophobia—Fear of diabetes.
Didaskaleinophobia—Fear of going to school.
Dikephobia—Fear of justice.
Dinophobia—Fear of dizziness or whirlpools.
Diplophobia—Fear of double vision.
Dipsophobia—Fear of drinking.
Dishabiliophobia—Fear of undressing in front of someone.
Domatophobia—Fear of houses or being in a house (Eicophobia, Oikophobia).
Doraphobia—Fear of fur or skins of animals.
Doxophobia—Fear of expressing opinions or of receiving praise.
Dromophobia—Fear of crossing streets.
Dutchphobia—Fear of the Dutch.
Dysmorphophobia—Fear of deformity.
Dystychiphobia—Fear of accidents.

E

Ecclesiophobia—Fear of church.
Ecophobia—Fear of home.
Eicophobia—Fear of home surroundings (Domatophobia, Oikophobia).
Eisoptrophobia—Fear of mirrors or of seeing oneself in a mirror.
Electrophobia—Fear of electricity.
Eleutherophobia—Fear of freedom.

Elurophobia—Fear of cats (Ailurophobia).
Emetophobia—Fear of vomiting.
Enetophobia—Fear of pins.
Enochlophobia—Fear of crowds.
Enosiophobia or Enissophobia—Fear of having committed an unpardonable sin or of criticism.
Entomophobia—Fear of insects.
Eosophobia—Fear of dawn or daylight.
Ephebiphobia—Fear of teenagers.
Epistaxiophobia—Fear of nosebleeds.
Epistemophobia—Fear of knowledge.
Equinophobia—Fear of horses.
Eremophobia—Fear of being oneself or of lonliness.
Ereuthrophobia—Fear of blushing.
Ergasiophobia—(1) Fear of work or functioning. (2) Surgeon's fear of operating.
Ergophobia—Fear of work.
Erotophobia—Fear of sexual love or sexual questions.
Euphobia—Fear of hearing good news.
Eurotophobia—Fear of female genitalia.
Erythrophobia or Erytophobia or Ereuthophobia—(1) Fear of red lights. (2) Blushing. (3) Red.

F

Febriphobia or Fibriphobia or Fibriophobia—Fear of fever.
Felinophobia—Fear of cats (Ailurophobia, Elurophobia, Galeophobia, Gatophobia).
Francophobia—Fear of France or French culture (Gallophobia, Galiophobia).
Frigophobia—Fear of cold or cold things (Cheimaphobia, Cheimatophobia, Psychrophobia).

G

Galeophobia or Gatophobia—Fear of cats.
Gallophobia or Galiophobia—Fear of France or French culture (Francophobia).
Gamophobia—Fear of marriage.
Geliophobia—Fear of laughter.
Gelotophobia—Fear of being laughed at.
Geniophobia—Fear of chins.
Genophobia—Fear of sex.
Genuphobia—Fear of knees.

Gephyrophobia or Gephydrophobia or Gephysrophobia—Fear of crossing bridges.
Germanophobia—Fear of Germany or German culture.
Gerascophobia—Fear of growing old.
Gerontophobia—Fear of old people or of growing old.
Geumaphobia or Geumophobia—Fear of taste.
Glossophobia—Fear of speaking in public or of trying to speak.
Gnosiophobia—Fear of knowledge.
Graphophobia—Fear of writing or handwriting.
Gymnophobia—Fear of nudity.
Gynephobia or Gynophobia—Fear of women.

H

Hadephobia—Fear of hell.
Hagiophobia—Fear of saints or holy things.
Hamartophobia—Fear of sinning.
Haphephobia or Haptephobia—Fear of being touched.
Harpaxophobia—Fear of being robbed.
Hedonophobia—Fear of feeling pleasure.
Heliophobia—Fear of the sun.
Hellenologophobia—Fear of Greek terms or complex scientific terminology.
Helminthophobia—Fear of being infested with worms.
Hemophobia or Hemaphobia or Hematophobia—Fear of blood.
Heresyphobia or Hereiophobia—Fear of challenges to official doctrine or of
    radical deviation.
Herpetophobia—Fear of reptiles or creepy, crawly things.
Heterophobia—Fear of the opposite sex (Sexophobia).
Hexakosioihexekontahexaphobia—Fear of the number 666.
Hierophobia—Fear of priests or sacred things.
Hippophobia—Fear of horses.
Hippopotomonstrosesquipedaliophobia—Fear of long words.
Hobophobia—Fear of bums or beggars.
Hodophobia—Fear of road travel.
Hormephobia—Fear of shock.
Homichlophobia—Fear of fog.
Homilophobia—Fear of sermons.
Hominophobia—Fear of men.
Homophobia—Fear of sameness, monotony or of homosexuality or of
    becoming homosexual.
Hoplophobia—Fear of firearms.
Hydrargyophobia—Fear of mercurial medicines.

Hydrophobia—Fear of water or of rabies.
Hydrophobophobia—Fear of rabies.
Hyelophobia or Hyalophobia—Fear of glass.
Hygrophobia—Fear of liquids, dampness, or moisture.
Hylephobia—Fear of materialism or the fear of epilepsy.
Hylophobia—Fear of forests.
Hypengyophobia or Hypegiaphobia—Fear of responsibility.
Hypnophobia—Fear of sleep or of being hypnotised.
Hypsiphobia—Fear of height.

I

Iatrophobia—Fear of going to the doctor or of doctors.
Ichthyophobia—Fear of fish.
Ideophobia—Fear of ideas.
Illyngophobia—Fear of vertigo or feeling dizzy when looking down.
Iophobia—Fear of poison.
Insectophobia—Fear of insects.
Isolophobia—Fear of solitude, being alone.
Isopterophobia—Fear of termites, insects that eat wood.
Ithyphallophobia—Fear of seeing, thinking about or having an erect penis.

J

Japanophobia—Fear of Japanese.
Judeophobia—Fear of Jews.

K

Kainolophobia or Kainophobia—Fear of anything new, novelty.
Kakorrhaphiophobia—Fear of failure or defeat.
Katagelophobia—Fear of ridicule.
Kathisophobia—Fear of sitting down.
Katsaridaphobia—Fear of cockroaches.
Kenophobia—Fear of voids or empty spaces.
Keraunophobia or Ceraunophobia—Fear of thunder and lightning (Astraphobia, Astrapophobia).
Kinetophobia or Kinesophobia—Fear of movement or motion.
Kleptophobia—Fear of stealing.
Koinoniphobia—Fear of rooms.
Kolpophobia—Fear of genitals, particularly female.

Kopophobia—Fear of fatigue.
Koniophobia—Fear of dust (Amathophobia).
Kosmikophobia—Fear of cosmic phenomenon.
Kymophobia—Fear of waves (Cymophobia).
Kynophobia—Fear of rabies.
Kyphophobia—Fear of stooping.

L

Lachanophobia—Fear of vegetables.
Laliophobia or Lalophobia—Fear of speaking.
Leprophobia or Lepraphobia—Fear of leprosy.
Leukophobia—Fear of the colour white.
Levophobia—Fear of things to the left side of the body.
Ligyrophobia—Fear of loud noises.
Lilapsophobia—Fear of tornadoes and hurricanes.
Limnophobia—Fear of lakes.
Linonophobia—Fear of string.
Liticaphobia—Fear of lawsuits.
Lockiophobia—Fear of childbirth.
Logizomechanophobia—Fear of computers.
Logophobia—Fear of words.
Luiphobia—Fear of lues, syphilis.
Lutraphobia—Fear of otters.
Lygophobia—Fear of darkness.
Lyssophobia—Fear of rabies or of becoming mad.

M

Macrophobia—Fear of long waits.
Mageirocophobia—Fear of cooking.
Maieusiophobia—Fear of childbirth.
Malaxophobia—Fear of love play (Sarmassophobia).
Maniaphobia—Fear of insanity.
Mastigophobia—Fear of punishment.
Mechanophobia—Fear of machines.
Medomalacuphobia—Fear of losing an erection.
Medorthophobia—Fear of an erect penis.
Megalophobia—Fear of large things.
Melissophobia—Fear of bees.
Melanophobia—Fear of the color black.

Melophobia—Fear or hatred of music.
Meningitophobia—Fear of brain disease.
Menophobia—Fear of menstruation.
Merinthophobia—Fear of being bound or tied up.
Metallophobia—Fear of metal.
Metathesiophobia—Fear of changes.
Meteorophobia—Fear of meteors.
Methyphobia—Fear of alcohol.
Metrophobia—Fear or hatred of poetry.
Microbiophobia—Fear of microbes (Bacillophobia).
Microphobia—Fear of small things.
Misophobia or Mysophobia—Fear of being contaminated with dirt or germs.
Mnemophobia—Fear of memories.
Molysmophobia or Molysomophobia—Fear of dirt or contamination.
Monophobia—Fear of solitude or being alone.
Monopathophobia—Fear of definite disease.
Motorphobia—Fear of automobiles.
Mottephobia—Fear of moths.
Musophobia or Muriphobia—Fear of mice.
Mycophobia—Fear or aversion to mushrooms.
Mycrophobia—Fear of small things.
Myctophobia—Fear of darkness.
Myrmecophobia—Fear of ants.
Mythophobia—Fear of myths or stories or false statements.
Myxophobia—Fear of slime (Blennophobia).

N

Nebulaphobia—Fear of fog (Homichlophobia).
Necrophobia—Fear of death or dead things.
Nelophobia—Fear of glass.
Neopharmaphobia—Fear of new drugs.
Neophobia—Fear of anything new.
Nephophobia—Fear of clouds.
Noctiphobia—Fear of the night.
Nomatophobia—Fear of names.
Nosocomephobia—Fear of hospitals.
Nosophobia or Nosemaphobia—Fear of becoming ill.
Nostophobia—Fear of returning home.
Novercaphobia—Fear of your step-mother.
Nucleomituphobia—Fear of nuclear weapons.

Nudophobia—Fear of nudity.
Numerophobia—Fear of numbers.
Nyctohylophobia—Fear of dark wooded areas or of forests at night.
Nyctophobia—Fear of the dark or of night.

O

Obesophobia—Fear of gaining weight (Pocrescophobia).
Ochlophobia—Fear of crowds or mobs.
Ochophobia—Fear of vehicles.
Octophobia—Fear of the Figure no. 8.
Odontophobia—Fear of teeth or dental surgery.
Odynophobia or Odynephobia—Fear of pain (Algophobia).
Oenophobia—Fear of wines.
Oikophobia—Fear of home surroundings, house (Domatophobia, Eicophobia).
Olfactophobia—Fear of smells.
Ombrophobia—Fear of rain or of being rained on.
Ommetaphobia or Ommatophobia—Fear of eyes.
Omphalophobia—Fear of belly buttons.
Oneirophobia—Fear of dreams.
Oneirogmophobia—Fear of wet dreams.
Onomatophobia—Fear of hearing a certain word or of names.
Ophidiophobia—Fear of snakes (snake phobia).
Ophthalmophobia—Fear of being stared at.
Opiophobia—Fear medical doctors experience in prescribing needed pain medications for patients.
Optophobia—Fear of opening one's eyes.
Ornithophobia—Fear of birds.
Orthophobia—Fear of property.
Osmophobia or Osphresiophobia—Fear of smells or odours.
Ostraconophobia—Fear of shellfish.
Ouranophobia or Uranophobia—Fear of heaven.

P

Pagophobia—Fear of ice or frost.
Panthophobia—Fear of suffering and disease.
Panophobia or Pantophobia—Fear of everything.
Papaphobia—Fear of the Pope.
Papyrophobia—Fear of paper.
Paralipophobia—Fear of neglecting duty or responsibility.

Paraphobia—Fear of sexual perversion.
Parasitophobia—Fear of parasites.
ParaskaVedaekatriaphobia—Fear of Friday the 13th.
Parthenophobia—Fear of virgins or young girls.
Pathophobia—Fear of disease.
Patroiophobia—Fear of heredity.
Parturiphobia—Fear of childbirth.
Peccatophobia—Fear of sinning or imaginary crimes.
Pediculophobia—Fear of lice.
Pediophobia—Fear of dolls.
Pedophobia—Fear of children.
Peladophobia—Fear of bald people.
Pellagrophobia—Fear of pellagra.
Peniaphobia—Fear of poverty.
Pentheraphobia—Fear of mother-in-law (Novercaphobia).
Phagophobia—Fear of swallowing or of eating or of being eaten.
Phalacrophobia—Fear of becoming bald.
Phallophobia—Fear of a penis, especially erect.
Pharmacophobia—Fear of taking medicine.
Phasmophobia—Fear of ghosts.
Phengophobia—Fear of daylight or sunshine.
Philemaphobia or Philematophobia—Fear of kissing.
Philophobia—Fear of falling in love or being in love.
Philosophobia—Fear of philosophy.
Phobophobia—Fear of phobias.
Photoaugliaphobia—Fear of glaring lights.
Photophobia—Fear of light.
Phonophobia—Fear of noises or voices or one's own voice; of telephones.
Phronemophobia—Fear of thinking.
Phthiriophobia—Fear of lice (Pediculophobia).
Phthisiophobia—Fear of tuberculosis.
Placophobia—Fear of tombstones.
Plutophobia—Fear of wealth.
Pluviophobia—Fear of rain or of being rained on.
Pneumatiphobia—Fear of spirits.
Pnigophobia or Pnigerophobia—Fear of choking of being smothered.
Pocrescophobia—Fear of gaining weight (Obesophobia).
Pogonophobia—Fear of beards.
Poliosophobia—Fear of contracting poliomyelitis.
Politicophobia—Fear or abnormal dislike of politicians.
Polyphobia—Fear of many things.

Poinephobia—Fear of punishment.
Ponophobia—Fear of overworking or of pain.
Porphyrophobia—Fear of the color purple.
Potamophobia—Fear of rivers or running water.
Potophobia—Fear of alcohol.
Pharmacophobia—Fear of drugs.
Proctophobia—Fear of rectums.
Prosophobia—Fear of progress.
Psellismophobia—Fear of stuttering.
Psychophobia—Fear of mind.
Psychrophobia—Fear of cold.
Pteromerhanophobia—Fear of flying.
Pteronophobia—Fear of being tickled by feathers.
Pupaphobia—Fear of puppets.
Pyrexiophobia—Fear of fever.
Pyrophobia—Fear of fire.

Q

R

Radiophobia—Fear of radiation, X-rays.
Ranidaphobia—Fear of frogs.
Rectophobia—Fear of rectum or rectal diseases.
Rhabdophobia—Fear of being severely punished or beaten by a rod or of being severely criticised. Also fear of magic (wand).
Rhypophobia—Fear of defecation.
Rhytiphobia—Fear of getting wrinkles.
Rupophobia—Fear of dirt.
Russophobia—Fear of Russians.

S

Samhainophobia—Fear of Halloween.
Sarmassophobia—Fear of love play (Malaxophobia)
Satanophobia—Fear of Satan.
Scabiophobia—Fear of scabies.
Scatophobia—Fear of faecal matter.
Scelerophibia—Fear of bad men, burglars.
Sciophobia Sciaphobia—Fear of shadows.
Scoleciphobia—Fear of worms.

Scolionophobia—Fear of school.
Scopophobia or Scoptophobia—Fear of being seen or stared at.
Scotomaphobia—Fear of blindness in visual field.
Scotophobia—Fear of darkness (Achluophobia).
Scriptophobia—Fear of writing in public.
Selachophobia—Fear of sharks.
Selaphobia—Fear of light flashes.
Selenophobia—Fear of the moon.
Seplophobia—Fear of decaying matter.
Sesquipedalophobia—Fear of long words.
Sexophobia—Fear of the opposite sex (Heterophobia).
Siderodromophobia—Fear of trains, railroads, or train travel.
Siderophobia—Fear of stars.
Sinistrophobia—Fear of things to the left or left-handed.
Sinophobia—Fear of Chinese, Chinese culture.
Sitophobia or Sitiophobia—Fear of food or eating (Cibophobia).
Snakephobia—Fear of snakes (Ophidiophobia).
Soceraphobia—Fear of parents-in-law.
Social Phobia—Fear of being evaluated negatively in social situations.
Sociophobia—Fear of society or people in general.
Somniphobia—Fear of sleep.
Sophophobia—Fear of learning.
Soteriophobia—Fear of dependence on others.
Spacephobia—Fear of outer space.
Spectrophobia—Fear of spectres or ghosts.
Spermatophobia or Spermophobia—Fear of germs.
Spheksophobia—Fear of wasps.
Stasibasiphobia or Stasiphobia—Fear of standing or walking (Ambulophobia).
Staurophobia—Fear of crosses or the crucifix.
Stenophobia—Fear of narrow things or places.
Stygiophobia or Stigiophobia—Fear of hell.
Suriphobia—Fear of mice.
Symbolophobia—Fear of symbolism.
Symmetrophobia—Fear of symmetry.
Syngenesophobia—Fear of relatives.
Syphilophobia—Fear of syphilis.

T

Tachophobia—Fear of speed.
Taeniophobia or Teniophobia—Fear of tapeworms.

Taphephobia Taphophobia—Fear of being buried alive or of cemeteries.
Tapinophobia—Fear of being contagious.
Taurophobia—Fear of bulls.
Technophobia—Fear of technology.
Teleophobia—(1) Fear of definite plans. (2) Religious ceremony.
Telephonophobia—Fear of telephones.
Teratophobia—Fear of bearing a deformed child or fear of monsters or deformed people.
Testophobia—Fear of taking tests.
Tetanophobia—Fear of lockjaw, tetanus.
Teutophobia—Fear of German or German things.
Textophobia—Fear of certain fabrics.
Thaasophobia—Fear of sitting.
Thalassophobia—Fear of the sea.
Thanatophobia or Thantophobia—Fear of death or dying.
Theatrophobia—Fear of theatres.
Theologicophobia—Fear of theology.
Theophobia—Fear of gods or religion.
Thermophobia—Fear of heat.
Tocophobia—Fear of pregnancy or childbirth.
Tomophobia—Fear of surgical operations.
Tonitrophobia—Fear of thunder.
Topophobia—Fear of certain places or situations, such as stage fright.
Toxiphobia or Toxophobia or Toxicophobia—Fear of poison or of being accidently poisoned.
Traumatophobia—Fear of injury.
Tremophobia—Fear of trembling.
Trichinophobia—Fear of trichinosis.
Trichopathophobia or Trichophobia—Fear of hair (Chaetophobia, Hypertrichophobia).
Triskaidekaphobia—Fear of the number 13.
Tropophobia—Fear of moving or making changes.
Trypanophobia—Fear of injections.
Tuberculophobia—Fear of tuberculosis.
Tyrannophobia—Fear of tyrants.

U

Uranophobia or Ouranophobia—Fear of heaven.
Urophobia—Fear of urine or urinating.

V

Vaccinophobia—Fear of vaccination.
Venustraphobia—Fear of beautiful women.
Verbophobia—Fear of words.
Verminophobia—Fear of germs.
Vestiphobia—Fear of clothing.
Virginitiphobia—Fear of rape.
Vitricophobia—Fear of step-father.

W

Walloonphobia—Fear of the Walloons.
Wiccaphobia—Fear of witches and witchcraft.

X

Xanthophobia—Fear of the color yellow or the word yellow.
Xenoglossophobia—Fear of foreign languages.
Xenophobia—Fear of strangers or foreigners.
Xerophobia—Fear of dryness.
Xylophobia—(1) Fear of wooden objects. (2) Forests.
Xyrophobia—Fear of razors.

Y

Z

Zelophobia—Fear of jealousy.
Zeusophobia—Fear of God or gods.
Zemmiphobia—Fear of the great mole rat.
Zoophobia—Fear of animals.

Reference

www.ttp://phobialist.com

REFERENCES

1. Subba, Desh ed. *Tapu Shringkhala*—1, Hong Kong, 2005.
2. Basanta Kumar Sharma, *Nepali Shabdasagar (Nepali Word Dictionary)*, Nepal, 2061 v.s.
3. Thamsuhang, Prakash ed. *Vayabad Baicharik Chintan (Opinion on Fearism)*. Dharan, 2066 v.s.
4. Swami Ananda Arun, *Santa Philosophy*, Osho, *Tapoban*, Kathmandu, 2008.
5. Yuwa, *Monthly Magazine for Youth*. Mulyangkan Publication, Kathmandu, Year 10 Issue 97, 2005.
6. Adhikari, Bishnu, *Darshanka Kehi Anautha Pakchha (Some Strange Aspect of Philosophy)*. Ratna Book Store, Kathmandu 2064 v.s.
7. Rahul Sangkrityan, *Sketch of the World*, trans. Narayan Giri. Marxbad Study-Research Academy, Kathmandu, 2066 v.s.
8. Bhandari, Mohan Prasad, Bhumi Prasad Dahal eds. *Purbiya Chintan ra Parampara (Eastern Thought and Trend)*. Student Publication, Kathmandu, 2066 v.s.
9. Mishra, Birendra Prasad, *Darshan Shastrako Parichaya (Introduction of Philosophy)*. Nepal Charity Foundation, Kathmandu, 2065 v.s.
10. Arjundev Panta, *Bedanta-Darshan Sar (Brief Vedaanta Philosophy)*. Ratna Book Store, Kathmandu, 2062 v.s.
11. Sachchidanda Mishra, *Ishwar Marisaky (God is Dead)*. trans. Balkrishna Shrestha 'Nebha', Utsarga Publication Baranasi, 2009.
12. GovindaRaj Bhattarai, *Creator and Digital Talk*. International Nepali Literary Society, Washington DC, 2066 v.s
13. Sanskrityayan, Rahul, *Samyabadnai Kina? (Why Communism?)*. trans. Kashi Ram Gaire. Pragati Book Sadan, Kathmandu 2034 v.s.
14. Panday, Madhusudhan, *Freudko Manobislesan (Freudian Psychoanalysis)*. Pairavi Publication, Kathmandu 2061 v.s.

15. Mohan Raj Sharma, Khagendra Prasad Luitel, *Eastern and Western Literary Theory*. Kathmandu, 2063 v.s.

16. Gurung, Kedar, ed. *Creator.* Western Sikkim Literature, Sikkim, India. 2006, Issue 56, Year 28,

17. Prasain, Punya Prasad, *Sukarat (Socrates).* Dikura Publication, Kathmandu, 2065 v.s.

18. Plato, trans. Ram Hari, *Sukaratko Atmakatha (Autobiography of Socrates).* Banjara Madhuwan Publication, Kathmandu 2065 v.s.

19. Subedi, Dipak ed., *Vayabad Chintan and Bimarsha (Thought on Fearism and Discourse)*, Fearism Study Centre, Dharan, 2067 v.s.

20. Puma, Prabin, *Hetchhakuppa* a Drama, Kathmandu, 2010.

21. Sunuwar, Naresh ed., *Srijanshil Sahitya (Creative Literature)*, Hong Kong, 2007.

22. Various critiques on indigenous novel by Desh Subba 2064 v.s.: Hangyuk Agyat, 'Sahityama Vaya Bimarsha (Discourse on Fear in Literature' in Srijansil Sahitya Samaj, Hong Kong; Krishna Dharabasi, 'A novel based on the search for cultural and mental problem'; and Dharmendra Bikram Nembang Rangabadi Perspective on a novel based on Limbuwani aestheticism or based on fearism.

23. Gobinda Raj Bhattarai, *Uttaradhunik Bimarsha (Postmodern Discourse).* Modern Books, Kathmandu: 2064 v.s.

24. Pande, Rabindra, *Nepal Pakchhik.* Kathmandu, *Bhadra* 13, 2067 v.s.

25. Upreti, Aruna, *Mahilama Manasik Awasad.* Kantipur Daily, Falgun 11, 2067 v.s.

26. Ghimire, Jhamak, *Jivan Kanda ki Fool.* Online Nepali Sahitya Manch, Kathmandu, 2067 v.s.

27. Upreti, Sanjiv, *Sidhantaka Kura.* Akshar Creation, Nepal 2068 v.s.

28. Gobinda Raj Bhattarai, *Uttaradhunik Aina (Postmodern Mirror).* Ratna Book Store, Kathmandu, 2062 v.s.

29. Pramila, *Dr Nirakarman Shrestha Inteviewed. Naya Patrika National Daily*, September 2, 2011

30. Jagadishchandra, Tarakanta Pande ed., *Nepali Samalochana.* Bibek Srijansil Publication, Kathmandu, 2068 v.s.

31. Karna Shakya, *Khoj (Search)*, Author and Publisher, Kathmandu, 2065 v.s.

Other Reference Books

1. Jean Paul Sartre, *Being and Nothingness.* Routledge, London, c1958.

2. Rush W. Dozier, Jr. west Lifayette, *Fear Itself.* Ind.:Purdue University Press. 1998.

3. Christopher Want, Andrzej Klimowski, *Kant for Beginners*. Icon, Trumpington, 1996.
4. Mel Thompson, *Eastern Philosophy*, Hodder & Stoughton, UK, 1999.
5. Car Gustav Jung, *The Undiscovered Self.* Routledge Classics, London and New York, c1958.
6. Abraham H. Maslow, *Motivation and Personality*. Longman, c1987.
7. Abraham H. Maslow, *Toward a Psychology of Being*. J. Wiley & Sons, New York, c1999.
8. Charles Darwin, *The Origin of Species*. Penguin Books, London, 1968.
9. Thomas Malthus, *An Essay of The Principle of Population*. Oxford University Press, 1999.
10. Karl Max, Friedrich Engels, *The Communist Manifesto*. Penguin Books, London. 1967.
11. Malcolm Penny, *The Food Chain*. Wayland, Hove, 1987.
12. Eric Fromm, *The Fear of Freedom*. Routledge and Kegan Paul.1942.
13. Bertrand Russell, *In Praise of Idleness*. Routledge Taylor & Francis Group, London and New York, 2008.
14. Eric Fromm, *The Fear of Freedom*, Routledge Classic. 2001.

Index

Manufactured by Amazon.ca
Bolton, ON

11983967R00210